SLAVE TRAFFIC IN THE AGE OF ABOLITION

Florida A&M University, Tallahassee
Florida Atlantic University, Boca Raton
Florida Gulf Coast University, Ft. Myers
Florida International University, Miami
Florida State University, Tallahassee
University of Central Florida, Orlando
University of Florida, Gainesville
University of North Florida, Jacksonville
University of South Florida, Tampa
University of West Florida, Pensacola

Slave Traffic in the Age of Abolition

Puerto Rico, West Africa, and the Non-Hispanic
Caribbean, 1815–1859

Joseph C. Dorsey

University Press of Florida

Gainesville   Tallahassee   Tampa   Boca Raton
Pensacola   Orlando   Miami   Jacksonville   Ft. Myers

07 06 05 04 03 02   6 5 4 3 2 1

Library of Congress Cataloging-in-Publication Data
Dorsey, Joseph C., 1948–
Slave traffic in the Age of Abolition: Puerto Rico, West Africa,
and the non-Hispanic Caribbean, 1815–1859 / Joseph C. Dorsey
p. cm.
Includes bibliographical references and index.
ISBN 0-8130-2478-1 (c: alk. paper)
1. Slave-trade—Puerto Rico—History—19th century.
2. Slave-trade—Caribbean Area—History—19th century.
3. Slave-trade—Africa, West—History—19th century. I. Title.
HT1086 .D67   2002
306.3'62'09729–dc 21
2002075495

The University Press of Florida is the scholarly publishing agency for the State
University System of Florida, comprising Florida A&M University, Florida Atlantic
University, Florida Gulf Coast University, Florida International University, Florida
State University, University of Central Florida, University of Florida, University
of North Florida, University of South Florida, and University of West Florida.

University Press of Florida
15 Northwest 15th Street
Gainesville, FL 32611–2079
http://www.upf.com

To my mother,

Madeline Bunn Dorsey,

gentlest of teachers,

and in loving memory of my father,

Harry Eugene Dorsey, Jr.,

1921–1982

Contents

Tables and Maps

Preface

Origins

This book results from my interest in the history of the Spanish seaborne empire and the variety of syncretic cultures deriving from it. Within these broad borders, I focused my concerns on slavery and race relations in locations rightly or wrongly identified as small, obscure, and therefore less important to the economic affairs of the Spanish Crown. In this vein, Puerto Rico proves ideal. Between the sixteenth and eighteenth centuries, Puerto Rico was important to imperial security as one of several Caribbean "keys to the Indies." But its frontier isolation rendered it incomparable to the wealth, grandeur, raucousness, and corruption that stimulated the urbanity of Mexico City, Panama City, Quito, and Lima, replete with the ubiquitous presence of Native Americans and African slaves in various stages of assimilation and resistance.

Even in the seventeenth and eighteenth centuries, when Havana developed an international reputation for the colorful and lucrative excitement of its urban decadence—"the boulevard of the New World," as Abbé Raynal described it—Spanish authorities continued to underestimate Puerto Rico's economic potential. Though a great deal changed between the 1760s and the 1820s, when numerous forces compelled Spain to acknowledge and act upon the island's worth, it played second fiddle to Cuba throughout the nineteenth century. Yet long before the Spanish government began to realize that Puerto Rico was more than a sentinel, more than another distant presidio, it exhibited many of the same cultural, ecological, sociopolitical, and sometimes economic features seen in other Spanish colonial settings large and small. These features included staunch loyalty to the king, the hegemony of Roman Catholicism, the uneven development of natural resources, political corruption, international smuggling, and black slavery.

In 1952, Arturo Morales Carrión's groundbreaking book *Puerto Rico and the Non-Hispanic Caribbean* revealed intricate patterns of legal and illegal commerce. It also demonstrated that both systems of exchange—the legal and the illegal—included the trafficking of slaves, especially African captives. Hence, it confirmed the island as a full-fledged member of the Atlantic community. However, inasmuch as his study closes in 1815, when Great Britain began to globalize its abolitionist convictions, existing historiography tends to downplay, overlook, or even negate continued trade relations between Puerto Rico and its Eastern Caribbean neighbors for the acquisition of both Creole and African-born slaves once Anglo-Spanish treaties outlawed the African slave trade, first between 1817 and 1820 and again in 1835. In this sense, my work follows one of Morales's many leads.

While the present study focuses on slavery, it centers more on the structures of its form as an illegal traffic and less on the structures of its content as a legal institution. It therefore deviates in some respects from the original version, a dissertation from the University of California. Though many slaves resisted the contradiction of tyrannies that punctuated their existence in the Age of Abolition, I removed chapters that constituted case studies of individual slaves and their families, for example, and published them elsewhere. Thus, the book does not explore shifting relations between slave commerce and the centrality of subaltern identity. Nonetheless, as a system-centered examination of slave acquisition processes, its primary aim is the same: to address a number of fundamental issues about Puerto Rican participation in the illegal trafficking of slaves that remain largely unexplored.

My work is aimed at students and professors of history and culture, as well as audiences with general interests in Latin American, Caribbean, and African studies. I have attempted to identify and integrate several overlapping subtexts. First, as an exercise in Caribbean history, seen through the lens of strategic essentialism, this study blurs colonial boundaries, sociocultural peculiarities, economic objectives, and political idiosyncrasies from one island to the next. Second, it suggests a chronological blurring of boundaries between moribund mercantilism and rising capitalism as they related to slave formation. Though recast as a series of treaty violations and criminal acts, clandestine slave trading remained dependent on multinational cooperation. It thereby continued to undermine notions of national identity and the promotion of unifying myths that sustained them by underscoring the political fluidity of Atlantic societies as a community bound exclusively by neither capitalism nor mercantilism. Last, as a different framework for the study of black slavery as a process of modern ethnogenesis, or cultural and biological hybridity, my efforts contribute, I hope, to the deflation of theoretical anxieties occasioned by tensions between quantitative and qualitative analysis.

Langue et Parole

I am exclusively responsible for all translations from Spanish and Portuguese to English. I have tried to give them as modern an interpretation as possible without losing the original essence of expression. However, correspondence from Spanish- and Portuguese-speaking officials found in London's Public Record Office and in the compilation of extracts published as the *Parliamentary Papers*, on which the same documents are based, were already translated more than a century ago. I make these distinctions because my own translations of Spanish and Portuguese archival materials differ from the literary fashions of nineteenth-century functionaries responsible for translating documents found in British sources. Also, accent marks in Spanish and Portuguese follow different rules and practices, even though many words are spelled identically and carry the same meaning—but not the same pronunciation. While *gloria historia río*, Rosario, Antonio, and Estanislao are Spanish, for example, *glória história rio*, Rosário, Antônio, and Estanislão are Portuguese.

Richenel Ansano, Leontyne Hillenaar, and Eliane van Vliet translated all Dutch archival documents and newspaper articles. Their efforts helped me substantiate closing arguments central to this study. For translations from French to English, there were occasions when I sought help to verify semantic accuracy and accent protocols. I am grateful to Jocelyn Garlington, Phillipe Paultre, Sharon Shelley, and David Wilkin for their help.

African, Asian, and European immigration played a variety of roles in Spanish American history during and after the colonial period. Puerto Rico is no exception. At the risk of disapproval, I have taken a few liberties with the given names of non-Spanish subjects who settled in Puerto Rico. In cases of certainty of foreign birth, where Spanish records listed "Guillermo," "Manuel," "Pedro," or "Juana María," for example, and natal countries were known, I refer to them as "William" (English), "Emanuele" (Italian), "Pieter" (Dutch), or "Jeanne-Marie" (French). There are two reasons for doing this. Most immigrants continued to sign legal documents with their original given names. More important, insistence on the legal use of their original given names defines limits they imposed on new boundaries of national identity by indicating how they wished that identity to be inscribed. However, this subtle brand of resistance to assimilation did not carry over to their island-born progeny. There were (and are, of course) many native Hispanophones with Spanish given names and non-Hispanic surnames. In such cases, I left given names unaltered.

Sentences such as "Spain lost the remainder of its American empire in 1898" and "America's first major slave revolt occurred in Santo Domingo in 1522" may confuse non–Latin Americanists. In this study, "America," "the Americas," and "American" refer to all lands and peoples between Canada and Argentina, including Mexico, Central America, and the Caribbean. In essence, they are used as hemispheric referents. They do not identify any particular nation. On the other hand, the term "United States" refers to the republic that lies between Canada and the Río Grande. With the occasional (and problematic) exception of "Anglo-American," the United States is not identified by any other term.

Though my interests in formalism, structuralism, poststructuralism, and postmodernism are keen, for this study I have made an effort to avoid language associated with any particular theory, method, or school of thought. There is, however, a rather simple exception. Occasionally I use the term "discourse" or its derivatives, "discursive" and "discursivity." "Discourse" has several uses in philosophy, law, political theory, cultural studies, and text analysis. In this study, I use it to refer to established conventions of communication, foremost in the context of social engineering for the purpose of population control.

Acknowledgments

I have benefited from the assistance and encouragement of many people in many places. For archival research in Europe and the Caribbean from the 1980s to the 1990s, grants and fellowships from the Santa Barbara Division of the University of California, the Research Foundation of the City University of New York, the Shuster Foundation of Lehman College, and various sources from Hamilton College supported a year's stay in Spain, two months in Portugal and Great Britain, six nonconsecutive months in Cuba and Puerto Rico, and a week in the Netherlands Antilles.

Archival administrators and staff members provided invaluable direction and services. For their cheerful and efficient cooperation, and not infrequently their domestic hospitality, I wish to thank: Antonio Estéban, María Teresa de la Peña, and Manuel Ravinia in Madrid; Wayne Lewis and Felipe Romero in London; Cora Vaz Pereira do Amaral Aguiar, Ida Maria Carvalho dos Santos, and Ezequiel Batista de Souza in Lisbon; Luis de la Rosa Martínez, Hilda Mercedes Chicón, Carmen Alicia Dávila, Eduardo de León, Aidita Laureano García, José Flores, Milagros Ortiz, and Milagros Pepín in San Juan; Armando Mal-Lía, Isabel Fernández Santana, Zoila Lapique, Tomás Fernández Robaina, and Georgina Baró Arencibia in Havana and Santiago de Cuba; and Richenel Ansano and Emy Maduro in Curaçao.

At the repositories I visited, I was fortunate to find a host of scholars steeped in the archival dust of their own projects. At the Archivo del Ministerio de Asuntos Exteriores in Madrid, I met Germán Rueda, who helped me gain rapid access to several collections in other cities in central Spain. At the Archivo General de Puerto Rico, the director introduced me to Ricardo Alegría, Gervasio García, Neville Hall, Jay Kinsbruner, Arturo Morales Carrión, Benjamín Nistal Moret, Andrés Ramos Mattei, Fernando Picó, Raquel Rosario, and

María Consuelo Vázquez Arce. I was fortunate to have the opportunity to interact frequently with Guillermo Baralt, Carlos Casanova Izaguirre, Nelson Fernández, and Teresita Martínez Vergne during earlier visits and Eileen Findlay several years later. At the Archivo Nacional de Cuba, I met the venerable José Luciano Franco and Pedro Deschamps Chapeaux, and for four unforgettable weeks I conversed daily and greedily with Fé Iglesias García and Walterio Carbonell. I am also grateful to Miguel Barnet and Isaac Barreal who helped arrange permission for me to use various archival collections in the course of my first visit to Havana in 1983. The skills, perspectives, and good company these scholars and archivists shared with me helped make each visit to Europe and the Caribbean a rewarding experience.

My mentor, Francis Dutra, paid meticulous attention to the development of this project as a dissertation. For the endless generosity of their time, counsel, and steadfast confidence in this effort and others, I extend warm thanks and heartfelt *abrazos* to César Ayala Casás, Irma MacClaurin, and Robert Paquette. Other friends and colleagues, old and new, lent their ears, eyes, and shoulders to the preparation of this book at various stages. For their support and encouragement, sincerest thanks to Cándido Ayllón, John Blassingame, Carolyn Buxton, Digna Castañeda, Douglas H. Daniels, Jean D'Costa, Eric Dorsey Sr., Nancy Jane Fairley, Vicente González Loscertales, Shelley Haley, John Hondros, Evelyn Hu-DeHart, Larry Knop, Arnold C. Lewis, François Manchuelle, Samuel Martínez, Luis Martínez-Fernández, Chandra Mohanty, Joseph Mwantuali, Boubacar N'Diaye, Charles Peterson, Peter Pozefsky, Randolf Quay, Manuel Ramos Otero, Palmira Ríos González, Cedric J. Robinson, Juan Rodríguez Acosta, Terry Rowden, Fanny Teresa Rushing, Birgit Sonesson, Rosemary Stevenson, Roslyn Terborg-Penn, Begoña Toral, Jorge Ulibarri, and Thomas A. Wilson.

I owe a great deal to Barbara Hetrick, Madonna Hettinger, and Alphine Jefferson at the College of Wooster, Emita Hill and James Jervis at Lehman College, and Dorothy Nagarán at the University of California, Santa Barbara, for their moral and administrative support, and to Dale Catteau, Roger Collier, Karolyn King, Jim Murray, John Sell, Charlotte Wahl, and especially Cathy Breitenbucher at the College of Wooster, Sally Carman and Carol Freeman at Hamilton College, and Renée Nurse at Lehman College for their tireless secretarial and technical support. The energy, enthusiasm, and dependability of student research assistants were also gratifying. At various stages of the book's development my eager aides included Betty Branch, Mauro Castro, Sandra

Cepeda, Virginia Brent Clarke, Zuleika de Jesús Agramonte, Tony Martelly, Victor Rodríguez González, Teresita Romero, Michael Suszter, Jason Suárez Villanueva, and Juan Valdés Núñez. I must acknowledge the editorial staff of the University Press of Florida for their cooperation, efficiency, and goodwill. I am also indebted to the anonymous external readers for their detailed commentaries. They exhibited a force of assessment that was broad, incisive, and energetic. While they approached the project with required detachment and frankness, their rigor was consistently constructive and supportive. I greatly appreciate the clarity of their vision and the strength of their expertise.

A grant from the National Endowment for the Humanities gave me an opportunity to meet with other historians for a six-week seminar at the University of Wisconsin in Madison in 1996. Under the direction of Francisco Scarano, lively discussions on Caribbean history bore fruit. I learned, in summary, that enunciatory splits in the location of culture always regroup at the confluence of discourse, theory, textuality, consciousness, and—all too often—ideology. Resistance to the growing interdisciplinarity of historical research and teaching enriches the production of knowledge in ways at once anticipated, refreshing, and surprising. Many thanks to Dr. Scarano and my fellow *seminaristas* for what has turned out to be an ongoing intellectual experience.

Endless thanks to my wife, Janet, our daughter, Jana, and my son, Clifford, for their loving and lively blend of patience, outrage, understanding, and indignation as I struggled—often unsuccessfully—to balance family needs and pleasures with the external demands and internal obsessions of this project and my profession as a whole. I credit my maternal grandparents, Charity Bullock Bunn (1899–2000) and Elias Bunn, Sr. (1895–1968), as my first history teachers and my first professors of oral tradition. The many accounts they inherited and shared with me about slavery, emancipation processes, and the social economy of race contributed to the foundations of my perceptions about difference, resistance, contradiction, and change. I also wish to acknowledge my brother, Leonard Patrick Dorsey (1961–1994), who taught me that pedagogical relations between older and younger siblings are based on mutual exchange. I dedicate this book to my parents, Madeline Bunn Dorsey and Harry Eugene Dorsey, Jr. (1921–1982). Their love of history, language, and people helped shape my worldview and the human economies that constitute its content. I am responsible, of course, for all flaws and infelicities in the pages that follow.

Introduction

Approaches, Directions, and Concerns

What is the masochistic urge to revel in one of the worst crimes of modern Western imperialism? Why treat this horrible period with seemingly scientific detachment and concern ourselves with its minutiae of ships, ports, and persons?

Herbert Klein, *The Middle Passage*, Introduction

This book contains a miscellany of themes that center on the clandestine slave trade to Puerto Rico. In it, I examine the extent to which forces of doubt, disunity, and incoherence served a single branch of an outlawed enterprise described then and now as small. From 1817 to 1859, the illegal slave trade to Puerto Rico operated in the shadow of larger and wealthier competitors. Furthermore, until 1835, British policy-makers identified the organization of Puerto Rican slave traffic as haphazard and segmented. This miscalculation was based on the superficial interpretation of numbers on the part of British officials and practices of deception on the part of slave suppliers, their customers, and their governments. The double illusion of inconsequential participation and organizational disarray did more to mask the success of Puerto Rican slave commerce than to reveal its shortcomings and failures. Both errors corroborate the assertion that the impact of British abolitionist politics on Spanish, West African, and non-Hispanic Antillean contributions was never consistent.

Despite varied patterns of European occupation, settlement, and exploitation in the Caribbean, slave labor and sugar production shaped the same colonial discourse. Temporal and circumstantial differences dictated similarities in the use of slave labor from one island to the next. Though sugar dominated agrarian enterprises in the non-Hispanic islands from the second half of the 1600s, its rise to preeminence in Cuba and Puerto Rico did not begin until later.

To cite but one example of comparative chronology and opportunity, the collapse of slave-based sugar production in St. Domingue (Haiti) between 1791 and 1804 accentuated its new centrality in the Spanish islands of Cuba and Puerto Rico. For the smaller of the two islands—in the wake of commercial and political reforms—the organization and implementation of mechanisms to increase royal profits from legitimate colonial industries were slow and difficult. Thus, an earlier history of metropolitan neglect, low slave fertility, and practices of slave manumission combined to favor dependency on the external acquisition of slaves. The Spanish Crown corrected the shortsightedness of its Caribbean vision by moving sugar production from the margin to the center of its economic agenda between 1765 and 1815. When sugar finally came to reign in Puerto Rico, with coffee as its consort, its sovereignty accelerated emphasis on access to slaves.

After a century and a half of profitable dependency on slave labor in its Caribbean colonies, Great Britain made efforts to stop international slave traffic. Its ministers negotiated bilateral treaties involving all Western nations engaged in maritime trade—from Denmark, Sweden, Russia, Greece, and Italy to the United States, Haiti, Mexico, most of Central America, and the whole of South America. From the 1820s to the 1850s, slave-holding interest groups in Puerto Rico enacted numerous plots and schemes to maintain access to foreign-born slaves. The combination of local and foreign-born slaves rarely exceeded a tenth of the population for the whole of the island's history—roughly 50,000 out of 450,000 to 500,000 by midcentury. Nonetheless, by way of mixed channels with mixed success the influx of slaves endured.[1] About 6,000 Africans per annum landed at Puerto Rican ports by the mid-1820s. Though British observers asserted that some 7,000 arrived in 1836, annual estimates dipped to 2,000 by the close of the decade, with few reliable estimates for subsequent years. And, as far as we can tell, the external slave traffic to the island stopped in 1859. When Spanish slave commerce was a legal affair, from 1510 to 1817, the influx of African captives to Puerto Rico was even smaller.[2] Therefore, relative to Brazil, Cuba, the non-Hispanic Caribbean, and the United States (or for that matter, two centuries earlier, Mexico, Panama, Colombia, Venezuela, Ecuador, and Peru), tracking the history of illegal slave traffic to Puerto Rico may seem less than worthy of pursuit, especially after its initial prohibition, in two stages, between 1817 and 1820.[3]

Legal cessation marked the end of pertinent government documents and bureaucratic minutiae that chronicled important features of the traffic for 300 years. Thus, records from participants in illegal slaving are few. Those that survive were written with ambiguity and deception in mind—in much the same way that illegal activities resulted in inaccurate records when the traffic was legal. For those seeking to examine the history of Spanish slave trading over time, major challenges lie in the contest between misinformation based on the mixing of legitimate commerce and contraband from the sixteenth to the eighteenth centuries and little reliable information because of antislave trade treaties in the nineteenth century. But smaller figures, stilted paper work, and heavily encoded messages are no less instructive than larger figures, ongoing serials, and unambiguous texts. Blind spots created by missing data and the cryptic language of secret reports are likewise embedded in the history of the period under review. Nonetheless, even if this were not the case, given the technical tensions of its execution, the internal dynamics of its social economy, and the external intricacy of its political design, the illegal slave trade to Puerto Rico is a story worth telling.

This study follows the Puerto Rican slave trade from the internationalization of the antislave trade campaign in 1815 to the arrival of the island's last known slave ship in 1859. It aims to identify the regional origins of African captives, on the one hand, and to assess the extent to which inter-Caribbean slave trading perpetuated commercial relations between Puerto Rico and non-Hispanic islands, on the other. These separate avenues of slave acquisition crossed paths frequently, forming conflated sources of involuntary labor and a third area of geopolitical concern: the extent to which the inter-Caribbean slave trade to Puerto Rico disguised the influx of African captives. Due to increased British opposition, the island's slave market faced waning numbers after 1830. However, it will be demonstrated at multiple levels throughout this study that inter-Caribbean cooperation, together with African and European brokerage, facilitated the endurance of the slave trade to Puerto Rico through the middle of the nineteenth century.

The shift from legal to illegal slave trading rendered the 1820s a period of trial and error. At some levels, however, transition is difficult to discern. The organization of transport not only remained in the hands of multinational fortune hunters, but British efforts failed to curb the activities of slave-trading firms. Until the 1850s, these firms continued to disguise themselves as French, Spanish, and Portuguese shipping companies with branch offices in Cuba, Puerto Rico, the United States, and England itself. Furthermore, until the late 1820s Denmark, France, and the Netherlands took their abolitionist agreements less seriously than they should have. Thus, for most of the first decade of prohibition, British maneuvers were less than impressive. The 1830s marked a greater period of strategic adjustment on both sides. Though many basic features of capture remained in place, due to the Equipment Clause of 1835, arrangements for transoceanic voyages did not. While this phase marked a turning point in the African slave trade to Cuba and Puerto Rico, change had different meanings for the two islands. For the larger, the second decade of clandestine operations spelled logistic change; for the smaller, it indicated both the firming of resistance policy and the advance of cessation.

This paradox, the approach of cessation on the wings of slave trade policy consolidation, may be divided into three overlapping stages. First, between 1834 and 1840 British protests against the export of newly emancipated English slaves to Spanish dominions underlined the necessity of shaping a watertight policy to silence international complaints. In addition to the Anglo-Spanish treaty of 1835—which for the first time permitted British naval officers to capture vessels based on evidence of slave-trading equipment alone—four years later, without consulting Brazil or Portugal, Great Britain began to seize all slave ships bearing the Lusitanian banner. Luso-Brazilians, long linked to Spanish American slaving activities, could no longer provide vessels bound for Cuba and Puerto Rico with the protection of the Portuguese flag. During this period Great Britain began to press for a consulate at San Juan, as a result of the enslavement of black Britons in Puerto Rico.

Second, the period 1840 to 1844 was fraught with internal uncertainty. Great Britain's discovery of English slaves in Puerto Rico embarrassed and angered the Spanish metropolitan government. The revelation not only publicized problems in local communication based on internal struggles for power, it forced the Spanish monarchy to authorize a British, abolition-oriented consulate. As bureaucrats in Madrid began to iron out the wherewithal of a reinforced slave trade policy, a concurrent series of liberationist slave revolts and conspiracies in Cuba and Puerto Rico dashed the hopes of metropolitan officials. Island security was an obvious concern, but another loomed large beside it. Who provoked the unrest—slaves born locally, African-born slaves, or slaves from the non-Hispanic Caribbean? This uncertainty challenged the wisdom of continued quests for external slaves.

Third, from late 1844 to late 1847, authorities assumed that slave militancy was largely under control. Thus, in 1845 Spain punctured the surface of its antislave trade law with enough loopholes to permit the traffic to continue.

For Puerto Rico specifically, the new code allowed enough leverage to reconnect African and inter-Caribbean channels. But 1848 marked the beginning of an extended lull. That year, slave revolts in Martinique, St. Croix, and Puerto Rico, along with the appointment of Puerto Rico's first abolitionist governor (after the revolts), combined to discourage further importations of slaves. In 1855, slave deaths from cholera renewed interest in the traffic. It was not until 1859, however, that a full-scale expedition succeeded, by accident, in landing over a thousand Congolese slaves on the island's eastern shore. This was the last documented arrival of African captives in Puerto Rico.

The Generation of 1973

In 1973, the centennial celebration of the abolition of slavery in Puerto Rico inspired a great deal of academic activity there. In 1974, Luis Díaz Soler's pioneering *Historia de la esclavitud negra en Puerto Rico* went through its fourth edition. An expanded version of Manuel Alvarez Nazario's linguistic study, *El elemento afro-negroide en el español de Puerto Rico*, was issued the same year, along with the controversial study of literature, orature, and the politics of race, *Narciso descubre su trasero: El negro en la cultura puertorriqueña*, by Isabelo Zenón Cruz. In 1978, Arturo Morales Carrión published *Auge y decadencia de la trata negrera en Puerto Rico, 1820–1860*, an important introduction to the ways and means of clandestine slave commerce through diplomatic history.[4] There were also several important doctoral theses authored by Puerto Rican scholars trained in the United States, Great Britain, and France. In this category, Francisco Scarano's published dissertation, *Sugar and Slavery in Puerto Rico*, distinguishes itself as a probing exercise in Spanish colonial economics. In a different fashion, the same may be said of Guillermo Baralt's *Esclavos rebeldes*, an examination of militant resistance that reinforces the history of the slave initiative. A larger group of Puerto Ricans earning master's degrees from the University of Puerto Rico and doctorates from the University of Valladolid made significant contributions to Afro–Puerto Rican historical literature by way of essays in such scholarly journals as *Caribe, Hómines, Cuadernos, Anales de Investigación Histórica, Revista del Instituto de Cultura Puertorriqueña*, and the *Latin American Research Review*.[5]

The "Generation of 1973" was largely an internal collectivity of scholarship that foregrounded the African origins of Puerto Rican history and culture. While it established slavery and race relations in Puerto Rico as integral components of Latin American and Caribbean studies, it had little impact on historiographic developments in the United States or elsewhere at the time. With the exception of Scarano's work, which was written in English, few scholars outside the island were aware of the Generation and the importance of its productivity.

Changing Theories and Debates

Concurrent with—and in many respects theoretically allied to—the Generation of 1973, changing trends encouraged the examination of forced servitude with more forward-looking approaches in mind. These new ideas crossed systems, generations, and institutions. Stanley Stein planted the seeds as early as 1957, but they did not begin to root until later, when scholarly emporia were inundated with publications that stemmed from energetic debates on comparative slavery in the Americas. The debates owe their origins to earlier works by Gilberto Freyre, Frank Tannenbaum, and Eric Williams.[6] Freyre's work on Brazilian slavery and its legacy lay at the heart of Tannenbaum's thesis.

Tannenbaum was inspired by Freyre's conviction that Portuguese colonial practices—including slavery in Africa, Brazil, and Portugal itself—were relatively free of racist elements. Thus, in *Slave and Citizen*, he asserted that the combination of Roman Catholicism and the *Siete Partidas*—a body of thirteenth-century laws compiled under the auspices of Alfonso the Wise—rendered Spanish and Portuguese slavery less rigorous compared to its practice elsewhere in the Americas, especially in English-speaking polities such as the United States and the British Caribbean. As imperial expansionists beginning in the fifteenth and sixteenth centuries, Spain and Portugal carried with them the traditional force of such Catholic mandates as baptism, confirmation, and marriage, on the one hand, and the justice of medieval Castilian law, on the other. And both—Catholic sacraments and Alphonsinian law—applied to slaves. By Tannenbaum's reckoning, the Catholic Iberian background also accounts for differences in race relations in Latin America and non-Latin America after the abolition of slavery. According to him, because the transition from slavery to freedom was relatively facile in Brazil and Spanish America, in bold contrast to the United States after Reconstruction, negative race relations in contemporary Latin America are less evident by comparison.

Despite an impressive following initially, the backlash against Tannenbaum's "friendly master" thesis was relentless. Among his most ardent attackers were scholars who switched sides. Problems in the thesis are fairly easy to recognize today. Lack of juxtaposition between time and space and theory and practice punctured his work repeatedly. Legal inscriptions designed for the Spanish kingdom of Castile in the 1200s were not meant for the Spanish American colonies between the 1500s and the 1800s. Though influenced by ideas found in Catholic and Alphonsinian canon, the distance between the spirit and the letter of Spanish and Portuguese colonial legislation was great. Tannenbaum was correct in his assertion that slave codes in the British, Danish, and Dutch Caribbean and in the United States were harsh compared to Spanish America and Brazil. But his argument does not question the extent to which Spanish and Portuguese colonial laws were implemented. Furthermore, he saw the institution of slavery in the Americas as a series of national systems rather than a single system of hemispheric, transnational proportions. It was the combination of these drawbacks that sparked virulent scholarly protest.[7]

In 1969, Eugene Genovese identified variables in American slavery that crisscrossed national and colonial divides. They included conditions of daily life, job diversity, the retention of African value systems, and access to manumission. In material and nonmaterial terms, he offered tools of measurement for gauging the severity of bondage in different places in the Americas. His essay provided level-headed insights that moved toward a resolution of the Tannenbaum controversy by outlining a quasi-structuralist framework for the study of slavery as sociocultural morphology.[8] In spite of the soundness of his suggestions, some scholars concluded that comparative projects were too confined, not by geography but by conceptualization. In 1974 and 1978, John Lombardi and Magnus Mörner promoted the diversification of slave studies.[9] The works of Verena Martínez-Alier, David Cohen, Jack Greene, Warren Dean, Fernando Picó, Laird Bergad, and Rebecca Scott rank among successful attempts to move away from polemics that isolated comparative slavery as a singular focus.[10] Grounded on intellectual, interdisciplinary, and transmillennial history, David Brion Davis and Orlando Patterson offered broad-based syntheses that also contributed to the diversification of slave studies.[11] However, rather than displacing the types of monographs that kept editors so busy in the 1960s and much of the 1970s, foci on multiple institutions, the internationalization of abolitionist politics, postabolition processes, and transgenerational concerns served to enrich them, as instanced in studies by Mary Karasch, David Eltis, Robert Conrad, A.J.R. Russell-Wood, and Robert Paquette in the 1980s.[12] Yet research devoted to the chronological confines of individual American slave regimes continued. Diversification and cross-fertilization helped put to rest the tense and sometimes bellicose arguments that comparative approaches seemed to provoke. The 1980s also marked rising interests in the study of slave systems in Africa and other parts of the non-Western world.[13]

Feminist investigations of slavery made gains in the 1980s and 1990s, but the same years witnessed a decline in an analysis of slavery from Marxist points of view.[14] Due to their reluctance to fathom historical uncertainty, indeterminacy, contradiction, and other cryptic spaces of epistemology as viable constructions of social oppression and resistance to it, many scholars who focused on the social relations of slavery vis-à-vis economic determinism reached an impasse or, at the very least, a series of mergers, absorptions, and dilutions. The halt, faltering, or blending may be due in part to the intellectual upheavals of postmodern thought, along with Louis Althusser's rather subversive reassessment of Marx's basic model for the social relations of labor. Rooted in intellectual history, philosophy, linguistics, feminism, postcolonial theory, counter-Freudian criticism, and Althusserian studies, these rebel readings underscore uncertainty, indeterminacy, and contradiction as useful voids of ambivalence.

While traditional Marxists revile ambivalence as antidialectical, postmodernists—and their text-centered constituents, the poststructuralists—glory in it precisely because it is, among other things, antidialectical. Whether rightly or wrongly associated with the nonlinear, counterdiscursive strategies of postmodern thought, Althusser's ideological state apparatuses, Hayden White's tropic foundations of metahistorical discourse, Roland Barthes's lexical sexualities, Julia Kristeva's genotextual semiotics, the symbolic capital of Pierre Bourdieu's habitus, Homi Bhabha's optical énoncé, Michel Foucault's social grids of biopolitical intelligence, and, above all, Jacques Derrida's grammatological folds, footprints, and traces sent many historians—Marxist or not—into an intellectual tailspin.[15] Obviously, problems in basic communication sufficed to encumber the movement of postmodern ideas among historians of slavery.[16] Only a few books fully constitute postmodern critiques of slavery, and they are limited almost entirely to the history of the United States.[17] Yet together with ideas emerging from the comparative analysis of slavery and the Generation of 1973, postmodern studies had an impact on the study of slavery and emancipation in Puerto Rico for the remainder of the twentieth century.

In 1985, Manuel Moreno Fraginals co-edited a collection of essays that focused on socioeconomic transitions from slavery to freedom.[18] Foregrounding abolitionist processes as overlapping histories of social, cultural, and political phenomena in Puerto Rico, the Dominican Republic, and Cuba, contributors identified the Spanish Caribbean as three autonomous components of a single entity unified by their differences from both the non-Hispanic Caribbean and the Spanish American mainlands. In the 1990s, Luis Martínez-Fernández, César Ayala, and Christopher Schmidt-Nowara expanded the Spanish Caribbean dimensions of geopolitical similarity and sociocultural unity with themes that range from abolitionist politics and diplomacy to the structural transformations (spatial, fiscal, technological, and ultimately, sociopolitical) of sugar production.[19] Works focusing on Puerto Rico alone integrated slavery, emancipation, and race relations in general with themes that include foreign policy, local and international market relations, literacy and public education, gender relations, and the social economy of individual cities and towns. Emma Dávila-Cox identifies the changing politics of commerce and finance in her history of the British consulate of San Juan. While Eileen Findlay and Félix Matos Rodríguez consider labor systems, slave and free, as they relate to the history of women's struggles against job bigotry and domestic violence, Teresita Martínez-Vergne works with Foucauldian vistas of knowledge, power, and agency in her institutional examination of public charity. Spotlighting the sociopolitical performativities of colonial identity, Fernando Picó's examination of late Spanish colonial class formation, subaltern resistance, and criminal justice includes both municipal and islandwide perspectives. Like Picó's study, Jay Kinsbruner's work on racial prejudice against the island's free black population is a microhistory that is not one. Complementing the chronology of slavery, it emphasizes San Juan but with input from other municipalities, especially Ponce.[20] While authors such as Pedro San Miguel, Luis Antonio Figueroa, and jointly Mariano Negrón Portillo and Raúl Mayo Santana adhere to slavery and emancipation exclusively, by focusing on municipal accounts they, too, accentuate the delicate interplay between macro- and mircrohistorical approaches.[21]

Since the 1970s, then, research on Puerto Rican slavery and its aftermath falls into three broad categories: (1) regional integrationist studies, as seen in works that examine Spanish Caribbean history as a cultural, nationlike entity consisting of three units bonded by language, religion, imperial rule, and foreign industrial exploitation—first Spain, then the United States—and similar but not identical local social groups; (2) municipal integrationist studies, microhistories that demonstrate constituent relations between local history and the history of the island as a whole—a division that subsumes slavery, emancipation, and emancipation adaptation under other institutions and industries such as marriage, public welfare, foreign trade and diplomacy, conscripted nonslave labor, the justice system, and the social relations of housing; and (3) overlapping the second, microhistories of individual municipalities that focus on slavery and its destruction alone.

Since the Generation of 1973, historical examinations of Puerto Rican slavery have used synecdochic approaches, a rhetorical construct that denotes the figurative uses of wholes for parts or parts for wholes. Despite the political differences that separated the Dominican Republic from Cuba and Puerto Rico for most of the nineteenth century and Puerto Rico from Cuba and the Dominican Republic from the early twentieth century onward, cultural and linguistic unity informs the regional integrationist histories of these Spanish Caribbean polities. Scholars in this category present individual islands as parts of an epistemic, quasi-national whole. In this sense, notions of political contiguity operate as figurative devices that displace the physical realities of geographic separation. Municipal integrationist histories—here, microhistories of slavery and numerous institutions that include slavery—suggest brands of local history likewise capable of using parts to represent wholes. Though authors in this double category emphasize that their site-centered foci do not speak for islandwide phenomena, the potential for contiguitive interpretation is always present. But this presence is less menacing than it appears. Contiguity and synonymity refer to different types of proximity. They are not interchangeable terms. As with any history of behavior, motivation, or consciousness, nonetheless, Spanish Caribbean slavery and commerce operated as a kind of *continuum interruptum*, a chain of discontinuities grounded in the disequilibria of human difference and change. Like contiguity and synonymity, language and history are not interchangeable signs. Unlike contiguity and synonymity, however, they are codependent, if not inseparable. Plots do not exist without stories; stories do not exist without sequences; synchrony resides within diachrony; and what is stated—from utterance to impact—cannot be separated from the process of stating it.

Between the insular projects that characterized Puerto Rican scholarship on slavery in the 1970s and the transinstitutional projects that outlived them, two conflicting concerns were never resolved: quantitative and qualitative approaches to the study of slavery. In the 1980s, new directions in qualitative research began to focus on individual narratives and collective biographies, while quantitative research since the 1960s continues to emphasize cliometric analysis.[22] Historical culturalists, social analysts, and text analysts charged that statistical studies, what scholars of slavery call "the numbers game," impersonalize the human tragedy and devastation of slavery. They asserted—and continue to assert—that numbers should not form foundations for historical narratives about slavery. With specific reference to slave commerce and transport, David Eltis and David Richardson defended the role of quantitative specialists when they said, "[W]e ... believe that it is difficult to assess the significance or representativeness of personal narratives or collective biographies, however detailed, without an understanding of the overall movement of slaves of which these individuals' lives were a part."[23]

Tied to the pursuit of essences predicated on the primacy of science, the "numbers game" bears a striking resemblance to the linguistic, literary, and cultural aims of structuralism (and its more abstract predecessor, formalism). Conversely, the fluid, free-playing dynamics of change and difference in individual narratives and biographic collectives, including narratives by or about slaves, are increasingly difficult to separate from the independent—and often picaresque—agents of poststructuralism. As with modernism and postmodernism, however, many experts now believe that structuralism and poststructuralism do not constitute separate worldviews. They are instead a series of critiques of the former by the latter. They are not intrinsically hostile to each other. In some ways the same holds true for relations between words and numbers. Just as postmodernism and poststructuralism need modernism and structuralism to validate their existence, quantitative analysis depends on qualitative explanations to decode or recode its messages. At the same time, among other things, words are inherently quantitative, as any exercise in content analysis will demonstrate.

John Thornton's analysis of maritime corridors as conduits of cross-fertilization between African and Iberian cultures in the Americas underscores the importance of synthesis between quantitative and qualitative research. He not only reminds us that words and numbers go hand in hand, he reaffirms that neither type of text is foolproof. However, considering the lack of information needed to formulate relations between African demographic trends overall and the numbers of Africans enslaved before and during the Atlantic slave trade, Thornton suggests that some statistical discussions are "manipulative assumptions."[24] His misgivings about postcolonial reconstructions of precolonial demographics are well informed. Citing numbers sparingly, he prefers to engage quantitative ideas as copious narratives based on primary texts in languages that range from Latin to Fulfulde. The results are dense yet porous weavings that avoid the foregrounding of one approach at the expense other. Thus, qualitative and quantitative tools are capable of building persuasive narrative structures. Authorial aims and strategies guide words as much as numbers.

Recovering the Slave Trade

Due to gaps in documents that point both to proslave trade policy and the inner spheres of slave acquisition, our understanding of Puerto Rican slave commerce is sketchy at best. While experts on this branch of the traffic are few, their contributions are diverse and rewarding. In his study of slavery and sugar production, Francisco Scarano noted that official records for slave imports to the island have never been found, that the island has no counterpart to the Cuban register of slave imports through Havana, and that the lack of such a counterpart is remarkable given that the two colonies fell under the same imperial administration and that in general their archival collections closely resemble one another.[25] But he remedied many areas of this problem. Relying on business transactions and census data for Ponce, Scarano determined that African-born slaves numbered as high as 53.4 percent by 1838, outnumbering locally born slaves by 12 percent and non-Hispanic Caribbean slaves by 48.2 percent. He estimated that the African influx reached its peak between 1821 and 1828, with an average of 225 slaves per annum. It then declined to 128 between 1834 and 1846.[26] In this manner, his work establishes guidelines for historians with economic and demographic concerns for other Puerto Rican municipalities in mind. In addition, noting that it behooved local officials to distort records destined for Madrid as much as possible, apparently to relieve the Spanish government of British abolitionist pressure, he corrected the position of earlier specialists who maintained that the Puerto Rican slave population increased during the 1820s as a result of birth rates.

Demonstrating the ways and means of slave demographic increase, Scarano underscores the extent to which microeconomic studies inform the history of the traffic during its illegal years. By proving that African captives in Ponce formed over half the slave population at the peak of the island's participation in the transatlantic slave trade, he reaffirms that sugar production, the colony's most important source of agrarian wealth, was squarely dependent on slavery, not on free labor as earlier theses maintained.[27] His findings are also significant because they modify earlier generalizations that attempted to explain why transatlantic slave traffic endured. While others argue that the rigors of plantation labor, together with sex imbalance, worked against natural reproduction—more so for Africans than Creoles irrespective of the setting—Scarano diversifies the oversimplified theme of Creole labor vis-à-vis African labor as a determining factor in plantation production. Dividing slaveholders into three groups—large, intermediate, and small—he affirms that large-scale sugar producers, who owned the greatest number of slaves, preferred foreign-born slaves, presumably African, to those born locally. Most evident among the reasons for this preference were planter links to international slave-smuggling networks. Midrange slaveholders used equal numbers of Creoles and Africans, while Creole slaves dominated among small-scale holders. Therefore, regardless of British antislave trade initiatives, Puerto Rican planters continued to seek transatlantic solutions to remedy labor shortages in the plantation sector. He also reveals a remarkable surplus of Puerto Rican–born male slaves among top-tier producers in Ponce, thus paving the way for further examinations of the internal slave market.[28]

Morales Carrión, in his diplomatic history of the Puerto Rican slave trade, identified Captain General Miguel de La Torre y Pando, who governed from 1822 to 1838, as the island's great catalyst in illegal slave trade operations.[29] Stressing the relationship between immigration and the non-Hispanic islands as depots for the importation of Africans to Puerto Rico, from different perspectives Scarano and Morales Carrión define problems with the clandestine traffic in its formative years. Morales Carrión's emphasis on Dutch and Danish Antillean intermediaries stems evidently from their free port status, of which many immigrants bound for Puerto Rico took advantage. On the other hand, his discussion of the importation of English slaves, roughly for the same period, serves to preface his perspective of Anglo-Spanish diplomatic conflicts. While Scarano also assesses the role of the non-Hispanic islands during the 1820s, he places greater emphasis on French conduits. Most Francophone newcomers to Puerto Rico came from Europe. But, intimates Scarano, the proximity of French Caribbean slave-holding colonies facilitated the importation of African slaves. Following this line of reasoning, French immigrants linked Puerto Rico to a colonial power in a greater position to resist British antislave trade demands. Though in the long run France proved to be Great Britain's greatest ally against the traffic, their alliance was far from evident in the 1820s.

Scarano and Morales Carrión do not explore the cultural specificities of Puerto Rican slave provenance. Therefore, in relation to planter accessibility to servile labor and international relations, neither author privileges slave origins beyond contrasts between Creole and African birth. However, without the quantification that supports Scarano's work, the demographic significance of Puerto Rico's position as the smallest slave-holding polity in the Greater Antilles would have remained distorted. His rearrangement of conceptual spaces of wealth, power, and slave labor enabled him to concentrate on complex and vicissitudinous business relations among players and agents within Ponce, between Ponce and other Puerto Rican municipalities, and ultimately, between Puerto Rico and the world beyond. In this manner, with quantitative and qualitative evidence, he corrected the misguided belief that the intensity of slavery in a given country or colony was contingent on the strength of slave numbers. Revealing the mutability of local, regional, and state history as social, political, and cultural variables, he shows where and how slave-holding in Ponce did and did not represent an islandwide phenomenon. Despite the Anglophilia that permeates Morales's diplomatic focus, he silenced the assertions of those who viewed Puerto Rican abolitionism as an unencumbered undertaking.

Framing the Issues

From the 1940s, but more noticeably from the 1960s, approaches to the study of slavery in the Americas relied on comparative methodologies, quantitative analysis, Hegelian-Marxian dialectical strategies, macrohistories, microhistories, transgenerational theory, transinstitutional practices, and women's history, along with droplets of postmodernism, narratology, and other text-centered concerns. However, there is more to be said about slavery in the history of Spanish colonial Puerto Rico, in particular the origins and organizing structures of the traffic that fed it during the years it was illegal. For a host of legitimate reasons, our understanding of the foundations that shaped the market patterns of acquisition and distribution in Puerto Rico is fragmented for this period.[30]

The 1820s marked the first decade of the clandestine trade. As such, it was critical. We know that the island's early period of economic transformation extended into the first decade of the illegal influx, but without Spanish maritime records it is difficult to determine how merchants and mariners organized the traffic and how bureaucrats handled the subterfuge. Hence, informational fissures block our access to the internal dynamics of the trade as an ongoing, transoceanic enterprise. As in previous centuries, American colonies and European metropoles synchronized their attention on Africa. In this context, at the conceptual level, nothing changed. Until the 1840s, British efforts failed to discourage the flow. Yet because of the campaign—despite its slow and controversial progress—our knowledge of the contours and protocols of illegal slave acquisition is limited. Archival gaps today stem from the secrecy of the trade at the time. Obviously, participants and their supporters were sensitive to paper trails. Therefore, those seeking to draw the Puerto Rican slave trade into the larger world of South Atlantic affairs are faced with many blanks in the data.

African captives were people who, as individuals and groups, played major roles in the shaping of Puerto Rican culture. But beyond sub-Sahara provenance, we know little about their natal cultures—simply because we have not been able to identify most of them without resorting to guesswork. We know even less about circumstances leading to their capture. The challenge remains to identify their origins beyond regional points of shoreline departure and to plot patterns of acquisition associated with their enslavement. Southwest Nigeria distinguishes itself as a case in point. We still lack evidence to verify what chain of logistic premises determined that Yoruba captives would flood slave markets in Cuba and Brazil but not Puerto Rico. Sources illustrating specific African locations of commercial interaction, social behaviors, political practices, and technical operations used to implement such interaction for the Puerto Rican branch of the outlawed traffic would reveal important information about developing trends and changing patterns of slave acquisition for the trade overall.

Between the Anglo-Spanish antislave trade conventions of 1817 and 1835, documents on Puerto Rican participation are especially sparse. Failing to recognize the island's leadership as significantly transgressive for most of this period, Great Britain, once again, was responsible for the paucity of records. Nonetheless, between 1835 and 1844 the Foreign Office took steps to correct the oversight. Therefore, from the mid-1830s onward, even without the elusive shipping records, many European and American collections—both libraries and archives—contain alternate sources that aid partially in reconstructing the organization of the Puerto Rican slave trade. Such materials reveal political barometers that measured the irregular flow of the traffic over four decades. While these sources are, for the most part, silent on the formation and implementation of illegal Spanish slave trade policy between 1817 and 1835, they shed considerable light on the theory and practice of slave acquisitions for the next fifteen years.

The following concerns outline my objectives in this book.

(1) Puerto Rico played a vital role in the formative years of the "Atlantic Community," a geo-historical designation within the intercontinental complex of slave-based agrarian industry and trade that, transcending the equatorial divide, Philip Curtin first identified as the "South Atlantic System." As a member of this community and as a participant in the system that fostered its growth, Puerto Rico cannot be separated from the history of slave trading as a behavioral economy predicated on a host of internal and external variables. Vis-à-vis slave trading in the Age of Abolition, this basic premise begs the basic question, What role did Puerto Rico play in the production of counterabolitionist politics as an applied practice, first and foremost in the context of international slave commerce?

(2) With special reference to distinctions between Puerto Rican and non–Puerto Rican input from the Caribbean to West Africa and back, how did Puerto Rican interest groups grapple with the mechanics of slave acquisition and transport? To be sure, by comparison, the trade did not thrive, but in fractured forms it continued. What forces and plans of action permitted it to go on after its prohibition, albeit in bursts and trickles? In other words, what were the organizational nuts and bolts of transatlantic and trans-Caribbean expeditions undertaken in the name of the Puerto Rican slave market? In addition, what glitches were endemic to Puerto Rican efforts, and who devised what methods to overcome them?

(3) To what extent did Spain endorse Puerto Rican slave suppliers and consumers in their efforts to keep oceanic corridors open in the face of British opposition to and Cuban hegemony in the outlawed traffic? More specifically, what were the combined roles of Spain, Cuba, and the non-Hispanic Caribbean, especially Curaçao and the eastern bulge, in executing these operations and the removal of obstacles that encumbered them?

(4) In view of both African and inter-Caribbean arrivals, who were the slave newcomers? What politics and market discourses facilitated the influx of Dutch-, English-, French-, and patois-speaking Creole slaves from the non-Hispanic Caribbean? How do their numbers compare with African-born slaves? And, as separate commercial

behaviors under different forms of duress, under what circumstances did the two flows of traffic converge? Furthermore, beyond the blanketed, reductivist concept of the "Coast of Africa," what were the specific origins of Puerto Rico's African-born slaves? What African polities—hamlets, villages, towns, cities, city-states, nations, and empires—supplied the island with its African-born captives, its *bozales*, its *negros de nación*, as they were called alternately for four centuries wherever they were found in the Spanish seaborne empire?[31] What forces precipitated their involuntary migration; what were their points of transoceanic departure; and what directions did their journeys take—their routes and junctions from capture to arrival on Puerto Rican soil?

(5) What combination of conditions and events in Spain, West Africa, and the Caribbean heralded the decline of Puerto Rican participation in the international slave trade?

Cuba outdistanced Puerto Rico as a participant in the Atlantic slave trade. Many scholars believe that the smaller island was forced to settle for whatever remnants happened its way, especially after 1830. Spain favored Cuba because of its size, its larger population, and consequently its greater taxability. But sibling concerns for metropolitan attention did not always result in Cuba emerging as the victor. The Real Cédula de Gracias of 1815, effective 1816 to 1830, was designed to bring Puerto Rico up to exploitable par. Upgrading included measures to encourage the influx of greater numbers of white immigrants and black slaves. When Spain granted a similar *real cédula*, or royal decree, to Cuba in 1817, the decree held but a fraction of the latitude found in the one granted to Puerto Rico. Nor did the Crown grant the Cuban decree freely. Powerful planters had to lobby for it.[32] The expiration of the Puerto Rican *cédula* coincided with a decline in the reexport of African captives from the non-Hispanic islands. When this source slowed to a trickle between 1828 and 1830, planters in Puerto Rico found it increasingly difficult to obtain African captives. Conversely, the Cuban slave trade—which sometimes exploited but never depended on inter-Caribbean connections—endured for another forty years.[33]

Less can be valid, and sometimes less is more. But when we compare the volume of slave traffic to Cuba and Puerto Rico, along with its short- and long-term effects, differences between greater and smaller numbers are staggering.

The impact of Cuba's quantitative and chronological edge extended beyond agrarian and fiscal concerns. These advantages resulted in separate processes of alienation and integration. The greater size and diversity of Cuba's African-born population sufficed to render creolization processes distinct. In Puerto Rico, the most noticeable result of demographic difference is the absence of African-based institutions, such as church-authorized *cofradías*, brotherhoods, or mutual aid societies, and the apparent (but not proven) absence of definitive and cohesive practices of ethics based on African systems of spiritual belief. Documents have yet to surface to suggest that nineteenth-century Puerto Rico had anything comparable to Cuban Santería from eastern Dahomey (Benin) and southwestern Nigeria, Abakuá from southeastern Nigeria, or Palo Mayombe, a conflation of religious beliefs and practices from the geographic extremities of Sierra Leone and the Congo. By far, African-born slaves formed the largest foreign-born group in Puerto Rico for the first half of the nineteenth century, but their numbers did not suffice to duplicate or approximate the proliferation of neo-African institutions that permeated Cuba.[34]

Behaviors and practices associated first with marginalization, then integration, acculturation, and assimilation—that is, creolization—differed between the two islands. The African presence in Puerto Rico was—and continues to be—felt. In terms of music, cuisine, folkloric couture, vocabulary, certain regional pronunciations, and on occasion surnames, Africans left indelible marks on the culture of the island. But tracing these legacies to specific African locations remains a challenge. Though ethnogenesis occurred in both Cuba and Puerto Rico, the impact of its blending effects was more pronounced for the latter. In addition to smaller numbers of slaves overall, it is apparent that patterns of demographic concentration, resocialization among linguistically and geographically disparate African groups, and procreation with Spaniards and Creoles, white and black, altered the cultural characteristics that delineated African heterogeneity.[35]

The slave trade to Puerto Rico is least documented between 1817 and 1835. Given that these years may have been the most intensive period of African influx, it is difficult to discern patterns of acquisition and ethnic representation for the whole of the illicit traffic. More favorable years for data fall between 1835, when Spain acquiesced to Great Britain's equipment clause, and 1845, when Spain promulgated its own antislave trade code. It will become apparent in the course of this study that the majority of captives imported to Puerto Rico during this period departed from the Upper Guinea Coast. Slave traffic to Puerto Rico may have passed its prime by the late 1820s, but much of Upper Guinea—Liberia (except Monrovia), Sierra Leone (except Freetown), and Guinea-Conakry (between Futa Jallon and the Pongo River)—yielded slaves for transatlantic export in the 1830s and 1840s. With the jolting exception of the Congolese captives who arrived on the *Majesty* in 1859, slave traffic to the island ceased by 1850.[36] Therefore, the analysis of issues surrounding how and why Puerto Rican interest groups came to favor Upper Guinea provenance begin with this study and will continue with others.

Themes and Descriptions

Chapter 1 considers the growth of Puerto Rican slave acquisitions from 1815 to 1830 by way of African and inter-Caribbean routes, the changing conditions that threatened slave acquisitions, and the maneuvers metropolitan officials began to devise to meet the challenge of decline. It also weighs the impact of immigration from Europe and the Eastern Caribbean on both channels of the traffic. Chapter 2 examines the developing politics of Anglo-Spanish diplomacy during the first decade of the first antislave trade treaty. Chapter 3 examines the impact of Anglo-Spanish diplomacy on the expansion of pro-slave trade legislation in Madrid from the late 1830s to the early 1840s. Chapter 4 considers the supportive roles of Denmark, France, and the Netherlands in the modus operandi of Puerto Rican slave-trading activity. While these nations are cited initially for their support in the first chapter, here greater attention is given to the relationship between their strategic positions as holders of Caribbean colonies and the political implications of their commercial affairs on the West African coast. Chapter 5 extends from the previous chapter to illustrate how the same metropolitan powers—Denmark, France, and the Netherlands—resisted British abolitionist diplomacy in favor of the Spanish slave trade. Moreover, it demonstrates the extent to which these powers lacked the means to control the commercial activities of their subjects residing on the coast of West Africa. Chapter 6 relies heavily on statistical illustrations to explore the depths of Puerto Rican participation in the transatlantic slave commerce. It scrutinizes the island's links to larger slave-holding polities after 1835, within the context of its ability to carry out independent expeditions. Chapter 7 focuses primarily on the Upper Guinea Coast to offer examples of the social, political, and cultural milieux that represented slave acquisitions in the 1840s. Particular attention is given to the shifting configurations of African affairs, especially in coastal enclaves linked directly and indirectly by politics and trade to major cities and towns in the hinterlands. Chapter 8 analyzes the abolitionist efforts of Great Britain's first consul in Puerto Rico. It serves as a multilateral prolegomenon to the revival of the inter-Caribbean slave trade discussed in the next chapter. Chapter 9 asserts that the arrival of captives between 1845 and 1847 marked a return to inter-Caribbean reexport maneuvers, which countered Spain's new but ever-evasive commitment to end the African slave trade.

I

Strategies and Stratagems

1

"Such an Obscure Colony"

The origins of Puerto Rican participation in the clandestine slave trade are found in patterns established from the earliest years of Spanish settlement. They begin with blind spots that prevented the Spanish government from recognizing the island's worth beyond its use as an isolated sentry to check foreign encroachment. Despite the nautical appeal of San Juan's layout, for example, which could have facilitated the development of large-scale enterprises, the Crown never elevated the capital city above the level of a secondary port. Due to a history of this kind of imperial negligence, many historians failed to recognize that isolation creates its own dynamic. This changed when Arturo Morales Carrión published his seminal work on Puerto Rican relations with the non-Hispanic Caribbean. He demonstrated that, with the cooperation of resident Spanish officials, Spanish settlers and Puerto Rican Creoles developed the means to survive, and sometimes thrive, through contraband commerce despite blatant metropolitan indifference from the 1520s to the 1790s.[1]

In his report to Charles III in 1765, royal envoy Alejandro O'Reilly complained that the inhabitants of Puerto Rico had little spirit for surplus production. According to him, the island's natural wealth—an abundance of fruits, vegetables, livestock, and waterways fat with fish—discouraged industrial incentive. He also complained that Spanish soldiers abandoned their quarters in favor of domesticity with black women, with whom they had many children and gave the whole of their modest income. Above all, he observed that coastal contraband trade with foreigners was well organized and beyond the reach of imperial control.[2] O'Reilly saw a great deal of surplus industry, of course, but most of it was destined for the non-Hispanic islands, in clear violation of fool-hardy but long-standing Spanish commercial restrictions. In this sense, many Puerto Rican harbors, beaches, bays, and other shoreline features were no less international pathways and crossroads than the "New World Boulevard" that was Abbé Raynal's Havana.[3]

Smuggling thrived on the southern, eastern, and western shores of the island but less in the north and rarely if ever in the capital. From Jamaica to Curaçao, English, Danish, Dutch, and French interlopers depended on Puerto Rico for lumber, dye woods, ginger, cattle, pigs, horses, mules, hides, coffee, tobacco, and prized Spanish silver, which colonists exchanged for salt and cassava, some-times strong spirits, but mainly textiles and slaves. Thus, from approximately 1670 to 1765, Puerto Rico was the center of international contraband trade in the Caribbean. The colony's character was rural to be sure, but the economic features of its isolation were limited to the walled city of San Juan. The rest of the colony had a life of its own.[4] The epistemological function of this spatial divide reminds us that meanings and definitions are only determined in com-parison to other meanings and definitions. As seen in Puerto Rico's early history of isolation, rurality and underdevelopment are always contingent.

In 1777, Governor José Dufresne expelled a Benedictine friar on false charges of commercial fraud. The ousted cleric was Iñigo Abbad y Lasierra, Aragonese secretary of the governor's nemesis, Bishop Manuel Jiménez Pérez. Back in Spain, Abbad published a comprehensive history of the island in 1788. Over the course of his tenure in Puerto Rico, he paid detailed attention to all he observed, including social relations within and across class lines. While he noted that social slippage through racial divides was not uncommon, he con-cluded that Africans and their descendants were the most abused and degraded: "A white man will insult any one of them, using the most contemptible language with impunity; some slave masters treat them with despicable cruelty."[5] He also understood the politics of contraband trade. Like O'Reilly, Abbad concluded that metropolitan neglect encouraged illegal and legal practices among the free inhabitants of the island: inter-Caribbean smuggling at the external level in the first instance, and sociocultural contradictions at the internal level in the sec-ond instance.[6] Thus, in spite of metropolitan neglect, by the eighteenth century Puerto Rico had the basic features necessary to develop and perpetuate a slave-based economy in the nineteenth century. Social and commercial patterns es-tablished between the 1530s and the 1790s were clearly visible and deployable in the 1820s. Even in the face of Anglo-Spanish treaties that twice banned international slave traffic, the illegal influx persisted with perforated success from 1817 to 1859.[7]

This chapter touches on an assortment of topics examined with greater detail and thematic integration in subsequent chapters. Discussions here address slaving activities at the intersection of Spanish resourcefulness and foreign succor to facilitate both the inter-Caribbean influx of Creole slaves and the transatlantic influx of African captives. The first section explores immigration as an expedient that encouraged and protected the slave trade to Puerto Rico between 1816 and 1830. King Ferdinand's immigration initiative anticipated arrangements with Great Britain to abolish the slave trade from Africa two years later. The decree included articles that encouraged foreign newcomers to purchase slaves from neighboring non-Hispanic Caribbean ports before settling in Puerto Rico. The Spanish government insisted on the legality of this avenue. Despite British pressure, it never outlawed inter-Caribbean slave traffic. Though some slaves who entered Puerto Rico by this channel were Creoles, most were newly landed Africans who were quickly rerouted or "reexported" to the island.

The second section considers small-scale inter-Caribbean slave acquisitions between 1835 and 1846. Most slaves in this traffic were bona fide Creoles from Brazil, Venezuela, the Danish Caribbean, and the United States. Their masters owned them and, for the most part, knew them prior to having filed petitions for their entry. Therefore, Great Britain had no grounds for inquiry or protest. Still, Spanish officials exercised caution in landing procedures in order to separate African identity from Creole or creolized identity and to avoid the introduction of slave rebels. The influx seemed quiet and innocuous. Yet this movement of Creole slaves (and one nominally free West African) underscored two conflicting realities. On the one hand, Spanish authorities feared slave revolts, especially those led by the African-born. On the other hand, the Creole influx proved to be a preface or dress rehearsal for the return to reexport maneuvers, which, earlier, under the auspices of the immigration decree, brought many African captives to Puerto Rico by way of non-Hispanic ports.

The chapter's final section outlines the course of Spain's bid for direct involvement in the African slave trade. Black slavery was not new to imperial Spain, but until the latter half of the eighteenth century, it relied on foreigners to provide captives for its colonies. Based on perennial complaints of insufficient servile labor from colonists, dependency on foreign slave traders was in itself a problem. But even after the Crown encouraged private Spanish companies to carry out slave expeditions to Africa, labor shortages in Puerto Rico remained acute. It becomes apparent why Puerto Rico, almost always compelled to play second fiddle to more prosperous Spanish colonies, relied on mixed channels of acquisition—African and inter-Caribbean—for as long as the slave trade endured.

Newcomers, Slave and Free

In 1815, Ferdinand VII promulgated the Real Cédula de Gracias, an immigration decree designed to stimulate the Puerto Rican economy. At the Congress of Vienna, which convened between 1814 and 1815, Great Britain announced the internationalization of its crusade against the slave trade. Anticipating British pressure, Ferdinand enticed foreigners with land grants and the tax-free importation of slaves. It behooved immigrants to bring family members and slaves, for the *cédula* granted white immigrants approximately six acres of land for each family member and about three acres to heads of households for each slave they brought. It granted free nonwhite immigrants half the lands allotted to whites. But few newcomers arrived with families. Most who did brought one or more brothers, cousins, or nephews, not spouses and children. Thus, it was wise for them to enter with as many slaves as possible, for once admitted under the provisions of the decree, subsequent slave acquisitions would not qualify for additional concessions of land. However, allowances were made for predecree resident foreigners to leave and return, as if for the first time, preferably with slaves. Though the decree authorized numerous commercial concessions to de facto foreign newcomers as well as to incoming non–Puerto Rican Spanish subjects, it did not provide land grants for the latter group.[8]

When Thomas Abraham, a New Yorker, landed in Puerto Rico with thirty slaves, mainly from the non-Hispanic Caribbean, he qualified for approximately 96 acres and the brother who accompanied him an additional six. En route from Genoa to Puerto Rico, Michele Saliva brought only a few slaves and therefore qualified for much less land. But the fortunes of the two men translated differently in settlement. Abraham did not need so large a coffle of bondsmen for his intended profession. By the time he settled down to coffee production in the highlands of Utuado in 1817, only 7 of the original 30 slaves remained. Apparently he sold the others to start his coffee business. In comparison, by 1826 Saliva owned 52 slaves, valued at 16,015 pesos. He was also a supplier, and in the same year, in concert with other Italians, he sold 104 slaves to local consumers for a total of 27,964 pesos.[9] Three groups of non-

whites arrived long after the decree expired: Asian workers who were probably Vietnamese, convicted Chinese contract workers from Cuba, and non-
Hispanic Antilleans, first and foremost Kittisians, Nevisians, and Virgin Island-
ers. Had they arrived earlier, when the decree was in force, few would have
qualified for its provisions.[10]

The lapse of the Cédula de Gracias in 1830 did not discourage white immigrants with slaveholding in mind. Some of them employed resourceful—
albeit illegal—means to establish themselves. In the mid-1840s, as a result of
financial difficulty, Seymour Boulogne and the Bellevue brothers, Fincer and
Forville, were about to lose their estates in Marie Galante, an islet dependency
of Guadeloupe. They fled to Puerto Rico with their twenty-three slaves. The
governor of Guadeloupe alerted the French consul in San Juan that the men
were trying to defraud their creditors and directed him to enlist the aid of the
governor of Puerto Rico to return the slaves. Governor Rafael de Arístegüi
promised his support, but when a steamer arrived to retrieve the bondsmen, he
would not allow them to leave. He reasoned that because the matter exceeded
commercial concerns, he could not authorize the return of the slaves. By 1851,
Boulogne and the Bellevues were established Puerto Rican residents. Another
French settler made a career of slave trading. A native of Bordeaux, Joseph
Beaupied arrived in Puerto Rico in his late teens, at some unknown date, with
neither money nor property but some training in engineering. He was not a
cedulario immigrant. Whatever his earlier fortunes, by the late 1840s, while still
a young man, he was a logistics expert for the transferal of slaves from the
French Antilles to Puerto Rico. For the next twenty years, he authored and
executed schemes to sell Puerto Rican slaves to Cuba. He was also implicated in
a plot to kidnap free Afro–Puerto Ricans to enslave them in Cuba.[11]

Many immigrants purchased slaves, but market rivalry often depended on
the degree to which they interacted with conationals. Some formed strong
affinities with compatriots and organized slave-purchasing activities around
them. Others, by choice or circumstance, did not bond with conationals and
thus Hispanicized rapidly. Still others operated in both worlds, marrying into
modest and often well-to-do white Creole families while maintaining natal
identity through social and economic liaisons with their expatriate communities.[12] Geography also segmented *cedulario* settlement. French nationals, for
example, including Italian-speaking Corsicans and French colonials who fled
the Haitian Revolution, competed with Spaniards and Spanish Creoles in the
sugar-producing centers of the south and west. Anglophones, almost exclu-

sively Britons and Irishmen—unable to compete with Spanish Creoles, Spaniards, and Francophones at the top level of the sugar industry—opted to settle in areas in the northeast and east. Irish concentration was noticeable between Fajardo and Humacao. It was especially dense in Loíza, Río Piedras, and Cangrejos (Santurce), where there existed a tightly woven Gaelic community based on client-patron relations between older immigrants and newcomers. Few Irishmen came with capital or spouses. Though many of those already established sponsored their brothers, nephews, and godsons, liquid assets among them were largely unimpressive, or undeclared, at the time of arrival. Furthermore, as subjects of the British Crown, slave purchases for Irishmen en route to Puerto Rico posed a problem. They could not depend on British Caribbean support. Unlike the French and Corsicans, who—in theory at least—enjoyed the conational cooperation of the French Caribbean islands, the Irish had to rely on Danish and Dutch Caribbean slave markets, where competition with Puerto Ricans and wealthier *cedularios* was keen.[13]

The prospects of slave-based wealth did not mesmerize all immigrants. Businessman Pieter Hosman emigrated from Amsterdam in 1817. In Puerto Rico, he purchased Liberato, Benito, Valeriano, and María del Carmen for domestic service. He outlived his Creole wife, María Josefa Guevara, and they had no children. When he died in 1843, he left his entire estate to the slaves.[14] In another case, Emanuele Laura (or Lauria) left Italy alone in 1815 but arrived in Puerto Rico with a young slave, María Estanislá. They settled in Ponce, where he opened a general store. María bore him three children, each of whom he freed at birth. In his will, he bequeathed all his assets to his mulatto children. He also freed their mother, "in compensation for her demonstrated affection and good behavior."[15]

The immigration decree was neither novel nor radical in its efforts to bolster the island's agricultural industry. Innovation was found in the attempt to build a loyal, solvent, assimilable, landed aristocracy dependent on the Spanish system of trade.[16] Slaves entering with *cedulario* settlers between 1816 and 1830 outnumbered slaves imported through other inter-Caribbean channels between 1821 and 1845. However, a certain problem in terminology is critical here. In the purest sense, a slave entering under any provision of the royal decree was a *cedulario* slave. The term did not distinguish slaves accompanied by immigrant newcomers—who would therefore qualify to receive additional land as stipulated in Article 10—from slaves imported either by foreigners or Spanish subjects after having already settled in Puerto Rico, as stipulated in Article 23.

When we attempt to discern the degree to which foreign settlers stimulated the slave trade, this lack of distinction presents itself as contrived indeterminacy. Slaves imported under Article 10 were never intended to replace or even supplement other forms of slave importation. The Crown offered land grants to coax the immigration of foreign slaveholders, nothing more. The blandishments of Article 23 were designed to encourage all residents—Spanish subjects, pre-decree resident foreigners, and foreign newcomers—to import slaves. Article 10 motivated the licit arrival of only a small number of slaves. At the same time, by subsuming the identity of all free foreigners under *cedulario* status, Article 23 promoted the illicit arrival of much larger numbers. It is necessary to highlight these differences because Governor Miguel de La Torre y Pando is credited for disguising the illegal influx of African captives by way of the 1815 *cédula*. This suggests that he thwarted the efforts of British abolitionists by the legitimacy of Article 10, which allowed *cedularios* to bring slaves with them. But few immigrants seemed impressively wealthy when they landed.

Table 1.1 shows that forty-nine heads of household entering Puerto Rico between 1816 and 1830 brought 9.7 slaves each, totaling less than 500 overall. Out of 335 French *cedularios*, 32 introduced fewer than 9 slaves each. Trailing considerably, 122 Italian *cedularios* brought 4.5 slaves each. By comparison, few immigrants came from the United Kingdom; out of thirty-five Britons, five brought a total of 83 slaves. These figures also problematize certain assumptions about the longevity of national identity, affinity, and privilege vis-à-vis immigration and slave commerce. Though it seems that Europeans emigrating from governments with Caribbean colonies were likely to bring more slaves, initial imports were far from staggering. Thus, in theory, La Torre's immigration pretext could only sustain itself within the context of Article 10. But considering that only 7.1 percent of immigrant heads of household brought slaves when they first entered, the majority of those who wanted slaves must have made their purchases after they arrived—be they new or preestablished immigrants—within the guidelines of Article 23, at which point such acquisitions were illegal and liable to prosecution according to the Anglo-Spanish treaty of 1817.[17]

Forecasting industrial progress based on the stimulation of capital, the government assumed that with proper encouragement, all *cedularios* would have a positive impact on the metropolitan treasury. To be sure, some capitalistic-oriented newcomers did generate wealth from their investments in the slave trade, providing Spanish merchants with the means to continue African expe-

Table 1.1. Foreigners entering Puerto Rico with slaves under the Real Cédula de Gracias, 1816–1830

	Total entrants	Household heads with slaves	Slaves
France	335	32	281
Mainland	280	23	216
Cayenne	2	1	2
Corsica	9	2	12
Guadeloupe	11	2	9
Haiti	24	1	15
St. Barthèlemy	9	3	27
Italy	122	7	32
Mainland	97	2	10
Sicily	25	5	22
United Kingdom	35	5	83
Dominica	1	1	1
Ireland	31	3	79
Scotland	3	1	3
Portugal	29	1	1
Mainland	28	0	0
Macao	1	1	1
Santo Domingo	6	3	34
Venezuela	3	1	1
Totals	530	49	432

Sources: Cifre de Loubriel, *Catálogo de extranjeros residentes en Puerto Rico en el siglo XIX* and *La Inmigración a Puerto Rico durante el siglo XIX.*

Notes: Figures reflect *cedulario* immigrants only. Other figures from Cifre's published inventories include sailors, visitors, convicts, and other transients, as well as immigrants who arrived after the decree expired in 1830. For example, for all of nineteenth-century Puerto Rico, French and Italian immigrants total 1,577. Figures for the British Caribbean during the *cedulario* years are understated.

Most newcomers from Haiti (St. Domingue) were refugees who had fled to Cuba, Florida, Louisiana, and the Spanish side of the island (Santo Domingo) between 1791 and 1804. Spanish Dominican totals were much higher. As Spanish subjects, they did not qualify for the concessions of the 1815 decree. Some were able to feign Haitian (i.e., French) identity and were listed as such.

Nearly 500 Venezuelans settled in Puerto Rico in the 1800s. At least half came between 1816 and 1830, in the wake of the Spanish American wars of independence. Those in this group were also Spanish subjects. Thus, they did not qualify as resident foreigners. Spanish subjects born outside Puerto Rico—first and foremost Spaniards directly from Europe and Spaniards and Creoles in flight from the independence wars—were granted resident privileges under a separate decree.

Before settling in Puerto Rico, the Dominicans and Venezuelans listed here must have fled to Louisiana or Florida first, but after these regions became territories of the United States in 1803 and 1819. Only by this route could they have settled in Puerto Rico under the Cédula de Gracias. In 1816, for example, eighty Spanish families left Louisiana for Puerto Rico under the Fernandine decree. BHPR, 11:137.

ditions and to finance the development of agriculture. After the *cedularios* arrived, the tax-free import of more slaves offered sufficient incentive to invigorate the local slave market—even without added land grants. But non-Hispanic newcomers had a relatively minor hand in the direct influx of slaves. The French slave trader Joseph Beaupied marked the exception, not the rule. Distinctions lay in the ability of some newcomers to supply local slave markets and to exploit slave labor at the plantation level. Regardless of vessel ownership, vessel registration, crew nationality, or the nationality of intermediaries on either side of the Atlantic, the organization of Spanish Caribbean slave commerce was a Spanish affair.

Traffic in Creole Slaves

Between 1835 and 1845, the relationship between immigration and slave importation in Puerto Rico changed. At the beginning of the ten-year span, Great Britain and Spain signed their second antislave trade agreement. At the end of the period, Spain legislated its own cessationist code. The second bilateral treaty found Miguel de La Torre in the twilight years of his long and prosperous reign as the island's most effective supporter of the slave trade.[18] His success was based in part on the rather awkward beginnings of the British international abolitionist campaign, which inadvertently allowed offenders sufficient time to map out stratagems to prolong the trade. Immigration continued, but fewer newcomers came with slaves. The localized version of Ferdinand's Cédula de Gracias reduced the profitability of arriving with them.[19] However, the spirit of the decree allowed Governor La Torre enough abstract leverage to promote a policy of unlimited slave importations after it expired in 1830. Though the second treaty was almost as ineffective as the first, it was forceful enough to encourage more Spanish subjects to take hands-on responsibility for the clandestine influx. In addition, as France, Denmark, and the Netherlands began to honor their abolitionist contracts with Great Britain, direct landings in Puerto Rico from the West African coast began to supersede, though not eclipse, reexport traffic from the non-Hispanic Caribbean.

Table 1.2 lists the names of applicants for permits to import slaves. Spanish law required them to include motives. An assortment of visitors, foreign immigrants, and resident Spanish subjects applied. Despite exceptions for the wealthy and the influential, the bureaucracy favored the importation of more than five slaves at a given time. Natal Spanish identity offered no edge. Seven applicants were foreigners, of whom five were legal residents, one was a naturalized Spanish subject, another a transient. Of the Spanish-born nationals, two were from Venezuela; the rest were either born in Puerto Rico or Spain. Mary Wallace Henny, a Thomian resident and widow of unnamed nationality, solicited permits to bring two slaves with her to Puerto Rico. Considering a permanent move, she wanted to survey the prospects. In July 1835, she arrived with her retainers, Celestina and Montgomery. The license stipulated that their stay not exceed three months and that they return with her. In September, she purchased a home and applied to bring six more slaves, three males and three females, who formed part of her estate in Martinique. She declared that they were all "labor-acclimated Creoles." Permission was granted within a week.[20]

Internal security was a recurrent theme in all the petitions. The aborted Ducourdray-Holstein Conspiracy of 1826 bore out not only the fear that no

Table 1.2. Small-scale slave imports to Puerto Rico, 1835–1846

Year of petition	Petitioner	Petitioner's national origins	Slaves	Immediate slave origins
1835				
	Pedro Basbe	Spanish	1	Vieques
	Mary Wallace Henny	United States	8	St. Thomas
	Fortunato Benallo	Brazilian	2	Brazil
1842–43				
	Juan and José García	Spanish	20	St. Thomas
1843				
	Mattheu Guède	French	4	Guadeloupe
	Julia Flavanger	United States	1	New York
	Pedro Novato	Spanish	1	Venezuela
	Jeanne-Marie Souffront	French	1	St. Thomas
	Antonio Aubaredes	Spanish	1	St. Thomas
	Nicolás Larraz	Spanish	2	St. Thomas
	Pierre Danois	French	1	St. Thomas
1845				
	Ana María Espinosa	Spanish	1	Venezuela
	Joseph Dizac	French	1	St. Thomas
1846				
	Francesco Margotti	Corsican (Fr.)	2	St. Thomas
	Laureano de Castro	Spanish	1	Cuba

Sources: AGPR, GE:E, caja 66, and GE:C, cajas 66 and 222.

Caribbean island was immune to antislavery activity; it also suggested, albeit erroneously, that sympathetic foreign whites were willing to provide assistance, if not leadership.[21] For the widow Julia Flavanger, who emigrated from New York in June 1843, the procedure was simple. Her lone slave, Henrietta, posed no threat to the system because she was only six years of age. On the other hand, the transfer of an older slave from one town to another required safeguards. Pedro Basbe of Humacao wanted to bring Juan Félix del Carmen from Vieques. The petition hinted at government concerns for security. Revealing neither the age nor birthplace of his slave, Basbe's wording suggests that Juan Félix was an African-born adult. To strengthen the request, Basbe swore he had owned him "a long time before initiating passport procedures."[22] As a person of means, Basbe did not need to address the conduct of his servant.

Army officer and merchant-planter Juan Martínez died in February 1843. He left his widow, Inés María Novato, and six children local property in Aguadilla and in Cumaná, Venezuela. Shortly before his death he sent his son Pedro to Cumaná to administer the family business. The Venezuelan estate included a slave, Natividad. Martínez's survivors were indecisive about the slave's future. Novato instructed her son to bring Natividad to Puerto Rico to determine his suitability to serve the family. As with Basbe's request, the petition contained no promise of good behavior. Instead, it included the endorsement of a family friend, Coronel Ramón Méndez, commandant of Aguadilla. Permission was granted in a few days.[23] In a somewhat similar fashion, the firm of Capetillo, O'Kelly, and Company, founded by a Spanish slave trader and an Irish immigrant, vouched for the conduct of two Brazilian slaves, María and Gerónimo, who accompanied their master, Fortunato Benallo, from Pará to San Juan. Benallo, a client of the local enterprise and a merchant in his own right, stopped in San Juan en route to Europe. Soon he revealed his wish to sell María to the company, stating that her companionship in Europe would be inconvenient. Permission was granted almost immediately.[24]

While the wealthy and influential did not need to spell out assurances for good slave conduct, in at least one case it was recalcitrance that prompted an arrival, as Infantry Commander Laureano de Castro stated in his petition to the governor. Though the Catalonian-born Spaniard made Cuba his home, he was called suddenly overseas—perhaps to Ceuta, in consequence of hostilities that led to war with Morocco—and he expressed concern over his wife's ability to handle their servant in his absence. Pedro Cayetano was an *emancipado* from southwest Nigeria. Freed by the Havana branch of the Court of the Mixed Commissions (which got its name from the British and Spanish judges who presided), he was consigned to the Castro household, but he took his free status literally and refused to remain with his guardians after dark. Despite efforts to "raise the level of his morals," Pedro continued to practice night flight and concubinage. Castro was oblivious to the possibility that the infractions he cited were related. Ultimately, it was inconsequential whether Pedro's nocturnal sojourns stemmed from a desire to be with his family or from, as Castro suggested, his incorrigible rebelliousness and concupiscence. Like other *emancipados*, Pedro was regarded not as a state ward but a slave. As such, Castro had the right to have him quartered in Puerto Rico in his absence. But Pedro proved dauntless. While he was held temporarily at the slave depository in San Juan but slated for long-term confinement in Vieques, warden Antonio Talavera boasted that he was perfectly capable of controlling him. Thus, the transferal was unwarranted. But he soon changed his tune. Within two weeks he requested Pedro's immediate removal to Vieques.[25]

Motives on applications for slave arrivals varied. Pierre Danois was a French national residing in the Danish Virgin Islands. He had strong ties to the Puerto Rican planter class. His brother, Joseph, was the second-largest slaveholder in eastern Fajardo, which ranked among the island's second-tier sugar-producing municipalities. From St. Thomas he requested permission to bring a domestic slave to serve him during a three-month visit.[26] Of the same status but requesting Spanish residency at the time, Jeanne-Marie Souffront was granted permission to import one slave to care for her four children.[27] Corsican-born Francesco Margotti left Puerto Rico for St. Thomas to recover from an undisclosed illness. He requested the reentry of his Creole slaves, María Teresa and Carmen. The latter had two free children, apparently fathered by the petitioner.[28] Shortly before retiring from a career as an army accountant, Antonio de Aubaredes purchased Luisa Pardo, a Thomian mulatto. He requested permission to bring her to San Juan as a domestic. Nicolás Larraz, who arrived from Spain in 1839 as second commandant of the Puerto Rican Carabineer Reserves, applied for two domestics.[29] Of the fifteen petitioners listed in table 1.2, he was the only one to cite "the notorious scarcity of personal slaves in the San Juan area." Mattheu Guède, a naturalized Spanish subject, lost his plantation in Guadeloupe in an earthquake in February 1843. Because he was a reputable, university-trained pharmacist long established in Humacao and possibly due to the urgency of his application for the immigration of his family, customs officials at the port of

Naguabo waived the required guarantee of good behavior for his four domestic slaves—whom he could not have known very well due to years of absence.[30]

Preoccupation over island security and slave importation took on curious dimensions where the reentry of Puerto Rican Creole slaves was concerned. In the spring of 1843, Jean Dizac created a stir when he took Juliana, his sister's eight-year-old slave, to France. Yielding finally to family pressure, he sent her back in 1845. It is not stated whether she was chaperoned. Due to complications, the child was detained in St. Thomas. On learning of her plight, Jean's brother, Joseph, solicited the governor to lift the restrictions that encumbered her return. He stated that the Dizacs missed the child, who was born and raised in their home, and that she longed to return to them. Because Juliana was born in Puerto Rico and was a minor taken away without the consent of her legal owner, the government agreed that potential dissident deportment was not an issue. But her return was delayed on confused evidence that Jean sent another child in her place. The proceedings included a dramatic court appearance by Juliana's grieving mother. The case was not resolved until an astute advocate, José María Vázquez, pressed the fact that laws governing the arrival of new slaves were not applicable to the reentry of either Creole or creolized slaves.[31] His argument fortified the supposition that fraudulent identity and illegal ownership were less likely to occur among slave returnees than slave newcomers. The former, especially lone Creoles, were more readily identifiable than the latter. Thus, in addition to preventing the import of potentially rebellious slaves, port authorities were concerned with rightful slave ownership to discourage the theft of property. Moreover, inasmuch as slave owners paid higher head taxes for newcomers than for returnees, verification of true ownership also had an impact on maritime revenues. A case from the municipality of Guayama best illustrates this point.

For a trip to St. Thomas in June 1837, Juan and José García solicited passports for themselves; their mother, María Palmira; and fifteen slaves: Agustina, nursing an unnamed son; María Geneveva, also nursing an unnamed son, and her daughter, Simona; Marta and her son, Alejandro; and Celestino, Matilde, Petrona, Clotilde, Victoriana, Alejandrino, Benito, and Francisco. The Garcías did not disclose the reason for the trip; they did not approximate a date for their intended return, nor does the record reveal when most of the party returned. The Garcías stated that the slave entourage, valued at 4,300 pesos, was for the domestic care of their family. In spite of professed need, the tenor of the application smacked of conspicuous consumption. "Necesitamos llevar algunos esclavos para nuestros servicios y comodidades en el viaje."[32] By flat distribution undifferentiated by age, each member of the García family had five domestic slaves for the trip.

Several slaves remained in St. Thomas with José García until 1843. Due to their extended absence, compounded by other difficulties, their return was impeded. Alejandro and Simona could not reenter until certified copies of their baptismal records were presented to the customs officer. This simple procedure took six weeks. Complications arising from the entry of five remaining slaves point to carelessness, fraud, and government corruption. María Rufina, a sixteen-year-old Puerto Rican–born slave, and African-born Manuela, age thirty-three, did not form part of the original party in 1837. In addition to providing passports with apparently altered dates of transit, family advocate José Meynieu produced a copy of María Rufina's baptismal record, attesting her age and verifying that she was born and reared on the García estate. For Manuela, he obtained a copy of her bill of sale, which showed that at age eighteen she was part of a coffle of newly arrived Africans the elder García purchased in 1825. The age discrepancy of three years on her passport and the duplicate sales receipt, which only identified her as "slave #64," did not seem to matter. Decorative scars on her face and buttocks matched those noted on the two documents.[33]

Clotilde, also African-born, presented a different challenge. In St. Thomas, she gave birth to a daughter, Rosario, in early 1842, and a son, yet unnamed and unbaptized, fifteen days prior to her return in December 1843. Records revealed that, at age thirteen, she was one of fourteen African captives the García brothers purchased in 1836. Though the transaction was in blatant violation of the Anglo-Spanish treaties of 1817 and 1835, the revelation caused no alarm in court. As with Manuela, corroborating evidence was the primary issue. Clotilde's sales receipt listed neither her name nor her number, but its physical description of her matched that on her passport. Nor did anyone question the fact that her exit papers were dated 1839, when she had left Puerto Rico with the Garcías in 1837. Furthermore, her reentry papers stated that she was accompanied by a third child, Ramón (age not given), though no such person landed with the García party when it returned on December 23, 1843. Meynieu avoided the remaining problem that could further delay Clotilde's reentry by verifying the ownership and identity of her infant son. He asserted that lactation, along with the infant's strong resemblance to her, sufficed to prove that he was her son and therefore the legal property of the García estate. Of Ramón, the judge stated that even though his name appeared on the passport, because Meynieu did not mention him and because he did not arrive, there was nothing further to adjudicate.[34]

The influx of Africans peaked during the tenure of Miguel de La Torre, whose rule nearly paralleled the first fifteen years of the illegal trade. By the close of 1848, statistics for Brazil, Cuba, Suriname, and the United States rendered Puerto Rico a distant fifth among remaining slave-based economies in the American hemisphere. Yet many features of Puerto Rican slavery were indistinguishable from those associated with larger slaveholding societies. These parities included a multidimensional slave trade. The Spanish monarchy courted foreigners with generous favors, calculating that the skills, capital, and new technology they introduced would increase profits from the island's agricultural economy. But regarding the degree to which they stimulated the slave trade, the verdict is still out. We only know that 481 family members and 432 bondsmen accompanied 49 immigrant heads of households. Without figures that distinguish the slave purchases of local and incoming Spanish subjects from foreign settlers while the Cédula de Gracias was in effect, it is not possible to measure the decree's impact with precision. Though the orientation of *cedularios* toward modern agrarian enterprises invigorated several municipalities, some *cedularios* brought more relatives than slaves, and many arrived alone. Thus, the decree played a minor role in the immediate stimulation of slave acquisitions. It was not a failure, but its limitations combined with other factors to signal the need to hammer out measures related directly to the influx of slaves.

All slaves were internal outsiders. Yet there was an element of structured disingenuousness in the miniscule movement of largely American-born slaves discussed in the second section and illustrated in table 1.2. Creoles and creolized Africans cost more than new African captives. While bureaucratic procedures reflected concerns that the conduct of the former had a negative impact on the latter, thus warranting careful screening before entry, such vigilance was not duplicated when larger numbers were involved. Whether African or Creole, greater numbers invalidated alleged privileges afforded to masters who owned "familiar strangers." The government was less concerned about screening the behaviors of incoming slaves than sending a message to the men and women who brought them: more slaves, less bureaucracy. As we shall see in subsequent chapters, when larger numbers of "true strangers" were at stake, familiarity bred more than contempt. It bred indifference.

2

Early Anglo-Spanish Diplomacy

Duplicity as Discourse

The first section of this chapter examines the Anglo-Spanish treaty of 1817 vis-à-vis the politics of its preparation, wording, and timing. Subsequent sections focus on changing conditions and unforeseen events that prompted Spain to reappraise and reaffirm its commitment to assist Puerto Rican planters in the acquisition of slaves through African and inter-Caribbean channels.

Knowledge, Power, and Word Play

Captured as a runaway slave on February 5, 1833, thirty-year-old Justo Vizcarrondo found himself in the Royal Jail of Toa Baja, a municipality near the capital of Puerto Rico. Notary public Julián García took the inmate's deposition in preparation for his first appearance in court. Justo swore to tell the truth "in the name of Our Lord" and sealed his oath with the sign of the cross according to juridical protocol. He gave his motive for marronage, that is, slave flight: fear and resentment for having received a hundred lashes followed by handcuffed confinement when he fled once before. He then outlined his path of flight through numerous towns before he was caught. The notary filed the deposition along with duplicates of other documents pertinent to the case. Among them were Justo's vital statistics. On October 8, 1819, his master, Nicolás Vizcarrondo, bought him from the cargo master responsible for the Africans disembarked in San Juan from the *Fama Habanera*, a Spanish frigate. At the time of purchase, he was a nineteen-year-old Manding captive known only as "Slave #309."[1]

Justo's enslavement was illegal. The treaty of 1817 called for the immediate cessation of the African slave trade north of the equator. The Manding homeland lies between the Niger and Senegal Rivers. In earlier times, the might of the Manding Empire centered at the southern fringe of the Sahara Desert in Timbuktu on the Niger Bend in Mali. These areas lie between ten and sixteen degrees north of the stipulated divide. As merchants especially, migratory branches of Mande-speakers spanned the width of West Africa proper as far as the Hausa states of northern Nigeria. Whatever Justo's specific origins in the Mande-speaking world, he came from above the equator. But neither his illegal enslavement nor his subsequent quest for freedom circumstantiated the criminal charges and punishments he faced. Authorities viewed him as one of too many impertinent maroons whose flights from bondage were acts of rebellion that threatened the status quo.[2]

At the Congress of Vienna in 1815, Spain and Portugal resisted British efforts to sign an accord with the allied powers to abolish the African slave trade immediately. Though British representatives secured a joint agreement, its text provided the Iberian nations with the delaying power they needed. Each nation that signed would be free to determine the most convenient date to outlaw the traffic.[3] Spain advanced two arguments to justify its place within the wiggle room of the stalling provision. First, in 1788 Great Britain announced its intention to prohibit the international slave trade early in the next century. British Caribbean planters had nearly twenty years to prepare for its abolition in 1807. Spain did not have comparable time to ready its colonies for the same move. More important, Spain was in the throes of full-scale independence wars in Mexico, Central America, and South America. With massive military reinforcements from the king, Cuba and Puerto Rico remained loyal, though both had their share of factions sympathetic to the anticolonial cause. An immediate declaration against the slave trade could undermine Spanish Caribbean loyalty to the Crown.[4]

Notwithstanding pledges of moral support from conservative European governments, Spain had to prepare for the treaty quickly. Ferdinand recognized the urgency before the Congress convened. A slave-trading license granted to Spaniards in 1804 was due to expire in 1816. Thus, before the treaty of 1817 went into effect, he pursued the resolution of three problems to alleviate both internal and external pressure: geography, slave reproduction, and taxation. First—following the counsel of his advisers, who observed and appropriated the Portuguese idea of dividing abolitionist proposals on equatorial terms—he agreed to outlaw African slave traffic from above the equator immediately.[5] This designation forbade the taking of captives from Senegambia and Upper and

Lower Guinea, that is, Senegal, Gambia, Guinea-Bissau, Guinea-Conakry, Sierra Leone, Liberia, Ghana, Togo, Dahomey, and Nigeria. The Ivory Coast separated Upper and Lower Guinea. For the most part, a history dictated by geo-ecological difference limited Ivorian participation in the transatlantic slave trade. Between 1817 and 1820, Cameroon, Gabon, the Congo, Angola, and Mozambique were Spain's last legitimate sites for slave acquisitions from Africa directly. But the equatorial divide proved inconsequential.

Second, before signing the treaty, Ferdinand gave secret instructions for his agents to urge the organizers of Cuban and Puerto Rican expeditions to reserve no less than a third of the cargo space for female captives to encourage, in his words, the "propagation of the species" so that "the abolition of the slave trade may be less noticeable in the future."[6] The centrality of this concern cannot be overstated. In the Americas, slave men cost more than slave women. But in Africa, slave women were not only more expensive, local brokers restricted their availability for overseas sale. Furthermore, according to Western laws, only slave women were capable of bearing slave offspring. White women and free women of color could not bear slave children. While race and social condition guided the maternity of a slave, paternity was irrelevant. Hence, in the context of procreation—as opposed to external acquisition—slave women alone bore the physical and psychological onus of reproducing the slave population.[7]

Third, with regard to financial concerns, in January 1815 Intendant Alejandro Ramírez, chief officer of Puerto Rican Economic Affairs, announced the creation of a 4 percent surcharge, payable in silver or paper money, for first-time rentals of private residences, warehouses, shops, and wine cellars. The new tribute did not apply to owners. This move anticipated the cessation of the external slave trade and its subsequent deficits.[8] In more direct terms, Ramírez authorized a one-time head tax of 1 peso on male field slaves age fifteen and older and 2 pesos for male slaves engaged as domestics. The tax exempted all females and any male slave who was elderly, under fifteen, or permanently incapacitated by disease or injury. It also exempted African slaves brought to the island within one year of the effective date.[9] The twelve-year license forbade the arrival of foreign Creole slaves. Therefore, the current owners of slaves from Tortola, St. Maarten, and Martinique, for example, were charged a one-time fee of 2 pesos. The levy applied to all foreign-born Creoles, regardless of age, sex, or physical condition. For the sake of authoritative propriety and nothing more, Ramírez concluded the announcement with two interconnected points. The new tax did not exculpate masters who violated the African-centered license of 1804 by purchasing Creoles, nor was it meant to compromise the African focus of the license, which was still in effect.[10] Inherent conflicts in these treaty preparations took a number of interesting turns. Though the Crown emphasized female slaves, it taxed and conceptually penalized the owners of all foreign-born Creole slaves, male slaves assigned to duties outside sugar production, and male slaves in general, excepting the African-born. On the other hand, the preparations reinforced a strategic given that lasted for the duration of the external trade: the procurement of slaves from any source by any means necessary.

The treaty of 1817 was a dead-letter document from the outset (see maps 1, 2, and 3).[11] Despite its somber opening, Article 1 set the tone for evasion:

From this day forward, as applicable to those in Spain as to those in America, I forbid forever all my subjects from going to the coasts of Africa, north of the equator, to buy slaves. Slaves purchased from said coasts shall be declared free at the first port within my dominions to which the ship arrives that carried them. My royal treasury will confiscate such ships, and what remains of their cargo. The buyer, the captain, his first mate, and the pilot shall be sentenced to ten years confinement in the Presidio of the Philippines.[12]

Article 2 amended the penalties stipulated in Article 1 by allowing a six-month grace period for expeditions undertaken prior to November 22, 1817. Under the same directives and penalties in the first article, Article 3 forbade slaving south of the equator after May 30, 1820, with a grace period of five months for ventures undertaken prior to that date. Article 4 stipulated that vessels used in voyages started before May 30, 1820, must maintain a ratio of five slaves per ton, stipulating the confiscation and liberation of slaves belonging to those found guilty of violating this "safety factor." Article 5 readjusted the slave ship weight ratio to five tons per two slaves to accommodate slave births, slave crew members, and slave valets for officers. Article 6 stipulated that foreign ships in Spanish ports were subject to the same prohibitions and penalties as Spanish ships. Article 7 lay the groundwork for the creation of bilateral courts in Cuba and Sierra Leone for the purpose of judging illegal slave trade operations. It also required that the decree be published in all American and Asian territories of the Spanish seaborne empire. Soon this simply meant Cuba, Puerto Rico, and the Philippines.

The treaty was an exercise in disingenuousness. First, by silence, Ferdinand

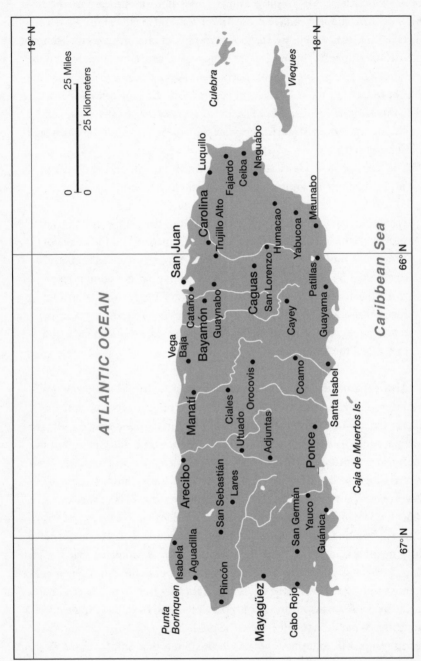

Map 1. Puerto Rico.

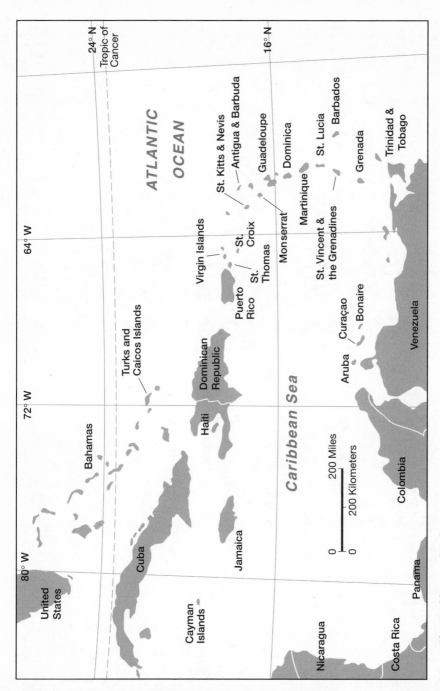

Map 2. The Caribbean archipelago.

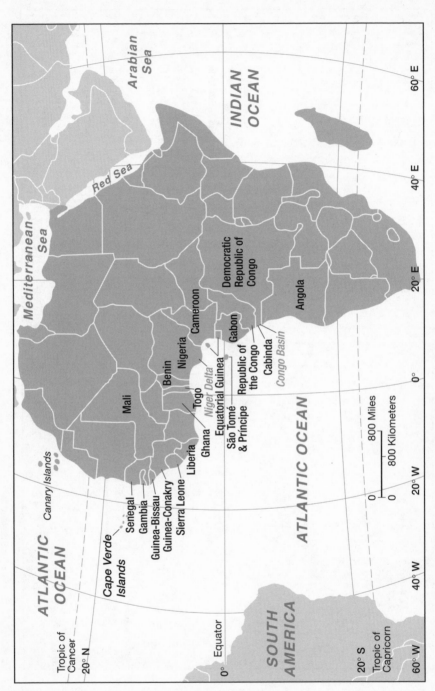

Map 3. Atlantic Africa: Upper Guinea, Lower Guinea, the Congo, and Angola.

maintained the legitimacy of reexport transfers by way of non-Hispanic Caribbean ports. For example, Africans who landed at Danish St. Thomas rarely stayed there. They were transferred to different vessels, and Puerto Rico was almost always their final destination. Second, his silence repeated itself by permitting Spanish subjects to outfit and supply slaving vessels of any nationality in foreign ports. Participants prepared for Cuban ventures in Cádiz, Barcelona, Baltimore, New Orleans, and Havana.[13] Preparation for Puerto Rican expeditions was usually undertaken in St. Thomas or any number of Dutch ports. On the African side of the Atlantic, vessels bound for Cuba and Puerto Rico took on supplies and forged identification papers in the Portuguese archipelago of Cape Verde in Upper Guinea or Portuguese São Tomé or Príncipe in equatorial waters. Third, if used at all, adjustments in the ratio of tonnage to persons was not meant to account for slave crews or slave infants born in transit. It doubled the space for able-bodied captives. Fourth, until the *Majesty* affair in 1859, Spain rarely pursued Spanish subjects, or anyone else, for complicity in the illegal slave trade. There were certainly trials and sentences, with defendants frequently in absentia, but few paid fines or served time in prison. Early in 1829, for example, British diplomats complained that participants viewed legal threats as a joke because Spain never prosecuted violators.[14] Fifth, though the British government paid the Spanish government 400,000 pounds sterling (10 million pesetas) to quit the slave trade, complaints about treaty infractions were rather naive.[15] One does not bite the hand that feeds it. However generous, bribes from Great Britain did not fill Spanish royal coffers; revenues from slave labor in the Caribbean did. As abolitionist Domingo Delmonte lamented, despite the palatial splendor slave labor permitted him to enjoy, Cuban residents—Spaniards and Creoles—paid the highest taxes in the Western world.[16]

Text analysts will appreciate Ferdinand's deployment of language. First, his pluralization, "the coasts of Africa," acknowledges both African heterogeneity and geographic difference. More than a sophomoric demonstration of spatial intelligence at the level of semantics, his recognition of Africa's littoral plurality operates politically as a preventative that intercepts the interrogative, "Which coast?" Second, the word "buyer" bifurcates between semantic and syntactic function. Syntactically, it establishes a hierarchy of criminal transgression from ship's owner to ship's pilot, an arrangement of words that is ultimately inconsequential given that all the participants named are subject to the same verdict. Semantically it splits again. Its first subdivision operates ambiguously, for the reader is uncertain as to whether "buyer" refers to the owner of the ship or the owner of its captives. This is not clarified until the sentence is completed. Although captains and first mates were often the co-owners of slaves in transit, as well as owners or co-owners of the vessels that carried them, pilots rarely had the means to participate in these voyages at the level of ownership. Furthermore, as illustrated in Chapter 6, vessel ownership and slave cargo ownership were divisions contingent on the proprietary structure of each expedition, and each expedition was an enterprise unto itself. Whether slaves-as-property and vessels-as-property were mutually exclusive varied from one voyage to the next.

The second subdivision is an exercise in selectivity. The king's choice of "buyer" (*comprador*) over "owner" (*proprietario, dueño,* or *poseedor*) suggests the idea of temporality and its connection to the intersection of word meaning and word function. It intimates a time factor that conveys a sense of newness and ultimately the innocence of ignorance. While "buyer" is a temporal designation that identifies a recent transaction, "owner" is devoid of temporality. The time factor is inherent in one and absent in the other—unless accompanied by other words that date it. The selection of the independent, time-bound newness of purchase over the dependent, time-contingent experience of ownership promotes a false sense of immediacy and naïveté, resulting in a unsuccessful effort to thin the density of the adage, "Ignorance of the law is no excuse." The effort was, however, less unsuccessful than segmentary.

Rhetoric is a third factor. The king never missed an opportunity to fire figurative barbs at the British. Great Britain was Spain's ally, and Ferdinand owed its government for several favors. British forces helped drive the French out of Spain, and with loans and grants, Great Britain helped Ferdinand gain the upper hand in a series of dynastic struggles over succession. But his resentment over British pressure to accept the treaty of 1817 was less than subtle. "Aún el bien que resultaba a los habitantes de Africa de ser transportados a países cultos, no es ya tan urgente y exclusivo desde que *una nación ilustrada ha tomado sobre si la gloriosa empresa de civilizarlos en su propio suelo.*"[17] Though his racist apology for the history of the Atlantic slave trade was typical, what followed, "the glorious enterprise of civilizing them [Africans], on their own soil," was not. Mixing recent history with mordant wit and a hint of prophecy, he associated the "enlightened" leadership of Great Britain—*una nación ilustrada*—with current and future African affairs. Silently, he acknowledged British commerce along the Gambia River and the British purchase and settlement of Freetown in Sierra Leone, where the Spanish government was now obligated to send judges for the abolitionist Court of the Mixed Commissions. With derision, however, he predicted Great Britain's dominant role in the European partition of Africa sixty-eight years later.

The treaty, as it appeared in the *Gaceta Oficial de Puerto Rico*, deleted references to British compensation to Spain and the creation of bilateral antislave trade courts in Havana and Freetown.[18] The omissions function discursively as a presence of absence. What was voiced in the treaty was silent in its manifestation as a royal decree. The missing words mark an absence, a separation, or communicative gap between the British government and the Puerto Rican slaveholding class. Though the silence was short lived and upheld by local authorities, it lasted long enough to achieve the desired results. It enabled Spain to reassert itself as the only broker between slave commerce and slave ownership. Once again Ferdinand confounded the direction of British hegemony with a preemptive strike. He promoted the illusion of treaty conformity and concern, while strategic omissions and volley upon volley of royal and diplomatic loquacity combined to favor continued Spanish participation in the outlawed trade. Threats of punishment, concerns for vessel safety, and other treaty stipulations resulted in the international articulation of empty intentions, a sly but typical production of Fernandine drivel.

Equatorial provisos are especially instructive, for they delineate the beginning of consistent abolitionist inconsistency in maritime operations. British distinctions between Cuban and Puerto Rican treaty violations were almost immediate. In the winter of 1819, in West African waters above the equator, British naval officers seized *Nuestra Señora de las Nieves*, a Puerto Rican schooner. Though its captain produced a permit that allowed him to take captives below the equator, forty Africans were on board at the moment of seizure.[19] The expedition violated the first article of the treaty of 1817. On the other hand, British naval forces did not begin to capture vessels bound for Cuba on either side of the equator until 1823.[20] This was an extraordinary grace period, for it surpassed treaty stipulations by three years.

Furthermore, why enlist the aid of complicated juridical and diplomatic procedures over a Puerto Rican slaver with 40 captives when, depending on vessel size, Cuban slavers carried 400 to 800 or more captives per voyage? One two-sided possibility comes to mind. First, the British Royal Navy lacked sufficient cruisers to monitor the African coastline. This was a problem in the best of times, but at the beginning of the campaign the shortage was acute. Second, British diplomats understood that under the leadership of Francisco

Arango y Parreño—a wealthy Creole and the founder of Cuba's slave-based sugar economy—Cuban slave owners were more interested in, and more capable of, demonstrating greater resistance to the treaty than their counterparts in Puerto Rico.[21] Thus, between 1819, with the capture of the *Nieves*, and 1823, when the pursuit of Cuban-bound vessels finally began, British naval officers divided Spanish Caribbean expeditions along figurative lines of owning and buying. For a short period at least, the timelessness of Puerto Rican ownership was more offensive then the time-dependency of Cuban purchase. In this manner, with a combination of stalling, bullying, incompetence, and indifference, the case of the *Nieves* characterized British maritime strategy for the first years of prohibition. More significant, it did not discourage other Puerto Rican expeditions planned prior to the treaty's deadline of May 30, 1820. Naval notary Antonio de Vega certified that the forty-four-ton schooner *Nuestra Señora de la Merced* was fully authorized to sail from San Juan for subequatorial Africa on February 10, 1820. This voyage, however, was also Puerto Rico's last legitimate slaving expedition to Africa.[22]

Early assaults against smaller Puerto Rican expeditions allowed British naval forces sufficient time to gear up for assaults on larger operations later. By the mid-1820s, British pursuits of slavers bound for Cuba outnumbered pursuits of those bound for Puerto Rico.[23] This reversal resulted in the creation of a diplomatic blind spot. After exhibiting apathy toward Cuban operations between 1820 and 1823, the Royal Navy locked its focus on them. The readjustment placed Puerto Rican activities at the center of abolitionist neglect. Despite reports of single and joint Puerto Rican expeditions from British cruisers patrolling West African waters, the British Foreign Office seemed incapable of dealing with Cuban and Puerto Rican infractions simultaneously. Until the mid-1830s, little altered its perception of Puerto Rican benignity. However, as we shall see, the weight of the British government's blind spot came to collapse on itself.

Between Treaties, 1817 to 1835

Puerto Rico received captives directly from Africa from 1817 to 1830. In conjunction with inter-Antillean reexport maneuvers—which by silence the treaty of 1817 endorsed—these expeditions were undertaken with and without the help of foreigners. In 1818, the Puerto Rican Royal Board of Sanitation reported that the *Jacinta*, a Spanish brigantine, arrived directly from the Niger Delta, between four and five degrees latitude north of the equator.[24] Though the delta fell within prohibitive parallels, the slaver escaped British cruisers. In reference to what precipitated a large slave revolt in Bayamón in 1821, one observer commented that the pueblo was flooded with new captives. Bayamón's slave population more than doubled between 1815 and 1821. The increase resulted from neither immigration nor reproduction. By 1821, its African-born population surpassed the number of slaves who entered under the immigration decree of 1815 by 60 percent.[25] Dictating his memoirs from his deathbed, Philip Drake, a retired slave trader, recalled the voyage of the ill-fated *Panchita*, which sailed from the Bight of Benin in 1828. The vessel was not only Spanish-owned, it had a Spanish crew. Drake described its captain as an aged Spanish slave smuggler who made his home in Puerto Rico.[26]

Though captives reached Puerto Rico by way of reexport maneuvers within the Caribbean and by voyages directly from Africa, is not possible to determine which route was the more favored in the first decade of the treaty. However, if inter-Caribbean lanes overshadowed direct arrivals, French abolitionist functionaries stationed in Puerto Rico would not have complained as loudly as they did. French consular protests in San Juan verified Governor La Torre's complicity. They also offer a glimpse at the mechanics of clandestine landings in the 1820s. On April 23, 1827, a French slaver laden with African captives landed in Aguadilla in the northwest. Authorities advised the captain to change the standard from French to Dutch. When consular agents went to verify the machination, they were only allowed to peruse the ship's false registration papers; direct communication with the captain failed because they were prevented from boarding the ship. The agent who reported the incident could not verify whether the captives came directly from Africa or whether they were reexported from a nearby non-Hispanic Caribbean port. But the voyage was probably transatlantic. The vessel's false French identity protected it in oceanic waters because British policy-makers were skittish about tackling French offenders. False Dutch identity gave the venture the appearance of legitimate commerce with Dutch Antillean free ports. Inter-Caribbean ventures required neither secrecy nor mendacity. Hence, Consul Levieil reported:

> Not only did local authorities refuse to assist in the inquiry, the island government procures the means for French slaveship captains to escape our vigilance. I was convinced of it, My Lord, when the captain general told me that he tolerated consular agents in obligatory deference to me, and that their function is limited to the inspection of maritime papers only. He said he forbade their involvement in official matters because he

wants nothing more to do with their protests, and that foreign ships are under his protection. Insomuch as slaveships arrive at the southern and western shores of the island, we cannot monitor our commercial and navigational activities without the aid of these agents. But even with the knowledge that our antislave trade ordinances are violated by French mariners themselves, I fear that a solution to the difficulty may be too late.[27]

Levieil did not name the ship, but he made generalizations about the structure of the subterfuge, including the avoidance of landing slavers in the bay of the capital. He also named local officials who, in lieu of monetary bribes, received one slave each for their silence: the customs inspector, the port captain, the comptroller, the chief of customs, and, depending on the political organization of the port town, the military commandant or the head of the municipal council. All the more damaging was his revelation that two slaves were allotted to the chief adviser of the colonial treasurer: the intendant, a royal commissioner whose office was considered incorruptible. Above all, he raised a topic that not only substantiated the vitality of direct slave-trading expeditions between Puerto Rico and West Africa, he struck a fiscal nerve. Bearing in mind that Great Britain lacked the diplomatic force to argue against Spain's insistence that inter-Antillean slave commerce was legal, he touched a spot that became a major issue in the reformation of Spanish slave commerce two decades later. After his lengthy lamentations, the consul identified a possible remedy when he said, "It would be easy, My Lord, to persuade the Spanish government to understand that the impediments we suffer are due to its own employees, who do not wish to publicize the indelicate if not scandalous manner in which they cheat foreigners and the Spanish treasury as well."[28]

Spain promoted illegal slaving, but penalties for evading taxes associated with it were severe: a heavy fine compounded by slave confiscation. Two interlocking forces motivated Spain's demand for the international recognition of the legality of inter-Caribbean slave trading: the assurance of a continued supply of workers and a steady flow of revenues. Licit or not, government-authorized slave landings in Puerto Rico during the 1820s were heavily supervised to ensure proper payments of tolls, tariffs, and head taxes. The trend Levieil depicted suggests that many taxable pesos from international slave commerce did not reach Madrid. With immigrants making relatively insignificant contributions to the Puerto Rican slave population until after they arrived and in the absence of serialized evidence to support the theory that they—together with local Creole elites and newcomers from Spain and its lost colonies—relied exclusively or even almost exclusively on non-Hispanic Caribbean networks for slaves, it is clear that mixed methods of acquisition continued to characterize slave commerce from 1821 onward. Hence, Spanish lawmakers were compelled to shape legislation around African and inter-Caribbean avenues.

Great turning points marked the history of Spanish slave trading in the 1830s. In 1831, France agreed with Great Britain to the mutual right of search. In 1835, Spain accepted the equipment clause, and Great Britain began to protest the reenslavement of its emancipated subjects in Puerto Rico. And in 1839, the British navy began to pursue the Portuguese flag. From then on, Spanish slave ships could no longer rely on the false identity of Portuguese registration and ownership, as shown in table 2.1.[29] These events, however, cannot be linked to Spain's initial participation in African expeditions. To do so would be chronologically late. Spanish control over African importations increased, as Spaniards, and a few Spanish Creoles, shared slaving operations with Lusophones and Francophones in Lower Guinea and gradually usurped the influence of Lusophone and Anglophone slave merchants in many areas of Upper Guinea. Though by the 1820s Spanish seamen were seasoned buyers and transporters of slaves directly from the African coast, the events cited called for drastic changes in stratagems. Quite by accident, however, one of them, British diplomatic protests in Puerto Rico, spearheaded the reevaluation of slave trade policy and the reorganization of acquisition tactics. But irony inscribed these meticulously formulated measures, for once they were ratified, Puerto Rican slave traffic almost came to a halt.

Table 2.1. Slave ships intercepted by the British Royal Navy in African waters per annum, 1839–1844

Year	Number of ships
1839	61
1840	43
1841	32
1842	11
1843	17
1844	17

Source: Great Britain, *Parliamentary Papers,* vols. 20, 21, 25, 29, 32.

Black Britons in Puerto Rico

The British government did not begin to contest the presence of Anglophone slaves in Puerto Rico in earnest until 1838. Earlier pressure on La Torre was weak and pointless. Delays were probably associated with the complexities of slave emancipation and apprenticeship in the British Caribbean between 1834 and 1838. Experts interpret the repatriation mission differently. Díaz Soler and Coll y Toste connect it to the reenslavement of runaways. Archival evidence does not corroborate this assessment. Morales Carrión sees it as an example of Spanish proslavery resistance to valiant British abolitionist philanthropy. As a political reading, this interpretation is a judgment call. Scarano links it to diminishing inter-Caribbean avenues of slave acquisition, a plausible generality, albeit English-speaking blacks, slave and free, began to appear in Puerto Rico as slaves more than a decade before British abolition.[30] The following discussion fleshes out the affair and its impact on Puerto Rican slave trade policy.

Though the Foreign Office received several reports about wrongfully enslaved Afro-Britons in Puerto Rico as early as 1823, larger numbers of such slaves did not appear until the mid-1830s.[31] Contrary to La Torre's assertion that they accompanied their masters to Puerto Rico as immigrants, most were sold by British planters fearful of inadequate compensation in the wake of systemwide emancipation. With the exception of a few from Trinidad, British intelligence reported that all the slaves were natives of Anguilla, Tortola, St. Kitts, and Nevis, and most were sold in Danish St. Thomas before being reexported to Puerto Rico. A small number remained enslaved in Danish dominion.[32]

When Great Britain raised its first official protest, both Denmark and Spain agreed to return the slaves as long as full compensation was granted to slaveholders possessing proof of legal ownership. Because neither government promised to supervise the settlement of slave value, Great Britain feared that publicized concerns would lead to price gouging and the continuity of the traffic.[33] The affair was handled locally. Officials in London delegated responsibility to British Caribbean bureaucrats and naval officers stationed in Barbados. To prevent fraud and to discourage criticism over the sinister methods used to take the Anglophones to Puerto Rico, officials agreed on a set price of 20 pounds per slave imported before August 1, 1834—the effective date of British abolition. British representatives expressed anxiety over the clarification of this point insomuch as Spain recognized the inter-Antillean trafficking of slaves as legal. As a consequence, freedmen were alerted throughout the English islands. Because slavery still existed in the French, Dutch, Danish, and Swedish Antilles, British consuls there were also advised to maintain vigilance. Four naval officers made six attempts to retrieve their "black compatriots," as they called them. Yet not more than seven of the forty-five identified as bona fide British subjects were freed and repatriated.[34]

La Torre's tactics were true to form. He feigned full cooperation while evading British emissaries. Later, he professed fear that the slaves in question were contaminated with abolitionist ideas. Moreover, he declined to advise his supervisors in Madrid that the problem existed, and he omitted the issue altogether in instructions to his successor.[35] Miguel López de Baños had barely taken over as governor when the British showered him with protests. He seemed eager to remedy the crisis. Table 2.2 shows the list he circulated throughout the island. After supplying British officials with evidence of his efforts, he swore continued cooperation "with all possibility to carry into effect Her Britannic Majesty's philanthropic views, and those of Her Illustrious Government."[36] One naval officer noted that he was impressed with López's measures, but he had reservations: "I much doubt the efficacy from such experience as I possess of the workings of the Spanish Government in all matters related to Negroes, and I am of the opinion that he considerably overrated his own abilities to ensure their bona fide execution."[37]

Though López continued to act in good faith, it became apparent that he, like his predecessors and successors, would not yield to British pressure. After declaring he had no control over La Torre's decision to correspond with Danish and Leeward Antillean authorities, rather than consulting his superiors in Madrid, he accused British officials of handicapping his efforts by furnishing vague evidence. He avowed that he could not find the slaves without knowing their corresponding names given in Puerto Rico, their distinguishing corporal features or scars, the names of conducting vessels, and precise dates of arrival.[38] Moreover, as with most high government officers, he was a Spaniard, a newcomer, and therefore an outsider. The combination was a challenge. López had to learn for himself that Puerto Ricans, including members of the planter class, were less than awed by his imperial authority. After issuing islandwide orders that all Anglophone slaves be sent to San Juan for repatriation, specifying generous remuneration, he added, "Anyone shall be deprived of all indemnity, and shall be severely punished, for incurring criminal disobedience to my authority and the orders of the Supreme Government, should it be known that he holds

Table 2.2. British subjects reported enslaved in Puerto Rico, 1834–1838

Municipality	Slave	Slave owner
Juana Díaz	Pedro	Teresa Lara
	Andrés	Gregorio Dávila
	Agustina	Petrona Ortiz
Luquillo	John	Manuel Román
Naguabo	Tom Bom	William Bedlow
	Fanny	
	María	The Butrio Brothers
	Luis	
	Opio	Cristóbal Ramírez
Juncos	Francisco	Town Mayor (not named)
Trujillo Alto	Jorge	Louis Couvertier
Las Piedras	Belén	Josefa Ortiz
Humacao	John	López and Magueti
	Juan	José María Ríos
	Johnny	Juan Antonio Miranda
Aguadilla	Pedro	Louis Duprey
	Silvestre	
	Florencia	Bruno Moreu
	Rosa	José (surname illegible)
	Jacobo	Town Mayor (not named)
Toa Baja	Enrique	Francisca Dávila
Añasco	Enrique	Gabriel Rodríguez
	Santiago	Vicente
	Manuel Eduardo	Andrés Basilis
	Carlos	Manuel Pagani
Patillas	James	Pedro Bodini
Fajardo	Carlos	Thomas O'Neill
	Flora	
	Moriah	
	Tom White	Juan Campos
	John	
	Francisco	María de Jesús Delgado
	Guillermo	Antonio Gotay
	Santiago	
	Dick	
	Lupeni [*sic*]	
Río Piedras	Luis	Jacobo de Castro
	Sofía	
	Norberta	
	Pedro	
	Domingo	

continued

Municipality	Slave	Slave owner
San Juan	Pedro	The Aranzamendi Family
	Pedro	Juan Guillén
	Abelina	Joseph Giraud
	Nancy	
Ponce	José	Mora (no given name)
	Isidoro	
	Luis	
	Juan Luis	
	Federico	
	Rita	
	Janet	
	María Agustina	Ana Bire
	Louis Creole	Jules Du Bocq
	Juan de Velis	
	Guillermo	The Martorell Brothers
	Isabel	Francisco Salas
	Susana	N. Vignuit
	María	
	Tomás	Thomas Souffront
	Juliana	Manuel Rosario
	Gweny (?)	
	Johnny	James Fraser
	María	Felicita Ferrer
	Julián	Father Joaquín Ollería
	Adelaida	Juan Salomas
Hatillo	Pedro	Patricio Gandía

Source: Archivo Histórico Nacional, Madrid, Gobierno de Puerto Rico, 5.070/29, 23. Orthography corrected where possible, e.g., Souffront (Soufron), John and Johnny (Yan and Yanni).

any English subjects in slavery, or that he assisted in any way to hold them for the purpose of impeding their emancipation."[39]

The British gave him the names and origins of 40 slaves, most of whom were reputed to have been sold in Mayagüez and Cabo Rojo by a branch of the Monsanto family—an Italian Sephardic clan from Curaçao—that lived temporarily in St. Thomas before settling in Puerto Rico between the 1790s and the 1830s.[40] Other sources suggested that some 500 had arrived since 1834. Whatever the true figures, fewer than 100 were sent to the capital.[41] The experience humiliated López, for he had just written to the governor of the Leewards, expressing his confidence in the passive character of the Puerto Rican people: "Well convinced of the submission of the inhabitants of this country, and of the docility with which they all hasten to fulfill the orders of the Supreme Government of the island, I do not doubt there should be any English subjects here who will not be found."[42]

From La Torre onward, compensation was the principal issue. Yet at major moments of reckoning, for there were several, British instructions were confusing. Commander J. Hope was the third naval officer sent to recover the slaves. During his second attempt, López informed him that seventy-three slaves were sent to the capital to await repatriation. Following the precedent established in St. Thomas, Hope was instructed to pay 20 pounds per slave. Unaware of this arrangement, López followed an agreement he found in La Torre's archive, which stipulated remuneration according to each bill of sale. Only two of the slaves had the necessary receipts. Hope reported that López declined his offer to pay whatever price the governor asked. According to López, the commander did not take the slaves because more appeared than he anticipated and he lacked the funds to cover all of them. Whichever version is closer to accuracy, both men grew exasperated. López returned the slaves to their owners, and Hope, returning to Barbados, rejected orders to make another attempt.[43]

Replacing Hope, Lieutenant Ellman was instructed to pay whatever the Spanish government asked and to secure the funds from Sydney Mason, a former diplomat for the United States but currently president of the Banco Colonial de San Juan. Though the British government planned to reimburse Mason, no one approached him before Ellman arrived. Mason's rejection of the role of intermediary should have come as no surprise. He married into a family of Hispano–Puerto Rican military elites and became a wealthy planter with many slaves.[44] Perhaps the British misjudged the extent to which Anglo-Americans identified with their Anglo-Saxon heritage.

Like Cuba and Brazil but unlike the U.S. South, Puerto Rico relied heavily on African labor in the nineteenth century. Sustained reliance on foreign-born Creole slaves was both risky and futile. Despite shrinking profits from slave labor in the Danish, Dutch, and French islands, most planters there frowned on the idea of selling their slaves to the Spanish islands. Obviously, some British planters were willing to sell them to Puerto Rico shortly before abolition and during the four-year apprenticeship period that followed. To discourage the outflux, Great Britain monitored the movements of its newly emancipated subjects. But few Britons ranked among immigrants between 1816 and 1830, and few slaves of British Caribbean origin arrived with slave masters, British or otherwise, between 1834 and 1838. Therefore, the enslavement of English-speaking Antilleans in Puerto Rico after the abolition of British slavery underscored the limits of the Cédula de Gracias. The presence of Anglophone blacks also highlighted a series of visible and invisible relations that marked a tense and awkward transition from the first to the second decade of the clandestine slave trade.

However faulty and ultimately disappointing to slaveholders in Puerto Rico, strategic liaisons between immigration and the traffic of Anglophone slaves were visible and audible. But these connections augured poorly for the British diplomatic front, for they reduced the visibility and the audibility of a greater problem, Puerto Rico's ongoing participation in the African slave trade. For the duration of the traffic, British officialdom found it difficult to monitor both African and inter-Caribbean lanes. Frequently, diplomats, administrators, and naval officers were compelled to follow orders that concentrated on one route or the other rather than on both.

Despite the plaudits British officials exchanged with each other over the capture of the Puerto Rican *Nieves* in 1819, slave ships bound for Cuba occupied center stage in Anglo-Spanish relations. The flaccid treaty of 1817 gave Puerto Rico a modicum of leverage by stipulating that Havana, not San Juan, would host the western branch of the Anglo-Spanish Court of the Mixed Commissions. Though common sense dictated the establishment of the Court of the Mixed Commissions in Cuba, abolitionist diplomats could have lobbied for a subcourt or some other form of official British presence in Puerto Rico. Their failure to do so contributed to the lack of historical evidence to document Puerto Rican participation, especially in the 1820s. Until Great Britain negotiated for consular representation in San Juan in 1844, the Foreign Office regarded Puerto Rico as an insignificant player. Compared to Cuba, Puerto Rico certainly played a minor role. The problem, however, was the misreading of "minor" as "insignificant." Though much energy was spent on efforts to identify, liberate, and repatriate black Britons enslaved in Puerto Rico, at the same time, with the boon of the Portuguese flag throughout the 1830s, African captives continued to reach Puerto Rican shores.

The interlude of the Anglophone slaves thus constituted an unusual diplomatic crisis. It sidestepped the uncertainty of Puerto Rican transgressions against Anglo-Spanish antislave trade accords, replacing them with the certainty of Puerto Rican transgressions against nascent notions of British imperial unity and national integrity based on racial equality. For the brief span of this remarkable ideal—though barely visible to British Antilleans themselves—

the blacks in question were more than people wrongfully enslaved in a foreign colony. By British law they were free subjects of the British Crown, with all rights, duties, and privileges therein.

We may never know what occasioned Governor López's solicitous behavior at the beginning of the affair, but he quickly changed his tune. His initial gush of cooperation, however, is less important than the appearance of the entire episode as a stratagem to hide the direct acquisition of African slaves by diverting British attention from transatlantic to inter-Caribbean corridors.

3

Friendly Fire, Enemy Fire

Policy Consolidation and Reform

The significance of Great Britain's attempt to liberate its black subjects from Spanish bondage cannot be overstated. Marking the first major diplomatic (but not military) confrontation between Spanish and British representatives on Puerto Rican soil, it had far-reaching consequences for both governments. On the one hand, high-ranking Spanish colonial officers paid dearly for Governor López's moment of cooperation with the British Royal Navy. Though he recognized his error quickly, it was too late. Governing bodies recalled him to Spain and generated a legislative furor. On the other hand, despite Spanish recentralization initiatives, the failed mission forced Great Britain to recognize the strength of the governor's office. No matter how ludicrous the attempt made López appear to his own government, by removing the flimsy surface of his diplomatic righteousness, he resumed the inflexible posture of his counter-abolitionist mandate and maintained it under mounting British pressure. His refusal to acquiesce to international abolitionist politics sent a crisp message to London: in matters of slavery and its commerce, Puerto Rico, as much as Cuba, warranted surveillance from within. Naval monitoring did not suffice. Thus, the liberation and repatriation fiasco formed one of several links that led to the creation of British state representation in Puerto Rico.[1]

The López initiative helped set the stage for a redistribution of political fronts as much in London, Madrid, and Havana as in San Juan. In this chapter, I delineate the direct and indirect impact of his failed mission. In the first section, I consider the changing currents of internal Spanish politics and its effects on abolitionist diplomacy. Summarizing the contradictions of internal relations among Spanish bureaucrats in Puerto Rico, I offer examples of administrative tension and instability that promoted and discouraged the slave trade. In the second and third sections, I reveal efforts to stabilize slave traffic through policy consolidation and reform. The fourth section centers on Anglo-Spanish relations vis-à-vis the creation of the British consulate in San Juan. As Great Britain's first fixed diplomatic mission in Puerto Rico, it doubled as an abolitionist sentinel. The origins of its function in this capacity are linked directly to Cuban politics and to the misjudgments of Governor López.

Conflagrations of Internal Politics

While the Anglo-Spanish face-off revealed a problem tied to inter-Caribbean channels of slave traffic, international tensions also contributed to internal discord. López played into the hands of recentralization politics in Madrid by providing the Junta de Ultramar (Colonial Board) with an excuse to curb gubernatorial authority further. Since the earliest days of seaborne expansion, the simplest disagreement among high-level colonial bureaucrats could become hostile. By the nineteenth century, little changed in this regard. The international collision between slave commerce and abolitionist politics underscored structural flaws in the Spanish colonial administration.

The intendancy was a strident economic office that ostensibly marked administrative distinctions between Hapsburg and Bourbon Spain. In reality, it drew perforated lines of bureaucratic discontinuity between the old order and the new.[2] The blurring of jurisdictional authority with overlapping duties and prerogatives was as much the legacy of the expansionist Hapsburgs as it was of the efficiency-oriented Bourbons. From the inception of the intendancy in Puerto Rico, top officials jockeyed for primacy. The course was set when Captain General Salvador Meléndez expelled Alejandro Ramírez, the island's first appointee to the Bourbon-created post.[3] From 1812 to 1822, the intendancy was separated from and reunited with the governor's office no less than four times. Recurrent change reflected not only power struggles that characterized the Bourbon Reforms in other colonies in the previous century; it also punctuated the uncertainty of the Spanish monarchy during the disruptive period of Napoleonic hegemony. Napoleon's final defeat—along with the wars of Spanish American independence—translated into the reorientation of Spanish ideas about imperial rule, ideas that augmented the importance of slavery and the commerce on which it depended.[4]

Ferdinand VII united the colonial offices of governor and captain general, endowing the joint post with sweeping authority. With only Cuba and Puerto Rico remaining in its American empire, Spain terminated the office of viceroy; the captaincy general became the highest colonial post. In Cuba, the central and eastern divisions had their own governors; only the governor of the western division was likewise captain general. Puerto Rico had but one gubernatorial office, which was simultaneously the captaincy general, with the exception of a brief period between 1822 and 1823. Miguel de La Torre was the island's first chief executive to hold both positions. As a result of the merger, the power and prestige of the intendancy diminished further. Though La Torre kept his intendants under tight control, they were not quite yes-men, for he respected their expertise in economic affairs, and he needed their counsel to facilitate the slave trade. Therefore, unlike his predecessors, he invigorated the office with the budgetary faculty it was originally designed to have. As long as the intendants agreed that slavery and its commerce were "necessary evils," he allowed them to perform their duties with little interference.

La Torre's charisma lent itself to the expanded authority Ferdinand VII granted his colonial chiefs, but it was neither his duty nor his intention to establish a lasting sense of cooperation between his office and the intendancy. At the close of his incumbency, the harmony he imposed collapsed. Limited further by the brevity of their terms, a succession of governors wrestled with their intendants over administrative dominion no sooner than they arrived. When La Torre left in 1836, Madrid set recentralization mechanisms in place. While there were important changes based on agreements between local leaders and the Junta de Ultramar—among them, municipal redistricting and penal reform—little altered the course of the metropolitan squeeze that followed La Torre's departure. The brief term of La Torre's replacement, Francisco Moreda y Prieto, was largely inconsequential, though it served as a foreboding political segue. An upstart who believed he would replace the incumbent intendant, José Domingo Díaz sent a letter to Moreda that doubled as a warning. He revealed irregularities in the payment of appropriate taxes and fees when a coffle of slaves from an unnamed island entered Puerto Rico through Guayama in the spring of 1836. Among other things, delicate relations between illegal slave traffic and the payment of taxes plagued the next governor for the duration of his office.[5]

Though the politics of slave commerce rewarded smart governors, it destroyed those less astute. Miguel López de Baños was neither weak, shrewd, creative, nor ethical, but he lacked the clout, charm, wit, and time required to develop the political dexterity associated with La Torre, the most agile and flexible of dictators. Moreover, because his term corresponded to the curbing of colonial authority, López was the first of many governors trapped by new politics emanating from Madrid. Though the intendancy of José Domingo Díaz overlapped with the tenure of several governors, it was La Torre who molded him to conform with Fernandine legislation, which promoted the ad hoc combination of gubernatorial autonomy and autocracy—poor preparation for changing times ahead.

Slavery played into governor-intendant relations. As expected, the intendant and the new governor did not work well as a team. Strained relations began as an exchange of barbs over billing responsibilities for the Anglophone slaves. Instead of making an effort to settle the minor dispute, Díaz sought the intervention of metropolitan authorities. Their mediation exceeded his expectations. The junta blamed both of them for the diplomatic confrontation with the British Admiralty. Remittances for per diem costs in San Juan—where the Anglophone slaves waited futilely to return to their homelands—extended from the jurisdiction of the local government to local justice rather than to the local treasury, a clear sign that the junta cast López and Díaz in the same negative light.[6] The showdown with the British earned the intendant low marks when he came under review. He faced charges ranging from nepotism to the creation of new tariffs without approval from Madrid.[7] But he did not lose his job. The buck stopped with López, and Díaz made sure that it did.

While López's enemies were hardly abolitionists themselves, they used his connivance in the slave trade to embarrass him. When his term came under metropolitan review after his dismissal in 1840, criticisms included the authorization he granted for three slaving expeditions. During his term, the *Constancia*, the *Caballo Blanco*, and the *Urraca* arrived safely in San Juan, Humacao, and Ponce with a total of 743 captives.[8] There were certainly other such expeditions, and his hands were full because of them. Addressing both slave commerce and slave treatment, two major lawsuits challenged his fitness to rule.

The Audiencia Territorial—the Puerto Rican High Court of Appeals—initiated both suits. Led by Attorney General Fernando Pérez de Rosas in 1839, the first case opposed López's ruling against vagrancy. Copious transcripts speak to the Audiencia's dissatisfaction with the waffling and frenetic contradictions that characterized Puerto Rican slavery and slave trading in the Age of Abolition. The plaintiffs produced a list of officials who received kickbacks from the illegal trade—from the chief of customs (2 pesos) to the governor and the intendant (8 pesos each). For a calculated influx of 2,000 slaves per annum by the late 1830s, each slave who landed represented 30 pesos in bribes. The governor and the intendant jointly received more than 50 percent of the bribes required. However, given that the intendant was obligated to give 25 percent of his share to the assessor, the governor received the largest portion of all.[9]

The second suit involved the death penalty pronounced against the five leaders of a slave conspiracy in Guayanilla in September 1840, one month before López was compelled to resign. Politically clumsy, brutal, and direct, rather than graceful, astute, and evasive, he supported the sentence of the Military Council: death by strangulation. The military advocate who led the defense protested the sentence and enlisted the aid of an Audiencia judge and other high-level officials to form a special tribunal. Basic arguments challenged the authority of military courts to try slaves. The tribunal reduced the sentence to an assortment of lesser ones, none of which included exile.[10]

The two suits and the British repatriation initiative combined to explode, resulting in legislation that made high colonial officers painfully accountable for their actions. Such concerns signaled the end of the semiautonomous character of the captaincy general in evidence since 1822.[11] Though the suits and the repatriation effort indicated that local politics still tempered the iron fist of metropolitical authority, the verdict was clear: Madrid would continue to tolerate—and encourage—quibbling among overseas bureaucrats. But if their discord proved injurious to the colonial system, criminal prosecution would follow. Thus, López's term defined a political discourse in transition, replete with trial and error at the level of local chicanery and foreign diplomacy.

"Fruitless and Arbitrary Excesses"

As a consequence of López's dealings with the British, the Madrid-based Junta de Ultramar held a series of meetings that generated considerable correspondence over how to handle the international slave trade. These sessions created new measures and fortified old ones to safeguard both inter-Antillean and African slave traffic. More specifically, the junta set out to address three problems revealed by the British repatriation conflict: public policy and the culpability of Spanish subjects; the financial responsibility of colonial agencies; and the responsibility of high colonial officers in foreign policy and diplomacy.[12]

First, there were misunderstandings over which office was responsible for debts incurred by the army, which fed and housed the black Britons summoned to San Juan for repatriation. Remittances included travel costs from various municipalities to the capital. The chief army accountant sent the bills to the intendant, who forwarded them to the governor, who sent them back to the Office of Army Accounts. The cycle was repeated. After exchanging several polite unpleasantries with the governor and the army accountant in the course of the third round, the intendant wrote to Madrid for instructions from the royal treasury, whose officers notified the Junta de Ultramar.[13] Members of the junta and the treasury expressed displeasure over how the problem was handled. The British government claimed eighteen slaves, but seventy-three appeared at army headquarters in San Juan. In addition to an excess of fifty-five slaves, metropolitan officials learned that an unspecified number spoke French or French-based patois.[14] Furthermore, because forty-six of the slaves were from the capital, junta members suspected that travel expenses amounting to 587 pesos and 97 centavos were padded. They argued that other arrangements could have been made without dependence on the royal treasury and without compromising the agrarian productivity of slave labor. They declared that the metropolitan exchequer would only cover expenses for the exact number of slaves the British government claimed. They charged López and Díaz for all remaining costs. Their first remonstrance concluded, "To avoid the repetition of these fruitless and arbitrary excesses, the superior authority of that island and the intendant must be made to understand that should cases such as these arise in the future, they must bear the weight of the responsibility, in acting without metropolitan authorization. The royal economy must always be the prime concern."[15] The matter was not resolved until 1846, when Intendant Manuel José Cerero acknowledged authorization to remunerate the Office of Army Accounts for funds used to care for the slaves at the correctional presidio in the capital.[16]

Next, the Colonial Board cross-listed the issue of tax evasion with illegal slave imports. As if finally heeding the warnings spelled out by the French consul nearly twenty years before, the government came to realize that un-monitored slave smuggling represented a substantial loss in royal revenues. While supporting the clandestine trade, measures were needed to promote the idea that Spain would not tolerate violations of colonial and international law. Though only nine of the seventy-three slaves arrived without payment of port duties and head taxes, this figure was too high for the junta. Nor did it seem to matter that La Torre addressed this problem when he issued an order in September 1836 that spelled out tolls, tariffs, capitation, and other charges levied in the illegal introduction of slaves, and that López followed it to the letter—as instanced in the arrivals of the *Caballo Blanco*, the *Constancia*, and the *Urraca*. But López, not La Torre, was the primary object of the junta's dissatisfaction.[17]

Along with other metropolitan agencies, the junta authorized a tariff amnesty program. Outstanding among the articles of the nine-point plan were the following: (1) Owners of illegally imported slaves need only register them within ten days of the proclamation and pay a small tax to prevent confiscation. (2) To discourage the landing of rebels, slave behavior must be authenticated by municipal officers, who would provide slaves with a certificate of good conduct if they qualified. (3) Masters were obligated to expel slaves identified as troublemakers, *esclavos revoltosos*; if not, the government would do so. (4) Masters continuing to import slaves without registering them and paying taxes for them, as well as masters who retained known militant slaves, would be fined 100 pesos for each slave, plus 50 pesos awarded to the person who reported them to the government. Slaves were free to denounce law-breaking masters. (5) Duties were to be paid within forty-eight hours after registration.[18]

The death of Ferdinand VII in 1833 heralded administrative reversals, which included metropolitan moves to control the delegation of seaborne authority. But the geographic distance between Spain and the Caribbean still made it necessary to allow local officers to have their say in the shaping of legislation. Thus, the junta did not specify the amount to be charged in its amnesty plan, nor did it cite the criteria for what constituted grounds for slave expulsion beyond "los de carácter revoltoso."[19] Free-flowing cabotage—trade between different ports, states, or colonies ruled by the same government—was not implied in the plan. Cuba did not import slave militants knowingly unless they were convicted prisoners. Legal action against such slaves was a different matter. But sale procedures for adjudicated rebels were not mentioned at all. Therefore, the directive "Masters must get rid of rebellious slaves by selling them away from the island" required further refinement in Puerto Rico.

The next assertion also required local refining and clarification. "If masters do not rid the island of rebellious slaves through external sales, the government will do so and charge the masters for all costs incurred." The expulsion of slave recalcitrants at their owners' expense could be understood to apply to future and successive illegal imports only. Without local amendments, it could mean that past transgressions would be forgiven and that one-time importations in the future would go unpunished. More important, in this instance and others for the remainder of the century, metropolitan directives tended to display a remarkable naïveté about the quotidian realities of life in the colonies. In the tax amnesty plan, for example, rewards and punishments presented special problems, problems outside the purview of the junta in Madrid. Therefore, high-ranking bureaucrats with years of experience in Puerto Rico were free to make appropriate changes in the reformation of proslave trade policy.

Regarding rewards, without the promise of anonymity, manumission, or resale to another master, 50 pesos to slave informants was poor compensation for the inevitable wrath they would face from their law-breaking owners. Regarding punishments, the detention of—and harsh measures against—militant slaves was acceptable, but the confiscation and expulsion of an able-bodied foreign-born slave for minor offenses were unlikely. Whether for petty infractions or overt rebelliousness, justice was of little import. The intervention of colonial authority always resulted in losses to the slave owner, who alone bore the cost of food, clothing, and shelter for preadjudicated slaves as well as detained slaves not destined for trial—such as captured runaways at the level of small-scale marronage. Masters were also responsible for some but not all court fees. Thus, many did not report slave transgressions unless lives and property were at stake. When slaves threatened personal or islandwide security—and a defendant's execution or exile figured in the outcome—it was cheaper for slaveholders to kill them rather than report them for due process of law.[20]

Some of the plan's provisions were absurd. But to achieve the larger objective—the shaping of a policy that supported both slave commerce and foreign diplomacy—it was necessary to include measures that seemed incomplete or nebulous if not antithetical to that goal. The aim, in effect, was the construction of practices guided by a policy of metaphysical deconstruction, the inscription of nonclosure, the creation of fixed and flexible openings in a newly formed cul-de-sac. The idea was not to locate and ferret out the contradictions of the plan but to create them and embed them within it in order to counteract external protest.

Outsiders were privy neither to the plan's fine-tuning nor the rationale that endorsed its implementation. This point is borne out further by the junta's third concern: Anglo-Spanish relations. Profoundly annoyed that López circulated notices for the recall of Anglophone slaves, junta members fell just short of branding him with imbecility.[21] During La Torre's incumbency, Commander Hope observed that repatriation agreements between the two countries would not work because Spain would never acknowledge treaty violations.[22] Indeed, the junta asserted that López's actions were tantamount to a declaration of guilt and that he was motivated by "imprudent zeal." The board was least impressed with his attempt to maintain Spanish honor by returning the Afro-Britons or, more apparently, his efforts to increase royal coffers by exacting a tax on the money due the masters of repatriated slaves.[23] If it were true that English-speaking slaves in Puerto Rico numbered from 400 to 500 men, women, and children, British compensation to their Spanish owners could not make up for the loss of slave labor, slave reproduction, and revenues, which over time would have proved injurious to both local production and the metropolitan treasury.

The junta divided its reprimand into two parts. The first identified colonial administrative friction. "Sadly, this is not the first time that island authorities have taken Madrid for granted by not consulting us on matters beyond their jurisdiction. Unless the government wants to see itself frequently compromised, as it is today due to lack of communication between the offices of the Puerto Rican intendancy and the captaincy general, this abuse must stop."[24] Because Spain encouraged poor relations between intendants and governors, when Díaz reported his disagreement with López, he acted as expected. The junta's scolding was superfluous given that its target was the governor.

The second section of the reprimand addressed slave traffic more directly. Here, with structural cohesion, the junta began to spell out its position for the first time by stating, "We cannot imagine how it was possible that in order to increase the treasury, island authorities publicly admitted that slaves were clandestinely imported in open violation of the law."[25] Then functionaries were told how to interpret the Anglo-Spanish treaty of 1835 in favor of the slave trade and how to impart this unique understanding to the British. The continuity of African slave commerce to Puerto Rico was reinscribed with full metropolitan approval. In an effort to sever his connection to the governor's diplomatic faux pas, Díaz set the tone for policy consolidation when he wrote, "It is a shame that agriculture demands that the government support and protect slavery, but it is an evil without remedy. Without it the colonies would be destroyed. This form of servitude must be tolerated, as well as the continued importation of slaves, who, in the main are Africans, excepting those whose importation is prohibited by our treaties with England."[26] He was not guilty of double-talk. He followed Spanish imperial logic.

The joint Ministry of Colonial Governance, Commerce, and Naval Affairs named a committee to study "this important and delicate matter ... to prevent further English claims of illegal enslavement." Hence, the amnesty program and other initiatives were implemented. Endorsing the counsel of the ad hoc committee, Díaz reiterated his position almost verbatim: "[Q]ue se introduzcan aquellos que por lo regular son africanos, y no de los que está prohivida [sic] su introdución [sic] por los tratados de Inglaterra."[27] The echo was simple and long-lived. Treaties forbade direct slave traffic from Africa, but because Spain never agreed to close inter-Caribbean channels, the non-Hispanic islands would remain significant sources of slaves—some Creoles but mainly reexported Africans. The only difference would be the absence of English-speaking slaves. The precision of his assertion merits closer examination.

Fine-Tuning

Spanish legislators and diplomats designed the exclusion of Anglophone bondsmen to curtail British abolitionist interference. It did not matter that in the eighteenth century, Spain encouraged marronage to Puerto Rico from the non-Hispanic islands, offering freedom to runaways in exchange for loyalty to the Spanish Crown and conversion to Roman Catholicism. Though the town of San Mateo de los Cangrejos was a haven for working-class Irish immigrants in the early 1800s, in the 1700s it was a settlement for foreign runaway slaves.[28] Selective oversight allowed junta members to rely on Hapsburg law from the sixteenth and seventeenth centuries, which stated that the importation of foreign Creole slaves was illegal. It mattered not that many Hapsburg laws were nullified or amended during the Bourbon Reforms of the eighteenth century. By referring to Creole slaves as *ladinos* (westernized Africans), the Colonial Board resolved a potentially troublesome technicality. Be it cabotage or foreign, from the 1820s to the 1870s Great Britain contested the legality of inter-Caribbean slave traffic. Vociferous British opposition fell silent on Spanish ears. This diplomatic stalemate allowed junta members to posit that the exclusion of Africans in favor of Creoles ran counter to Spanish law.[29] In other words, by the deliberate slippage of their reckoning, the abolition of the African slave trade was illegal.

Coupled with the fact that French, Dutch, and Danish Caribbean planters did not demonstrate a willingness to sell their slaves, despite their troubled sugar economies, Spain's resuscitated respect for older imperial decrees justified the continuity of the trade. Be they African or Creole slaves—as long as bondsmen were not imported into Spanish dominions from the British empire, as long as slaves were introduced from neighboring Caribbean islands where slavery still existed, and as long as the governments of these islands provided permission, support, and protection—Great Britain had no right to impede the slave trade. Without spelling out this detailed rationale to the British, Spain engineered a diplomatic coup.

The joint ministry's ad hoc committee advised that the amnesty plan be reduced to three areas of concern, all centering on prerequisites for slave imports. Their recommendations illustrate ongoing relations between narrow economic agendas and broader concerns for social relations within the politics of local and metropolitan control. Committee members presented their criteria with a preamble that outlined the need to balance logical policies with economic reality. In other words, they sought to amend external antislave trade agreements with internal measures "that do not jeopardize our national standards." Members then equated British abolitionism with political hyperbole, fully admitted Spain's efforts to circumvent bilateral accords, and once more lambasted López for his efforts to repatriate Anglophone slaves.[30]

The committee advised that importations be judged according to the status and character of individual slaves from neighboring ports, be the source intra-imperial or foreign. The proposed divisions were foreign runaways, exiles, and dissidents; victims of kidnapping; and small coffles of newly arrived Africans acquired through foreign merchants. The first was a proscription; the second and third were adornments. Reasons for the exclusions in the first category differ little from concerns outlined in the nine-point tax amnesty program as seen in the stipulation, "[E]l país no permite que se añadan más elementos de peligro a los que [ya] desgraciadamente existen." The second measure did not outlaw the kidnapping and enslavement of foreign blacks. It upheld the efforts of the nine-point plan to guarantee the ownership of kidnap victims through tax amnesty. Kidnapping for enslavement was a crime of necessity. To avoid British denouncements, they advised greater caution in dealing with these types. For the third measure, the entry of Africans via the non-Hispanic, non-Britannic Antilles, the committee fashioned a double justification: the need to sustain the Puerto Rican economy through agricultural development and the right of tax-paying Spanish subjects and residents to own private property. Again, caution was advised, but as long as buyers paid import duties and head taxes, the Spanish government would not permit British seizure.[31]

There were no instructions for cases of direct landings from Africa, cases initiated with the spotting of suspicious vessels that British agents and their Puerto Rican abolitionist informants verified as slavers.[32] It was of little consequence that no Foreign Office employee ever witnessed a landing of African slaves on Puerto Rican soil. Unlike Cuba, Puerto Rico had no juridical base from which to launch procedures for the liberation of Africans landed illegally on its shores. Slavers bound for Puerto Rico but intercepted by British cruisers on the American side of the Atlantic were escorted to Havana for proceedings. The treaty of 1817 called for the creation of a court to adjudicate all transatlantic slave ship ventures involving Spanish ports. If the arbiters agreed that a given vessel was a slaver—a simple task with captives on board—it was condemned and the captives declared *emancipados*, or liberated Africans. In addition to allowing vessel seizure based on slaving equipment alone, the treaty of 1835 required the relocation of *emancipados* to British Caribbean colonies. But more of them remained in Cuba as state wards entrusted to morally upright subjects, a trait determined by each applicant's ability to pay the local treasury. Diplomats, travelers, and sympathetic white Creoles agreed that Cuban *emancipados* suffered a fate worse than slavery. Thus, by the 1830s their plight became another bone of contention in Anglo-Spanish diplomacy.[33]

For administrators in Puerto Rico, the absence of *emancipado* politics was a blessing. But their counterparts in Cuba believed that Puerto Rico should share the burden. In Madrid, silence radiating from the ad hoc committee spoke volumes in this regard. The committee could not make recommendations for procedures to handle Puerto Rican *emancipados*. As a legitimate designation in Puerto Rico, *emancipados* did not exist. In other words, as a social category and a legal condition, the term had no local reference point until the landing of the *Majesty* in 1859. Without the legitimacy of institutional structures to negotiate the freedom of Africans enslaved illegally in Puerto Rico, the illegality of their welcomed presence remained a nonissue at this point. Obviously, after African captives landed in Puerto Rico, the possibility of rerouting them to Cuba to pursue their liberation was nil. Motivated by avarice and other forms of self-aggrandizement endorsed by the social economy of slavery and the politics of the day, slavists were cautious and shrewd. Hence, for the junta and the ad hoc committee in Madrid, as well as island administrators, sugar producers, and other entrepreneurs, the only option was to prevent the British detection of inbound slave ships in Puerto Rican waters.

Throughout the session, the ad hoc committee members echoed the junta's disapproval of López's orders to circulate government notices without metropolitan consultation, emphasizing that it would never happen again. To assure this end, they enjoined the junta to create the most stringent recentralizing measure taken since the Cortes (Parliament) voided Cuban and Puerto Rican representation after Ferdinand's death.[34] "Hence forth, as applicable to the colonial authorities of Cuba and the Philippines as it shall be to those of Puerto Rico, it is forbidden to publish any circular, ordinance, or disposition without the approval of the Crown, no matter how advantageous it may seem to their government or their property... and if these authorities continue to abuse their responsibility by ignoring this command, their actions will be equated with usurpation and they will be tried for treason."[35]

The old viceregal expedient, "Obedezco pero no cumplo" (I obey but I do not comply), was legislated out of existence. Rougher sides of the law were softened somewhat. Intendants and governors were still free to act autonomously in emergency conditions, but they were held accountable for independent actions that endangered imperial security. Only incumbents were responsible for decisions deemed careless or unwise; retired officials could not be tried.[36]

The committee saved the best for last. Following a precedent the British government established in its Caribbean colonies, it authorized the recruitment of free Africans for contract labor in Puerto Rico. Committee members promised that laws to regulate the program would duplicate the British model to the letter.[37] They further stipulated that the Foreign Office be notified of the project, anticipating no grounds for protest because Anglo-Spanish treaties did not prohibit free African immigration and because the British government itself set the example. But the project failed before it started. Though the Junta de Ultramar authorized it in 1843, four years passed before its members submitted it to the Spanish Caribbean governors for consideration. A myriad of events contributed to the delay, not the least among them, a chain of slave disturbances on both islands in 1843, the establishment of British consular representation in San Juan in 1844, and the Spanish penal code of 1845.

Flatly rejecting the African immigration idea, Governor Rafael de Arístegüi counted on the junta to implement measures already adopted for the facile import of slaves. He based his reasoning on a mounting climate of fear in evidence since 1841. In May 1841, his predecessor, Santiago Méndez de Vigo, informed the Ministry of Colonial Governance, Commerce, and Naval Affairs that Haitian propagandists sent subversive literature to the island by way of British steamers from Santo Domingo. According to Méndez, the intention was to repeat the Haitian Revolution in Puerto Rico, "a fin de fomentar la revolución de negros como había ocurrido en Haití." He issued decrees that required the

registration of all incoming persons and parcels to prevent the landing of anyone suspected of Haitian identity.[38] His precautions paid off; seven months
later, vigilant forces in Ponce uncovered a slave-based conspiracy to revolt.
The ringleaders were African-born. Though trans-Caribbean networking gave
them every reason to count on armed support from Haiti, the plot was betrayed
locally.[39]

Arístegüi's objection to the African immigration bore fruit as well. In his last
year of office, the Colonial Board worked out the final stage in the reformation
of slave trade policy. Ideas that motivated this phase and their application—
both products of his orchestration—are detailed in Chapters 8 and 9. At this
juncture, suffice it to say that he not only eclipsed the "Africanization" of Puerto
Rico by rejecting the free immigration plan; he facilitated the continuous
trickle of slave imports on his own terms without jeopardizing his position.[40]
Influenced by new laws that would incriminate him for decisions that put the
colony at risk, he controlled all phases of slave importations. But his caution
also helped spearhead the end of the traffic. Following his return to Spain in
December 1847, there were no documented landings of African captives until
February 1859. The end of his tenure inaugurated a twelve-year hiatus.

Madrid, London, San Juan, and Havana

In 1817, Great Britain assumed the superior side in its binary opposition with
Spain. For its perceived lack of bilaterality, Spain countered the discourse by
ignoring the agreement. Great Britain countered the counter by placing an
equipment clause in the treaty of 1835. Spain responded by relying on the
flags of Portugal and the United States for the remainder of the decade. The
British responded by creating the post of superintendent of liberated Africans. The position, designed by Viscount Palmerston, the British foreign secretary, seemed tailor-made for David Turnbull, a Scottish abolitionist with
strong, Christian-based, problack sympathies that set him on a collision course
with Spanish authorities in Cuba. Palmerston upgraded the consulate to consulate-general, merged it with the new superintendency, and gave the double
office to Turnbull as a result of aggressive self-lobbying and the accolades he
received for his published report on slavery and the prospects of abolition in the
Caribbean.[41] Great Britain agitated Anglo-Spanish relations further by (1)
docking a hulk, the *Romney*, in the harbor of Havana to receive and care for
Africans newly emancipated by the Cuban branch of the Court of the Mixed
Commissions; (2) tolerating and often encouraging Turnbull's brash, disrup-

tive, and relentless behavior, first and foremost while Palmerston headed the Foreign Office; (3) prosecuting Spanish slave ships flying the Portuguese flag; and (4) aggravating the United States to the point of armed hostility.[42]

In the spring of 1842, Lord Aberdeen, the earl of Clarendon, Great Britain's new foreign secretary, removed Turnbull from his consular post, replaced him with Joseph Crawford, and dissolved the superintendency of liberated Africans. Turnbull left in August, returned by stealth at least once in October, and continued to circulate among black people, slave and free. In November 1842, Governor Gerónimo Valdés expelled him permanently, vowing to have him shot on sight if he returned. Between March and November 1843, slave revolts rocked the island from Cárdenas to Matanzas. The new governor, Leopoldo O'Donnell, received reports about an international, race-based conspiracy against the Spanish colonial government. However real or imagined, he was certain Turnbull was at the root of it. By January 1844, the Conspiración de la Escalera, the governor's Afro-Cuban bloodbath, was in full swing.[43]

As a consequence of slave trade politics in Cuba, between the treaty of 1835 and O'Donnell's excesses in 1844, Puerto Rico became a pawn between Great Britain and Spain. Nearly overwhelmed with slave trade infractions in Cuba, neither British consular agents in Havana nor British naval agents in Barbados noticed the increase of English-speaking slaves in Puerto Rico during the apprenticeship period of British emancipation between 1834 and 1838 until it was too late. Cognizant of its failure to free its subjects enslaved on Spanish soil, on the one hand, and in an effort to end a decade of bellicose politics and diplomacy, on the other, Great Britain pushed for and won consular representation in Puerto Rico. Though interest in legitimate trade weighed in the decision to press Spain for a consulate, diplomats cited the liberation of enslaved Afro-Britons as the primary motive.[44] However, the origins of the quest are embedded in Cuban politics, with the Court of the Mixed Commissions at its controversial core.

On numerous occasions between 1826 and 1844, Spanish and British officials promoted the transfer of the Mixed Court from the larger island to the smaller. In August 1826, two British men-of-war chased the schooner *Minerva* into Cuban waters, captured it in Cabañas Bay, and escorted it to the port of Havana. Spanish authorities alleged that it carried no slaves. That evening, British authorities witnessed the unloading of African captives in the presence of urban police units at the dock. It was also evident that the schooner disembarked some of the Africans in Puerto Rico before the venture terminated in

Cuba. Though British arbiters from the Mixed Court ordered a hearing, Spanish arbiters prevailed. Thus, the record shows that the ship arrived to Cuba from Puerto Rico without slaves. Charging corruption among local officials, British diplomats in Havana petitioned the Spanish government to transfer the Mixed Court to San Juan.[45]

In July 1832, the governor of Cuba, Mariano Ricafort, informed the secretariat of the Department of Justice in Madrid (el Despacho de Gracia y Justicia) that a Dutch merchant, H. van der Meulen, obtained permission from his government to extract slaves from Curaçao and sell them to the Spanish islands. On these grounds, Ricafort requested that the Mixed Court be transferred to Puerto Rico.[46] Given that Puerto Rico enjoyed special diplomatic relations with Dutch Curaçao—where Spanish government funds paid private agents to report anticolonial activities—Ricafort's rationale was less flaccid than it appears.[47] In October 1833, the theme surfaced again. Both George Villiers, British ambassador to Spain, and Cuba's new governor, Miguel Tacón—a crafty pseudo-intellectual with remarkable oratory skills—rejected the proposition. Villiers cited the physical and emotional hardships involved in removing newly landed captives from Cuba to Puerto Rico. Tacón agreed, adding that voyages from Cuba to Puerto Rico were as arduous as those from Africa to Cuba. His exaggerated comparison not only typified his diplomacy, it also prefaced his subtle assertion that he was willing to entertain the idea of moving the court. He identified Puerto Rico as the only alternative because "any other site on Cuban soil would result in the same inconveniences." Whose inconveniences? Like all good statesmen, Tacón spoke with more than one tongue. Yet here his double entendre was clear.[48]

Turnbull's reputation for ardor preceded him. Though he did not occupy the joint post of consul-general and superintendent of liberated Africans until November 1840, in August 1839, on orders from Madrid, Governor Valdés approached interim officers at the British consulate to ascertain the possibility of transferring both the Mixed Court and the hulk *Romney* from Havana to San Juan. He cited Turnbull's abolitionist infamy as the motive.[49] By October 1841, Valdés was fed up with the intrepid Scottish Afrophile. Citing an uprising that involved forty southwest Nigerian slaves at a construction site in the heart of Havana—which soldiers crushed by killing six of them and injuring ten—he linked the fray to Turnbull's "spirit of insurrection" and asked that the Mixed Court be transferred to Puerto Rico immediately.[50]

Palmerston responded that the transfer of newly arrived Africans from Cuba to Puerto Rico would cause them further suffering after the Atlantic crossing. This was, of course, old news. Tacón and Villiers said as much in 1833. His real motives were transparent. He knew that the change would work to Cuba's advantage, for all manner of local chicanery would have prevented the safe transfer of captives and vessels from Havana to San Juan for Mixed Court proceedings. But it would cut into British designs as well. Despite the force of its equipment clause, which allowed the Mixed Courts of Havana and Freetown to condemn slave vessels without captives on board, the treaty of 1835 was nearly as ineffective as the treaty of 1817. However, it permitted British agents to send liberated Africans in Cuba to work as wage earners in underdeveloped or recently settled British colonies such as Belize, the Mosquito Coast, the Bahamas, Bermuda, Demerara, and Trinidad, though older and wealthier colonies such as Jamaica, Barbados, and Antigua were also recipients.[51] Relocating the court would slow the flow of *emancipados* to British dominions. Turnbull endorsed consular representation in Puerto Rico. He based his support on the advice of naval officers who attempted to recover the black Britons enslaved there. Suggesting that the idea be raised in Madrid, La Torre and López cited their lack of authority to approve it. Shifting gears, Palmerston recognized the plan as essential in 1838, but British leaders did not broach it again until 1842.[52]

As the Turnbull connection corroborates, the origins of the British consulate in Puerto Rico cannot be separated from Cuban affairs. The two colonies were determined to ignore the treaties of 1817 and 1835. But the Foreign Office still underestimated Puerto Rican violations until Turnbull published his exposé in 1840, which included slave data for both islands. While historians have yet to exonerate the energetic Turnbull for complicity in a series of slave revolts between 1841 and 1844, few doubt that he brought Anglo-Spanish diplomacy to an all-time low.[53] Though Valdés ousted Turnbull two years before Spain appointed O'Donnell as governor, Turnbull's problack legacy led the new chief to suspect him of continued liberationist activity. The sanguinary persecutions that followed were based on O'Donnell's conviction that such activity was meant to destroy both slavery and Spanish colonial rule in Cuba. Accusations against the fiery Scot were plausible, for if he did not participate in the plot, he inspired rebellion within Cuba's diverse black population. While nothing suggests his complicity in slave unrest in Puerto Rico between 1839 and 1844, his inter-Caribbean networking, in evidence since 1835, sufficed to raise suspicion.[54]

As Cuban slaveholders hoped, Consul Crawford lacked the undisciplined passion of his predecessor. The Mixed Court grew increasingly unsuccessful in many respects.[55] With Turnbull gone, treaty infractions multiplied. On these grounds, Crawford requested the court's transfer. His logic rested on the erroneous supposition that more cases would result in favor of British judges in San Juan. Officials in Havana and Madrid favored the idea as well. Finally, for the first time, Spain and Great Britain agreed to the move simultaneously.[56] But nothing came of this memorable moment until O'Donnell arrived in Havana in late 1843.

Before Turnbull's tenure, Palmerston opposed the change. When Turnbull held joint diplomatic positions, Palmerston supported the idea, while Spain did not. When Palmerston's Whig government fell in 1841, Tories named Aberdeen foreign secretary. Palmerston paid a form of loud, anti-Spanish lip service to British abolitionist politics that was, at times, less than convincing. Aberdeen, on the other hand, was overtly conciliatory toward Spain. When O'Donnell became governor of Cuba in October 1843, the time was propitious to resume talks about the court's transfer.[57] First, though only next door in Jamaica, Turnbull was expelled from Cuba, and his replacement, Crawford, reflected the less confrontational policies of the new Tory government. Second, Spain's short pro-British regency headed by Baldomero Espartero had fallen. (Isabel II was underage, and her mother, Queen-Regent María Cristina, fled Spain in disgrace for a host of unsavory reasons.) Third, slave traders found ways to make up for the loss of protection from the Portuguese flag. Fourth, the British government had already agreed to the transfer before O'Donnell arrived. Only the details remained. If the transfer became a reality, high colonial officers, governors above all, could enrich themselves further with slave trader bribes.[58] Relocating the court to Puerto Rico would free Cuba from the strain of close British surveillance.

Though Madrid backed O'Donnell's proposal, opposition came from London and San Juan. Palmerston courted enmity in his public and private affairs. Lord Aberdeen, Earl of Clarendon, ranked among his worthiest detractors. Puerto Rican affairs figured impressively in Aberdeen's efforts to undo everything Palmerston had achieved in the politics of abolitionist diplomacy when he succeeded him in October 1841. The following example ranks among the best. Estéban Balaguer was one of many Spanish slave traders who established residency in Puerto Rico. He helped supply the local slave market, owned slave ships, and captained them. With considerable experience in West African systems of barter, he also dabbled in the gold trade in Upper and Lower Guinea.

When officers of the Royal Navy confiscated one of his vessels and plundered its stores in Sierra Leone, he sued the British government. With Aberdeen's backing, he won, though Palmerston overturned the decision when he regained his post in 1845.[59]

Notwithstanding his support for Balaguer, Aberdeen could not countenance O'Donnell's bid to transfer the Mixed Court. Though he was labeled a moderate in Madrid's liberal government, the Foreign Office recognized the governor correctly as a conservative with a reputation for military excess. Aberdeen based his decision to reject the idea of transfer on recommendations from Mixed Court judges themselves. He directed British agents in Havana and Madrid to resist O'Donnell's pressure because "[t]he move to such an obscure colony, where communications with Havana are so poor, would signal the Commission's loss of moral influence."[60]

No less alarmed was Puerto Rico's new captain general, Governor Rafael de Arístegüi, the Count de Mirasol, who equated the presence of the British flag with the evils of foreign influence, that is, the conflation of antislavery and anti-Spanish colonial politics. Furthermore, at this point all requests for transferal automatically included the relocation of another nemesis—the *Romney*. Thus, Arístegüi concluded that the presence of the Mixed Court and the hulk in Puerto Rico would amplify expansionist designs on the Spanish Caribbean emanating from the U.S. South.[61] Both the British Foreign Office and the Puerto Rican captaincy general faced two choices: buckle under the dominating influence of Leopoldo O'Donnell in Cuba or seek a middle ground. Authorization to establish a British consulate in Puerto Rico was, therefore, a double compromise: one, between San Juan and Madrid; the other, between London and Madrid.[62] The Mixed Court and the *Romney* remained in Havana.

As with most governors of the Spanish Caribbean islands in the nineteenth century, O'Donnell was a military man. He was also a hero in the first Carlist War.[63] Cuba, however, was his first overseas post. Arístegüi was far less decorated militarily, but he had years of administrative experience as an army officer in Cuba when he was named to govern Puerto Rico.[64] But in spite of his record of service to the Crown, he could not compel Madrid to recognize his ability to resist Cuban pressure without agreeing to the presence of a British consulate in his jurisdiction. At the same time, the idea of guarding against the further influx of emancipated Afro-Britons provided the British government with a face-saving pretext to insist on consular representation after its failure to rescue its people from Puerto Rican captivity.

Neither before nor after the arrival of the first consul in 1844 was the British government privy to elaborate measures the Spanish government formulated to advance slave trade entrenchment. Debates over the destiny of the Court of the Mixed Commissions eclipsed concerns for the repatriation of Afro-Britons still enslaved in Puerto Rico, the main reason given for establishing a consulate. Instead of pressing for the freedom of those who remained, the Foreign Office reasoned that the consul should concern himself with other matters—such as the landing of Africans. By this time, British officials believed that the trafficking of black Britons had ceased, an unfortunate miscalculation, for the theme perforated relations with Spain up to the mid-1850s.

After Ferdinand's death, Spanish liberals began to undermine the authority of high officials sent to the colonies. By the close of the 1830s, metropolitan forces had eroded much of the hegemony associated with captains general, governors, and intendants, as instanced in the fallout that resulted from Great Britain's failed efforts to liberate and repatriate Puerto Rico's English-speaking slaves. Though the intendant was reprimanded, the governor, Madrid's perfect scapegoat, bore the full weight of the episode. The totality of López's blundering record played into the hands of recentralization politics. In their scathing review, authorities blamed him for the concession of British consular representation. But the erosion of gubernatorial authority was contrived in uneven terms. Separate considerations for slave trade politics divided the curbing of power between Cuban and Puerto Rican affairs.

Though Cuba and Puerto Rico shared the international spotlight in this theater of counterabolitionist horrors, the former was always the main protagonist. For supporting performances, Puerto Rico earned no more than honorable mention. Disequilibrium notwithstanding, slave commerce—but not slavery—rendered Cuban and Puerto Rican politics inseparable, as evidenced in the creation of British state representation in San Juan. The consulate was crucial because it fell under the supervision of the foreign secretary, who headed the Foreign Office. British victory, however, was less than complete inasmuch as it strengthened Spanish resolve to protect the slave trade to Cuba. Spain's triumph over hard-line British abolitionism was no less fractured. The internal politics of Spanish colonialism turned on itself at the expense of sound, proslave trade measures applicable to both islands. Spanish politics reduced the consolidation of slave trade policy and reform to a state of functional futility.

Because of the episode of the Anglophone slaves, Spain granted Cuba its nod of approval to continue the traffic in African captives. It did not deny the smaller island similar approval; it simply continued to place less value on its participation in the trade. However, given the waning vigor of abolitionist enthusiasm in the Foreign Office, along with the decreasing effectiveness of the Mixed Court in Havana, the consequences Spain paid for the presence of a British consulate in San Juan were small.

The Foreign Office created the position of superintendent of liberated Africans in Cuba without Spanish approval. The governors and planters of Cuba had much to gain by transferring the Mixed Court, but because the Foreign Office forced the short-lived superintendency on them, they translated British support for the move as detrimental. Turnbull, the consulate-general of Havana, and the Foreign Office gave them every reason to believe that British endorsements of anything ran counter to slaveholder interests. Be it Whig or Tory, if the British government agreed to it, something had to be wrong. Years of mutual distrust resulted in an impasse that only Puerto Rican input could navigate. Hence, British consular representation in San Juan negotiated, but did not resolve, two sets of political conflict. At the international level, as a token of Aberdeen's conciliatory diplomacy, it reduced tensions between Great Britain and Spain by ending more than a decade of waffling dialogue over the transfer of the Mixed Court. At the colonial level, it reaffirmed Cuba's position as favorite in the eyes—and the treasury—of the Spanish central government without alarming or offending the governor of Puerto Rico. In essence, better a consulate than the Mixed Court and the black-manned *Romney* that served it.

II

New Routes, Old Remedies

4

Teamwork

Frenchmen, Dutchmen, and Danes

The inter-Caribbean trafficking of Creole slaves was small compared to African influxes. English-speaking slaves in Puerto Rico heightened political stress between Great Britain and Spain, Puerto Rico and Spain, and Puerto Rico and Cuba. In Puerto Rico, some 500 English-speaking slaves were concentrated mainly in the south in Ponce, in the north between San Juan and Río Piedras, and the east between Fajardo and Naguabo.[1] In Cuba, about 5,000 English-speaking slaves lived in Oriente Province, especially Holguín, which locals nicknamed "Little England." Excepting sporadic cases of kidnapping, Anglophone Creole slave traffic to the Spanish islands ceased in 1838, though complex, gender-based litigations for their freedom continued into the 1850s.[2] Other islands sold Creole slaves to Puerto Rico but on a scale much smaller than the influx associated with the abolition of slavery in the British islands.

Greater profits lay in the transfer of new African arrivals from non-Hispanic Caribbean ports to Puerto Rican ports under the guise of Creole identity. But clothing Africans according to Caribbean slave couture was an unconvincing ploy that only a few reexport strategists used in the final stage of transatlantic slave smuggling. No British abolitionist naval officer ever mistook a newly arrived African captive for a Creole. More useful deception involved good paperwork. As long as sales receipts, lading papers, and other documents stated that incoming slaves were purchased from nearby islands, Africans continued to reach Puerto Rico legally as non-Hispanic Creoles.

This chapter examines direct landings from Africa, inter-Caribbean reexport subterfuge, how both were deployed, and which situations favored one over the other. Different nations serving the Spanish Caribbean used different methods to bypass antislave trade treaties with Great Britain. Escape depended as much on the location of European trading posts on the West African coast as on the location of European colonies in the Caribbean. By direct acquisition from West Africa and reexport maneuvers in the Caribbean, French, Dutch, and Danish auxiliaries devised joint and independent schemes to transport Africans to the Spanish islands long after slavery was accepted as moribund in their own colonies.

Expeditions discussed in this chapter show how Puerto Rico benefited from the support of its non-Hispanic neighbors. While most of the examples lack final proof that the island was involved, circumstances for each case leave little room for doubt. By 1820, Cuba and Puerto Rico were the only Caribbean colonies still dependent on African slaves. Their planters were also the only ones in the region with the will and the means to pay for them. But Cuba did not rely on aid from the non-Hispanic islands for African slaves. Conversely, Puerto Rico did, and it was better situated to do so given its proximity to the Eastern Caribbean. It also had a history of lucrative market relations with its foreign neighbors for more than 200 years.

Maritime Diplomacy

After 1815, Danish St. Thomas served as a principal junction for newly arrived Africans destined for reexport, but having evolved as a clearing house for foreign markets, it was more than a depot. Its economic romance with San Juan predated the abolitionist era.[3] Despite the conveniences of Dano-Spanish trade relations, diplomacy compelled Puerto Rican slave merchants to rely as much on direct Spanish means. Though avenues remained mixed, Spanish-run slave junctions along the West African littoral proliferated in the 1830s, especially in Sierra Leone and Liberia. Therefore, Thomian complicity underwent expansion as well as evolution. In *Trata*, Morales Carrión emphasizes the importance of non-Hispanic Caribbean cooperation in the slave trade to Puerto Rico. But in addition to attributing traffic decline to augmented British pressure, he connects it to the exit of Miguel de La Torre in 1836. Though subsequent governors supported the trade up to 1848, Spanish politics allowed La Torre—but not his successors—greater freedom to promote it.[4]

W.E.F. Ward agrees that the 1830s marked a turning point, but stressing changes in antislavery techniques and proslavery resistance, he assesses the period from a different perspective. At its inception, the British abolitionist machine "did not have to deal merely with a few desperadoes who were willing to risk defying their own country's laws. It had to deal with big business: with large firms owning fleets of vessels and secretly condoned by their governments." He notes further that improved treaty composition, combined with "the incessant work of the Royal Navy, gradually weeded out the law-abiding and the faint-hearted. It left the business to tough and desperate men, those who were prepared to fight their way through the naval patrol."[5] Ward's evaluation of illegal slave trading before and after the 1830s raises questions about corollaries and cohorts during the period of transition. On the one hand, the transport segment was always in the hands of desperate ne'er-do-wells, thugs, and impoverished multinationals seeking to earn a living as mariners. On the other hand, the British abolition of slavery and British efforts to secure more effective treaties in the 1830s failed to shut down slave-trading firms. Into the 1850s, such organizations continued to disguise themselves as legitimate shipping companies in Europe, the Caribbean, and the United States.[6] Despite the treaty of 1817, business nearly proceeded as usual.

The second decade of maritime abolitionism saw scrambles for adjustment on both sides. Many basic features of acquisition remained, such as kidnapping and the enslavement of war captives. But the equipment clause in the treaty of 1835 compelled merchants and captains to modify the organization of transport. On the basis of chains, excessive rations, superfluous shelves in the hold, and other indications, the clause permitted the capture and adjudication of slave ships without slaves on board. It also saved lives. Desperate and ruthless captains under chase no longer found it necessary to toss captives overboard to avoid capture.[7] Now, even without slaves, antislave trade officers could take ships equipped for the traffic. The need for speed and efficiency separated clandestine slave operations from previous centuries when the trade was legal, and the equipment clause separated the first Anglo-Spanish treaty from the second. Nonetheless, while the 1830s marked a turning point for both Spanish colonies, change had different meanings for them. For Cuba, the decade spelled logistic change; for Puerto Rico, it heralded the advance of decline.

Spain and Great Britain were allies since the French occupation of the Iberian Peninsula early in the century. The British government used the Napoleonic upheavals to intervene in Spanish affairs. At the external level, it assisted in restoring the Spanish Bourbon monarchy. At the internal level, in a series of dynastic disputes, Great Britain helped guarantee the line of succession through the descendants of Ferdinand VII. With grants, loans, and military aid, the

British exploited the alliance to secure abolitionist treaties from Ferdinand and his widow, Queen-Regent María Cristina.[8] Other European slave-holding polities—first and foremost France, Denmark, and the Netherlands—were either less trapped or not trapped at all by diplomatic pressure from Great Britain. As Antillean neighbors, fellow imperialists, and fellow slaveholders in better positions to resist British exertions, these powers supported, albeit indirectly, Spain's resolve to continue illicit slaving expeditions. Since the seventeenth century, all three countries had coastal settlements that spanned from Senegal to Liberia and from the Gold Coast to the Bight of Benin. These bases were crucial in view of British initiatives to destroy Spanish slave factories in West Africa during the 1840s.[9]

France competed with Great Britain and Portugal for legitimate trade along the Senegal and Gambia Rivers.[10] Spaniards based at Gallinas and Sherbro in Sierra Leone dominated coastal slaving activities in most of Upper Guinea from the Pongo in Guinea-Conakry to Cape Palmas, Liberia, almost in full view of Monrovia and Freetown, West Africa's Anglophone bastions of antislavery.[11] In Accra on the Gold Coast of Lower Guinea in present-day Ghana, Danes, Dutchmen, and Britons occupied massive stone fortresses, which the Portuguese built in the fifteenth and sixteenth centuries. Europeans used them to guard against the encroachment of each other's trade agreements with African kings and merchants. By 1810, Accra declined as a reliable source of captives for export. But its eastern neighbors from Ouidah to the Niger Delta rose to prominence, with French, Spanish, and Luso-Brazilian agents and resident intermediaries working with and against each other to secure slaves for oceanic shipment. However, British vigilance made multinational cooperation among lawbreakers essential.

Treaties between Great Britain and other powers with Caribbean holdings reflect similar and dissimilar concerns. All agreed to suppress the African slave trade, search suspected vessels, and, if appropriate, escort them to predetermined ports for adjudication. France and Denmark amended agreements with Great Britain for mutual search and detention. While France refused to establish a mixed court, which required bilateral consent, the Netherlands resisted multilateral accords.[12] Such conventions would have subjected the Dutch colonies to surveillance by neighbors with whom they were not always on the best of commercial terms.[13] Denmark had three Caribbean colonies; France, four—including St. Martin, which it shared with the Dutch, who called it St. Maarten. The Netherlands had seven, including Suriname in South America.

Denmark had no further interests in expansion. In fact, in 1850 it began negotiations with Great Britain to sell its leases on the Gold Coast.[14] While the Dutch expanded no further in Africa, they increased their political and economic interests in Southeast Asia. Despite rivalry for legitimate trade in West Africa from the 1840s to the 1880s—and a host of treaty violations in Africa and the Antilles—France became Great Britain's most reliable European ally against slave traffic.[15] Had the Netherlands assented to mutual search rights with France along with Great Britain, Dutch merchants would have been vulnerable to all manner of intrigue with additional foreign competitors. Between 1831 and 1833, France agreed with Great Britain, Sardinia, and Tuscany to the mutual right of search. This treaty, and subsequent accords, excluded Ouidah, which rivaled Lagos as the most notorious slave emporium in the Bight of Benin. Agreements also excluded East Africa, where French, Portuguese, and Swahili slave traders served Brazil, the Near East, the French islands of the Indian Ocean, and, to lesser degrees, the Far East and the Spanish Caribbean.[16] But France refused to ratify an equipment clause and a bilateral court of adjudication with any nation for the same reason the Hague rejected multinational accords—fear that rivals would be privy to the details of legitimate maritime trade. Thus, French abolitionist cooperation was selective, as instanced in the inter-Caribbean voyage of the Spanish schooner *Diosa* from French Guadeloupe to the Bay of San Juan.

In 1825, the Puerto Rican firm of Goenaga y Cartagena sold twenty slaves to Eugenio Jiménez of Loíza, a northeastern town between San Juan and Carolina. The slaves—six females between twelve and twenty-five years of age and fourteen males between eighteen and forty-five—cost Jiménez 7,607 pesos. They landed with full government authorization. They were African captives and under no circumstances could have been mistaken for Creole slaves. Paperwork identified them by numbers, not names; there was no mention of previous owners in Guadeloupe; and nearly all their bodily descriptions included reference to decorative scarifications, some simple, others elaborate. Cloaked in the legitimacy of intercolonial Franco-Spanish commerce, there was nothing secretive about the trip. As a result of this front, among other issues discussed later, British authorities never raised the landing to the level of diplomatic intelligence.[17] Although British protests against the inter-Caribbean trafficking of African and Creole slaves began in earnest in the late 1820s, they maintained silence when the French were involved.

The British occupation of the Dutch Caribbean islands during the Napoleonic period influenced the Hague's decision to withdraw from the slave trade officially. In 1814, most of these possessions were returned to Dutch sovereignty. When William I ascended the throne, he abolished slave trading in all Dutch ports. Four years later, he signed the first of several treaties with the British.[18] As a consequence, few slave ships apprehended were actually Dutch-owned, and only in a few instances were Dutch nationals known to dominate slave ship crews.[19] Still, and probably without the king's knowledge, Dutch connivance was far from marginal.

Structures of Pursuit

The use of double identification papers was common from the 1820s to the 1840s. Franco-Dutch teamwork established the precedent. Before 1830, most slavers flying the Dutch standard aided French interests. For handsome fees, Dutch officials provided permits and identification, while Nantes, Bordeaux, Martinique, Guadeloupe, and Cayenne provided capital, ships, and crews. Between August 1825 and March 1826, seven slavers obtained papers in the Dutch Caribbean. One was certified by Governor Paulus Laar of Curaçao and six by Governor William Von Sprengler of St. Eustatius. Culpability was not limited to bilateral machinations. Spaniards and Danes also benefited from the fraud.[20]

During the proceedings against Jean Blaise, a French schooner master from Guadeloupe, he confessed to the Anglo-Dutch tribunal at Freetown that he purchased the vessel *Gallant* from a North American residing in St. Thomas. In St. Eustatius, for 5,000 guilders, Von Sprengler supplied Blaise with Dutch naturalization, Dutch registration for the ship—renamed the *Vogel*—a certified muster roll for the fifteen Frenchmen who formed its crew, and a license that allowed it to carry cannon. On September 17, Dutch customs cleared it for passage to Portuguese São Tomé. It is not clear whether the *Vogel* intended to reach the Portuguese equatorial island, because when it was captured in Sierra Leone, its French identification papers, calling it the *Oiseau*, stated that it was also bound for São Tomé. In addition, the papers stated that its owner was a Jean Lafosse and that it cleared customs at Pointe-à-Pitre, Guadeloupe, on the same day as the *Vogel*, with the same schooner master.[21] Motivation for its dual identity was based on international treaties. If the British detained it at Freetown, it could not be subject to trial without slaves because France had not yet agreed to an equipment clause. Dutch papers were useful in the event of French of detention. The Netherlands had no antislave trade agreement with France. Despite the fact that it was not intercepted on the high seas—a violation of the

Anglo-Dutch treaty of 1818—its trial by the Mixed Court demonstrated Dutch efforts to cooperate. It was condemned to confiscation for many reasons—outstanding among them, Blaise could not have been in St. Eustatius and Guadeloupe at the same time, as both sets of papers indicated. There was also a weight discrepancy of twenty-eight tons on the two manifests. In essence, there was no *Oiseau*.

The *Fortunée* offers a more detailed study of inter-Caribbean cooperation in the late 1820s. Its condemnation also shows the extent to which the British were willing to bend their own rules. But unlike the *Oiseau*, added evidence increases the probability that the voyage was slated to end in Puerto Rico. After a twelve-hour chase, the schooner was captured on May 15, 1826, with 252 captives. Mastered by Jean-Jacques Gimbert of St. Tropez, with a multinational crew of fifteen, including Francophone slaves, it reached Freetown on June 8 for adjudication by the Anglo-Dutch tribunal.[22]

Gimbert declared that the voyage began in Guadeloupe and was to end there. Jacques Laborde had commanded the French-built vessel, but on his death in Cape Verde, Gimbert took charge. The second master was first hired as supercargo in St. Thomas by Jean Baptiste Gay, president of the Gay Company and principal stockholder of the ship. Gimbert also stated that Gay's business arrangements so delayed embarkation that the crew from Guadeloupe deserted. Recruiting replacements caused further delay. Finally the vessel sailed from St. Thomas to São Tomé for legitimate trade and then to the Bonny in the Niger Delta for slaves.[23] Because Gimbert could not determine the nationality of the pursuing vessel, he had Dutch and French flags hoisted alternately throughout the chase. Confined to his cabin by illness, he issued commands from there. Once the aggressor was identified as British, he ordered his slave-valet to toss the tin box of Dutch papers overboard and his Dutch ensign to keep the French standard aloft. The Dutchman misunderstood the order and raised the flag of his own country. After he corrected the error, the French flag flew about six minutes before British officers boarded.

British judges faced the task of proving that the *Fortunée* was Dutch.[24] The Anglo-Dutch equipment clause was of no concern because the schooner was caught with slaves. The captain sought to avoid French identity because that would mean proceedings in a French court, and the slaver would have to be taken to Senegal. Experience taught them that under such circumstances, authorities at Gorée usually declined juridical procedures without positive proof that suspected vessels were French.[25] Such proof was impossible without a trial.

It was, therefore, imperative that the British side of the Mixed Court identify the vessel as Dutch.

Even before other witnesses proved Gimbert perjured himself repeatedly in his first deposition, British arbiters doubted his story for several reasons. First, Gay's affairs alone delayed the ship's departure. St. Thomas was the last Caribbean site where captains had difficulty recruiting crews. It was a hub for multinationals of all characters and interests, including steady streams of mariners looking for work. As early as 1823, the British asserted that Puerto Rico imported newly arrived Africans from St. Thomas on an average of thirty shiploads a year.[26] Delays probably stemmed from the need to accommodate agents and merchants working on behalf of Puerto Rican slaveholders. Second, a ship en route to São Tomé from the Caribbean would not need to enter Cape Verdian latitudes unless a stop was planned or there was an emergency, which would have been recorded in the log. Jean-Jacques Gimbert was Jacques Laborde.

Third, Gimbert stated that there were several men in his cabin in addition to his valet, Victor, whom he ordered to discard the Dutch papers. Citing Victor was essential. The French *Code Noir* forbade slaves to testify against their masters unless in cases of capital crimes. Piracy was a capital offense in most Western countries, but France, along with most governments at this time, refused to equate it with slaving. If the *Fortunée* proved French and thus subject to French litigation, Victor could not be called on to swear that Gimbert directed him to pitch the Dutch papers overboard.

In the 1500s, the Portuguese islands of São Tomé and Príncipe were popular entrepôts for slave traffic from Angola and the Congo to the Americas. Though foreign ships still called to purchase sugar, by the mid-1600s the islands had fallen on hard times. By the early 1800s, thanks to local coffee and cacao production and the outlawed slave trade, they regained popularity. It is unlikely that Gimbert went to São Tomé for legitimate trade, though he would not have acquired slaves there either. He stopped to purchase supplies and items with which to barter for slaves in the estuaries of the Niger Delta. With the exception of Corisco, up to 1840 most smugglers operating in equatorial waters acquired slaves directly from the mainland.[27]

The stopover in São Tomé suggests another pattern. In the 1820s, French slave traders along the Bonny monopolized the area to the point that Spaniards and Luso-Brazilians sought captives elsewhere.[28] Conversely, merchants from the French Caribbean, acting in the interest of foreign slave merchants and slave trade investors, as well as their own, seemed to undermine the profit-making potential of their African-based compatriots. Frenchman at Bonny sent vessels away without slaves, guarding the area against Iberian interlopers, who by the 1830s displaced them. The Lusophones, on the other hand, despite the risk of deception, were willing to accommodate their foreign Antillean neighbors.[29]

Gimbert's crew was his undoing. When queried individually, none recalled anyone on board named Laborde, nor could they remember going to Cape Verde or anywhere else in Upper Guinea. Though none was certain whether the final stop was to be Suriname, Puerto Rico, or Cuba, none mentioned Guadeloupe as the starting point, and only two stated that it was to terminate there, as Gimbert testified. English steward Christopher Westcott stated that Gimbert recruited him in St. Thomas with the rest of the crew. Two of the three black sailors from the French Caribbean who boarded at Bonny testified that they only accepted work on the *Fortunée* because they were told that its final destination was St. Thomas, where they resided, and that the voyage originated there as well. Most concurred that all the ship's officers were French, that there were two Dutch ensigns, and that the sailors were Spaniards, Italians, and assorted Antilleans. Jean Vincent, a black Francophone who exchanged his culinary skills for passage, declared that he saw the crew members retrieve letters and identification papers from their bags and pockets and throw them overboard once it was certain that the British cruiser would overtake them. No one remembered Gimbert's being infirm. The consensus was that throughout the chase, while shouting orders, he held stone-weighted boxes in each hand, and when he gave the final order to maintain the French flag, he gave the "Dutch box" to the ship's English carpenter—not to his slave—to cast overboard.[30]

When first depositioned, Gimbert swore that while all the ship's stockholders were French nationals, neither he nor any of the officers or crew held shares in it or had an investment in its slaves. But once his testimony proved spurious, the British judges dismissed his subsequent statements, one of which reaffirmed that Jean Baptiste Gay was the principal shareholder and the primary investor in the ship's captives, an assertion verified by confiscated correspondence between French residents and transients at Bonny and French residents in Dutch Suriname and Danish St. Thomas. True to their aim to prove the ship's Dutch nationality, British judges ignored this evidence and the assertions of the officers and crew when they swore that Gimbert was both captain and part owner of the ship.[31]

Because the deponents could not agree as to whether the vessel was French or Dutch, the British and Dutch judges were deadlocked. At this point, the

Britons declined to accept the testimony of those who stated it was French on the grounds of hearsay and literacy. Deponents with reading skills who saw Dutch papers outnumbered those with like skills who saw French.[32] The Dutch judges protested that because the slaver was the property of French subjects, it was illegal for it to be tried by a commission of Anglo-Dutch arbiters. Overriding Dutch dissent, the British judges postulated that a ship's ownership was immaterial vis-à-vis its nationality. The plot thickened as the mixed tribunal was presented with evidence that the vessel was owned by a Mr. Pardo, a Curaçao-born Dutchman residing in St. Thomas. Rather than sinking in their own argument about the vessel's nationality, the British used Pardo's birthplace to support their stance that the *Fortunée* was Dutch. They ended the case by stating that the flying of a French flag for six minutes did not suffice to sustain a vessel's national identity.[33]

While it is tempting to label the Dutch with acquiescence, the Hague had nothing to lose. Overwhelming evidence showed that the venture was entirely French. Though Dutchmen were involved, their energies were not invested in Dutch affairs. Dutch commissioners in Sierra Leone boasted a clean slate, unlike their counterparts in Paramaribo, Suriname.[34] Thus, their protests were merely a matter of form. By destroying the Dutch identification papers, Gimbert knew the case would have a greater chance of acquittal in French Gorée than in British Freetown.

Anticipating a cumulative impact, the British opted for short-lived victories over long-term solutions. In view of the appalling conditions of slave ship holds, which had direct bearing on mortality during and after the middle passage, more Africans would have died en route to Senegal and in the course of dilatory French litigation. Nor was Gorée equipped to handle the medical needs of captives intercepted and liberated by abolitionist cruisers. Further, had the Foreign Office spent less time wrangling uselessly with Spain and Brazil and directed more effort on diplomatic negotiations with France for the authorization of Anglo-French tribunals, a more effective campaign against the transatlantic and inter-Caribbean trafficking of slaves could have resulted.

Concrete proof for the destination of the *Fortunée* is wanting, but calculations based on the ports named point to Puerto Rico as the most plausible location. One witness stated that the slaver was to go to Paramaribo. If the slave market did not prove lucrative there, it was to proceed directly to Havana. (If the ship were Dutch, its captain would have known the state of Dutch colonial slave markets.) Both cities may be eliminated for several reasons. The Dutch did not need to rely on the French—who dominated the vessel numerically—

to acquire slaves. The Dutch government provided the means for foreigners to carry out expeditions from the free ports of St. Eustatius and Curaçao, and when Surinamese planters could afford to, they ordered newly arrived Africans from those islands, introducing them as Creoles. Furthermore, a voyage from Suriname to Havana would have thwarted the profit motive. Since Spanish planters were willing to pay more for slaves than were the Surinamese, it made little sense to stop in Paramaribo first. Even if they stopped there initially on the return voyage, Havana would not have been targeted as the next port. Arduous winds would have augmented slave mortality.

Between 1821 and 1825, 111 vessels cleared Cuban customs for Africa. All of them returned with slaves, and almost all flew Spanish or Portuguese colors.[35] Between 1825 and 1826, 32 ships left Havana for West Africa, and only 3 were caught and condemned. Cuban planters were not dependent on Suriname for reexport trade, for it was neither a slave entrepôt nor an international center for the transformation of black identity from African captive to Creole slave. Depositions from the crew of the *Fortunée* named Puerto Rico repeatedly as the final destination. Witnesses for many Mixed Court trials named Puerto Rico as a port of call for water and supplies, before and after Atlantic crossings.[36] This was ludicrous, of course, especially for foreign ships. Why pay expensive Spanish tolls and tariffs when the Danish free port of St. Thomas lay only thirty-six miles from Puerto Rico's eastern shore? While few corroborated Gimbert's assertion that the voyage was to end at Guadeloupe, a year earlier, two North Americans residing in Ponce received permits to import 1,000 slaves from the French islands. Under this license, 511 slaves arrived from Martinique between September and October 1825. Moreover, between 1825 and 1833, almost all slaves landing at Ponce were Africans reexported from Martinique and Guadeloupe via French and Dutch transports.[37]

For the early years of the illegal slave trade, proposed final destinations reveal little about the itinerary of slave trade expeditions. Merchant vessels, whether in the business of slaving or legitimate commerce, were not obligated to end voyages in ports of national registration. With the exception of Paramaribo, where the voyage could have been expected to terminate—without cargo— all ports mentioned could have been scheduled to receive slaves. Therefore, considering all these factors, it seems certain that the *Fortunée*'s Carabalí captives from southeast Nigeria were slated for Puerto Rican cane fields, either directly or indirectly via reexport operations from St. Thomas or one of the French or Dutch islands of the Eastern Caribbean.

After 1835, slavers continued to rely on Dutch identity or any other willing nationality, but by that year blatant misrepresentation based on Franco-Dutch amalgams had ceased. Due to a lack of evidence of habitual treaty infractions and accurate conclusions from the Foreign Office that Dutch planters could no longer afford to buy slaves, the Surinamese branch of the Court of the Mixed Commissions closed in 1845. The slavocracy of the Netherlands Antilles collapsed as early as 1841. Suriname, stronghold of Dutch slave-based agriculture, could not compete with slave-based agrarian production in Brazil and the Spanish Antilles.[38] Yet Dutch complicity in the acquisition of captives destined for other Caribbean plantocracies was another matter. For Puerto Rico, Dutch connections remained important.

Mixed Channels of Acquisition

With the exception of Dutch Aruba and Franco-Swedish St. Barthèlemy, the Danish Virgins were the smallest slave-holding colonies in the region. Of these islands, the well-developed plantation sector was limited almost exclusively to St. Croix. St. John and St Thomas were underexploited as slave-based economies. However, in contrast to St. Croix and St. John, the environment of St. Thomas was urban and international. The port of Charlotte Amalie was the richest point of transshipment in the Caribbean. Its success was rooted in a fusion of Danish administration, Spanish military dependency, and the commercial hegemony of foreigners. During his long career as an international merchant, George Coggeshall visited the Danish Virgins often. On his last voyage to St. Thomas in 1831, he observed, "The government officers and garrison are Danes and converse in the Danish language. The mercantile classes generally speak English, French, and Spanish, while the masses speak Creole French, English and Spanish, intermixed with the African lingo. So when a stranger visits the marketplace, or any other public assembly, he is almost deafened with the confused jargon of discordant sounds, which remind one of ancient Babel."[39] Later in 1860, novelist Anthony Trollope shelved his celebrated literary elegance to assess the Thomian ambience as "Hispano-Dano-Niggery-Yankee Doodle."[40]

St. Thomas and other free ports were constant sources of abolitionist frustration. In 1802, Denmark distinguished itself as the first European nation to outlaw the external slave trade in the nineteenth century. In 1848, it ranked with France as the second Western slave-holding government to end the institution of slavery itself. However, as long as influxes were transitory and in the hands of foreigners, St. Thomas continued to broker the slave trade. As late as the

1860s, Danish functionaries in West Africa and the Caribbean were willing accomplices in the trafficking of African captives. St. Thomas's reputation as a slave emporium and entrepôt began with its free port status in 1764. From 1789, when the Spanish Crown relaxed tariffs on slave importations, to 1815, when it decreed the Cédula de Gracias, St. Thomas's commercial relationship with Puerto Rico strengthed.[41] It is difficult, however, to discern changes in that relationship after international slave commerce was declared illegal. The Anglo-Spanish prohibition of 1817 ran into the immigration decree of 1815, which depended on the inter-Caribbean slave trade with the non-Hispanic islands—especially the Danish Virgins.

Though St. Thomas declined as a slave junction after 1830, it remained important for the outfitting of slave ships and as a point of embarkation for Africa.[42] By this time, Spanish merchants depended more on vessels of their own nationality, as table 4.1 illustrates. But the question remains whether captives bound for Puerto Rico landed there directly from Africa or first in St. Thomas or elsewhere. In support of ruse modifications after the treaty of 1835, Danish input did not wane, though substantiating this assertion is an onerous task. On the one hand, documentation is scanty. On the other hand, though easily detected, some traders continued the practice of switching slave identity from African to Creole.[43] But with the exception of cases such as the *Amistad*, legal occasions to expose the switching of slave identity declined. Legal opportunities to board suspected vessels were less frequent on the Caribbean side than on the African side.

Table 4.1. Ports of registration for Spanish slave ships intercepted by the British Royal Navy in 1839

Port	Number of ships	Percentage
Havana	26	63.4
Matanzas	2	5.0
Santiago	2	5.0
Puerto Rico	4	9.7
Havana-Matanzas	3	7.3
Havana-Puerto Rico	1	2.4
Havana-Coruña	1	2.4
Havana-Barcelona	1	2.4
Havana-Cádiz	1	2.4

Source: Great Britain, *Parliamentary Papers*, vol. 20.

When merchants used the paper deception of false slave identity, especially during the fourteen-year course of Puerto Rico's immigration decree, British protests were useless. The need to clothe new captives as Creoles for inter-Caribbean transit was exaggerated. Traffickers relied more on other loopholes and protocols to prevent abolitionist agents from entering slave ships once they reached Caribbean ports, as instanced in the case of the *Minerva* in Havana in 1826 and the complaint filed by the French consul in San Juan in 1827. These strategies decreased after the 1820s. In the long run, the plantation was to be the best offense, for it provided the most enduring obstacle to foreign investigations. The cry of national sovereignty and private ownership—and the use of common sense for personal safety—discouraged antislave trade agents from entering the very places where the greatest numbers of African slaves were found.

Coggeshall's observations exemplify the need to differentiate the landing of captives at inter-Caribbean junctions from landings directly from Africa. In 1831, he noted how much Puerto Rico had changed since his first visit. He attributed these changes to foreign immigration and the expansion of slavery.[44] During his four-day visit to Mayagüez in early February 1831, he witnessed a slave sale. Though he said the captives came from Africa directly, parts of his narrative suggest that they were reexported from neighboring non-Hispanic islands. He observed instances of both resistance and poor health. But he noted that small schooners carried 150 to 200 captives at a time.[45] A few days later in Ponce, he witnessed another landing and a series of sales. His description of the slaves and the protocols surrounding their purchases differed from his observations in Mayagüez.[46]

In 1840, another visitor had a close encounter with the slave trade. En route from New York to Fredericksted, St. Croix, aboard the schooner *Eliza*, James Smith entered the occasion in his diary on December 10.[47] His account leaves little doubt as to the origin and destination of the vessel. The *Eliza* was scheduled to enter the archipelago from the Atlantic by way of St. Maarten. On the evening of Wednesday the tenth, it was coordinated at 19° 29' and 61° 40' when the captain informed his passengers that they would maintain a speed of six knots once entering Caribbean waters. On Thursday morning at eight o'clock, they were 130 miles from St. Croix, sighting St. Maarten at noon and passing Saba and St. Barthèlemy forty miles to the southeast. On Friday at 9 A.M., following the encounter with the nameless brig, Smith saw Virgin Gorda at 18° 25', and at 7 A.M. the next day they passed Christiansted at the northeast end of St.

Croix. Without stopping, they reached their destination of Fredericksted to the southwest, facing southeast Puerto Rico. Latitudinal reports for Wednesday and Friday—together with the rate of speed Thursday evening when the *Eliza* met the slaver—show that both vessels were less than a hundred miles northeast of Christiansted.

Because the slave ship was closer to Cruzian waters and because it ran parallel to the *Eliza* in the same direction, it is certain that it did not embark from St. Thomas as a short, reexport voyage but from the Atlantic as a lengthier, transoceanic voyage. Under these circumstances, Puerto Rico was the only possible destination, and Africa was the only point of departure. The vessel could not have come from Dutch St. Maarten because it was not yet a free port, and it was too close to British surveillance from Anguilla. While occasionally Puerto Rican slaveholders imported individual Creole slaves from St. Maarten, merchants rarely designated it as a port for reexporting Africans. Finally, if the brig had come from the free port of Dutch St. Eustatius or one of the French islands to the southeast, it would have been spotted northeast of St. Croix.

Written nine years apart, the two narratives tell us that Puerto Rico relied on direct slave acquisition from Africa from one decade to the next. From Smith's account we are able to deduce that the slaver was bound for Puerto Rico without the mediation of reexport. However, Coggeshall's reports are more problematic. Parts of his story are lucid and direct, while others are marked with gaps and ambiguities. At best, his observations only hint at trends in slave conveyance and the special features that defined them. Though he was against slavery, and said so repeatedly in his memoir, he never allowed his opposition to enter the public arena of abolitionist politics. His hosts and business associates in Puerto Rico were slaveholders. As such, Coggeshall had to disguise their identities and omit the specific names of the sites to which they escorted him to witness their illegal purchases. Thus, his accounts combine clarity, curiosity, pragmatism, and naïveté. His description of the uniformity of appearance and condition within the larger set of captives in Ponce—compared to the mixed appearances and conditions he observed among the three smaller sets in Mayagüez—results in a fairly accurate portraiture of circumstantial diversity. Nonetheless, Coggeshall does not name any non-Hispanic Caribbean island associated with reexport maneuvers because he seems to believe that all the captives he described came directly from Africa.

Considering the varied health conditions of the group that landed in Mayagüez and the varied manner in which they were treated, according to degrees of resistance, it is apparent that they came directly from the African coast, as did the brig Smith described. The Mayagüez report also indicates that masters purchased the slaves in advance. Those who landed at Ponce were auctioned to buyers arriving from all parts of southern Puerto Rico. Coggeshall also distinguished vessel types. Most scholars agree that slave ship captains preferred swift schooners with smaller cargo capacity to larger and slower brigs and brigantines.[48] This may have been the case, but data gathered for this study show no indication that larger vessels declined in importance for the overall period of the illegal slave trade. The 350 Africans whose landing Coggeshall witnessed in Ponce arrived by brig at one time. Conversely, the captives he saw in Mayagüez formed part of three small expeditions that totaled 500 captives disembarked over two months. Though the Ponce landing opposes the consensus that points to preferences for schooners and smaller cargoes of slaves when crossing the Atlantic, Coggeshall's account of the Mayagüez captives supports it.

Foreign assistance in the slave trade to Puerto Rico did not end between the treaties of 1817 and 1835. Cooperative nations, more specifically, cooperative subjects from three particular nations, tested strategies new and old in their continued roles as distributors. By 1830, Frenchmen, Dutchmen, and Danes developed tactics based not only on the content and context of their governments' treaties with Great Britain; they also redefined the importance of their commercial presence in West Africa. Predating the Age of Abolition by more than a century, this presence, in the abstract, decriminalized the traffic by reaffirming the right to travel and trade between ports of the same nationality.

As evidence revealing circumstances that divided inbound expeditions from Africa between direct landings in Puerto Rico and indirect landings courtesy of inter-Caribbean aid, travelers' accounts have their uses and drawbacks. Coggeshall's last visit to Puerto Rico coincided with La Torre's long tenure. The presence of government officers at Ponce—to collect head taxes, tolls, and duties—proves that the governor issued permits for the trip. It also demonstrates Spain's insistence on the legitimacy of inter-Caribbean slave commerce. Though Coggeshall tells us that the Ponce landing was direct, the captives must have rested and regrouped somewhere else in the Caribbean before reaching their final destination. Along with the presence of revenue agents, the healthy condition of the *ponceño* captives supports the view that, between treaties, the governors of Puerto Rico granted few permits to import slaves directly from Africa.

The Mayagüez report opposes this view. In addition to the sickly slaves

Coggeshall saw for sale among the ranks of the healthy, their disembarkations were shrouded in secrecy, as seen in the various points where the vessels landed, along with the absence of tax collectors. Government connivance was public, legal, and therefore inter-Antillean vis-à-vis the landing in Ponce but surreptitious, illegal, and therefore transatlantic for the landing in Mayagüez. As to timing, the voyages must have begun shortly before the expiration of the Cédula de Gracias, which allowed applicants to buy and bring captives from other ports. There was no need for La Torre to court international flack by making a habit of authorizing African expeditions. He relied on the legitimacy of the immigration decree, which relied on the legitimacy of the inter-Caribbean slave trade.

Smith's nautical precision establishes that the brig he saw marked the close of an inbound voyage from Africa to Puerto Rico directly, while the landings Coggeshall reported—one based on his own observation and three on second-hand accounts—came from direct and indirect channels. Unfortunately, his observations are fragmented; together, they constitute three-fourths of a whole. Though he witnessed the landing and selling of slaves at Ponce, half his report for Mayagüez is based on what he saw—the auction of the captives—while the other half—the arrival of three groups of captives—is based on what he was told. Thus, as an eyewitness, 25 percent of his story is missing, rendering his narrative less reliable than it appears.

The distance Coggeshall establishes between logistic diversity and logistic contradiction is extremely short. Though the polarity of health conditions—and attitudes—among the Mayagüez captives corroborates his assertion that they had just crossed the ocean, their having landed in different vessels over an eight-week period suggests that reexport strategies segmented an original, large-scale, transoceanic voyage, about which he knew nothing—despite his familiarity with Danish St. Thomas and other parts of the non-Hispanic Caribbean, especially the islands of the southeastern curve. It seems, therefore, that the schooners he mentions were used for inter-Caribbean rather than transatlantic purposes. Regarding the *ponceño* captives, despite his certainty of direct African provenance, he spotted no sickly slaves and no explicit form of resistance. And there is nothing, of course, in either of his reports to suggest that the slaves had begun to undergo the process of Western socialization. They were neither Creoles nor *ladinos*; nor was there an effort to impart the idea that they were. The absence of visible dissent, trauma, illness, and mortality suggests that they reached Ponce by reexport from a nearby island, where they were separated from the militant, the dazed, the sickly, and the deceased and given an opportunity to refresh themselves after the Atlantic crossing.

Because Coggeshall's reports are incomplete, they shed little light on the extent to which mixed channels of slave acquisition remained accessible before the treaty of 1835. Insomuch as they correspond chronologically to Franco-Dutch and Franco-British agreements for the mutual right of search, they likewise offer inconclusive evidence for the proliferation of direct African importations after 1831. Furthermore, the collusion of Danish, Dutch, and French nationals in the Spanish slave trade from West Africa is absent from the narrative. Paralleling cooperation from officials in the non-Hispanic Caribbean islands under the colonial authority of the same three governments is less implied in the text than imposed on it by the reader's deduction.

Coggeshall's memoir contributed to the conspiracy of slave trade silence. Though circumstantially limited, Smith's vignette is more candid. In terms more obvious, it supports the historiographic consensus that between the late 1820s and the early 1830s, Spanish slave traders began to rely more on Spanish carriers and direct importations. However, the assertion of national self-reliance through direct landings is more applicable to Cuba than to Puerto Rico. Though Smith witnessed the closure of a direct voyage, his sojourn took place during the tenure of López de Baños, who relied as much on reexport operations from St. Thomas.[49]

5

Moving Meridians and Parallels

With continued emphasis on the girth of Danish, Dutch, and French af fairs along the West African coast, this chapter illustrates the uniformity of slaving interests among metropolitan governments, their colonial officials, and their multinational cohorts. The first section examines communication prob lems between Great Britain and its allies against the slave trade, especially allies with colonial interests in both Africa and the Antilles. The second section fore grounds Dutch military recruitment. This theme prefaces developments that culminate in Chapter 9, wherein it is asserted that Dutch military recruitment on the Gold Coast in the 1830s formed links to slave acquisition schemes in Puerto Rico via Curaçao in the 1840s. Marking differences between public policy and private initiative, the third section examines new forms of French labor recruitment and their impact on diplomacy between Great Britain and France, and Spain. The final discussion considers African provenance in Puerto Rico based on linguistic evidence, with particular reference to captives from present-day Ghana. These discussions show that statistics currently accepted for Spanish participation in the illegal slave trade warrant reevaluation.

Sustaining "The Grand Evil"

After 1820, overt Danish participation in the slave trade to Puerto Rico was marginal and elusive on the supply side. But Dutch and French activities were still linked to direct African access. Denmark began to compete for the use of coastal West African real estate comparatively late. It did not establish a trading community in Accra until the eighteenth century.[1] But neither the lag of its entrance into African affairs nor the diminutive size of its Caribbean colonies compromised its participation in the slave trade. Census data for 1804 and 1805 show that nearly 50 percent of the slave population of the Danish Virgin Islands was African-born.[2]

Of all European states with Caribbean territories, Denmark appeared the most cooperative in carrying out the spirit and the letter of its antislave trade treaties. Appearances, of course, are deceiving. Given the centrality of St. Thomas in the inter-Caribbean slave trade to Puerto Rico, Danish abolitionism offered a special form of paradox—as much in Africa as the Antilles. Envoy and Minister Plenipotentiary Krabbe Carisius acknowledged Palmerston's reminder that in the space of two years, Danish diplomats and other agents had yet to receive instructions from Copenhagen regarding the Anglo-Spanish accords of 1835.[3] He promised to hasten announcements of the new treaty and its implications. He also sent copies of prior Dano-British agreements to his consuls in Washington, Havana, Caracas, Rio, Tenerife, and the Azores. Resistance was not confrontational. For example, he did not mention Danish Accra on the Gold Coast.[4]

Abolitionist correspondence between Great Britain and Denmark revealed standard diplomatic duplicity. It was one thing for Danish public officials or Danish private subjects to be suspected of assisting the landing of Africans or Creoles at Spanish ports but quite another if such affairs involved British and Danish territories alone. In Demerara, British colonial officials openly encouraged runaway slaves from nearby Dutch Suriname to seek asylum under the protection of the Union Jack. Conversely, slaves fleeing Danish St. Croix for freedom in British Tortola were returned or sentenced to British Caribbean work camps on charges of vagrancy. In turn, the Danish government promised to extradite any British subject suspected of buying or selling newly emancipated Afro-Britons.[5] As with the trade itself, individual slave bids for emancipation across lines of European identity were contingent on diplomatic relations between the governments involved. Obviously, the British were on better terms with the Danes than they were with the Dutch—albeit Anglo-Danish diplomacy was less successful in West Africa than in the West Indies, as we shall see.

Writing from St. Croix, for example, in May 1837, P. V. Scholten, governor-general of the Danish Virgins, voiced his concern to Henry Light, lieutenant governor of Antigua and the British Virgins, that the magistracy of Tortola released thirteen Cruzian runaways. But he concluded by confirming that his government would continue to extradite Britons who reenslaved their freed, apprenticed compatriots within his jurisdiction. "I am happy... to inform your excellency that the vigilant and zealous exertions of the police at St. Thomas brought about the discovery of the revolting crime committed by an English subject, Mr. [George] White, from the Island of St. Christopher [St. Kitts], in selling as a slave, to a resident of St. Thomas, a free boy, Joseph Burgundy.... [T]he culprit has been apprehended."[6] Light responded that the release of the Cruzian slaves resulted from a misunderstanding between the Tortolian Privy Council and the magistrate. The former instructed the latter to issue a writ of habeas corpus, but he drew up a writ of habeas corpus ad subjiciendum instead. Though either writ resulted in adjudication, one required a bond, which allowed greater pretrial mobility. Functionaries corrected the error and issued warrants of arrest. The governor promised that the Cruzian escapees would be caught. He also assured Scholten that if the Danish government did not call for the return of the slaves, which it did not, they would be tried, found guilty of vagrancy, and sentenced to hard labor. He ended by confirming plans for the extradition of George White and the return of young Joseph to St. Kitts with full restoration of freedom and the resumption of apprenticeship.[7]

Despite three holdings in the Antillean archipelago, the Danish government exercised no control over nonadministrative affairs. Furthermore, with no standing army or on-call militia to speak of—only a small garrison of guards—Denmark relied on Spanish troops in Puerto Rico to crush the Cruzian slave revolt of 1848.[8] The free port of St. Thomas rendered it a haven for legal and illegal trade. Informal Danish hegemony in West Africa was even more pronounced. There, lack of imperial control fell within the overall scope of things European in Africa before the middle of the nineteenth century. Far from the tone of most diplomatic correspondence, few European governments could boast of conventional colonization anywhere in sub-Sahara Africa before the "pacification" campaigns that followed the Conference of Berlin in 1884–85. Various western European nations, charter companies, and individuals established coastal and riverine spheres of social and commercial influence before the nineteenth century, but as guests or rent- and tax-paying residents of African kings and paramount chiefs. The acclaimed Portuguese presence was at times little more than a patchwork of settlements over which the Lusitanian Crown exercised little authority until the nineteenth century.[9] British sovereignty in Sierra Leone was limited emphatically to Freetown. In Lower Guinea, an admiral complained in 1830, "The blacks are not by any means so much under the control of Europeans as it may be supposed in Europe. This may be inferred, among other proofs, from the fact that the Commandant of Cape Coast [in Ghana] was unable, in 1828, to prevent the negroes, under the jurisdiction of the English Government, from attempting to seize upon the principal Dutch fort on the coast, namely St. George d'Elmina and Fort Koenraadsburg."[10] The scarcity of Danish residents exacerbated the lack of government control. Fortifications were garrisoned by limited numbers of local recruits whose Europeanization—here, cultural identity with and loyalty to Denmark —was negligible. In addition, the Danish Crown remunerated its thin cadre of metropolitan-born civil servants stationed in Accra in ways that thwarted the politics of abolition and *mission civilisatrice*, for bona fide Danish subjects were often paid with slaves.[11]

This scenario provided a perfect channel for the flow of slave traffic. One eyewitness reported that the illicit commerce continued from Sierra Leone to the Niger Delta and that "there is no hamlet belonging to England, the Netherlands, or Denmark." He also affirmed that Africans residing within European coastal settlements were the main targets of local middlemen in the service of European, Euro-American, and mulatto slave dealers.[12] In 1840, William Tucker, commander and senior officer of the West African division of the British antislave trade squadron, asked Laird Dall, governor pro tem of Danish Accra, to verify that the territory of Atocco fell within Danish jurisdiction. The enclave was the recent scene of intense slaving activity. In order for Spain to use the settlement as a depot for slave coffles en route to coastal Ouidah, Popo, and Arang, displaced Spanish merchants incited the inhabitants of Atocco to revolt against the Danes. The previous Danish governor attempted to clear the Volta River of slave traders and their agents, called *mongos*. But due to insufficient men and firearms, the project was half completed. It was, however, intimidating enough to motivate the flight of such large-scale merchants as the Malagan Pedro Blanco and the Brazilian Francisco "Chacha" de Souza.[13] Ultimately, the maneuver was ineffective because the traders, mainly Spaniards, not only returned to the Volta, they expanded into Atocco.[14]

Once Dall confirmed that the enclave fell within Danish sovereignty, Tucker offered to supply it with British forces. Dall declined, thanked him, and assured him that while he was without means to fortify the area, he would do his best to discourage the trade. He concluded that a show of force would be useless, "as the slave-agents have different factories, and when they are driven from one, resort to another, till the military force is withdrawn."[15] Subsequent correspondence reveals new layers of conflict at both the diplomatic and domestic levels. Because the Danish Crown refused to permit British interference in its African affairs, the Foreign Office sought new ways to resolve abolitionist ineffectiveness on the Gold Coast. The British government gained a modicum of Danish acquiescence but not without several exchanges that demonstrated both Danish complicity in the slave trade and contention within the ranks of the British diplomatic corps.

Anglo-Danish tensions are central to understanding the forces that divided the origins of captives destined for the Spanish Caribbean. The Danish Virgins played little, if any, role in the African slave trade to Cuba. Conversely, they were crucial for Puerto Rico well into the 1840s. Palmerston instructed his ambassador at Copenhagen to advise the Danish government of his displeasure over its failure to act on his suggestion that Danes residing in slave-holding countries on official duty be prohibited from owning slaves.[16] The swift response was terse: (1) Danish consular agents are not salaried; (2) though most are former merchants, they were not subjects of the king of Denmark; (3) the charging of fees on Danish ships trading within their districts is the only compensation Denmark can provide them for their services; (4) to prohibit them from buying and selling slaves would result in the loss of services useful to Danish commerce and navigation; and (5) as long as slavery exists in the Danish Caribbean, it will be impossible to abolish it in Africa.[17] The reply spelled out Denmark's position clearly: no legal obstacles prevented Danish subjects or foreign residents from trafficking in or owning slaves. Anglo-Danish abolitionist treaties forbade the use of Danish vessels as carriers of slaves, nothing more.

Palmerston reiterated his instructions to Ambassador Wynn. The envoy responded that Denmark demonstrated sound reasoning in its decision not to prohibit its officials from owning slaves or engaging in slave commerce. He added that his superior's logic was beyond reckoning. Palmerston admonished Wynn for his impertinence and issued the directive a third time. Wynn obeyed.[18] Shortly after, Palmerston lost his office to Lord Aberdeen, the earl of Clarendon. Under his conservative authority as British foreign minister, Denmark agreed to ban its seaborne agents from participation in slave commerce. But despite the agreement, St. Thomas continued to broker the slave trade to Puerto Rico, though its link to Danish Accra remains unclear. The documents do not reveal whether Palmerston linked European settlements in West Africa to the flow of slave traffic to the Spanish Caribbean. To encourage European governments to prevent slaveholding and slave trading among their subjects, foreign agents, and local Africans residing in their districts, he expressed greater concern for proper example:

> The continuance of the practice of the purchase and employment of slaves by European settlers and residents on the coast of Africa tends to encourage and perpetuate on the part of African slave dealers all those barbarous practices and atrocious cruelties which are inseparably connected with the original procurement of the slaves in the interior of the country, and with their march to the coast; and it has also the effect of shaking the belief of the African chiefs in the sincerity of the desire professed by the Powers of Europe to put the Slave Trade down.... [I]t must be difficult for these uninstructed chiefs to comprehend how these same nations which make the Slave Trade an offense when carried on by sea, should permit and encourage it, and even partake in it themselves, when it is carried on by land.[19]

Renewed exertions on European nations with enclaves on the African coast coincided with the revival of reexport maneuvers. From 1845 to 1847, the governor of Puerto Rico authorized the landing of Africans under the guise of Creole slave imports from the Dutch, Danish, and French Caribbean. Thus, Palmerston may have suspected this type of foul play when he wrote earlier:

> With reference to my despatch, in which I instructed you to suggest to the Danish Government the expediency of prohibiting its subjects in its possessions on the coast of Africa, from purchasing and owning slaves, I beg to state to you, for your information, that I have instructed Her Majesty's Representatives at the Courts of Paris, Madrid, Lisbon, and the Hague, to make similar representations to the French, Spanish, Portuguese and Dutch Governments, each of which Governments holds possessions on the coast of Africa, or in islands off that coast, in which the purchase and holding of slaves is believed to be tolerated.[20]

Like the French but unlike the Danes, the Dutch had long and profitable experiences in West Africa, as well as in the Caribbean. In the first two decades of the nineteenth century, Dutch slave-trading operations extended from Sierra Leone in Upper Guinea to the islands of São Tomé and Príncipe, which, with Fernando Poo, extend into the Atlantic from the Niger Delta between the Bights of Benin and Biafra in Lower Guinea. Dutchmen also worked with private French firms that served the French and Spanish Antilles. By the 1830s, their efforts were confined to the Lower Guinea Coast between São Jorge da Mina and surrounding settlements in Accra—which remained their base of operations—and Old Calabar in the Niger Delta.[21] Like the Danes, the Dutch of circum-Mina had little influence over local African affairs. But the casting of European hegemony against local control distorts the nature of the conflict. Explicitly or inexplicitly, the British government accused its allies of failure to honor their treaties. They denied the charges and at times discovered embarrassing ways to puncture the self-righteousness of their accusers. Above all, British interventionism on the Gold Coast encouraged the outward flow of slave traffic.

Between 1829 and 1831, the British government placed itself in the middle of Fante-Asante warfare. This was the third of nine major interventions that culminated in the colonization of the Gold Coast.[22] The hinterland Asante relied on the coastal Fante to broker their dealings with Europeans, which included the buying and selling of slaves. But slave trade suppression signaled an economic crisis for West African leaders accustomed to the wealth and power the traffic generated. Firearms and ammunition Europeans brought to exchange for slaves, for example, were crucial for such governments as the Asante and the Fon of Dahomey to maintain control over annexed provinces and client states.[23] Increasing dependency coincided with Asante expansion to the coast, which resulted in the subjugation of the Fante, which eliminated them as middlemen. The Fante convinced the British that the Asante interfered with the advance of legitimate trade—a term guaranteed to stir the emotions of British abolitionists, capitalists, and missionaries alike. Compared to other areas of West Africa, the Gold Coast exported far fewer captives. Nonetheless, the Fante and the Asante were involved as suppliers, as the description "Mina" indicates in slave records from New York City to Veracruz and Managua to Montevideo. But during the Age of Abolition, to the chagrin of the Asante, the British always allied with the Fante.[24]

On December 16, 1839, Commander Edward Lucas arrived at Mina Castle from Freetown. The British Admiralty commissioned him to investigate reports of Dutch connivance in Atlantic slave commerce. His findings alarmed both the Colonial Office and the Foreign Office. Though local leaders confessed their role in the trade, they asserted that the accusations were not justified given that slaving was as current in the British settlements of Accra as it was in the Dutch settlements. One deponent reported that "the war between England and the Ashantee deprived them of every other means of subsistence but that arising from the slave trade."[25] Lucas cited such claims repeatedly in his report. In one example, he paraphrased the metaphoric lamentations of two Fante detainees, "Though they had engaged in the prohibited slave trade, it was only imputable to having been drawn into it by the offers of some Englishmen and . . . likening themselves to a woman deserted by her husband, and tempted by various persons, they alleged that . . . destitution, and want of all necessities of life, have driven them to it."[26]

In corresponding with Lucas, Lieutenant Colonel Last, commandant of Dutch Guinea, identified the social distribution of Afro-Dutch relations: Africans within Dutch quarters, some Creole, some not; Africans allied to the Dutch but residing outside Dutch quarters; Africans in the process of separating themselves from Dutch jurisdiction; and, residing in and outside of Dutch quarters, Dutch nationals in the employ of indigenous slave merchants. Together, these variants bred chaos. Last left Mina for other Dutch settlements in search of two compatriots, Thomas Lifling and Bart Frederick Plange, "whose want of subordination had afforded me reason to be dissatisfied with them." He also sought certain Fante slave traders who "thought themselves under no obligation to recognize the jurisdiction of the Netherlands Government." He attributed the slaving behavior of the Fante and resident Dutchmen to the havoc arising from British intervention in the second Fante-Asante War of 1824–26.[27]

Unlike their compatriots beyond Dutch quarters, the Fante of circum-Mina were on good terms with the Asante as well as with the British, who at times classified the Fante mistakenly as their subjects. Great Britain's hostile response to Fante complaints of Asante autocracy upset the delicate balance. Conflict and the promise of economic advantage occasioned shifts in loyalties. Attracted by the prospects of autonomy, British gunboats, and improved commerce—including slave exports—the Mina Fante ended entente cordiale with the Asante and left the Dutch settlements to join their countrymen and the British in assaulting Asante territories. These changing configurations antagonized the Dutch as much as the Asante, who attacked them as traitors.[28]

Mina Africans within Dutch boundaries were often targets of slave catchers slithering along the peripheries, and in such instances their loss was considered final. But when they were spirited away by members of local communities— communities that recently nullified their association with the Dutch—retaliation was swift. Last described one incident. "I marched with my troops up the hill that led to Great Cormantine . . . almost all the people were under arms to repulse us. We nevertheless succeeded in getting into our possession the two kidnapped females just mentioned, natives of Elmina. . . . We also seized two members of the Negro Government."[29] But espousing neither abolitionism, colonization, nor foolhardy bravura, Last admitted, "We preferred keeping the people of Accra in their present favorable disposition, and contented ourselves, this time, merely with severe exhortations and serious cautions for the time to come, without prejudice to any ulterior measures which we might think proper to adopt hereafter."[30]

Henry Hutchinson, a British resident of Fort Anomabu, was also given to hostage-taking in skirmishes over trade rights. He declared that his work was not only "beneficial, but necessary for the preservation of good order and the personal safety of the natives."[31] Subsequent observations lent credence to the belief that British intervention thwarted abolitionist aims on the Gold Coast by depriving local Africans and European residents of legal commerce. Dutch, Danish, and British subjects not only engaged openly in the slave trade—along with the ubiquitous Iberians—they discussed their activities freely in the presence of British naval officers. Hutchinson noted that British subjects, including officials, believed that slaving provided their "principal source of income."[32] His most damaging indictment had yet to come.

Fante slave merchants employed the Dutchmen Lifling and Plange in Dutch Apam and Kormantine. Recent accusations against the two men proved groundless. Though the Dutchmen wanted to continue working with local slave catchers, once the two towns severed relations with the Dutch government, the men declined to pay indigenous taxes, resulting in their expulsion from the towns. In Last's words, "They [Lifling and Plange] refused to pay that Negro Government some local imposts."[33] From Ouidah, a Spaniard named Fernández traveled to Dutch Accra to supervise a transshipment of slaves on an armed Spanish brigantine. Though Last expelled him, instead of leaving Accra, Fernández fled with the two Dutchmen to various English quarters. Lifling and Plange went with their coffles to Tantamkweri, a British fort a few miles east of Dutch Kormantine, shipped their captives from there, and proceeded to Winneba, another British settlement, to exchange Western-manufactured clothing for slaves. Last also pinpointed British corruption at higher and more specific levels. "It would perhaps not be denied that Dutch Accra had been fixed on, for want of a garrison, as a place from which to embark slaves; but it is remarkable that when Fernandez, the Spanish merchant, in consequence of my order to quit the Dutch territory at Accra, chose a retreat with Mr. Fry, the Commandant of the English portion, situated a small distance from thence."[34]

Looking for positive proof to indict Lifling and Plange, Last ransacked the compound of Ankra, the Fante slave merchant who employed the two Dutchmen as intermediaries. The trader's brother, also involved in the trade, confessed that Ankra had just marched a hundred captives to the coast for transshipment on an unnamed vessel of unnamed nationality. But authorities short-circuited the voyage when the ship passed the Danish settlement of Ningo. There officials intercepted it, escorted it to Fort Christianburg, and fined its unnamed captain for illegal slave trading. Since he was unable—or unwilling—to pay the penalty, the Danish governor demanded of the captain three slaves, warning him that if he entered Danish waters with slaves again, the same procedure would follow.[35]

Though this form of penalty was practiced widely, Last wanted the governor to verify it himself. He did not succeed because the governor had just left Fort Christianburg. The motive for his absence was even more puzzling than his interpretation of antislave trade policy. He went to Ouidah to call on its principal slave broker, the notorious Francisco de Souza.[36] We may conclude that the Danish governor was a most remarkable man, serving beyond the call of duty in his efforts to stamp out the slave trade. But Ouidah—a coastal Creole community and thriving slave depot subject to the hinterland kingdom of the Fon—would not have tolerated the presence of a bona fide abolitionist, least of all one who also represented a European government. So notorious was Ouidah that the British navy avoided gunboat diplomacy for fear that heavily armed slave ships would respond with equal vigor.[37] It is unlikely that Souza would have received a European official who was not involved in surreptitious activities.

Lucas was convinced of the marginality of Dutch complicity in slave smuggling on the Gold Coast, and the accounts of other British officers indicated as much. Last's report—which ended with an invitation to the British to bomb Dutch enclaves suspected as traffic junctions—strengthened Lucas's certainty of relative Dutch innocence. More convincing were the events he witnessed himself, leading him to warn, "You may burn their huts if you please, but this remedy is insufficient to put a stop to the grand evil." He concluded, "If England could make peace with the Ashantees, this event—to which the attention of the English Government seems not to have been sufficiently directed—might benefit the good cause [abolition], and I think this might be brought about by the Governments of England, Holland, and Denmark sending out impartial Commissioners."[38] But Lucas's concerns found audience in no quar-

ter of his government. British officials refused to admit that military intervention compromised the antislavery crusade. Nor were they willing to acknowledge the extent to which imperial interests in legitimate African markets and
raw materials now superseded the humanitarianism of their ideals. The third
Fante-Asante War ended with the Asante being forced to relinquish their coastal
dominions.[39]

Anglo-Dutch antislave trade diplomacy continued its multifaceted course.
The plight of the Africans liberated from the *Snow* after its condemnation in
1823 at the Surinamese branch of the Mixed Court dominated the Hague-
London-Paramaribo circuit for nearly twenty years.[40] But the enslavement of
Afro-Britons in Dutch Caribbean colonies through a variety of channels—including British planter connivance—was minor compared to Spanish schemes.
However, during Aberdeen's term, British diplomats were often forced to use
their creativity to free black Britons and emancipated Africans who continued
to labor as slaves in Dutch Suriname.[41] The Dutch government feigned tacit
approval when British intervention reversed Asante expansion to the coast.
Local hostilities spawned by the Anglo-Fante axis called for changes in multinational slave trade stratagems. Political circumstances in the neighboring
states of the Gold Coast made slaving for export more desirable than ever. But
the loss of the Asante littoral, which augmented British influence, sparked an
exodus of slave traders northwest to Upper Guinea, where international slaving
was thought to have been on the wane, and east to Ouidah, Lagos, and the
Niger Delta, where incoming smugglers created a bonanza for local merchants already profiting from the fall of the Oyo Empire. British intervention
temporarily discouraged but did not stop slave commerce on the Gold Coast.
It reshaped alliances among interest groups now obligated to rely on greater
resourcefulness.

Java and the Gold Coast

Dutch succor in the Atlantic slave trade—from the public and private activity
and passivity of its nationals in Africa to their roles as suppliers and brokers for
Brazil and the Spanish islands by way of their free ports in the Caribbean—
lasted until the Hague abolished slavery in 1863. Dutch intentions to continue
the brokerage of black exploitation were confirmed in 1831, after the third
Fante-Asante War. Precisely then, the Netherlands made its first attempt to
recruit "free" men from the Asante Empire to serve as soldiers and policemen
in the Dutch East Indies. Though good planning seemed to preclude abuses, it

is asserted here and later that Dutch merchants and Spanish slaveholders benefited.

Colonel Verveer, a Frenchman once in the service of Napoleon but now serving the Dutch, headed a Hague-authorized delegation to the Asante capital of Kumasi to secure permission from the Asantehene (ruler) to recruit his subjects for tours of military duty in Java (Burma) at a rate of 1,000 per year for six years.[42] The idea struck at the core of British interests in Lower Guinea. In South America, the Dutch were still chafing over the loss of lands along the Demerara and Essequibo Rivers in what became British Guiana (now Guyana). To add lexical insult to the political injury of these appropriations, editors of Georgetown newspapers openly encouraged marronage from Suriname to the new British territories.[43] Furthermore, despite surface civility, the Dutch were not amused over British interventions on the Gold Coast, which disrupted legitimate trade. For the Dutch, a treaty with the Asante would deflate British designs on the area. For the Asante—straining under an Anglo-Fante blockade—the Dutch arrangement prefaced accords that would bring them European goods heretofore denied them because of British enmity.[44]

Contending that all subjects of the Asantehene were slaves at the mercy of his whims, the British protested that the Dutch were reviving slave commerce because such an agreement would encourage wars between hostile governments for captives alone.[45] The Dutch replied that military recruitment was humanitarian inasmuch as it freed local slaves and provided the families of nonslaves with compensation for the loss of agricultural workers. Just as Lucas was mistaken in his judgment that the Dutch acquiesced to British abolitionism and economic expansion because they asked for aid to destroy slave markets in and around Dutch Accra, other British officers erred in predicting that the Asante would foment wars with their neighbors. Rather than retain for domestic consumption superfluous captives from earlier wars, the Asante sold them to the Dutch for 25 guilders per head. The Asantehene convinced his neighbors to follow suit, which they did but not to the letter. Local and European traders began to promote hostilities in order to acquire war prisoners to sell to the Dutch.[46] Neither Dutch nor British interests were philanthropic. To the embarrassment of the Foreign Office, the commander of British Accra openly endorsed Dutch efforts and helped recruit Africans from coastal British forts and settlements.[47] Beyond the cover of altruism, the Hague saw no reason to justify the training of African recruits in the Dutch West Indies for service in the Dutch East Indies.

Between 1836 and 1841, several thousand Asante subjects served in Java for a year or longer and returned home. But equal numbers, allegedly trained for the same tour, never left Suriname.[48] British authorities were distressed over this Dutch version of *mission civilisatrice*. Shortly after fifty African recruits landed in Suriname, Consul John Samo criticized the sluggishness of Dutch Westernization. He believed that twenty-five days crossing the Atlantic in an armed Dutch steamer and four days on Dutch American soil achieved neither acculturation nor assimilation. Revealing both the core of his liberalist training and his blighted faith in the merits of Dutch creolization, he complained, "These Africans appear to be in the same state of ignorance as they were when they left their native land."[49] His subsequent observations were more to the point, as he identified features of the new traffic that were reminiscent of the old.

> They [the recruits] seemed to have been selected from different nations and tribes as they do not all speak the same jargon, and their personal character indicates that several of them are from the interior parts of the coast of Africa, upon which the Dutch settlements are situated. The importation of these Africans has caused considerable excitement here [Suriname], and there is reason to believe that attempts may be hereafter made by individuals to enter into contracts with the natives of Africa to serve them for a stated period, under the denomination of free laborers, in which capacity they would venture to introduce them to this colony.[50]

It seems unlikely that the Dutch were making disguised attempts to reinforce slavery in their colonies. Though they did not abolish slavery until 1863 (1848 in St. Maarten), the numbers involved in military recruitment did not suffice to suggest a plot to reroute some recruits to plantation labor. Increasingly, Dutch uses of coerced labor would be limited to Southeast Asia. Nor was it likely that significant numbers were taken to Brazil and the Spanish islands as slaves. The Dutch government admitted that African regiments were being used to control labor forces in both Java and Suriname. Unlike demographic distributions in the Dutch Caribbean islands, free blacks in mainland Suriname never exceeded 7 percent of the total population, and slaves outnumbered whites sixty-five to one.[51] Responding to British accusations that black soldiers and black laborers were one and the same in Suriname, the Dutch minister of foreign affairs made the following distinctions: "The black soldier will not permit any negro slave to pass near him in the streets, unless the latter fronts and uncovers himself before him, an honor which the African receives with proud indifference."[52] Ironies continued. Raw data show that one in six African military recruits actually came from British Accra, which lay beyond Asante control. Furthermore, the recruits were used to capture runaway Surinamese slaves en route to freedom in British Guiana. After several meetings between the Dutch monarch and the British ambassador, the program was canceled in September 1841.[53] But considering what took place later in the decade, especially in Puerto Rico, Dutch West African recruitment cannot be dismissed as harmless to the abolitionist cause. Decreasing profits in Suriname did not buffer conditions for slaves. Brutal treatment and the uneven distribution of slaves to nonslaves increased the possibility of slave revolts. In Indonesia, the Dutch organized labor-intensive agriculture around slave traffic from the Bay of Bengal. In both colonies—Java and Suriname—Dutch officialdom saw the creation and deployment of African regiments as an expedient to curtail slave resistance.

Military recruitment could have disguised a small flow of African slaves into Dutch Indonesia as well as into the Dutch Antilles. But if this form of foul play had been a part of the program for Java, it was doomed to failure. Dutch officers complained that African enlisted men did not adjust to Asian climes.[54] Such a scheme had greater potential in the Dutch Antilles. A small number of Africans could have been—and probably were—reexported from Suriname by way of free port colonies to Puerto Rico and, to a lesser extent, Cuba between 1845 and 1847. Hence, Consul Samo was not off target when he asserted that military recruitment could develop into illegal slave traffic.[55]

New French Connections

Earlier I identified Franco-Dutch cooperation in Spanish slaving operations. Further evidence is more conclusive. Between 1819 and 1829, twenty-three vessels were confiscated as a result of Mixed Court proceedings in Paramaribo. Twenty of them were French.[56] Albeit after 1830 Franco-Dutch complicity is more difficult to verify, forces within the two governments continued to work together. First, it seems more than coincidental that the Hague selected a French expatriate to lead the Dutch mission to the Asante capital. Though Verveer requested Africans for free military service in Dutch colonial dominions, the French government sent a similar delegation to Kumasi to recruit free laborers for work in Martinique and Guadeloupe.[57] After several attempts, the plan came to fruition in 1848, the year France abolished slavery in the Caribbean.

Second, Anglo-Dutch abolitionist treaties permitted British abolitionist officers to board, search, and detain all vessels in Dutch West African waters suspected of slaving except for those flying the Dutch standard. However, without royal permission, Dutch authorities at Mina extended the privileged exclusion to French vessels.[58]

Third, France's first major bid for imperial domination in West Africa, armed conflict with al-Hajj Umar Tal, had yet to materialize. Nor had French traders negotiated with local governments to use lands on the Gold Coast in Lower Guinea, as they had done in Senegal and in Upper Guinea or as other Europeans had done elsewhere along both coasts. Therefore, they could not reciprocate Dutch favors granted them at Mina. Nonetheless, in Upper Guinea in the 1840s, all slavers intercepted by British cruisers at the mouth of the Pongo River, including those flying the Dutch flag, were laden with French-manufactured supplies.[59] Just as the Dutch of circum-Mina sold slaving equipment to any vessel in need, French merchants functioned similarly as they expanded commercial operations beyond the Senegal River into present-day Guinea-Conakry, as the following case illustrates.

Isabel Gomes Lightbourn was an African Creole from a family of slave dealers based in Faringuia on the Pongo. As her ship embarked to gather captives held in other parts of the river for transport to the Spanish Antilles, British officials destroyed it along with its contents, all of which she purchased on credit from Marc Valentine, a French shipper based in Gorée. Charging that the destruction of her ship and its goods prevented her from paying Valentine, she sued the British government and won. Aberdeen reasoned that remuneration was due because the vessel was intercepted in an estuary rather than the Atlantic proper.[60]

France caused Great Britain considerable discomfort. So delicate were matters of Anglo-French diplomacy that the authors of the Foreign Office List of Slave Ships, published in 1845, omitted the true character of French involvement by reporting only 31 vessels, or 1.3 percent, of 2,313 as French. Studies by Serge Daget reveal why the Foreign Office approached the problem with caution, if not with premeditated ambiguity.[61] He uncovered 763 French slavers; Nantes alone handled 261 of them between 1814 and 1845. His work shows that 47 percent of all slaving expeditions originated in legitimate French ports in France, the Caribbean, Gorée Island in the bay of Dakar, and Réunion in the Indian Ocean. He bases his theory of silence on Great Britain's position that it could not support the French restoration and publicly denigrate it at the same time.[62] This is not to say that the British antislave trade machine did not pursue and condemn French slavers, which it did, or that the French government wholly ignored its treaties, which it did not. It does mean—as opposed to rela-tions with Spain—that Great Britain could not pressure France for bilateral courts, multilateral treaties, or the mutual right of search. Though often, but not always, rigorous against French maritime infractions, the British preferred subtlety at home. It was this strategy, theorizes Daget, that led sentinels in London to downplay the sluggishness of French cooperation.[63]

By 1835, open French connivance in the Spanish slave trade was passé. But during the 1850s, new schemes appeared, cloaked in the pretense of contracted African labor. With official government approval, under the auspices of the Marseilles-based Régis Company and the firm of P. J. Maes of Nantes, French-men recruited Africans from kings, noblemen, war leaders, and merchants from Senegal to Benguela to satisfy the needs of planters in the French islands of the Indian Ocean, the French Antilles, and the Gulf plantations of the United States.[64] In 1858, a *New York Times* editor noted that "vessels engaged in the trade generally use the French flag because British cruisers on the African coast will not trouble it."[65]

British officials attempted to link the traffic of "free African laborers," or *éngagés*, to the Caribbean slave trade by suggesting that such a program would inspire Dutch, Danish, and Spanish subjects to undertake similar schemes to disguise slave traffic. They also asserted that articles in Brazilian and Spanish Caribbean newspapers that discussed the *éngagé* program were secret codes for slaveholders and slave merchants.[66] Their alarm, however, was selective. Great Britain built the model for African immigration to remedy the economic crisis of emancipation adaptation in its Caribbean colonies.[67] But if Franco-British antislave trade relations were prickly, many elements of Franco-Spanish pro-slave trade relations were murky. Other French connections will be explored in subsequent chapters, but in the context of French expatriates and renegades vis-à-vis their contributions to various slave-trading schemes in Spanish domin-ions. Here, suffice it to say that the beneficiaries of the *éngagé* program were Réunion, Martinique, Guadeloupe, Cayenne, and, to a lesser extent, Louisiana and Mississippi. Despite British suspicions, there is no proof that Africans reached the Spanish islands through initiatives authorized by the French gov-ernment, though the activities of individual Frenchmen were different matters altogether.

Diplomacy compelled Great Britain to recognize French authority in coastal Senegal and Dutch and Danish authority in parts of Ghana. The same force held true in the Caribbean. Spain's official colonial presence in the Gulf of Guinea was young and barely visible at this time. Great Britain hoped to purchase Spanish equatorial holdings. Failure to do so exaggerated its exasperation with Spain, but through the clandestine slave trade, France, Denmark, and the Netherlands recognized and amplified the Spanish presence in Africa—albeit in areas where Spain had no colonial claim. The quiet alliance between government-protected Spanish, Danish, Dutch, and French subjects—be they independent nationals or corrupt public officials—was neither facile nor uniform. Given the drama of frequent shifts, they formed a team that was not one. But throughout the period of transition, from the 1820s to the 1830s, cross-national threads of illegal cooperation remained strong enough to carry the Puerto Rican slave trade into the 1840s.

Nouns, Adjectives, Predicates

While the "Mina" were noted in nineteenth-century Cuba, they did not figure among the island's principal African-born groups.[68] Though texts documenting the slave trade to Puerto Rico mention the Gold Coast as a source, nearly all references predate the nineteenth century.[69] If British and Dutch eyewitnesses did not err, we must conclude that Spaniards in the 1830s made a habit of rerouting "Mina" captives from traditional Gold Coast points of departure to sites across the Volta River to Ewe territory and beyond to Popo and Little Popo in present-day Togo and Benin (Dahomey), where they were transshipped to the Caribbean as "Popó" and "Arará" captives (also called "Aradá"). These Spanish terms identified slaves embarked from areas in and around Dahomey. Though Cuban records indicate that the "Arará" ranked among the island's five largest African-born groups, many labeled as such could have been "Mina" from Ghana.[70]

Linguistic patterns and records on slave dissent are useful for pinpointing the origins of Puerto Rico's *negros de nación*, its African-born slaves. Studies by Alvarez Nazario and Baralt help define the limits. They show, for example, that "Arará" and "Popó," as well as "Mina," appeared as surnames for Africans and their descendants from the sixteenth to the eighteenth century, though the two scholars do not indicate the extent to which Ghanian and Dahomean ethnic groups were present in the nineteenth century. Indeed "Arará" and "Popó" do not appear at all. According to Alvarez Nazario, "Mina," as a surname, survived up to the twentieth century in Loíza Aldea, but it seems that most African surnames of ethnic or national origin faded from official records after the abolition of slavery.[71] He does not indicate what the most common surnames were, but searches in plantation inventories, penal records, some—but not all—bills of sale, and newspapers with notices of runaway slaves, along with edited compilations of documents, suggest that "Congo," "Gangá," "Mandinka," and "Carabalí" were cited with the greatest frequency.[72] On the other hand, both Alvarez Nazario and Baralt show that common given names from Ghana, between Kumasi and the coast, are found in nineteenth-century Puerto Rican records on militant slave resistance. They include "Cuacua," boy-child born on a Wednesday, and "Baha," boy-child born with a physical disability.[73]

Baralt's work on slave resistance underscores the dynamics of African identity in both homogenous and heterogeneous terms. Thus, his emphases point to the presence—however small—of "Mina" captives in nineteenth-century Puerto Rico after the prohibition of the African slave trade. With different objectives, Alvarez Nazario confirms the same presence. Though dated, the incomparable girth of his detailed study of language, African identity, and cultural diffusion, in its broadest sense, proves that from the early 1500s to 1859, Puerto Rico received captives from every African port known to have participated in the transatlantic slave trade, including the East African shores of Mozambique.[74] But because of the study's sweeping diachronic scope, it is less useful for specific patterns of nineteenth-century linguistic distribution. However, its comparative semiotic evidence corroborates important historical trends—first and foremost that Cuba and Puerto Rico exhibited similar and different patterns of African slave acquisition during the Age of Abolition. Determinants such as clout, strategies, opportunities, resources, chronologies of geographic preference, demographic concentrations, and the wholly unequal distribution of wealth rendered African slave acquisitions between the two colonies at once similar and separate experiences.

This chapter surveyed slave trading in areas where current research shows that it was on the decline: the Senegambia region above Upper Guinea and the Gold Coast area in Lower Guinea. The British Foreign Office distorted the true volume of French input. While we lack sufficient evidence to show parallel distortions vis-à-vis Dutch and Danish complicity, other British texts suggest that similar machinations and conspiracies of silence contributed to reduced figures for African captives exported from the Gold Coast. Serialized evidence—the basis for statistics we currently accept—does not show Spanish slave traders operating around European settlements in Accra, as Lucas had reported. Therefore, his eyewitness accounts, along with those by Last and Verveer, are especially important, given that statistics for Gold Coast exports from the 1810s onward fully contradict the assertions of their detailed reports. Neither Lucas nor Last named Spanish Caribbean destinations in their reports on slave traffic from the Gold Coast. Nor did Verveer name them as he lay the groundwork for military recruitment in Kumasi.[75] But when Lucas and Last cited Spanish slave traders, service to Cuba or Puerto Rico was their only possible aim. By combining these accounts with recent works in history and earlier works in linguistics, it becomes clear that new studies are needed on the Gold Coast for the early years of slave trade prohibition.

Great Britain attempted to tie Spain into political knots. Other Western slaveholding polities were less entangled in British accords. Less diplomatic and economic debt allowed them more wiggle room to defy, or at least dispute, British antislave trade pretensions. As Antillean neighbors, fellow colonialists, and fellow slaveholders in better positions to resist British pressure, France, Denmark, and the Netherlands found it advantageous to support, albeit secretly, Spain's resolution to continue illicit slaving expeditions. By the seventeenth century, all three had trading centers on the West African coast from Upper to Lower Guinea. In view of the British destruction of Spanish slave-trading posts in Upper Guinea in the 1840s, these older bases were crucial. The relationship between French, Dutch, and Danish commercial districts in West Africa and French, Dutch, and Danish colonies in the West Indies merits underscoring. Though British forces could never establish a solid link between French, Dutch, and Danish commerce on the coast of West Africa and the violation of Anglo-Spanish accords against the transatlantic slave trade, with good reason they suspected it, and with mixed results they maintained surveillance against it.

Due to the intrigues of European politics and diplomacy, British antislave trade engagements with France remained sore spots. Though British cruisers pursued offending French vessels, in too many instances, especially in cases involving French complicity in the Spanish slave trade, Great Britain was reduced to throwing up its hands to the tune of "cherché la France." The refrain was more than a deceptive recognition of national and cultural difference through mystification; it was a deployment to downplay British support of domestic French politics. Denmark seemed the most willing to honor its antislave trade agreements. Yet much like other slaveholding powers, when confronted by British diplomacy, the Danes responded with a mixture of sincerity, hostility, and futility. Unlike France and the Netherlands vis-à-vis their Caribbean territories—but like the Dutch or the British for that matter—Danish political control over the slave-trading affairs of its subjects on the Gold Coast was even less evident. British investigations of slave traffic from Danish Accra and Danish St. Thomas proved equally useless.

Of the three governments, the Netherlands provided Spain with the greatest maneuverability. British eyewitnesses not only reported the bona fide lack of Dutch hegemony vis-à-vis the slave trade from the Gold Coast in the 1830s and 1840s; they verified that Spanish slave traders operated easily in Dutch enclaves, that the Dutch government refused to prohibit foreign vessels from using their ports to export slaves, and that the Dutch government cultivated amicable relations with the Asante king to facilitate the recruitment of his subjects for military service in Java and Suriname. While the recruitment program ended in 1841, it left many questions unanswered. As the British observed, nothing prevented recruiters in Kumasi or bureaucrats in Paramaribo from designating a portion of the people as slaves for Spanish Caribbean markets.

6

African Rivers

Structures of Transport

Though sometimes less than forthcoming, memoirs by ex–slave traders reveal important facets of the traffic before and after it was outlawed. Few, however, discern Puerto Rican interests. Accounts by Theodore Canot and other smugglers would have us believe that slaves rarely landed in Puerto Rico. Thus, British parliamentary records and Spanish records from the Havana branch of the Mixed Court are valuable sources in this regard. Though neither source provides ample data for broader pictures that include the cultural dynamics of slave acquisition from the West African interior, they help identify the changing contours of Puerto Rican participation from the West African coast, the primary aim of this chapter.

Large-Scale Expeditions

Occasionally, British reports identified Puerto Rico as a junction for the African slave trade to Cuba. In this capacity, Africans were landed in Puerto Rico in one vessel, then transferred to the larger island in another. Such cases were usually limited to emergency situations, from which local merchants profited by skimming off captives, then rerouting the prepaid remainder to Cuba.[1] More common were deliberate joint ventures between the two colonies. Under these arrangements, reexports to Cuba were small. Yet no matter how often merchants from the two islands joined hands and funds to carry out African expeditions, Puerto Rico was not designated as a reliable depot for slave ships en route to Cuba.[2] Nor was it dependent exclusively on Cuba for African captives. Interested parties examined all options. The dexterity of the Puerto Rican slave trade narrowed down to two expedients: the Cuban-based Blanco-Martínez-Souza axis, with corollary firms in New York, New Orleans, Baltimore, Bahia, London, Madrid, and Freetown, as well as Havana and Matanzas; and the Puerto Rican circuit alone, which proved just as successful as the broader-based Cuban machine, if not more enduring.

Writers—observers, historians, novelists, and playwrights—have examined the careers of slave traders such as Theodore Canot, Pedro Martínez, and Francisco de Souza. Their infamous lives make good stories. But none compares to Pedro Blanco, whose vision and no-nonsense business savvy permitted him to retire from slaving, it is said, with the unusual combination of affluence and good health. Many of his known predecessors and contemporaries died in disease-ridden poverty, accelerated by drug and alcohol dependency.[3] His expanded notoriety is linked to Canot's associate and host, "Mongo John" Ormond, whose demise led to a decade of uncertainty along the Pongo River. Small indigenous kingdoms and chieftaincies revolted, and hostilities ensued among mulatto African families. Like Mongo John, these Creole dynasts courted the favor of hinterland Muslim potentates, who provided them with captives to sell to Europeans on the coast. Though the Lightbourns and the Fabers were victorious, instability lasted long enough to make Gallinas the center of slave trade operations on the Upper Guinea Coast.[4] Canot thought it better to work for Blanco than seek independence in troubled Río Pongo. Once Blanco semi-retired to Italy in the 1840s, as the story goes, Canot moved to New Cess, Liberia. Making no headway there, he abandoned the business. Río Pongo, along with Sherbro, reemerged to compete successfully with Gallinas, now in the hands of Blanco's numerous disciples.[5]

Blanco's expansion corresponded with the treaty of 1835, with its equipment clause. But the new agreement did not discourage the trade. Cuba and Puerto Rico relied on the Portuguese flag, which Britain did not pursue until 1839. Despite slumps linked to the withdrawal of the flag, slaving made a strong showing, as table 6.1 illustrates. However, computations by David Eltis show what raw British data did not. Although between 1811 and 1867 maritime agents intercepted one in five ships, for the same period only one in sixteen had slaves when captured or detained.[6] His findings deviate little from an older formula attributed to slaving tycoon Pedro Martínez: For every slave ship intercepted, twenty escaped. In this light, Table 6.2 illustrates the extent to which Puerto Rico benefited from the African slave trade. (Table 6.2 may be found at the end of chapter 6.) Between 1834 and 1859, twenty-nine attempts to land Africans in Puerto Rico came to the attention of British authorities. Records

Table 6.1. Slave ships intercepted in African waters without the Portuguese flag, 1839–1844

Year	Number of ships	Percentage increase or decrease
1839	61	—
1840	43	29
1841	32	−26
1842	11	−66
1843	17	+64
1844	17	—

Source: Adapted from table 2.1.

detail the success of only two, the *Vencedora* and the *Majesty*. But if we accept the calculations of Eltis and Martínez, failed slaving expeditions masked a host of successful ones.

The *Vencedora* eluded condemnation because it was a bona fide passenger ship. Prior to boarding travelers in Cádiz, it took on slaves at the Congo and Kwanza Rivers. They were prepaid and slated for reexport to Cuba. The scheme was fractured. Because of the ruckus Spanish passengers and British diplomats raised, the captives were sold in Puerto Rico and remained there.

There were several reasons why the *Majesty* probably escaped detection. First, though Spanish-owned, it was made in the United States and flew its flag. Albeit British cruisers pursued slave ships waving the Stars and Stripes without hesitation, such vessels were sighted in Upper and Lower Guinea, not subequatorial waters, where the United States had established a pattern of legitimate trade, especially between Cabinda and Luanda. Therefore it could have been mistaken for a merchant ship. Second, it carried an estimated 1,600 Congolese captives. Its dimensions were enormous. Due to its size alone, few would have thought it a slaver. Third, under political fire at home since the mid-1840s and fatigued by increased slave ship pursuits for most of the 1850s, occasioned in no small part by renewed succor from the United States in the slave trade to Cuba, the British squadron was losing momentum.[7]

Table 6.2 shows that Puerto Rico was drawn into Blanco's sphere between 1835 and 1836. Francisco de Souza reigned in the Bight of Benin. In theory, his influence from Ouidah to Luanda represented the southern half of a slaving empire whose northern portion Blanco headed from his base in Gallinas in Sierra Leone. But Souza was less talented in long-distance trade. Despite excellent relations with the Fon, suppliers in the Dahomean interior to whom he was subject, his ties to Angola and the Congo were exaggerated. Stressing speed and full stocks, Blanco used Souza to beat the equipment clause.[8] To guarantee that Sierra Leonian barracoons were filled with captives for shipment at a moment's notice, Blanco's association with him was vital. Vis-à-vis slave origins from West Africa proper, Upper Guinea, from Bissau to Liberia, was less populated than Lower Guinea, from the Gold Coast to southeastern Nigeria. Demographic losses from the slave trade were more acute in the savannas of West Africa, on whose coastal periphery Blanco planted himself. Souza, based in tropical West Africa, was constantly in Blanco's debt. To repay him, he shipped many of his captives north to Gallinas, where they embarked for the Spanish Caribbean.[9]

Emergencies modified this south-to-north pattern. In the case of the *Explorador*, Blanco sent captives to Souza's agents in Luanda to avoid British cruisers. Blanco and Souza owned the slave cargo jointly with two Spaniards, José de Inza and Cenón Ignacio de Aldeçoa, both of whom alternated as captain. Souza co-owned the vessel with Aldeçoa. On arrival in Puerto Rico, Pedro Guarch was designated to handle the sale of the slaves. At times listed as the captain of slavers bound for Cuba and Puerto Rico and at times listed as the fraudulent owner of Puerto Rican slave cargoes when British naval officers detained him, Aldeçoa testified that he was born and resided in Bilbao. José de Inza's quarter share was a front to disguise Aldeçoa's larger investment. Inza's background is a mystery. More information is available for Pedro Guarch, the Puerto Rican broker for the *Explorador*. His family migrated from Tarragona in segments between 1809 and 1831 and settled in Mayagüez. By 1829, he owned a bakery, employing his nephew as an apprentice. The lad's training linked with future plans. He left baking in the early 1830s to join the family's maritime business, also based in Mayagüez.[10]

Blanco's strained relationship with Souza is borne out in letters found on the *Explorador*. In his instructions to Inza he wrote:

> You are aware that Mr. Francis Felis de Sousa [*sic*] has one fourth share in the voyage, consequently it will be necessary to dispose of the whole invoice which is calculated to give at least 520 packages [slaves], costing about 44,000 dollars when embarked. Notwithstanding, the interest of said Sousa, you must not deliver to his agent any portion of said interest. . . . As Mr. Sousa, to complete his fourth interest in the voyage, has borrowed 5,000 dollars from us, it will be well that you send all vessels sailing from Ayuda [Ouidah] to this [Havana], any packages you have on freight, to enable us to reimburse ourselves of Mr. Souza's advance.[11]

For transport, Pedro Martínez was Pedro Blanco's most important ally. A shipbuilder based at Cádiz, with homes in Havana and Matanzas, Martínez owned thirty vessels alone and co-owned others with Blanco. But as a player in the slave trade to Puerto Rico, his role was limited. Of the ships listed in table 6.2, he owned only the *Temerário*, which had no visible link to Blanco. Martínez played a greater part as an adviser and a supplier of slaving equipment, as seen in the case of the *Brilhante*.

Depositions from the crews of the *Explorador*, the *Fénix*, the *Negrinha*, and the *San Nicolás* failed to mention Puerto Rico. But slaving was never an honest business, least of all after 1815. Captains destroyed evidence as quickly as possible before British officers boarded their ships. At the time of capture, three of the four ships carried little written evidence to tie them directly to slaving. And crews—unless intimidated by trial proceedings in Freetown, where they feared abandonment to the tempers of resident Western and Westernized blacks who abhorred the slave trade—withheld as much information as possible. To verify that the vessels were bound for Puerto Rico we must look at names cited in lading papers and in proceedings at the Mixed Court. In the case of these four ships, one name surfaced often. Pedro Guarch of Mayagüez brokered relations between suppliers and consumers. Resident Puerto Ricans were never ship owners, captains, or supercargoes for African expeditions unless the island figured in the itinerary.

There is further evidence to support the claim that these vessels were bound for Puerto Rico. On the one hand, Cenón Ignacio de Aldeçoa was the surrogate captain as well as the co-owner of the *Explorador*. On the other hand, both the *Fénix* and the *Negrinha* were captured off Grenada. No slave ship bound for Cuba alone would have run the risk of sailing in the thick of British colonies in the eastern Antilles unless Puerto Rico was the terminus, a designated port of call, or a site for emergency landings. In a chase, not even the most neophyte of captains would have followed such a course without Puerto Rico figuring in the venture. The captains of both vessels were veterans in the trade. There was no chase, nor were there reports of technical or climatic difficulties that would have called for an unscheduled stop. In addition, Juan Mariano de Aldeçoa, a peninsula-born resident of Puerto Rico and the brother of Cenón Ignacio de Aldeçoa, substitute captain of the *Explorador*, was found on board the *Negrinha*. When interrogated, he stated that he was the pilot of a slaver recently condemned at Freetown and that he boarded the *Negrinha* to catch a ride home. Had the ship planned to stop in St. Thomas, an unlikely port of call for an inbound slaver in 1836, or had it gone directly to Havana, he could have returned to Puerto Rico easily from either port. The only problem is that the ship's manifest listed him as a round-trip passenger.[12] Final proof of the true destination of the *San Nicolás* is based on a criterion for the *Negrinha*. Pedro Lafarque, a Puerto Rican resident, was the middleman and sole owner of the cargo.[13] Further, it was fitted and supplied *in* Puerto Rico. We have no evidence to suggest that Cuban ships prepared for the Atlantic crossing in Puerto Rico. Nor do records identify it as a port to outfit slavers slated to return to Cuba alone. To the contrary, with its dangerous proximity to the British islands of the southeast, Puerto Rico was easier to monitor. But once reaching Cruzian waters, it was clear sailing for slavers bound for its southern and western shores.

While entry into Caribbean waters from the Atlantic at any point in the eastern curve required special skills to outrun British cruisers, participants in Cuban ventures had no such cause for concern. Though Jamaica peered close from the southeast and the Bahamas from the north and northeast, neither British colony was close enough to Cuban shores to guard against the landing of African captives. While maritime supplies cost less in Puerto Rico than in Cuba, real bargains were found in the free port colonies of the non-Hispanic Caribbean. Savings to outfit a Cuban ship in Puerto Rico would have been insufficient to warrant the extra cost of paying sailors en route from the larger island, where the voyage of the *San Nicolás* began, to the smaller island, from which it sailed. Were it rigged and stocked at a Dutch or Danish port, a risky possibility for a Cuban venture, only then would savings have been substantial.

Crews destroyed paper trails for the *Fénix* and the *Negrinha* before British officers boarded them. A log was found on the *San Nicolás*, in French, a matter the British declined to pursue.[14] The *Brilhante* log was also destroyed, but damaging letters were found in the sleeve of the first mate, who was actually the captain, Francisco González Veiga of Puerto Rico. The letters reveal strong Cuban connections to the Puerto Rican slave trade. They disclose details about not only the *Brilhante* but the *Emprendedor* as well. The Pedro Martínez Company of Cádiz and Havana and the Blanco, Carvallo, and Company of Havana owned the two vessels jointly. When Juan Bautista Matías de Carvallo died shortly before the adjudication of the *Emprendedor*, Blanco bought the remaining stock from Lino, brother of the deceased, making him sole owner of the company and both ships.[15]

Papers confiscated from the *Emprendedor*—also captained by González Veiga—corroborate the fact that 1839 was a watershed. After years of protecting Spanish slavers, the British Parliament voted to prosecute the Portuguese flag north and south of the equator. Furthermore, false Portuguese clearance papers and passports, once easy and cheap to obtain in Cape Verde, were less readily available. Despite new British measures, Cape Verdian authorities suppressed counterfeiting operations to corner the market themselves. In addition, rather than freeing condemned vessels—which were sold to British merchants at Freetown, who resold them to Spanish agents from Gallinas and Sherbro—the Foreign Office now ordered them broken up and sold as timber to colonial lumberyards worldwide.[16]

A letter from the *Emprendedor* confirms Blanco's reputation as a tough-minded businessman. Blanco wrote: "You will be most careful in rendering me an account of all your transactions, showing the nature of your different purchases, and the result of them."[17] Another proves that Puerto Rico purchased Africans from Cuba, not the reverse, which British observers often and erroneously suggested. "Not only your duty, but your interests and inclinations should lead you to act with every precaution.... If by accident you should be prevented from landing the slaves at Trinidad [de Cuba], a certificate to this effect must be produced to satisfy the parties to whom they are consigned.... At Puerto Rico, Don Pedro Guarch; at Santiago [de Cuba], Don Rafael Masó; at Trinidad [de Cuba], Fernández, Bastido, and Company."[18]

Because top-level slave traders maintained civility and courtesy in their letters, tensions are not easy to detect. González Veiga did his best to prevent the capture of the *Emprendedor*. Following Blanco's orders, he recruited a Portuguese-speaking crew at Porto Praia, and when British officers detained it, he destroyed the log and hid all correspondence before they boarded. While Martínez recognized that capture could not be avoided and praised González for his efforts, Blanco was less understanding. The captain wrote to Martínez, "When I left this place [Gallinas], Señor Don Pedro Blanco was quite well and desired his best wishes to you."[19] But in closing, Captain González hinted at his true feelings and feigned ignorance that Blanco bought the remaining shares of Blanco, Carvallo, and Company: "I am now without any employment, as you may suppose, from the unfortunate loss [of the *Emprendedor*], and I do not know when I may again have the occasion to board a ship. Although I feel satisfied that I can always reckon on the friendship and protection of Señor Don Lino Carvallo, whom it always gives me pleasure to serve, I would prefer being once more engaged with you, provided you have any business you can employ me in."[20]

Blanco had already contracted González to captain the *Brilhante*, but he sacked him and blacklisted him for the loss of the *Emprendedor*. Because Lino Carvallo sold his stocks to Blanco, González also lost the company's patronage.

Apparently, the Carvallo brothers brokered tensions between Blanco and the Puerto Rican–based captain. When Juan Bautista died and Lino sold his share of the business, González lost the protective intercession of the Carvallos. Martínez replied that slave trading had become too precarious, "As vessels are constantly being lost. . . . [F]or the present, I think it desirable to be occupied otherwise."[21] González maintained deference and decorum toward Martínez: "Hoping you will always command my services." But while recruiting sailors for the *Brilhante* in Havana, he withdrew $2,815 from Martínez's company account in the name of Blanco's firm and advised the shipping tycoon that "this draft will be quite sufficient to close our account." He then proceeded to San Juan to outfit the *Brilhante*. In cryptic language, he acknowledged to Blanco that this voyage would be his last: "The amount of the expense attending the fitting of the bases of the hatches, which you will observe in the vessel's accounts, I beg you will be pleased to remit to Señor Don Pedro Guarch. . . . [U]ntil now I have not had the opportunity to write to you. I shall leave this to the care of Señor Guarch, as he has been so obliging as to offer to send a letter to you by the first opportunity."[22]

Considering how well González hid papers when the British overtook the *Emprendedor*, the easy discovery of those on the *Brilhante* owed perhaps to a desire for vengeance. Of the twenty-one letters found on the latter ship, dated from February 17, 1838, to August 27, 1839, he wrote ten of them respecting both ships. They were, of course, undelivered. Five were for Blanco and five more for Martínez. Blanco gave two others to González to deliver to João José Claudio Linares, a Cape Verdian middleman, and Julián Zulueta, one of Cuba's wealthiest slave merchants.[23] The letters were to go to Havana, Gallinas, Porto Praia, Cádiz, and London, Zulueta's main base of operations. González had ample opportunity to deliver the letters addressed to parties at the first three ports, as well as the means to see that those for the last two were safely dispatched to Europe. Yet the letters, and eight more he received from the same correspondents, were found on his person.[24] It was unusual for the captain of a clandestine slaver to carry such incriminating evidence. After the condemnation of the *Brilhante*, González disappeared from the pages of British Foreign Office reports, as did the Blanco-Martínez-Souza connection to the slave trade to Puerto Rico. The promising career of Pedro Guarch, whom González branded a sycophant, also came to a halt. In table 6.2, we see that in 1836 the peninsula-born Puerto Rican was no more than a liaison between the Blanco axis and the Puerto Rico slave-holding community. By 1838, he was on the cutting edge of success as the prospective owner of the *Brilhante* captives. Yet like González Veiga, he, too, bowed out of the business.

Little differentiated the Cuban-assisted slave trade from independent Puerto Rican initiatives. Both stood an equal chance of capture and home-free disembarkation. Until 1839, both used Spanish and Portuguese flags, albeit independent voyages relied less on this ploy. For both avenues, captains, vessel owners, and slave owners were almost always peninsula-born residents of Puerto Rico. Records of capture do not specify each sailor's nationality and place of residence, though Hispanophones made up the majority of the crews. For different reasons, the cross-referencing of instructions was another commonality. Expeditions with mixed Cuban and Puerto Rican interests were planned on a larger scale, and with the Blanco axis in motion, organization was often grandiose, as were problems.

The *Explorador* formed part of an elaborate two-year expedition involving Cuba, Puerto Rico, Brazil, and every major West African slave port from Sierra Leone to Angola, including Mina, where Captain Aldeçoa dabbled in the gold trade. But evidence is not conclusive enough to verify that the *Emprendedor* and the *Brilhante* formed branches of a single venture. In any event, despite Blanco's meticulous planning, González sabotaged the latter voyage. Confiscated letters offer further insight into the commercial mechanisms and social spaces of the Blanco machine. A letter to Claudio Linares of Porto Praia was meant to advise him of the roles two brothers were to play in the failed expedition. In different capacities, Domingo and Ignacio Pérez Rolo were slave caretakers. One resided in Puerto Rico but was listed as the lone passenger on the *Brilhante*. Therefore, if the vessel had loaded slaves, he would have been its supercargo.[25] The other was based in Gallinas, in Blanco's employ, perhaps as captain of the barracoon guard. Though González stopped at Porto Praia, he did not deliver the missive.

Additional briefs reveal that González and Vicente Sánchez—a Blanco disciple who figured in the 1840s in slave transport from Gallinas and Río Pongo to Puerto Rico—attempted to buy three condemned ships before deciding on the *Emprendedor*.[26] The briefs explained that problems finding a recycled slaver of good quality in Freetown delayed their arrival to Gallinas. In Blanco's last letter to González before the relationship soured, he congratulated him for loading 447 captives on the *Emprendedor*, adding that he forwarded González's pay to his wife as requested. Here we learn that the captain was on double payroll. Blanco and Martínez paid him separately. Shortly before Blanco's premature praise, Martínez informed the captain that his pay was deposited in his company's account at Havana, in Blanco's name. We also discover that while mariners were paid only for successful ventures, captains were paid regardless of the outcome.[27] Otherwise, González would not have claimed his salary for the interrupted voyage.

Letters for lone Puerto Rican ventures disclose different concerns. Internal organization freed participants from the complexities of tricontinental networking. Such freedom enabled Puerto Rican–based traders to concentrate on the island's greatest weakness—geographic vulnerability to British vigilance. The five letters found on the *Tejo*—all written from Puerto Rico in April 1838—expressed concern over the whereabouts of the *União*, a slaver long overdue to arrive. The Cuban connection was still evident but diminishing. José María Urrutia, captain of the missing vessel, was to deliver letters to Theodore Canot, Tomás Burón Rodríguez in Gallinas, and Cristóbal Aragón in New Cess—all employees of Blanco at the time. But the trio had nothing to do with the return voyage of either the *União* or the *Tejo*.[28] After the condemnation of the latter, two more letters were found, authored by Lorenzo Ruíz of Puerto Rico, first of two captains of the scandalous *Jesús María*. Ruíz wrote Urrutia, captain of the tardy *União* and later the *Carranzano*, to advise him that another slaver, the *Melchor*, arrived in Puerto Rico with its African captives after experiencing difficulty.

Ruíz also mentioned the *Comadrecita*, a slaver that ran into trouble not connected to British vigilance.[29] In addition, the letter sheds light on a man who played a significant role in the Puerto Rican slave trade for the next ten years. Casimiro Capetillo, slave owner of the *Zema*, which the British confiscated in Liberia in 1836, also owned the *Comadrecita*. He was the senior partner of a shipping firm in San Juan. In the late 1840s, he petitioned for slaves ostensibly from the Dutch Antilles.[30] Ruíz warned Urrutia of new methods to thwart landings. In the spring of 1839, Puerto Rican informants advised British agents of the anticipated arrival of the *Merced*, a Puerto Rican schooner built in Baltimore. On reaching the eastern side of the island, the Africans were to be transferred to the *Melchor* and taken to the southwestern side for distribution. To catch the *Melchor*, already laden with Africans from an earlier voyage, someone told its captain the *Merced* had arrived. This attempt to lure it out of hiding and into the path of a British warship failed. In Ruíz's words, the warship "left this port in time to allow the happy arrival of the *Melchor*, and we suppose some perverse person informed her that Urresti [captain of the *Merced*] was expected."[31]

The British vessel of which Ruíz spoke constantly cruised the British islands east of Puerto Rico from Anegada to Anguilla, often disguised as a merchant ship. Ruíz wrote to Urrutia in Gallinas to warn him, as well as to the missing captain in New Cess. He was anxious because he expected to hear from him by way of the *Merced*, which the British had just released at Freetown for want of evidence. He apprised Urrutia that British surveillance had stepped up around Puerto Rico. One ship operated between the northeastern towns of Fajardo and Loíza; two more, between Loíza and Culebra, a Puerto Rican islet facing the Danish Virgins; two others covered the southern shores, along with the camouflaged war brig. Ruíz also noted that British patrols stopped and searched all vessels, even packets, between Puerto Rico and the British Virgins. He cautioned against touching any Caribbean port—even the French and Dutch—because of the cruisers. "With your good chronometer," he advised, "you have no occasion to make land at any of these." Last, Ruíz advised, "It appears best to me for you to steer north as far as the meridian of the town where [your supercargo, Atanasio] Echavarría has his warehouse." His reticent reference indicated Dorado, several miles west of San Juan. He closed speculating that the *Merced* had been caught but that the *Carranzano* just arrived and was ready for the next voyage. Like all good slave smugglers, Urrutia ran trips back-to-back. Ruíz's updates aided him in landing the *União* in Puerto Rico. He was less successful with the *Carranzano*, which was captured without slaves in Liberia. Since Urrutia was the owner of the captives from that voyage, having an empty hold at interception must have softened the blow of his loss as the owner and captain of the condemned vessel, which the British destroyed.[32]

Independence and Interdependence

French links to the Puerto Rican slave trade recurred up to the abolition of slavery in 1873. Previous chapters addressed French general input to the early 1830s and the dwindling complicity of French merchants on the Upper Guinea Coast later in the decade.[33] In the present discussion of independent Puerto Rican expeditions, in at least three cases a Frenchman proved to be a central figure. In Freetown, Sierra Leone, in January 1838 the Mixed Court condemned the *Princéza Africana*. Despite its Portuguese orthography, it was a Spanish vessel. There was nothing unusual about the deception undertaken to promote its Portuguese appearance, nor was there anything extraordinary about its capture and the emancipation of its 222 African captives. But the co-ownership of the captives makes it worthy of note, for it links Puerto Rican interests to the fluidity of French identity. Half the would-be slaves were owned by the brothers Felipe and Juan Batista Lavaca, Basques who migrated from San Sebastián to Puerto Rico in 1810 to assist their uncle, Pedro de Arana, in an unspecified family enterprise.[34] By the 1830s, the brothers were slave smugglers. The other partner was Edouard Combelle, Haitian-born French national who lived in Puerto Rico and St. Thomas. Two months later he reemerged as a central figure in the case of the *Con la Boca*, a lengthy effort that failed to prove that Africans landed in Puerto Rico with the aid of Danish officers in St. Thomas. British authorities could not reconstruct the full itinerary of the expedition, nor could they establish the whereabouts of Combelle and his crew. But depositions confirmed that the Foreign Office continued to identify Danish Caribbean auxiliary until Denmark sold its Gold Coast leases in 1850, lacked the diplomatic leverage to confront cross-national slave expeditions, and remained squeamish about publicizing French participation.[35]

Paper trails fail to establish when Combelle began to traffic slaves for Puerto Rico. But by the time of his exit in mid-1839, he was a seasoned dealer. For his last mission, on the *Casualidade*, he was the captain, the vessel owner, and the owner of its slaves.[36] He commanded an all-French crew, and he was in league with an impressive group of scoundrels. Through Antonio de Brito, captain of the *Tejo*, he purchased the schooner from the Portuguese Italian mulatto, Caetano José Nozzolini, ex-governor of Bissau and cofounder of a slaving dynasty that dominated the Lusophone sector of the Upper Guinea Coast. The captives were provided by Henry (aka Harry) Tucker, a Creole African dynast and Bullom chief who, with others of like pedigree, brokered slave trading between Sherbro and the Spanish Caribbean. The machinations of Tucker and Nozzolini were hardly news to British agents, but records from Combelle's *Casualidade* are the first to link their activities to Puerto Rico.

Letters from the intercepted vessel affirm that Puerto Rican interest groups worked well without Cuban constituents. Heretofore, historians could only assume that Puerto Ricans, like Cubans, Brazilians, and North Americans, resided on the West African coast and negotiated deals with indigenous merchants and potentates. The case of the *Casualidade* offers proof. Pedro Lafarque, a veteran Puerto Rican slave smuggler, and Andrés Anglada, who in 1834 arrived in Puerto Rico from Gerona with his wife and two children, were not only responsible for distributing Combelle's captives on arrival; they went to Sherbro to arrange the current expedition and others.[37]

François Thomé, a Frenchman based in Monrovia, handled logistics for meetings with Chief Henry. Apparently, Tucker held Anglada and Lafarque in high esteem, for he wrote, "You are well aware that when you left my country for Puerto Rico, it was heartbreaking to see you part, but it could not be helped as your business called you home."[38] He then advised that Combelle died of abdominal disorders in May 1839 and that First Mate Joseph Gouy assumed command of the *Casualidade*. Tucker apologized for the small number of captives sent "for lack of wars in this country at the present time." But he promised the return of chaos to higher levels of armed hostility next year.[39] Though French-born Joseph Beaupied and Pierre Fourçade authored grand schemes to sell Afro–Puerto Ricans, slave and free, to Cuban buyers between 1858 and 1873, Combelle worked for Puerto Rico exclusively.[40] His death marked the end of private, individual French connivance in the influx of Africans to the island.

Great Britain's failure to pursue the French connection to the *Casualidade* was based, in part, on greater demands elsewhere. The Foreign Office had just learned that Manding, Peul, and Soninke (called Sarakole in the Spanish Caribbean) jihadists sent war prisoners to Gorée to sell to French settlers in coastal Senegal. Such traffic contributed to *éngagé* schemes in the 1850s, given that some of the captives went to the French Antilles. In an attempt to stop the transatlantic revival and extension of the Gorée trade, the British navy detained the Martinique-bound *Sénégambie*. Though empty, it was fully equipped for the middle passage. Its seizure led to another crisis in Franco-British relations.[41] Palmerston instructed his ambassador in Paris to advise the French government of the role of its subjects in the slave trade to Puerto Rico, citing Combelle, Gouy, and Thomé from the *Casualidade*. He advised the French ambassador in London of the same problem. He also denounced slave traffic in Gorée.[42] But his second missive did not mention the *Casualidade*. In view of the *Sénégambie* controversy, which dominated diplomatic dialogue between the two countries, Puerto Rico was relegated once more to the back burner of antislave trade affairs. Moreover, the directorship of the British Foreign Office fell to Aberdeen, who set about undermining everything Palmerston had achieved.[43]

Twentieth-century historians have commented a great deal on the intermittent Lusitaniazation of West Africa proper, from Senegambia to the equator, from the fifteenth to the nineteenth century.[44] With the exception of the western section of the Ivory Coast, the littoral of every modern-day West African republic was polyglottal in many western European languages, pidgins, and Creole amalgams.[45] The importance of Spanish, however, should not be underestimated. French outdistanced Portuguese in Senegambia by the eighteenth century, and English and Portuguese were more useful on the Lower Guinea

Coast—even in the present-day Francophone republics of Togo, Benin, and Gabon. But in the nineteenth century, Spanish was the lingua franca for much of the Upper Guinea Coast outside Freetown and Monrovia until the end of the Atlantic slave trade. The Manding, Susu, and Fula of the Pongo, the Fula of Futa Jallon and the girth of Sierra Leone; the Temne, Bullom Sherbro, Manding, and Vai of Sherbro Island and Gallinas, from Sierra Leone to Liberia; and the Kru of Liberia, who worked the entire coast as fishermen and slave trade auxiliaries—in essence, any African linked closely with the Atlantic transshipment of captives from Conakry to Cape Palmas—learned commercial Spanish by occupational necessity.[46] The significance of this Iberian language on the Upper Guinea Coast is borne out in two slave ship cases related to the Puerto Rican trade.

To educate the heirs of slave-trading empires in the ways of their clients, some Creole African dynasts sent their children abroad to learn the Spanish language as well as Spanish banking and marketing customs and skills. This strategy was not novel. English slave traders sent their mulatto sons to study shipping in Liverpool when slave commerce was legal. In 1835, the *Preciosa* was captured southwest of St. Thomas. Though the voyage began in Puerto Rico, the crew testified it was headed for Matanzas. Though it was to end in Cuba, Puerto Rico was the only immediate destination for inbound slavers in Danish waters. Ships did not go to Cuba by sailing southwest of the Danish Virgins. Mongo John Ormond's fourteen-year-old son was a passenger. He testified in Havana that his mother took over the business as regent while he trained in the Caribbean, and Spanish was to be the main feature of his studies.[47] In 1841, when the British intercepted the *Segunda Rosario*, also southwest of St. Thomas, two of Isabel Gomes Lightbourn's sons were on board. The trip was slated to end in Puerto Rico. Isabel directed Joseph and Santos to sell the slaves she contributed to the venture—40 out of 293—then proceed to Cuba for lessons to correct their fractured Spanish.[48]

Why did Puerto Rican expeditions favor less-populated Upper Guinea over more densely populated Lower Guinea? First, we must bear in mind that almost all voyages cited here were unsuccessful. As noted earlier, while British patrols intercepted one in five trips between 1811 and 1867, only one in sixteen captives was freed.[49] In view of his ratio and the illustrations in this chapter, there is little room to doubt that from the mid-1830s to the late 1840s—lulls and interruptions notwithstanding—most of the island's captives came from Sierra Leone and Guinea-Conakry. Though Cuban and Puerto Rican slave catchers sailed the Upper Guinea Coast between Conakry and Liberia, with Sierra Leone providing the greatest number of captives from the region—in full view of British-ruled Freetown—Puerto Rican suppliers had greater reason to minimize the risks of seizure.[50] Eltis and others offer this cue. The intricate river systems of Upper Guinea discouraged antislave trade operations. Río Pongo and Gallinas boasted mangrove swamps and sinewy waterways at once formidable and complex. Thus, slave ships escaped British patrols frequently.[51] Fewer captives from less-populated Upper Guinea allowed Puerto Rico to compete with Cuba in this region but not others.

Lower Guinea was a different matter. Togo, Dahomey, and the Nigerian southwest, whose captives embarked mainly from the Bight of Benin, were more vulnerable to British interference.[52] But parties serving Cuban interests could afford to take risks—and they did, thus marking the spectacular influx of Yoruba-speaking slaves from southwest Nigeria and southeast Dahomey. Those serving Puerto Rico could not and for the most part did not. However, they stood less chance of detection by seeking captives from the Niger Delta and the Bight of Biafra in the Nigerian southeast. Both the delta and the southeastern bight, in contrast to the southwestern bight, were cut with waterways that resembled the systems of Upper Guinea, which made abolitionist access similarly difficult.

Puerto Rican interest groups engaged in the same practices associated with slave commerce in larger polities. Slavery consumed lives—above all, the lives of slaves. Thus, slaveholders were slave consumers. As we have seen in Tucker's relations with Combelle, Anglada, and Lafarque, slave traders—be they Spanish, Portuguese, French, Dutch, Danish, or West African Creoles—recognized the behaviors of Puerto Rican slave consumption as something not unusual but typical. It was a market and they served it. But unlike the Dutch, Danes, and Lusophones, the French—especially expatriates—played special roles as hands-on facilitators, albeit their participation varied. Fourçade and Beaupied served Cuba and Puerto Rico, but in the long run they found their niche in cabotage traffic between the two islands. Conversely, Combelle served Puerto Rico alone, and only through the transatlantic corridors of the Upper Guinea Coast.

Cuba always outdistanced Puerto Rico in slave acquisitions. As a result, independent Puerto Rican access to African captives was limited to Gallinas, Sherbro, and the Pongo in Upper Guinea (which yielded Mande-speakers—some Vai but mainly Soninke, Susu, Manding, and especially Gangá); the Niger Delta in Lower Guinea (some Ibibio, according records from the *Temerário*, but mainly Ibo, called jointly "Carabalí"); and ill-defined areas on both sides of the

Congo but few from Angola. Thus, Cuba (and Brazil), not Puerto Rico, received large numbers of Yoruba ("Lucumí") captives from the Bight of Benin. Yet limitations notwithstanding, slaving interests in Puerto Rico overshadowed abolitionist politics until the late 1850s.

Table 6.2. Slave ships from Africa bound for Puerto Rico, 1834–1859

A. Name of vessel, date and location of capture, and nationality

Vessel	Detained/captured	Location	Nationality
Arrogante Mayagüesana	09/17/1834	Mid-Atlantic	Spanish
Josefa	12/04/1835	Sierra Leone	Spanish
Zema	01/25/1836	Liberia	Spanish
Explorador (1)	01/29/1836	Nigeria	Spanish
Luisa (2)	02/09/1836	Angola	Spanish
Vigilante (3)	03/08/1836	Jamaica	Portuguese
Preciosa	07/12/1836	Cuba	Spanish
Negrinha (4)	09/20/1836	Grenada	Portuguese
Fénix (5)	09/26/1836	Grenada	Portuguese
San Nicolás (6)	12/01/1836	Sierra Leone	Spanish
Descubierta	01/14/1837	Nigeria	Spanish
Temerário	01/20/1837	Nigeria	Portuguese
Cinco Amigos (7)	03/08/1837	Liberia	Spanish
Cobra de Africa	05/27/1837	Cameroon	Portuguese
Primoroza	09/25/1837	Príncipe	Portuguese
Vencedora	10/14/1837	Bahamas	Spanish
Felicidade	11/04/1837	Nigeria	Portuguese
Princéza Africana	12/26/1837	Sierra Leone	Portuguese
Con la Boca	02/25/1838	Cuba	Spanish
Gertrúdes	12/28/1838	Sierra Leone	Portuguese
Tejo (8)	01/31/1839	Gabon	Portuguese
Merced	06/18/1839	Liberia	Spanish
Carranzano (9)	06/27/1839	Liberia	Spanish
Casualidade	07/06/1839	Sierra Leone	Portuguese
Brilhante	10/16/1839	Sierra Leone	Portuguese
Segunda Rosario	01/03/1841	St. Thomas	Spanish
Jesús María (10)	01/09/1841	St. Croix	Spanish
Triunfo (11)	01/11/1845	Guinea-Conakry	Spanish
Majesty	02/05/1859	Puerto Rico	United States

Alias names of ships and their nationalities: (1) *Emilio*, Spanish; (2) *Julio*, Spanish; *Diana*, Spanish; *Duke of Genoa*, Italian; (3) *Manoel*, Portuguese; (4) *Norma*, Spanish; (5) *General Mora*, Spanish; (6) *Grande María*, Colombian; (7) *Monserrate*, Spanish; (8) *Fortuna*, Spanish; (9) *Christian*, Danish; (10) *Tres Hermanas*, Spanish; (11) *Atalanta*, Spanish; *Monserrate*, Spanish.

B. Vessel type, tonnage, and nationality

Vessel	Type	Tons	No. in crew	Nationality (no. passengers)
Arrogante Mayagüesana	schooner	96	31	Spanish
Josefa	schooner	55	21	?
Zema	schooner	?	18	Dutch
Explorador	brig	116	29	Spanish
Luisa	brig	?	?	?
Vigilante	brigantine	91	21	Portuguese
Preciosa	schooner	?	17	Spanish (8)
Negrinha	schooner	?	15	Portuguese (1)
Fénix	brigantine	170	27	Portuguese (3)
San Nicolás	brig	227	26	Spanish (1)
Descubierta	schooner	25	11	Spanish
Temerário	brigantine	140	31	Portuguese
Cinco Amigos	schooner	42	18	Spanish
Cobra de Africa	schooner	110	19	French
Primoroza	schooner	58	15	Portuguese
Vencedora	schooner	?	14	Spanish (51)
Felicidade	brigantine	150	26	Portuguese
Princéza Africana	schooner	?	17	Portuguese
Con la Boca	schooner	115	?	? (not given)
Gertrúdes	schooner	35	14	Dutch
Tejo	brig	200	26	Portuguese
Merced	schooner	?	16	Spanish
Carranzano	brigantine	90	16	Spanish
Casualidade	schooner	80	14	French
Brilhante	schooner	77	20	Spanish
Segunda Rosario	schooner	?	21	?
Jesús María	brigantine	?	10	Spanish (7)
Triunfo	brigantine	75	15	Spanish
Majesty	barkentine	?	34	Spanish

C. Captains

Vessel	Captain	Capt.'s nationality	Alternate capt.
Arrogante Mayagüesana	Bartolomé Ferrer	Spanish	—
Josefa	Miguel Calvet	Spanish	Claudio Alvarez
Zema	Agustín Morales	Spanish	Juan Zumárraga
Explorador	José de Inza	Spanish	Ignacio de Aldeçoa
Luisa	Juan Victor Jastram	Spanish	José Pereira Coutto
Vigilante	Miguel Bertinote[a]	Portuguese	Juan Bufo
Preciosa	Santiago Comas	Spanish	—
Negrinha	Manoel Soares[b]	Spanish	—
Fénix	João José António Barbosa	Portuguese	—
San Nicolás	Angel Calsamilia[c]	Spanish	—
Descubierta	Pablo Plá	Spanish	—
Temerário	Camillo Fonseca	Portuguese	—
Cinco Amigos	Pedro Ferrer	Spanish	Salvador Selles
Cobra de Africa	António José Conceição	Portuguese	—
Primoroza	Joaquim Xavier	Portuguese	Daniel Honório Barrozo
Vencedora	Antonio Lloret	Spanish	—
Felicidade	Antínio Guimarães	Portuguese	—
Princéza Africana	José Caragil	Spanish	Fernando Sá da Brandão[f]
Con la Boca	José Ferreira	Spanish	—
Gertrúdes	José António Foro	Portuguese	—
Tejo	António Brito	Portuguese	—
Merced	José Urresti	Spanish	—
Carranzano	José María Urrutia[d]	Spanish	—
Casualidade	Edouard Combelle[e]	French	J. Gouy & A.J. Brito
Brilhante	Francisco González Veiga	Spanish	Francisco García Machado[f]
Segunda Rosario	Francisco Peirano	Spanish	
Jesús María	Lorenzo Ruíz	Spanish	Vicente Morales[f]
Triunfo	Juan Carreras	Spanish	—
Majesty	Rafael Aguilar	Spanish	

a. aka Manoel de Barros.
b. Portuguese-born.
c. Danish-born.
d. aka Nathaniel Crane.
e. aka Edward Campbell.
f. Fraudulent captain.

D. Vessel owners and places of residence

Arrogante Mayagüesana	Bartolomé Ferrer, Puerto Rico
Josefa	Miguel Calvet, Puerto Rico
Zema	Casimiro Capetillo, Puerto Rico
Explorador	Ignacio de Aldeçoa, Spain[a]
Luisa	Estéban Balaguer, Puerto Rico[b]
Vigilante	Pedro Blanco, Cuba and Sierra Leone [c-1]
Preciosa	Edward Yousiff, Guinea-Conakry
Negrinha	Francisco Cardozo Mello, Cape Verde
Fénix	José António Barbosa, Cuba
San Nicolás	Angel Calsamilia, Cuba
Descubierta	José Balaguer, Puerto Rico [c-2]
Temerário	Pedro Martínez, Cuba and Spain
Cinco Amigos	Pedro Ferrer, Puerto Rico
Cobra de Africa	António José da Conceição, Cape Verde
Primoroza	Daniel Honório Barrozo, Cape Verde
Vencedora	?
Felicidade	António Teixeira Guimarães, Cuba and the Azores
Princéza Africana	José Caragil, Spain [c-3]
Con la Boca	?
Gertrúdes	Matías de Brito, Guinea Bissau
Tejo	Francisco de Souza, Dahomey (Benin)
Merced	?
Carranzano	José María Urrutia, Puerto Rico [c-4]
Casualidade	Edouard Combelle, Puerto Rico [c-5,d]
Brilhante	Pedro Blanco, Cuba and Sierra Leone
Segunda Rosario	?
Jesús María	?
Triunfo	Juan Carreras, Puerto Rico
Majesty	?

a. Francisco de Souza, Benin

b. Juan Victor Jastram, Puerto Rico

c. Fraudulent owners: (1) Francisco Cardozo de Mello; (2) Camillo Urbano da Fonseca; (3) Fernando Sá de Brandão; (4) Nathaniel Crane; (5) António José de Brito.

d. Joseph Gouy, Puerto Rico

E. Slave cargo owners and places of residence

Arrogante Mayagüesana	Bartolomé Ferrer, Puerto Rico
Josefa	Estéban Balaguer, Puerto Rico[a]
Zema	Casimiro Capetillo, Puerto Rico
Explorador	Juan de Inza, Spain[b]
Luisa	Estéban Balaguer, Puerto Rico[c]
Vigilante	Francisco Cardozo Mello, Cape Verde
Preciosa	Edward Yousiff, Guinea-Conakry
Negrinha	Francisco Cardozo Mello, Cape Verde
Fénix	José António Barbosa, Cuba
San Nicolás	Pedro Lafarque, Puerto Rico
Descubierta	José Balaguer, Puerto Rico
Temerário	José Ferreira, Portugal
Cinco Amigos	Pedro Ferrer, Puerto Rico
Cobra de Africa	António José da Conceição, Cape Verde
Primoroza	Daniel Honório Barrozo, Cape Verde
Vencedora	Bartolomé Ferrer, Puerto Rico
Felicidade	António Teixeira Guimarães, Cuba, the Azores
Princéza Africana	Juan & Felipe Lavaca, Puerto Rico[d]
Con la Boca	?
Gertrúdes	Rafael Vélez, Puerto Rico
Tejo	Domingo Valdés, legal residence unknown
Merced	?
Carranzano	José María Urrutia, Puerto Rico
Casualidade	Edouard Combelle, Puerto Rico
Brilhante	Pedro Guarch, Puerto Rico
Segunda Rosario	?
Jesús María	?
Triunfo	Juan Carreras, Puerto Rico
Majesty	?

a. Fraudulent owner, Miguel Calvet.
b. Co-owner, Francisco de Souza, Benin.
c. Co-owner, Juan Victor Jastram, Puerto Rico.
d. Co-owner, Edouard Combelle, Cape Verde and Puerto Rico.

F. Where vessels were fitted and supplied

Vessel	Fitted	Supplied	Last American port
Arrogante Mayagüesana	—	Puerto Rico	Puerto Rico
Josefa	Puerto Rico	Puerto Rico	Puerto Rico
Zema	Puerto Rico	St. Thomas	St. Thomas
Explorador	?	?	Bahia[a]
Luisa	?	?	Puerto Rico
Vigilante	—	?	(Cape Verde)
Preciosa	Puerto Rico	Puerto Rico	Puerto Rico
Negrinha	Puerto Rico	?	St. Thomas
Fénix	?	?	Cuba
San Nicolás	New York	St. Thomas	St. Thomas[b]
Descubierta	?	?	Puerto Rico
Temerário	Cape Verde	Guinea Bissau	(Cape Verde)
Cinco Amigos	—	Puerto Rico	St. Thomas
Cobra de Africa	Cape Verde	Cape Verde	(Cape Verde)
Primoroza	Cuba	Cuba	Cuba
Vencedora	?	?	(Cádiz)
Felicidade	Cuba	Cuba	Cuba
Princéza Africana	Puerto Rico	Puerto Rico	Puerto Rico
Con la Boca	?	?	Puerto Rico[c]
Gertrúdes	Puerto Rico	Puerto Rico	Puerto Rico
Tejo	—	Cuba/St. Thomas	St. Thomas
Merced	—	Puerto Rico	Puerto Rico
Carranzano	Puerto Rico	Puerto Rico	St. Thomas
Casualidade	St. Thomas	St. Thomas	St. Thomas[d]
Brilhante	Puerto Rico	Puerto Rico	Puerto Rico
Segunda Rosario	—	St. Thomas	Cuba
Jesús María	?	?	(Canaries)
Triunfo	Puerto Rico	Puerto Rico	Puerto Rico
Majesty	New York	New Orleans	New Orleans

Notes: Places in parentheses indicate a non-American port.

American agents and residences: (a) Pedro Guarch, Puerto Rico;
(b) Juan Martín Hidalgo, Cuba, and Pedro Lafarque, Puerto Rico;
(c) J. F. Dubourg, St. Thomas; (d) Pedro Lafarque and José Andrade, both Puerto Rico.

G. African ports

Vessel	African ports of call[a]	Last African port
Arrogante Mayagüesana	Loango	Loango
Josefa	Cape Mesurado	Cape Mesurado
Zema	C. Mesurado, New Cess, Grand Bass	Setta Kru
Explorador	Mina, Ouidah, C. St. Paul	Luanda[b]
Luisa	Grand Bass, New Cess, Loango	Loango
Vigilante	Gallinas, New Calabar, Bonny	Bonny
Preciosa	Río Pongo	Río Pongo
Negrinha	Gallinas	Gallinas
Fénix	Ouidah, Little Popo, Príncipe	Little Popo
San Nicolás	Sherbro	Sherbro
Descubierta	Bonny, New Cess	New Cess
Temerário	Bonny	Bonny
Cinco Amigos	New Cess	Setta Kru
Cobra de Africa	Príncipe, Bonny	Bonny
Primoroza	Bonny	Bonny
Vencedora	Congo	Congo
Felicidade	Cape Verde, Bonny	Bonny
Princéza Africana	Sherbro, Cape Palmas	Sherbro[a]
Con la Boca	Vicinity of Sierra Leone	Sherbro
Gertrúdes	Guinea Bissau, Sherbro	Sherbro
Tejo	Islands of the Gulf of Guinea	Cape Lopes[b]
Merced	Monrovia, Freetown	New Cess[c]
Carranzano	Monrovia, New Cess	New Cess[d]
Casualidade	Cape Verde, Banana Island	Sherbro[e]
Brilhante	Gallinas	Gallinas
Segunda Rosario	Cape Verde, Río Pongo	Río Pongo[f]
Jesús María	Cape Verde, Sherbro	Sherbro
Triunfo	Gallinas, Río Pongo	Río Pongo
Majesty	Ambriz	?

a. 2 stops at Sherbo; resident agent, Gallinas, Pedro Blanco
b. 3 stops at Cape Lopez, 3 at Gabon; resident agent, Monrovia, "Capt. Tam"
c. 2 stops at Freetown, 4 at New Cess
d. resident agent, Monrovia, N. M. Hick
e. Freetown, François Thomas; Sherbro, Henry Tucker
f. Río Pongo, Isabel Lightbourn and Manoel Porta

H. Slave sites and mortality rates

Vessel	Dominant site	Slaves[a]	Mortality[b]	% Mortality	Months in Africa
Arrogante Mayagüesana	Loango	357	68	19.0	6
Josefa	—	—	—	—	6
Zema	—	—	—	—	6
Explorador	—	—	—	—	6
Luisa	—	—	—	—	6
Vigilante	Niger Delta	248	111	44.7	6
Preciosa	Río Pongo	288	7	2.4	7
Negrinha	Gallinas	340	4	1.2	6
Fénix	Anecho	515	32	6.2	6
San Nicolás	—	—	—	—	6
Descubierta	—	—	—	—	3
Temerário	Niger Delta	358	98	27.4	1
Cinco Amigos	—	—	—	—	3
Cobra de Africa	Cameroon	164	63	38.4	?
Primoroza	Bonny	182	46	25.2	?
Vencedora	Kwanza River	26	0	0	?
Felicidade	Bonny	335	54	16.1	6
Princéza Africana	Sherbro	222	0	0	11
Con la Boca	—	—	—	—	?
Gertrúdes	—	—	—	—	?
Tejo	Sherbro	168	0	0	11
Merced	Gabon	116	0	0	?
Carranzano	New Cess	20	?	?	?
Casualidade	—	—	—	—	2
Brilhante	Sherbro	88	0	0	2
Segunda Rosario	Río Pongo	293	5	1.7	2
Jesús María	Sherbro	280	28	10.0	3
Triunfo[c]	Río Pongo	—	—	—	1
Majesty	Congo	1,050	214	20.4	?

a. Sex distribution omitted for lack of serials.

b. These figures represent slave mortality at the point of interception. They do not include deaths after the vessel's capture.

c. 650 captives were scheduled to board, but the process was interrupted by the British Navy.

I. Liberation site and African regions represented

Vessel	Liberation site	Represented African regions	Bound for Puerto Rico alone
Arrogante Mayagüesana	Freetown	Congo/Angola	yes
Josefa	—	Upper Guinea	yes
Zema	—	Upper Guinea	yes
Explorador	—	Lower Guinea, Congo/Angola	no
Luisa	—	Upper Guinea, Congo/Angola	yes
Vigilante	—	Upper Guinea, Lower Guinea	no
Preciosa	Belize	Upper Guinea	no
Negrinha	Grenada	Upper Guinea	yes
Fénix	Grenada	Lower Guinea	yes
San Nicolás	—	Upper Guinea	yes
Descubierta	—	Upper Guinea	yes
Temerário	Freetown	Upper Guinea	yes
Cinco Amigos	—	Upper Guinea	yes
Cobra de Africa	Freetown	Upper Guinea, Lower Guinea	no
Primoroza	Freetown	Lower Guinea	no
Vencedora	San Juan	Congo/Angola	yes
Felicidade	Freetown	Upper Guinea	no
Princéza Africana	Freetown	Upper Guinea	yes
Con la Boca	—	Upper Guinea	yes
Gertrúdes	—	Upper Guinea	yes
Tejo	Freetown	Lower Guinea, Congo/Angola	yes
Merced	Freetown	Upper Guinea, Lower Guinea	yes
Carranzano	Freetown	Upper Guinea	yes
Casualidade	—	Upper Guinea	yes
Brilhante	Freetown	Upper Guinea	no
Segunda Rosario	Freetown	Upper Guinea	no
Jesús María	Havana	Upper Guinea	yes
Triunfo	—	Upper Guinea	yes
Majesty	San Juan	Congo/Angola	yes

J. Additional remarks on each vessel

Arrogante Mayagüesana	Captain was the brother of Pedro Ferrer of Mayagüez and Barcelona.
Josefa	Detained first on November 17 but released for lack of evidence.
Explorador	In its second stage of a double voyage.[c,e]
Vigilante	Cabo Rojo PR named; a different vessel by the same name escaped in 1839.
Preciosa	Free Africans on board: 4 Kru sailors (Sherbro); 4 traders (Pongo).[a,d]
Negrinha	Future captain Juan Mariano Aldeçoa of Puerto Rico listed as passenger.
Fénix	Unnamed passengers: 2 Spaniards and 2 Frenchmen.[a]
San Nicolás	One Thomian passenger; logbook in French; slaveowner listed as supercargo.
Temerário	Ibo and Ibibio captives mutinied in the Niger Delta.
Cinco Amigos	Captain was the brother of Bartolomé Ferrer. See *Arrogante Mayagüesana* above.
Cobra	Voyage began in Havana, contrary to papers citing Cape Verde.[b]
Primoroza	Crew recruited in Puerto Rico and St. Thomas.
Vencedora	Cabotage: Cargo owner Bartolomé Ferrer sold 7 captives to Cuban buyers.
Felicidade	Included sailors shipwrecked at Bonny from previous slaving voyages.
Con la Boca	Edouard Combelle implicated; crew included men abandoned at Freetown.
Tejo	Letters from Puerto Rico name ships; slated to land 400 captives.[e]
Merced	British boarded 3 times before seizure; some captives secreted away.
Casualidade	Letters between African and Puerto Rican slave traders found on board.
Brilhante	Letters reveal business strains.[c,e]
Segunda Rosario	Letters reveal slaving procedures among mulatto dynasts in Pongo.[a]
Jesús María	Vicente Morales, only known Puerto Rican Creole to captain a slave ship.
Triunfo	References to Canot's slaving activities at Cape Mount, Liberia.
Majesty	Largest expedition in the history of the Puerto Rican slave trade.

Sources for table 6.2

PP: vols. 15, 16, 18, 20, 21, 23, 36, 40.

PRO: FO 84: 354, 355.

AHN: PRG, legajos, 5.079/16, 5.082.29, 5.088/25; Estado, legajo 8020/45.

AGPR: GE:E, caja 68.

ANC: RCO, legajos 101.85, 121.73, 121.75, 161.58 180, 164.396.

GSC, legajo 941.33176.

continued

GG, legajo 565.27942.

RC, legajo 148.7306.

Note: In neither structure, content, nor context does this table resemble the appendix provided by Morales Carrión in his *Trata*. Several vessels he named are omitted here for lack of detail, though he also made use of British source materials. There were efforts, for example, to land slaves between 1847 and 1859—the greatest chronological gap in records for the Puerto Rican slave trade—and some may have succeeded. Such undertakings, however, were documented sparsely or not at all. Whatever the case, proof for them is wanting. On the other hand, 20 of the 29 vessels in this table do not appear in Morales's list. In essence, what served the purposes of his appendix—to identify and annotate briefly 34 vessels directly and indirectly tied to the Puerto Rican slave trade between 1818 and 1864—do not serve mine. Thus, the illustrations above do not include all Puerto Rican voyages that came to the attention of maritime abolitionist authorities.

a. Escaped condemnation.

b. Freelance expedition; no prearranged contracts, purchases, or instructions; ordered to land slaves wherever expedient after crossing the Atlantic.

c. Pedro Blanco involved beyond vessel or cargo ownership.

d. Pedro Martínez involved beyond vessel or cargo ownership.

e. Francisco de Souza involved beyond vessel or cargo ownership.

III

Mare Liberum

7

South Atlantic East

Cycles of Revival and Decline

Three factors guided the Puerto Rican slave trade after 1835. All of them reflected changing conditions in Africa, Europe, and the Caribbean, which distinguished patterns of acquisition and transport from the earlier years. These factors were: religious upheavals and economic rivalries that triggered transformations in West African political structures from the savannas to the coast; increased Anglo-Spanish tension resulting from British consular reports from San Juan; and the culmination and disintegration of slave trade policy during the incumbency of Governor Rafael de Arístegüi. This chapter considers the first factor.

Compared to Upper Guinea, Lower Guinea, the Congo, and Angola played minor roles in the slave trade to Puerto Rico. Cuba relied heavily on all these regions, as well as on Mozambique. What militated against Puerto Rico's following Cuba's example of regional girth and diversity? At the same time, what constituted the Puerto Rico difference beyond West African water systems and a triad of European support hostile to British surveillance? Previous chapters addressed some of these concerns. Here, emphasizing social and commercial ties between the coast and the interior, I consider the forces of political change. After a brief overview, discussions will highlight three West African contingencies—polytheists, Muslims, and Christian Creoles—and their impact on the flow of west-bound traffic. These themes draw Puerto Rico further into the crosscurrents of its cultural formation by exploring the social, political, and economic origins of its African-born population.

Political Cultures of Slave Acquisition

The 1840s etched the limits of Anglo-Spanish abolitionist diplomacy in high relief. Slave traders proved as resourceful as ever. Declining abolitionist motivation, policy confusion, and tactical disorientation contributed to the success of Puerto Rican slaving activities in its final years. Inter-Caribbean slave traffic was always a sore spot between Spain and Great Britain, and Puerto Rico, not Cuba, was the principal transgressor. With centuries of legal and illegal trade relations with the non-Hispanic islands, it was better situated to benefit from the aid of its foreign neighbors.[1]

Despite its proximity to the Bahamas and Jamaica, Cuba was relatively isolated in its relations with other islands vis-à-vis slaving activities. Content with its sophisticated networks for direct imports from East, West, and Southwest Central Africa, Cuba did not rely on its neighbors for slaves. In terms of British vigilance, neither Jamaica—too distant and too busy—nor the Bahamas—comparatively underdeveloped and understaffed—threatened Cuban slaving operations. On the other hand, Puerto Rico was as much the alpha of the Lesser Antilles as it was the omega of the Greater Antilles. When necessary, it could rely on old links with its French, Dutch, and Danish Caribbean neighbors for African captives, in spite of the British Barbadian naval base. Direct African imports to Puerto Rico, including Cuban-assisted ventures, did not cease until 1847. But between 1845 and 1847, when Atlantic corridors proved too hazardous for direct landings and when internal forces in Puerto Rico militated against the continued feasibility of such voyages, non-Hispanic ports resumed reexport maneuvers. As we shall see in Chapter 9, there is incontrovertible evidence of the use of these maneuvers as late as 1850.

Table 4.1 demonstrates Puerto Rico's ongoing ability to launch independent expeditions. Havana remained the primary proprietary port for the Spanish Caribbean. But beyond the Cuban capital, with four ships charged to its own ports, Puerto Rico surpassed both Matanzas and Santiago by 50 percent. Yet naval reports for 1839 signaled the end of one era and the beginning of another. Regionally differentiated data for that year show that only eighteen out of sixty-one intercepted vessels had slaves on board. Lower Guinea, the Congo, and Angola lost ground as prime sources. Though Upper Guinea did not outshine other regions with consistency, statistics for 1839 suggest that it had come into its own. Table 7.1 shows that Upper Guinea not only achieved parity with Lower Guinea, but in the unexplained absence of Angola, both surpassed the Congo Basin.

Decline in the influx of Africans to Puerto Rico was evident by 1835. Morales

Table 7.1. Vessels captured by the Royal Navy with slaves on board, 1839

Port	Ships	Percentage
Upper Guinea		
Bissau (Guinea Bissau)	1	14.3
Pongo (Guinea-Conakry)	1	14.3
Sherbro (Sierra Leone)	3	42.8
Gallinas (Sierra Leone)	1	14.3
New Cess (Liberia)	1	14.3
Total	7	100.0
Lower Guinea		
Lagos (Nigeria)	2	28.5
Brass (Nigeria)	1	14.3
Nun (Nigeria)	1	14.3
Calabar (Nigeria)	3	42.9
Total	7	100.0
Congo-Angola		
Cape Lopes (Gabon)	2	50.0
Sette Cam (Congo-Brazzaville)	1	25.0
Cabinda (Angola)	1	25.0
Total	4	100.0

Source: Great Britain, *Parliamentary Papers*, vol. 20. <tnts>*Note:* Information in parentheses was added.

Carrión credits British persistence for the wane. Focusing on Ponce, Scarano substantiates the approximate start of the decrease. Foregrounding direct voyages, tables in the previous chapter support the conclusions of both scholars, for they demonstrate that after 1839, landings trickled to a minimum. Nonetheless, these two sources, with the tables in chapter 6, must be weighed within the context of their foci. We have seen that British efforts thwarted the arrival of many slave ships bound for Puerto Rico between 1834 and 1845. But we have no idea how many escaped.

Great Britain's war against the slave trade was as admirable and formidable as it was self-serving and segmented. Eschewing economic motives, Morales Carrión veils British economic incentives with a successful altruism that is not borne out in the record.[2] Scarano's statistics for Ponce are conclusive but not consistently representative. Albeit Ponce's influx of 225 African captives per annum between 1821 and 1828 dropped to nearly half that amount between 1834 and 1836, there are no comparable municipal studies to suggest that the decline was islandwide.[3] Nor in terms of slaveholding and its relation to sugar production did Ponce surpass neighboring towns by leaps and bounds. In the peak years of sugar production in Ponce, roughly 1830 to 1850, Mayagüez and Guayama were never far behind. Between 1812 and 1828, the slave populations of Ponce and Mayagüez were almost identical in size. Though Guayama had fewer slaves at that time, its percentage of slaves to nonslaves was higher than that of its principal municipal competitors. Thus, figures for Ponce's declining slave market are not always relevant to slave arrivals for the island as a whole. Indeed, there is proof that in the wake of Ponce's shrinking influx, Mayagüez and Guayama did not follow suit, for they made last-ditch efforts to obtain African captives for their own consumption by way of their own ports exclusively.[4] But these short-lived attempts to pick up where Ponce trailed are less important than the proslavery forces that continued to operate in the face of international opposition.

Littoral Dynasties: Creole Brokers on the Upper Guinea Coast

Pedro Blanco refined tactics for quick loading and embarkation. Stable relations with local suppliers—especially the Vai—helped entrench the Blanco machine in Gallinas. Because of him, Spaniards enjoyed some degree of influence in internal affairs, albeit they lacked any real authority or political control. On the other hand, slave commerce in Río Pongo rested delicately on coastal mulatto hegemony, royal indigenous matrilineality, and good relations with the leaders of inland Muslim polities. Hispanophone slave traders favored the Pongo no less than Gallinas or Sherbro, where the Afro-English Tuckers likewise served as intermediaries. Smugglers serving Puerto Rico targeted Río Pongo as an important source in the 1840s, when the African slave trade to the island began its irreversible decline. Thus, an examination of slave trade mechanisms vis-à-vis sociopolitical relations among the Pongo's indigenous peoples, Creole mixed-bloods, and Europeans is useful to help illustrate problematics of the period.

Many experts who have studied the decline of transatlantic slave commerce place greater emphasis on prepartition politics, the success of British abolitionism, and the impact of that success on African elites who relied on the external slave trade. As compared with the latter, a great deal of attention has focused on the changing dynamics of internal slave trading for internal consumption, especially the organization of slave plantations for the production of palm nuts, peanuts, and their by-products now in demand as items of legitimate trade for British and French industrial enterprises. But our understanding of continued slave acquisitions for transoceanic export remains perforated. We know little about the supply side of the trade as it was carried out by the Luso-Brazilians, Hispano-Cubans, and Hispano–Puerto Ricans. Nor do we have a sense of how African politics dictated changing commercial relations between these brokers and African brokers on the coast.

While quantitative patterns are fairly clear—thanks to the efforts of Philip Curtin, David Eltis, Martin Klein, Patrick Manning, and others—qualitative examinations are needed to shed light on the sociocultural and sociopolitical dimensions of the traffic, first and foremost in the context of Spanish Caribbean concerns. The problem is especially acute for the Upper Guinea Coast, where slaving was thought to have plummeted by the 1840s, and for the Congo-Angola region, where scholarly attention declines after the 1830s and stops in the 1850s, when Brazil ceased to import slaves. Despite the silence of Spanish texts on internal African affairs as they related to the export of captives, other sources reveal the changing contours of indigenous politics, Euro-African hybridity, and their connection to slave acquisitions in Puerto Rico.

Cape Verdean–born Caetano José Nozzolini, an indirect business partner of Edouard Combelle, was the son of a local mulatto and an Italian seaman. Like other foreigners in areas between Senegambia and Guinea-Conakry, his success in Guinea Bissau was based on a pivotal marriage.[5] Though his wife, Aurélia Correia, was a Creole mixed-blood, the inhabitants of Bissau and Cacheu awarded her family a great deal of prestige because of her royal Bijago lineage. It was only through his wife that Nozzolini, an outsider, became the undisputed lord of a slave-smuggling empire that spanned the Lusophone area of the Upper Guinea Coast.

The youth found on the *Preciosa*—cited in chapter 6—was John Ormond III. His grandfather, Ormond, *père*, was an English slave trader who won local recognition and prestige by marrying into Susu royalty. Ormond, *fils*, the infamous Mongo John, was born and educated in England. Treated rather shabbily in school, the mulatto went to Africa to assume his father's business. On the death of a maternal uncle, he became paramount chief of Bangalang, tucked safely in the complex waters of Río Pongo in Guinea-Conakry. The maternity of John Ormond III is not certain. His mother may have been Mongo John's favorite consort, Esther Tyler, the quadroon daughter of an English vicar turned slave trader. The mother to whom he referred in his testimony in Havana was probably a close Susu relative. Tyler died of poisoning at the age of twenty many years before.[6]

Unlike the case in other areas of the upper littoral, most women of circum-Bangalang were excluded from positions of leadership. However, the Lightbourn women ranked among the exceptions. Isabel was the descendant of Susu-Portuguese slave traders.[7] When Ambrósio Gomes, a Portuguese captain, married Bibiana Vaz, a Bissau mulatto, sometime in the 1680s, he joined her family's slaving business at Cacheu. At some point, the Gomes line began to Anglicize, as family members moved south to Bakin in Río Pongo. In 1788, for example, the mulatto chief Manuel Gomes studied maritime commerce in Liverpool rather than in Lisbon or Coimbra. Early in the nineteenth century, his daughter, Bailey Gomes, a slave merchant in her own right, married an Anglo-American, Paul Lightbourn, producing four children, including Isabel. Isabel married an unknown local, certainly a Creole, with whom she had four sons. On widowhood, she entered into professional and personal relations with Benjamin Campbell, the British merchant cited in Chapter 6.[8] At the professional level, he and a Gorée-based Frenchman supplied her with slave ship paraphernalia and provisions for slave barracoons. Though sensitive to British surveillance, as a supplier in legitimate (nonhuman) trade, Campbell was safe from prosecution. At the personal level, he was the father of Isabel's four additional children, including one of her two sons taken off the Puerto Rican *Segunda Rosario* in 1841. Their daughters were educated in France, England, and the United States. Both married Englishmen; one settled in Baltimore, the other in London. Both sets of Isabel's sons followed in the family business.[9]

Mongo John was succeeded by his brother, William.[10] Susu authorities recognized that William lacked the cunning and toughness of his brother. The deposition of Ormond III indicated that his uncle could not rule Bangalang alone. By identifying his "mother" rather than his uncle as a paramount potentate in Bangalang, he implied that leadership was divided into two spheres: William governed political affairs, and the unnamed Susu kinswoman took charge of economic affairs—that is, international slaving. Mongo John's death precipitated large-scale revolts involving several thousand slaves, some of whom were exploited locally, while others were destined for the Americas.[11] It also inspired armed struggles among Creole slave-trading families, such as the Lightbourns and especially the Fabers, who aspired to displace the heirs of Mongo John. Moreover, the Ormond faction was on the verge of open hostility with the Fula imamate as it expanded from Futa Jallon to the ports of Bangalang and the Susu capital at Thia.

Thus, young Ormond's absence had triple meaning: business training in

Cuba; preparation for succession in the wake of his uncle's feeble rule; and personal safety during the immediate crisis. The death of Kai Yende, king of the Kati, who worked with Ormond dynasts as intermediaries between Fula slave hunters and Spanish merchants, together with the death of William Ormond himself, sparked new slave revolts that Fula and Creole forces suppressed. To better monitor profits from both the slave trade with Spanish merchants and the peanut trade with French and British merchants, the Fula established themselves as direct rulers of Bangalang. They obliterated the Ormond-Susu-Kati power base and recognized the Lightbourns and Fabers as the only intermediaries between European buyers and themselves.[12] Bangalang lost its autonomy as a creoledom. Like Ouidah in Dahomey, it became a puppet polity subject to the varied interests of indigenous African lords in the interior.

When Pedro Blanco retired, Gallinas was taken over by his Spanish protégés, whose eastward expansion into Liberia undermined Canot's attempts to make it on his own. By the middle of the 1840s, the Lightbourns and their Spanish agents brokered much of the Upper Guinea Coast, with occasional assistance from French traders at Gorée.[13] The Tuckers of Sherbro lost considerable influence thanks to antislave trade treaties with British agents. The Lightbourns pulled vestiges of local slave trade interest groups into their orbit.[14] The Nozzolinis stood to be their only competition once the Brazilian slave trade slowed a halt between 1850 and 1854, though ultimately they posed no threat. The proximity of Guinea-Bissau to the British settlement at Bathurst (Banjul) on the Gambia discouraged Spanish traders from relying too heavily on Dom Caetano. Furthermore, he died of dysentery in 1850.[15] By the middle of the decade, occasional succor from independent French traders—linked to the Lightbourns and thus to the Puerto Rican slave market—gave way to the *engagé* program, which lasted until 1859, when the African slave trade to Puerto Rico ceased.[16] The Lightbourns supplied Cuba with captives until the late 1860s. French expansion in Upper Guinea, along with declining demands for African slaves in Cuba, encouraged them to rely on legitimate trade exclusively.[17]

War, Trade, and the Changing Taxonomy of African Identity

Early in the sixteenth century, Spain prohibited the landing of Islamic Africans in its American colonies. Authorities in Puerto Rico and elsewhere in the Greater Antilles labeled the Wolof of Senegambia—along with mulattoes, Maghribines, and Levantine Afroids—as catalysts in slave revolts. Stereotyped as *mala casta* who set poor examples for Amerindians and non-Islamic Africans, they were forbidden entry by the Crown under severe penalty.[18] But by the nineteenth century, Spanish laws and slaveholders were less fastidious in this regard. Experience proved that sub-Sahara Africans—be they polytheists or Muslims, "Guineamen" or Bantu—could be captured and molded into some semblance of submission, on the one hand, and given to sustained militant resistance, on the other.[19]

From the eighteenth century onward, Islamic revival and expansion in Senegambia and Upper Guinea rendered Muslims central to the process of slave acquisition as captives as well as suppliers. The rise of aggressive, imperialistic reinscriptions of Islamic politics in Upper Guinea corresponded to the Spanish crisis of British abolitionist politics. The results defined an important epistemological break. By the 1820s, Spanish slaveholders were largely indifferent to the diversity of African identity and the comparative value attributed to it. By this time, postcaptive taxonomies of precaptive origins did little more than describe. On legal documents, auction announcements, and runaway notices, reference to ethnic and national names for *negros de nación* no longer represented African heterogeneity. Declining in use, especially in sales notices in Puerto Rico, they functioned as codependent components of black representation itself—a new discourse that grouped, conflated, and ultimately subsumed all Africans and their Creole progeny under the rubric of *negros*, a singular sociocultural category undifferentiated politically by phenotype, language, or place of birth.[20]

Tables in chapter 6 verify that most African-born Puerto Ricans came from Upper Guinea in the 1830s. Though slave traffic to the island dropped in the 1840s, Upper Guinea, rather than Lower Guinea and subequatorial Africa, continued to be the main source. Thus, closer regional examinations are in order, in particular, those reflecting internal developments that influenced the continuity of slave acquisition as a transatlantic enterprise. British reports for the 1840s stressed that Sherbro and Gallinas were obstacles to maritime cessation. Though naval officers exacted treaties from paramount chiefs and burned Spanish slave factories within chiefdoms subject to suppressionist accords, success was often temporary. Up to the end of the decade, slave merchants simply fled to Río Pongo and Bissau where the Lightbourns, the Nozzolinis, and other African Creole families welcomed their business. Abolitionist aggression was equally inconsistent north of Sierra Leone. Several factors contributed to the contrast: the waterways of the Pongo; declarations of Portuguese suzerainty over Bissau, Cacheu, and the Bissago archipelago; and, despite a British presence along the Gambia, limited British influence between Senegal and Guinea-Conakry, where French forces exerted their interests. To the end of the 1840s, Sierra Leone, beyond Freetown, was an important but an increasingly mercurial source of captives—as was Liberia beyond Monrovia. By comparison, Río Pongo and circum-Bissau continued to function as sources and bulking stations for the Spanish slave trade.[21]

When the British bombed the harbor of Rio de Janeiro in 1850, the African slave trade to Brazil ended soon after. In Cuba, by the 1860s it slowed to a trickle, ending at some unknown date in the 1870s. With the exception of the *Majesty* in 1859, documented slave traffic to Puerto Rico ended in the summer of 1847. Though British naval aggressions ended the Brazilian trade, Lusophone brokerage for the Spanish islands declined before midcentury. In Lower Guinea, by the 1850s British abolitionism and expansionism discouraged slave exports from the notorious Bights of Benin and Biafra as well as from the Gold Coast, where slave exports were less voluminous than elsewhere before and after 1815. Other forces, however—such as the outcome of the Civil War in the United States and clashes between French and Muslim expansionists in Upper Guinea—combined with British energies to signal the close of the slave trade to Cuba. Earlier cessation in Puerto Rico was linked to different factors. In addition to professed fears of African-led slave revolts, for example, the island never recovered from the politics of its first abolitionist governor, Juan de la Pezuela, who rather perversely equated abolition with the selling of Puerto Rican slaves to Cuba.[22] As we explore the structures of slave acquisition in Upper Guinea, it will become clear that British diplomacy and maritime vigilance played ephemeral roles in ending the slave trade to Puerto Rico.

The arrival of John Ormond, *père*, to Río Pongo in the late eighteenth century coincided with the consolidation of a widely respected imamate in Futa Jallon. It consisted of nine multiethnic provinces—largely Fula (aka Peul), Susu, Manding, and Jallonke—united in the name of Islam.[23] Each provincial division was headed by an *alfa*, or chief. The movement toward the centralization of Futa Jallon was linked to the desire of its inhabitants to unite and fortify themselves against the slave trade and the devastation that always accompanied it. Yet each province enjoyed considerable autonomy, and a parliamentary Council of Elders kept the power of the imam, or *almami*, in check. In spite of its status as the official state religious culture, Islam spread slowly, especially among the cattle-herding Fula in the countryside. Furthermore, in 1751, after the death of the first almami, Karamoko Alfa, his successor, Ibrahim

Sory, launched a series of jihads against neighboring polities. His aggressions had nothing to do with Islam. They were raids for captives for both local use and for sale to Europeans on the coast. With power shared strenuously between two aristocratic, sedentary Fula families—the descendants of Alfa and the descendants of Sory—life in mountainous Futa Jallon followed Koranic precepts. By contrast, its economy was rooted in slave commerce for local consumption and export. This brand of state building—state formation for self-defense against the chaos of the slave trade, followed by the adoption of slave trading by the same newly formed government that sought to separate itself from it—was duplicated in other areas and regions of the African continent, before and after Great Britain inaugurated the abolitionist movement. Though polytheists and Muslims alike in Sierra Leone, Liberia, Ghana, Dahomey, Togo, Nigeria, the Congo, Angola, and the hinterlands of East Africa practiced state protection, or state emancipation, at the expense of their neighbors, after Sory's death in 1791 Islam was the only religious culture permitted in the imamate.[24]

The death of John Ormond, *fils*, early in the 1830s created fissures in a bond of cross-cultural interdependency that characterized slave trading in Upper Guinea. But in the long run, it merely marked a shifting of coastal hegemony among rival Afro-European slave-trading families. Between the early 1820s and the early 1840s, Afro-Portuguese mulattoes of circum-Bissau and their Anglicized counterparts of Río Pongo forged alliances with Muslim governments of the interior. In August 1843, Ahmed Sanha, shaykh of Manding Badora, ceded the territory of Ganjarra to Portuguese administration. It seems that the treaty formed part of a series of slave trade accords that Caetano Nozzolini initiated. With greater bearing on Puerto Rico, two clans based in the Pongo system—the Fabers and the Lightbourns—allied themselves with the Fula imam of Futa Jallon sometime between 1839 and 1841.[25] As with most inland suppliers of west-bound captives, be they Muslim or not, royal and theocratic leaders in Futa Jallon concerned themselves with commercial access to the Atlantic by way of political—if not outright autocratic—control over non-Islamic intermediaries and good diplomatic relations with Creole intermediaries, over whom they often exercised final authority.[26]

Summarizing the impact of slave traffic on Islamic state security between the interior and littoral, Martin Klein observed that jihad leaders often depended on access to horses and firearms. He also noted, with others, that the jihad lost its religious character by the close of the 1700s and that Muslim expansion became an excuse for the enslavement of non-Muslims on the frontiers of Futa

Jallon. According to Klein, the popular exchange of slaves for European goods explains the oppressive character of the new regimes toward non-Muslims, whom they enslaved en masse and sold on the coast or gathered into slave villages. Such interpretations of jihad affected political activity on the Pongo. Further inland, around the Niger, Klein noted that the Tukulor jihadist al-Hajj Umar Tal and his short line of successors needed guns to establish a vast Islamic commonwealth beyond their Senegalese homeland. They sought goods that could be exchanged for weapons, and they sought booty, above all slave women, to reward their soldiers. No commodity could bring as quick and as sure a return as slaves. They traded in slaves to survive. Boubacar Barry observes that slave labor in Futa Jallon "freed the aristocracy to take its hand off productive work, concentrating wholeheartedly on politics and slave raiding along with the study and explanation of holy scripture, while nurturing the social groups needed to shore up its domination and to perpetuate it."[27]

The ascendancy of John Ormond, *fils*, around 1800 was not without obstacles. Having reinforced his father's amicable influence with nominal control, he was supplied by the Kati and Baga with war prisoners and victims of kidnapping. He also nurtured his father's relations with the Fula imamate.[28] Since the jihads of the eighteenth century, the Susu and the Fula fought to control the Pongo slave trade. A matrilineal member of the Susu nobility, young Mongo John was declared paramount chief of Bangalang, some fifteen miles from the mouth of the river. To remove his domain from the path of recurring Fula-Susu conflict, he struck an agreement with Ibrahim Sory, imam of Futa Jallon, which gave him autonomy in exchange for connecting the imamate to markets for the export of gold, hides, rice, ivory, and slaves.[29] The accord proved sound. When the Fula suppressed the Susu, Bangalang remained independent. While Mongo John shared the Pongo trade with other Creole dynasts such as the Fabers of Sangha, the Lightbourns of Faringuia, the Fernandeses of Bereira, the Skeltons of Kissi, and the Gomeses of Bakia, his relationship with the imamate placed him in a class apart.[30] His objective and that of the Fula were one in the same: that Río Pongo remain linked to Futa Jallon as the prime terminus for Manding, Soninke, and Dyula caravans from Malian emporia and other commercial centers along the Niger Bend. Among Euro-African families between the Núñez and Scarcies Rivers, Ormond's primacy was firm.

Mongo John's demise alarmed the imamate. Given that other river outlets were more vulnerable to abolitionist surveillance, any upset in the balance of power would hem in Niger merchants and Fula brokers. Alternative outlets for the Fula of Futa Jallon had diminished. Moreover, internal hostilities could encumber slave traffic from the upper and lower Pongo to the coast. Along with slaves, the Kati, the Baga, and the Susu were in open rebellion on learning of Mongo John's death sometime between 1829 and 1833. Adding to the mix, Creole clans fought each other in 1838 with indigenous slave armies, which they formed in the wake of earlier rebellions.[31] Fula intervention settled hostilities in the Pongo creoledoms by displacing Ormond's brother, William, and occupying Bangalang as a prefecture. William died soon after, but the fate of his nephew, Mongo John's son, is unknown. Documents on the teenager's whereabouts end with his detention in Havana after the capture of the Puerto Rican–registered *Preciosa* in 1836.

In the absence of an Ormond heir, the Fula established Bangalang as a lowland administrative center and a watchtower to maintain peace among the Pongo's volatile factions and to keep tabs on commercial activities with Europeans. Thus, slave trading shifted from Bangalang to the dominions of the Fabers and the Lightbourns. Both clans turned their attention to native revolts, with military forces from highland Futa Jallon joining armies of clan-owned slaves. Reinforced vassalage quelled further rebellions among indigenous groups. Cultivating favor with the Fula imamate and tied to other Creole families by strategic marriages, the Lightbourns shared power and influence in upper Pongo with the Fabers. Despite continued clashes with rival families and ongoing resentment from local indigenous rulers over the administrative and military presence of the Fula in the Pongo area, the Fabers and the Lightbourns inherited the Ormond machine. The latter dominated the Pongo economy for the remainder of the century.[32]

Pongo struggles augmented slaving operations at Gallinas, which straddled the border of Sierra Leone and Liberia. This cluster of dubiously confederated Vai chieftaincies exported 9,000 to 10,000 slaves to Cuba, Puerto Rico, and Brazil in 1840. Exasperated, British forces blockaded Gallinas for several months. Twenty-one ships with 13,000 prepaid captives were intercepted, tried, and condemned by either the Vice-Admiralty Court or the Court of the Mixed Commissions. Five vessels escaped with 1,506 slaves. Taking action—which Aberdeen challenged when Palmerston left office—the British burned eight Spanish factories in Gallinas, liberated 840 slaves held for shipment, and destroyed the equivalent of $500,000 in property.[33] While some Spaniards joined Theodore Canot at Cape Mount, Liberia, others fled to Nozzolini's new stronghold at Río Núñez in Guinea-Bissau. But Nozzolini could not capitalize on temporary instability on the Pongo. At odds with non-Muslim middlemen and with the British for their occupation of nearby Bulama Island, he returned to Cape Verde to broker slave commerce from there.[34] Six ships with 1,500 captives left Bissau in 1842.[35] Though abolitionists reported that slaving between the Gambia and Sierra Leone Rivers had ceased, by 1843 Río Pongo returned to its former prosperity.[36] The following year, Puerto Rican slaving expeditions returned to Pongo waters.

In 1844, the Admiralty reported the revival of slave traffic from Gallinas. In Nozzolini's absence from Bissau, direct trading from there nearly ceased.[37] His return to Cape Verde provided added importance to his homeland in the 1840s. Prior to 1839, when Great Britain outlawed the use of the Portuguese flag to protect Spanish slaving expeditions, these Sahelian islands supplied slave ships with false papers and fresh provisions after crossing the Atlantic. Direct return voyages from the Pongo and Núñez Rivers, Gallinas, Sherbro, and Cape Mount were still evident in the mid-1840s. But many captives were also collected from these same outlets and taken to Cape Verde, where larger vessels were prepared for return trips. The islands were supply centers and counterfeiting markets for the outbound and bulking stations for the inbound. Thus, self-exile from Bissau and self-repatriation to Cape Verde suited Nozzolini well. When French settlers and merchants in Gorée disrupted Afro-French commerce, they had limited access to domestic slaves, often, but not always, polytheists captured in the wake of declining Bambara (aka Bamana) hegemony in the kingdoms of Segu and Kaarta, Fula politics in Macina, and Tukulor expansion from Futa Toro in Senegal to the Niger Bend in Mali.[38] From Cape Verde, Nozzolini not only filled slavers with captives from Río Pongo, Sherbro, and Gallinas, he also provided French communities in coastal Senegal with slaves for domestic use.[39]

Table 7.1 shows that activities in 1844 forewarned of antislave trade failures in the 1850s. Though many coastal leaders signed suppressionist treaties with the British government, for the next four years slaving flourished in all areas of the Upper Guinea Coast. Misinformation continued to be a source of the problem. In 1847, the Royal Navy reported that slaves were no longer exported from Río Pongo because of local interests in surplus farming.[40] The report stemmed from statistics stating that, of the five ships captured in Upper Guinea waters, none came from the Pongo. While the Lightbourns began peanut production for European markets in the 1830s, as we shall see in Chapter 8, between 1845 and 1847 they still shipped slaves to Puerto Rico. In other words, vis-à-vis slave traffic to the Spanish Caribbean, reports crisscrossing the British Admiralty, the

British Colonial Office, and the British Foreign Office failed to recognize the extent to which suppliers mixed slaving with legitimate trade. In 1848, of the thirty-one vessels seized between Senegal and Angola, fifteen came from the Upper Guinea Coast, eleven between Sherbro and Cape Palmas, two from Freetown, and one from Río Pongo. Yet the authors of that same report observed that Río Pongo was the only slave port remaining in Upper Guinea at the close of 1848. They seemed oblivious to data indicating that Bissau, Sherbro, and Gallinas, as well as Pongo, remained active slave entrepôts.[41]

In 1848, the Vai chiefs of Gallinas expelled all Spaniards after the British—once again—burned their slave factories. British naval officers lauded the action as a victory for the abolitionist cause, for they identified Gallinas as the favorite haunt of slave traders serving Cuba and Puerto Rico for the last 150 years. Their miscalculation is noteworthy given that Cuba and Puerto Rico relied on the British for slaves recurrently from 1713 to 1807. Furthermore, linguistic evidence for Puerto Rico does not support a noticeable presence of captives exported from Gallinas—mainly Manding and Gangá but also Vai—prior to 1780.[42] In another report, Nozzolini was also said to have returned to British-occupied Bulama in circum-Bissau, where he started anew as a respectable peanut farmer. This was another example of miscommunication. Other British reports continued to cite all of Portuguese Guinea, along with the Pongo, Sherbro, and Gallinas, as major depots for slaving expeditions destined for the Spanish Caribbean.[43]

Yet something was afoot. Between 1846 and 1848, patrols sighted fewer slave ships on the Upper Guinea Coast. But if British abolitionist energy or the Spanish penal code of 1845 had anything to do with the decrease, neither force proved crucial. Luso-Brazilian slaving activity declined in Upper Guinea. But the diminished Lusophone presence was insignificant there, given Portugal's history of greater activity in Lower Guinea, the Congo, Angola, and Mozambique.[44] Many Lusophone traders relocated to other areas, though, as we have seen, some remained to serve Spanish ports. Between 1846 and 1847, no slave ships were spotted leaving Upper Guinea for Brazil, though the Admiralty reported the shipment of some 1,000 slaves from Bissau, Pongo, Sherbro, and Gallinas and stated that Luso-Brazilians now worked for Cuban and Puerto Rican interests.[45]

The partial withdrawal of Luso-Brazilian traders alone should account for the drop in slave traffic by 1849, but new developments in Islamic affairs also contributed to a lull. Unlike the Fula imamate of Futa Jallon, which mixed theocratic doctrine with trade, the Fula emirate of Ahmed-ibn-Muhammad Bari (aka Seku Ahmadu Lobbo) was noted for the undiluted application of Koranic principles. After waging a jihad against his polytheistic Bambara over-lords and the fawning jack-Muslim chieftains who served them, he founded the state of Macina, in present-day Mali. His strict, pristine theocracy earned him the admiration of some leaders and the vexation of others. He did not claim to be the *mahdi*, or messiah, but he declared himself *mujaddid*, reviver of Islam, and sent letters to the sultans and caliphs of Morocco and Sokoto, in northern Nigeria, for their recognition of the honorific and for their allegiance. He of-fended the caliph of Sokoto by assuming the title of emir, commander of the faithful, basing this lack of deference on his belief that the Nigerian caliphate did not follow strict Muslim law. His views on slave commerce were even more offensive. He did not openly challenge his Fula kinsmen in Futa Jallon, hailed as sub-Sahara Africa's oldest jihad state, but he annoyed them by criticizing the business-oriented shaykhs of the Sahel, whose sources of wealth included tolls charged on caravans passing through their domains, and Futa Jallon itself.[46]

Slave caravans avoided austere Macina, for Shaykh Ahmed's adherence to Koranic writ meant the tighter application of laws that addressed the depriva-tion of human liberty. The great reformer refused to tolerate ill-defined con-cepts of enslavement. Such morality meant that Futa Jallon would have to bear greater responsibility in slave acquisitions for export—a major source of in-come. The Fula there had come to rely on the flow of slaves from itinerant Mande-speaking traders. Now they had to organize their own slave-hunting campaigns, as they had done a century before under Sory. And while their military force was strong enough to keep Río Pongo in check, it was small compared to other West African armies. Futa Jallon could ill afford to have its soldiers double as slave catchers indefinitely.[47] When the reformist shaykh-emir died in 1844, many breathed a sigh of relief, including financiers in Timbuctu and Jenne, who led a revolt against the successors of their pious critic and occasional overlord. Though the son and grandson of Shaykh Ahmed held Macina together, it was poised on the brink of conquest. Increasingly sur-rounded by other Muslims who neither respected its sovereignty nor observed Koranic specificities about slave owning, Macina was engulfed and consumed by religio-political strife and the growing interests of Western powers, first and foremost France.[48]

Another state-forming jihad was in the making. Al-Hajj Umar Tal, a Tuku-lor, was viewed with suspicion wherever he traveled in West Africa after his successful residence and advanced Koranic training in the Middle East. Though his mystic religiosity and sophisticated scholarship dazzled royal courts in the western Sudan, not to mention theologians in Mecca, he was branded a rebel for promoting the *Tijaniyya*, a revolutionary Sufic brotherhood founded in Fez in 1780 and outlawed in much of the Muslim world. He was detained, jailed in, or expelled from Timbuctu, Macina, and Bornu at Lake Chad. He was even ousted from tolerant, cosmopolitan Sokoto as well as from his native Futa Toro in Senegal, from whence he fled back to his base at Futa Jallon, where he had lived for several years.

In 1848, the Fula ousted the charismatic Tukulor. They could not reconcile the growth of his following with his purchases of firearms from the coast. From Futa Jallon, he made the hegira, replete with fervent entourage, to nearby Dinguiray in Kaarta, now a semi-Islamized satellite state of Macina. From his new base, he built a force of some 12,000 men, armed with his Sufic ideals, along with French- and British-made weapons from Dakar and Freetown. His army of full- and part-time troops could swell to 30,000 when summoned.[49] The aims of Umar Tal and other nineteenth-century West African jihadists are well documented and too copious to do them justice here.[50] They are, however, relevant to the state of Atlantic slave commerce at midcentury. After establishing himself at Dinguiray, Umar Tal continued to travel throughout western Sudan, recruiting followers and amassing firearms. In 1852, on a Koranic technicality, he declared a jihad, which within a few years carved out a short-lived empire that incorporated much of the savanna from the Sahelian fringe southwest to Senegal and from Timbuctu, at the Niger Bend, to the periphery of Futa Jallon.[51]

Between 1849 and 1851, the slave trade from Upper Guinea declined further. British gunboat diplomacy in Brazil was a major factor. Between 1849 and 1850, slave traffic to Cuba dropped from 7,400 to 3,300. While the decline may be associated with any number of factors—from slow recovery from the penal code of 1845 to the establishment of a British consulate in Lagos in 1850—Umar Tal's armed visits to numerous western Sudanese polities disrupted all manner of commerce. One such visit propelled his "hosts" to seek military aid from the French.[52] The interruption of trade was damaging because slaves destined for the Americas were captured in the interior or from areas close to the coast but not far enough from the inner regions to escape the unsettling forces of Umar Tal's campaigns.

Between 1852 and 1853, figures for the slave trade to Cuba rose from 7,000 to 12,500. Reasons for the comeback included adjustments to the Spanish penal code of 1845, renewed slave trade succor from the United States, and diluted British attention due to the Crimean War. Umar Tal factored into the increase as well. Thousands—Manding, Soninke, Susu, Fula, Tukulor, and others—responded to his jihad in 1852. Because he prioritized the stamping out of "paganism"—his drive to purify "tainted" Islam in established Muslim states came later—polytheists were the first to feel his force.[53] As Boubacar Barry observed, "[I]f Shaykh Umar attacked the *ceddo* [polytheistic slave-soldier] states first, his policy was dictated by strategic considerations. It enabled him to sell captives taken during his holy war in Futa Jallon. He then used the proceeds to buy arms from Sierra Leone and the Southern Rivers, far from Futa Jallon."[54] Thus, politics and slave traffic involving Futa Jallon, the Creole clans, and the indigenous states of Río Pongo linked Umar Tal's jihad to Spanish Caribbean slave markets. Though he conquered and absorbed Macina into his empire, Futa Jallon remained free of him. His brief success—followed by the quasi-jihadist forays of the Manding and the more successful French—kept the Lightbourns and their increasingly underenthusiastic allies at Futa Jallon in service to Cuban slave traders through the 1860s.

By the 1860s, nonetheless, between the Pongo and Núñez Rivers, Creoles and Muslims also favored peanut production as a substitute for slave commerce with Europeans. French interest along the Núñez was most evident. France established a military base there in 1866. Following this signpost, the Fula of Futa Jallon renewed brokerage with Creole blacks and mulattoes on the Núñez, who exported 4,000 tons of peanuts annually by the end of the 1860s. This figure surpasses rival production on the Pongo by 50 percent for the same period. Though the Lightbourns changed with the times, continued requests for slaves in Cuba deferred their response to changes in supply and demand. But deferral was brief. It is simply a question of when agrarian exclusivity started; some thirty years earlier the Pongo families began to mix slaves with coffee and peanut exports.[55]

What then was afoot in the mid-1840s, and what impact did it have on slave traffic to Puerto Rico? Many forces rested at the confluence of many events. Back-to-back African-led slave revolts and conspiracies in Cuba and Puerto Rico between 1841 and 1844 are worthy of note, as is the establishment of the British consular representation in San Juan in 1844. Shaykh Ahmed's death, also in 1844, and the Spanish Penal Code of 1845 were events that demanded immediate attention from dealers on both sides of the Atlantic. But Spanish Caribbean slave markets reacted differently to all these events. The

brief panic that marked Cuba's initial response to the penal code was not duplicated in Puerto Rico. Eltis shows us that in 1844 approximately 10,000 Africans
arrived in Cuba, compared to 2,600 in 1845, 1,000 in 1846, and 1,700 in 1847.
While slave trade serials for Puerto Rico are wanting, consular reports from
San Juan point to ongoing efforts to acquire African captives during those
years. It seems then that dire necessity predisposed brokers serving the smaller
island to respond resourcefully to both the Spanish penal code and political
changes in Upper Guinea, which included, among other things, a slow revival
of slave traffic from the interior between the reigns of the shaykh's son and
grandson, as well as the conquest of Macina by Umar Tal.

Often connected to international changes in the law of supply and demand, political shake-ups in the Muslim states of the West African interior
were certainly felt on the coast. From 1842 to 1848, the Fabers and the Lightbourns enjoyed unparalleled success as intermediaries between Fula suppliers and Spanish shippers. Between 1845 and 1847, Pongo slaving activity
figured prominently in diplomatic communications from San Juan. However,
British agents in Havana did not register like concerns for the region. In a pinch,
traders serving Cuba could rely on the Bights of Benin and Biafra. Given the
crisis at this time, Cuba—once an auxiliary but now a rival—squeezed Puerto
Rico out of Lower Guinea between 1845 and 1848. Brokers for Puerto Rico
formed a series of small, independent and semi-independent expeditions to
West Africa. They concentrated on Upper Guinea rather than on Lower Guinea,
where competition with Cuba for captives was most keen. Thus, toward the
close of its participation in the traffic, Puerto Rico was forced to make greater
efforts to wean itself from Cuban aid.

Still active in Upper Guinea despite dwindling numbers, wealthier Cuban
interest groups could always afford to spread slaving across African regional
divides. In Puerto Rico, smaller and less solvent interests groups did not have
this choice. For them, the near exclusivity of voyages to Upper Guinea was not
an option but a necessity. Cuba recovered from the uncertainty of the traffic
with bounding enthusiasm. This uncertainty—based on decline in the second
half of the 1840s—was followed by Cuba's "last hurrah," or what W.E.F. Ward
calls "The Roaring Fifties" of the slave trade. For Cuba, 1845 to 1850 marked the
beginning of the calm before the storm. Puerto Rico, at the same time, experienced the reverse.

British reports on slave traffic to Puerto Rico repeatedly cited the Pongo
River as a popular source in the 1840s. While fluctuations cannot be wholly

attributed to Creole power struggles on the coast or to Islamic expansion in the interior, the Pongo trade did not show serious signs of revival until Shaykh Ahmed died. His death corresponded to the return of commercial prosperity on the Pongo—with assistance from the imamate of Futa Jallon—after uncertain times following the death of Mongo John. Though Great Britain established a consulate at San Juan in 1844, the year of the shaykh's demise, Puerto Rico benefited from renewed traffic from the Pongo. While details on the extent to which Umar Tal's usurpations influenced coastal operations prior to his jihad in 1852 are lacking, between 1852 and 1853, 12,500 captives landed in Cuba, the highest annual figure for its African influx in thirteen years. On the other hand, Umar Tal's jihad and his conquest of Macina and other Sahelian polities had no impact on Puerto Rico. After 1847, no slaves of Upper Guinea origin were reported to have landed there. The death of Shaykh Ahmed stimulated the traffic between 1844 and 1847. Conversely, between 1848 and 1850, the prejihad activities of Umar Tal discouraged it. While power politics in West Africa had a hand in maintaining the slave trade to Puerto Rico in the 1840s, it also contributed to its decline.

8

South Atlantic West

A Stasis of Flux

This chapter identifies trends and events that led to the reopening of the inter-Caribbean slave trade to Puerto Rico between 1845 and 1847. The first section considers differences between Cuba and Puerto Rico vis-à-vis slave resistance and its perceived connection to African provenance, on the one hand, and abolitionist postures as they related to social divides among the free populations of the two islands, on the other. The second section assesses the early years of the British consulate in Puerto Rico as an abolitionist mission. It questions the competency of John Lindegren, who made serious mistakes in reporting slave traffic from both African and inter-Caribbean routes. Given Spain's steadfast refusal to outlaw the trade in Antillean waters, the final section explores the confused enunciations of Anglo-Spanish and Anglo-Dutch relations in relation to the inter-Caribbean trade. All three sections build foundations that link the Caribbean influx directly and indirectly to the last spurts of slave traffic from Africa.

Two Wings, One Bird

Slave rebellions rocked Puerto Rico between 1835 and 1847, resulting in loss of life among participants, slaveholders, and military units.[1] Though the island had yet to experience the last of these conspiratory events, serialized in 1848, local officials were disturbed over a chain of Cuban slave disturbances between 1841 and 1843, which led to the persecution of Afro-Cubans slave and free between late 1843 and early 1845.[2] Thus, before responding to planter complaints of insufficient slaves, Governor Rafael de Arístegüi weighed the possibilities. He knew Spaniards still operated in Upper Guinea and still had the means to supply Puerto Rico with captives. He also knew that certain non-Hispanic neighbors remained willing to broker the traffic.

Considering the history of militant slave resistance in the Caribbean and everywhere else in the Americas, why did Puerto Rican planters continue to seek African captives? Let us consider comparative social groups. Disturbances in Cuba linked slaves to British abolitionists as well as to the island's black bourgeoisie. Puerto Rico's ethnic composition was less varied. Unlike Cuba, it had no Mexican Indian labor force, and its Asian population seemed almost invisible until the mid-1860s.[3] Though poor whites lived and worked with poor free blacks—who interacted socially and sometimes politically with slaves—their ideas about slavery and abolition are largely unrecorded. In general, regardless of class differences among them, Puerto Rican whites could prove troublesome politically. However, the colonial government could not identify the island's small, Creole white, upper-class abolitionist intelligentsia as such until 1859, when its members founded the Sociedad Abolicionista Española in Madrid.

The extent to which the Afro–Puerto Rican middle class empathized with slaves is uncertain before the 1860s. Historically, where phenotype permitted, well-to-do free people of color were not considered, and did not consider themselves, colored, that is, of African descent. Though passing for white was as illegal in Puerto Rico as it was in Cuba—or for that matter, the United States—surveillance against it was less fastidious by comparison.[4] Yet in 1866, one year after the Sociedad Abolicionista received its charter from the Spanish Crown, Vice Consul Leopold Krug reported to the British Foreign Office from Mayagüez, "[T]here is said to exist a secret emancipation society whose members are mostly colored people of pretty good social positions, lawers [sic], physicians, etc. These persons liberate, out of their own means and by subscription, a good many new born slaves by paying to their owners, according to Law, 25 pesos for each of them the same day they are baptized."[5] Whatever the case—and the years 1859 to 1865 may prove to be the dividing line in this regard—Puerto Rico's black middle class was not only younger than its Cuban counterpart, it was less solvent, less segregated, and perceived as less of a threat politically.

Authorities in Cuba identified Yoruba militants as catalysts in several slave disturbances in the early 1840s.[6] Puerto Rico's Yoruba population was disproportionately small. A handful appeared in runaway slave notices in the 1820s, but neither they nor any other slaves from the Lower Guinea Coast were ever identified as participants in Puerto Rican slave revolts.[7] Though Spanish buyers grew disinterested in African heterogeneity, compared to their expertise in the past, in view of events in Cuba between 1843 and 1844—following the logic of crisis based on Spanish responses that date back to the sixteenth century, when Charles V forbade the importation of Wolofs after America's first major slave revolt in Santo Domingo in 1522—it behooved the governor of Puerto Rico to avoid the importation of Yoruba slaves. African-born slaves often led resistance movements, including marronage. Yet the government's belief in militant behavior on the grounds of African ethnicity or nationality is beyond reckoning because it did not discriminate on the basis of slave origin.

Africans from centralized states, acephalous agrarian societies, or metallurgical cultures may have been preferred to pastoral nomads or hunters and gatherers in Spanish colonies where farming or mining played significant roles—though captives with herding backgrounds were prized on cattle ranches in Cuba, Mexico, and South America—but it was the nature of slavery itself, not the heterogeneity of African identity, that caused conflict between masters and slaves. The Bambara and the Wolof were no more prone to revolt than were the Ibo or the Yoruba. Although abolitionist politics eroded slaveholder intelligence and pretentiousness regarding the geo-cultural origins of African slaves, misinformation dies hard. As late as the 1970s, some scholars still labeled the Congolese as docile, industrious, and more assimilable—though such stereotypes had little bearing on their market value compared to other Africans. Furthermore, in Cuba, Puerto Rico, Louisiana, and elsewhere, *los congos* headed social organizations and joined in militant liberationist activities.[8]

Though some data suggest that Cuba and Puerto Rico received proportionate numbers of African slaves from Upper Guinea, the Congo, and Angola, the two islands demonstrated forking paths of acquisition. Wealthier planters and merchants in Cuba capitalized on the greater availability of captives from Lower Guinea—due, in part, to its larger population compared to both Upper Guinea and the Congo-Angola region. With fewer resources, Puerto Rico's smaller planter class could not take advantage of the same regional accessibility. By self-centered necessity, as suggested in the previous chapter, Cuban succor in the slave trade to Puerto Rico had its limits. Assistance was one thing, competition was another. African captives from the Gold Coast, western Dahomey, and the Bight of Biafra—named generically in Spanish, *mina* (mainly Asante, Fante, Ewe, and Ga), *Arará* (mainly Fon), and *carabalí* (some Ibibio but largely Ibo)— appeared in both islands in accordance with the fluctuations of the day. But the parsimonious presence of Yoruba captives in Puerto Rico compared to their inundations in Cuba indicates that the latter reduced its aid to the former in the Bight of Benin from the 1830s onward. Governor Arístegüi must have borne these points in mind when he authorized the brief but potent influx of slaves in 1847 in full view of the British consulate. As long as Africans were accessible, their origins were inconsequential. Though it is asserted in the next chapter that some of the captives probably came from the Gold Coast in Lower Guinea, we shall see in this chapter that connections in Upper Guinea were more reliable.

Future research may show that Puerto Rican slave revolts in 1848 were less the product of inter-Caribbean slave dissidence—from Martinique, Guadeloupe, and St. Croix, as some scholars have argued, or the subsequent repressive measures that were sparingly implemented, as other scholars have overlooked —and more the result of the sudden influx of a thousand or more African captives the year before.[9] If the thesis of Upper Guinea predominance holds true, then slaves imported in 1847—added to those imported from 1835 to 1845—came not only from the same region, many were exported from the same ports, with origins in the same or neighboring polities, which facilitated interaction in Puerto Rico with kin, compatriots, coethnics, and colinguals. Common cultural origins, in addition to common sociopolitical grievances, must have encouraged the slave conspiracies of 1848.

Slaves were at once dreaded and desired. Though they were internal outsiders, their labor translated into wealth and prestige. Thus, concerns for slave unrest coexisted with efforts to continue the slave trade. While this schizogonous construct was not unique, in Puerto Rico it was exacerbated because slave numbers were small, by official count never more than a tenth of the population. In the Spanish Antilles in the nineteenth century, lower fertility rates among African-born slave women—reinforced by the continuous influx of more African men than women—kept sociopolitical tensions high, as African-led slave revolts have shown.[10] The risks involved in maintaining cadres of internal outsiders were as great as the profits of their involuntary labor. Laws inscribed preferences for assimilated Creole slaves over African newcomers —albeit the former were said to have corrupting influences on the latter. Yet adverse working conditions that augmented mortality, on the one hand, and comparatively easier access to manumission, on the other, challenged demographic growth among Creole slaves. As a consequence, as long as South Atlantic waterways remained open, African captives continued to be imported —irrespective of female underrepresentation and low fecundity among them.

Fear of slave revolts and the desire to minimize quibbling with Great Britain made the honing of Puerto Rican slave trade policy difficult. As discussed in the first chapter, the problem became greater when international politics sandwiched Puerto Rico between the British Foreign Office and the colonial government of Cuba, which led to British diplomatic representation in San Juan. The presence of the British consulate in Puerto Rico resolved Anglo-Spanish uncertainty over the future of the Cuban branch of the Mixed Court.[11] Though at times Great Britain proposed the court's transfer from Havana to San Juan on humanitarian grounds, the real issue was Spanish treaty violations.[12] The move would have augmented Cuban infractions and provided officials with more opportunities to exact bribes from slave traders.[13] For a while Spain ignored adamant protests from Puerto Rico. After several African-led uprisings between 1838 and 1843, island officials were less inclined to welcome shiploads of slaves on a regular basis—least of all Africans destined to be freed by the Mixed Court and settled in their midst. But in the long run, unbeknownst to Spain, Great Britain supported the move in theory only.

La Torre governed Puerto Rico from 1822 to 1836. None who followed could duplicate his promotion of illegal slave traffic. But the Foreign Office did not identify the island as recalcitrant until the tenure of López de Baños.[14] During his term, Great Britain learned of the extent to which Puerto Rico, like Cuba, exploited the labor of British Antillean ex-slaves. Such machinations may not have warranted the transfer of the Mixed Court, but the Foreign Office was alarmed enough to propose a fixed mission in San Juan to discourage it.[15] The new consulate enabled the British to keep an eye on Cuba by maintaining the mixed tribunal there while gaining diplomatic and economic toeholds in Puerto Rico as well. But it was more than a ploy against treaty violations; it was a victory in a face-off with Cuba, Spain's richest and most powerful colony.

The Consul and the Count

Discrepancies in import-export practices between Puerto Rico and Great Britain were enough to merit a consulate. Three years after the office opened, trade scales still tilted in Spain's favor. While Great Britain shipped 54,546 pesos worth of products to Puerto Rico in 1847, it sent 1,363,438 pesos worth of its goods to British dominions the same year. Spanish Puerto Rican exports to British ports rose 778,565 pesos over the previous year, though British imports increased by a paltry 242,247 pesos.[16] The official aim of the consulate was to secure the freedom of black Britons secreted away to Spanish servitude. This aim failed as much as quieter attempts to reach a more favorable balance of trade. The traffic in black Britons stopped long before the first consul arrived, but efforts to liberate and repatriate those still in bondage were never renewed. During the first four years, more consular energy was devoted to improving trade relations and preventing the landing of African slaves. With one impressive exception, the plight of enslaved British subjects in Puerto Rico was forgotten.[17]

As Puerto Rico's first British consul, John Lindegren deserves high marks for his indefatigable devotion to the cessation of external slave traffic. But he merits low marks for his inexplicable gullibility and naïveté. For the most part, he accurately assessed the political postures of several governors as they related to the slave trade—proslavery, antislavery, or neutral. But his misjudgment of Governor Arístegüi as a true friend of the abolitionist cause lies beyond comprehension. When it came to the governor, Lindegren's common sense retreated to parts unknown. In addition, his understanding of Puerto Rican slavery was, on too many occasions, far from cogent.[18]

As soon as Lindegren accepted the commission, Aberdeen obliged him to survey the state of slavery. Lindegren relied on Spanish public records, along with private sources.[19] His informants were fairly reliable. Structured as questions and answers, cardinal points of the survey reported the following. While slaves formed a numerical minority, nonwhites together—slave and free—nearly equaled the island's white population. The African influx reached its peak during the incumbency of Governor La Torre, though no estimates were available. Between 1837 and 1843, under the governorship of his successors, Moreda, López, and Méndez, some 1,600 Africans arrived, while thus far (five months) under Arístegüi, no slaves were smuggled in. The slave population was on the rise, owing to the combination of favorable male-female ratios and a slowing of individual manumissions rather than to external acquisitions.[20]

Many responses were based on misinformation and guesswork. Contrary to Lindegren's assertion that slaves could not testify against their masters, slave testimony could be admitted in both civil and criminal cases in local magistracies, the territorial appellate court, and, more commonly, in lawsuits slaves filed against their masters.[21] His failure to understand this aspect of Spanish law is strange, for in the same report he marveled at the very concept of a slave protectionist court, which was authorized for all of Spain's colonies in 1789 and implemented in Puerto Rico in 1826. Lindegren also erred in observing that slave policy had not changed in a decade. For example, in 1838, to disguise his support of the slave trade, Governor López ordered masters to report all slave deaths within three days to discourage the substitution of recent captives for dead slaves. And in 1841—ostensibly to distinguish foreign Antillean Creoles from Africans—Governor Méndez issued a circular to legitimize the presence of all fraudulently imported slaves.[22] Lindegren also misread the applicability of legal equality between whites and free people of color. Tax-paying property owners—among whose ranks blacks were few—always enjoyed greater legal protection than did the propertyless. Nor did he realize what motivated the absence of public abolitionist politics. Imperial policy not only banned political parties, abolitionism was equated with treason and subversion until 1860. Though it was rarely applied in Puerto Rico, except to soldiers and slaves, all traitors and subversives were subject to capital punishment.[23]

Hints of Lindegren's dilatory acclimation to current slave-trading affairs were evident almost from the outset of his appointment. In January 1845, he reported to the Foreign Office and the Vice-Admiralty that a brigantine recently left San Juan for Río Pongo. The British naval station at Barbados was alerted, and officers planned to capture the vessel on its return. But it was caught at the mouth of the Pongo after a six-hour chase, destroyed, and its crew abandoned in Freetown. The fate of its 650 captives was not yet known.[24] The report reveals the marvels of networking. Lindegren's informant knew the vessel's owner personally and had seen letters advising him of its capture—undoubtedly for the purpose of insurance claims. The reliability of his source is without question because the slaver was the *Triunfo*, captained by Juan Carreras of Puerto Rico and captured in February 1845. The consul was apprised of the situation long before the African squadron reported it to the Foreign Office.[25] More impressively—from Puerto Rican sources, not British consular agents in Havana—he learned about the revival of slave traffic from the Pongo. Abolitionist cruisers had not sailed its waters in two years. Again, Puerto Rican informants were on target. The British Admiralty filed no report for Río Pongo in 1843 and mentioned neither sightings nor captures in 1844.[26]

While the *Triunfo* gives further proof that slavists in Puerto Rico planned and executed independent ventures as much in the 1840s as in the 1830s, Cuba continued to play an occasional role. The peninsula-born brothers Mariano and Cenón Ignacio de Aldeçoa, absent from Puerto Rican slaving for nearly a decade due to greater opportunities in Cuba, reappeared in the 1840s in the business of mixed acquisitions.[27] Francisco Gandía, a Puerto Rican resident and apparent newcomer to the trade, used his Puerto Rican–registered ships to serve both islands.[28] The French-born Cuban Pierre Fourçade also began to combine Cuban and Puerto Rican interests.[29] Despite increasing Puerto Rican autonomy, overall operations remained mixed.

Lindegren's reports on Juan Carreras and the Pongo venture marked the beginning of his puzzling assessment of Governor Arístegüi, the Count de Mirasol. Throughout the count's tenure, Lindegren held him in highest regard, describing him ad infinitum as a defender of the antislavery crusade. Nothing was further from the truth. The consul should have been aware of the governor's duplicity from the beginning, as evidenced in the *Triunfo* report. "The Governor has positively refused leave for the slaver to land her cargo here when she returns, though the owners were previously led to expect that he would allow it. All he will permit is that they [Spanish officials] may hold communications with her when she calls off the port." "Communications" provided a hint that Lindegren did not recognize. On the flurry of ships that sailed for Africa from Cuba and Puerto Rico over the past year, he informed Aberdeen that Arístegüi had "in consequence of a private meeting held in the beginning of September last [1844] granted slave traders until the month of March to import slaves and wind up their concerns on the Coast of Africa, and this will account for the large number of vessels sent out at the time."[30]

Lindegren never understood that the Puerto Rican captaincy general operated in pendular oscillations between the certainty and uncertainty of administrative dexterity. He misjudged Arístegüi's political authority habitually. The Spanish government ratified the penal code of 1845 for immediate implementation in early March of that year. Contrary to the governor's statement, there was no grace period "granted [to] slave traders to . . . wind up their concerns on the Coast of Africa." He neither had nor needed the power to grant one. Thanks to the experience of metropolitan lawmakers and their faith in the practice of twenty-five years of illegal slave trading, delays and other "silent graces" were embedded in the code. Perhaps due to the newness of his office or the conservatism of his present supervisor, Lord Aberdeen, Lindegren preferred caution in his relations with the count. Or perhaps he truly believed that the aristocratic governor would keep his word and prevent slave landings after March 1845. Naïveté and undue hesitation were unusual traits among British consuls charged with antislavery responsibilities. Yet at this time, Lindegren's behavior was riddled with contradictions.

In the spring of 1845, consular agents revealed that "Spaniards concerned in the slave trade both here [in Puerto Rico] and in Cuba act from the same information without a doubt and hearing that part of the coast [of Río Pongo] did not appear to be watched, they hoped to carry on their Trade ... successfully and chose it for the best port of security."[31] Indeed, within a year's time Lindegren's informants told him that Puerto Rican traders established slave factories in Faringuia, Isabel Lightbourn's Pongo territory. Though it is not known whether her hospitality was without precedent, this is the first time since the treaty of 1817 that parliamentary records refer to independent Puerto Rican slave-collection stations in Africa. Thus, irrespective of penal codes and bilateral treaties, as late as the mid-1840s it seems that Puerto Rico had no intention of abandoning the African slave trade in the near future.

Again, in the fall of 1845 the governor demonstrated his penchant for mendacity, and again, revealing his naïveté, Lindegren speculated that the *Triunfo* Africans, who never boarded the captured vessel, were rerouted to Brazil.[32] By this time, the few Lusophones who remained in Río Pongo served Spanish markets exclusively. On October 28, a small schooner with 250 captives appeared in San Juan. Lindegren assumed that the owners declined to meet its captain, Juan Carreras of the ill-fated *Triunfo,* for fear that the governor would not permit them to land the captives. The unnamed vessel received provisions that evening and sailed the following morning. The consul predicted that it would go to Cuba or Brazil. The schooner arrived secretly. Lindegren was certain Mirasol knew nothing of it until he mentioned it the following day. The governor vowed to prevent the landing of any slaves and ordered a man-of-war to seize the offending vessel.[33] The battleship in question was a dilapidated brig. Undergoing refitting and with sails unbent, it could not pursue the slaver until 4 P.M. Then calm weather thwarted the possibility of chase until the next day, October 30. Before sunset the previous day, the ship was long out of sight. On November 1, Lindegren reported the incident to naval officials at the Barbadian station and advised them to alert their cruisers in Cuban waters. He failed to realize that the 250 slaves formed part of the aborted *Triunfo* expedition and that they were, in all probability, the last of the original group that had been divided up and transshipped in smaller ships because of the capture and condemnation of the larger.[34]

In a sudden burst of common sense, the consul rejected his earlier opinion that the *Triunfo* captives were redirected to Brazil. The epiphany, of course, was brief. He concluded with confidence that they were still being held in Río Pongo for shipment—after nearly a year's detention. Surely he must have known that since the 1820s, captives were rarely held on the African coast any longer than a few weeks. Still keeping these captives separate from the ones on board the unnamed vessel spotted in San Juan, he informed Arístegüi that they would probably land in the south or the west. The count responded that such a landing would be impossible without his knowledge and feigned ignorance of the nameless slaver that had anchored within half a mile of his palace. Lindegren learned later that the unnamed schooner took the slaves to Havana without complications.

In view of the governor's record for double-dealing—which went unchanged for the next three years—and considering that the Barbadian admiralty was often too short of cruisers to monitor Puerto Rico adequately in the 1840s, there is every reason to believe that the nameless vessel made a scheduled stop at San Juan; that, unable to unload its prepaid slaves there, it made an unscheduled stop at southwestern Cabo Rojo before proceeding to Havana; and that the count tricked the consul once again.[35] More specifically, the voyage of the *Triunfo* was a Puerto Rican venture from start to finish, as illustrated in Chapter 6. British intervention compelled its owners to modify their plans. The would-be cargo of 650 captives was divided for transport on small schooners, which arrived in Puerto Rico as planned. What remains uncertain is whether some of the slaves were originally slated for reexport to Cuba or if the maneuver was an impromptu arrangement based on last-minute changes occasioned by Lindegren's inquiries.

On February 24, 1846, Joseph Crawford, British consul-general to Cuba, wrote to Lord Aberdeen that the Spanish brig *El Conde de Mirasol* docked at Havana during the second week of the month. He believed that the voyage originated in Puerto Rico, landed 400 Africans at Cárdenas (in central Cuba), then proceeded to the capital in ballast. Though the ship was Puerto Rican–owned and registered, its slave cargo was consigned to Franco-Cuban Pierre Fourçade.[36] On March 2, from Jamaica, David Turnbull informed his government that a Mr. Goff, an Englishman visiting Puerto Rico, saw a slaver near the port of San Juan, which landed 160 African captives, and during a short junket by steamer, he met the man said to have captained the vessel in question. Aberdeen forwarded a copy of Turnbull's note to Lindegren with the following preface. "Her Majesty's Government consider it due the Governor of Porto Rico not to permit to pass without investigation a statement so vague. Such allegations could be seen to reflect unjustly and injuriously on the good faith of the authorities of Porto Rico."[37] He then expressed his trust in the consul's certainty that Arístegüi was a man of his abolitionist word, an amazing assertion given that the ship bore the governor's noble title.

After making inquiries, Lindegren's reply was escapist and defensive. He stated that he already knew of Goff's chat with Carreras in early February, though he did not mention it in his reports until late spring, after Aberdeen requested an investigation. He then asserted that the captain "must, I think, have referred to a circumstance which occurred shortly before the present governor arrived." Were Lindegren correct, the landing would have taken place three years prior to Goff's conversation with Carreras and nearly a year before his own appointment as consul and the count's appointment as governor. Lindegren also said that Carreras "was then returning to San Juan, where his family resided, when he made the statement to Mr. Goff."[38] Again he erred. Carreras and Goff were already in San Juan. They met on a local steam packet after landing in Puerto Rico from Cuba and Jamaica by different ships. They could not have landed together, as the consul suggested. He noted that the slaver Goff saw in February 1846 was the one the governor ordered captured by the decrepit man-of-war in October 1845, adding that it was slated for slaving in the Pongo in 1844, did not get papers, and was replaced by the subsequently intercepted *Triunfo*. It remained to shuttle new captives from one Puerto Rican port to another and from one Spanish island to other.[39] Crawford repeated that the *Conde* was a cabotage slaver—it only carried slaves for sale between Spanish ports. In spite of confirmations from Kingston and Havana, Lindegren labored to arrest Aberdeen's suspicions that the *Conde* and the vessel Goff sighted were the same. He denied any connection between the governor and the slave ship bearing his name. Thrice in the same dispatch he extolled Arístegüi's abolitionist virtues.

The matter of the *Conde* did not end there. Twenty days after Lindegren dismissed its activities, he reported that it was scheduled to pick up 600 captives from Río Pongo. Its owners, unnamed, were anxious for it to reach Upper Guinea during the rainy season, when British cruisers were likely to be absent. It was fitted in Curaçao, not St. Thomas, a hint that signaled possible links to Dutch collusion on the Gold Coast.[40] Were the *Conde* limited to cabotage, British protest would have been fruitless. But Lindegren reported later that it was also an international slaver. His delayed intelligence precluded the possibility of an effective confrontation with the governor.

When the vessel returned to San Juan, Lindegren said he demanded an audience with the count. Arístegüi claimed illness and declined to see Lindegren for several days. When the meeting took place the governor revealed that (1) the *Conde* sailed for West Africa for slaves, with his full approval, after the captain followed his order to solicit a license; (2) though Lindegren believed that its license came from Havana, the count stated that its owners applied to Madrid for authorization and that it would be granted; and (3) the governor imposed a bond equaling the vessel's value to guarantee that it would not embark for Africa. Lindegren challenged neither the spatio-temporal absurdity of the second point nor the discursive incompatibility of the first and third.

Arístegüi's contradictions and misrepresentations are worthy of note. Authorities in Madrid had not supervised the granting of slave ship permits exclusively since the eighteenth century. Such tasks were delegated to officers in the colonies. Furthermore, such permission would have violated the Spanish penal code of 1845 openly. Overt disregard for national laws under international scrutiny was not characteristic of the government. In addition, if metropolitan powers issued slaving permits, colonial governors lacked the authority to encumber them with restrictive bonds. Arístegüi was too astute to counter the politics of recentralization emanating from the Council of the Indies in Madrid.[41] Last, when he told Lindegren that permission from Madrid "would be granted," the ship had already left.

Once more Arístegüi deceived the consul. But he did not stop there. He assured him that his expensive bond would prevent any expedition. Then, regarding Goff's report, "he expressed great surprise, and said that it was impossible to have taken place." But Aberdeen solicited further proof of the count's antislavery cooperation. Lindegren did not waver in his defense. On July 11, 1846, in his last slave trade report for that year, he wrote, "I trust that this communication will quite satisfy Your Lordship as to the impossibility of the slave trade existing here in Porto Rico as long at least as the present governor remains here."[42]

The British consulate in Havana had its share of roguish, incompetent, and sensically challenged functionaries. Some were themselves slaveholders, and they, in conjunction with Spanish officials, subverted the efforts of those who took their mission seriously.[43] However, by the mid-1840s, corruption among them declined. But in San Juan, Lindegren's defense of Arístegüi was consistent enough to suspect his integrity, his intrinsic intelligence, or both. Seventeen times between 1844 and 1848 he described the governor as an enemy of the slave trade—even with irrefutable evidence that Arístegüi authorized slave expeditions. But proof of the consul's perfidiousness is hard to come by. Indeed, considering his improvements in the 1850s, it would be erroneous to brand the whole of his abolitionist record as inadequate.

In addition to Lindegren's admiration for the count, other matters sow seeds of doubt about his competence as an abolitionist officer. First, the consul painted Puerto Rican bondage in a flattering light. Like other abolitionist-oriented Britons, he read the misinformed accounts of Puerto Rican slavery and the slave trade in Turnbull's *Travels to the West*. So blithe was Lindegren's portraiture that Aberdeen—no stranger to counterabolitionist posturing—compelled him to submit statistical proof to clarify distinctions between the letter and spirit of Puerto Rican slave codes. But even with specific instructions, he made serious mistakes.

Second, he exhibited a marked curiosity for laws related to slaveholding among Britons residing in foreign domains. In the previous decade, Palmerston pressured British subjects in Latin America, the Maghreb, the Levant, East Africa, and tropical Asia to desist from all activity related to slave traffic and slave ownership. Aberdeen half-heartedly continued the policy. Thus, the identification and harassing of British slaveholders by British consuls in the Spanish islands were not unexpected. Nor was it odd that Lindegren, more than his counterpart in Havana, made repeated inquiries to the Foreign Office about that policy. But the tenor of some of his questions is disquieting. For example, "I should be glad, on this account, if you could point out to me by what Act the purchase or sale of slaves by British subjects in the island of Porto Rico, for purposes within the island, is prohibited."[44] His query floats somewhere between sublime ignorance and self-incrimination.

Third, though the first two points (along with his unshakable confidence in the governor) do not substantiate doubts about his honesty and personal interests, it is important to note that he had a resident kinsman in Puerto Rico, William Lindegren, who owned trustee contracts for Congolese *emancipados* between 1859 and 1864. The younger Lindegren not only bought the forced labor of liberated Africans, with a Spaniard fronting as the true "guardian," he was named in a lawsuit for the excessive cruelty he meted out to his African wards. Though the trusteeship began after the consul was replaced, the family connection intrigues as much as it alarms.[45]

Documents used for this discussion shed little light on Lindegren's personal affairs. Thus, we proceed from the continued assumption that he did not compromise his position as a royal official. Perhaps he was simply a man who saw the world through rose-colored glasses. Or perhaps his misjudgments marked the unusual longevity of his position as a consular neophyte. Whatever the case, his conciliatory, pro-Spanish behavior during his first years as consul aligned perfectly with the conservative abolitionism of the British Foreign Office during the tenure of Lord Aberdeen.

If Lindegren was slow on the uptake in his early years of service, by 1847 he began to see the light. Still careful not to implicate Arístegüi, he wrote on February 10, "As long as the present governor remains, no slave will be allowed to be landed on this island." He also crowned his own brow with abolitionist laurels. "I know privately that the slave dealers are supported by persons in authority here who would give their every encouragement, but the presence of a British Consul in the Island is their principal difficulty."[46] But despite his exaggerated trust, he reported two major schemes in the making: another shipment of 600 captives from the Pongo and a new plan for slave imports through inter-Caribbean channels. By 1847, with the exception of one reference to the Pongo trade—Puerto Rican slave runners and agents found it more expedient to purchase French schooners at Gorée for return voyages—direct African imports took a backseat to the inter-Antillean crisis.[47]

In his study of nineteenth-century slavery in Cuba, Franklin Knight observed that the Spanish penal code of 1845 seemed to be an earnest attempt to stop the African slave trade, but after a temporary panic, normalcy returned when it became apparent that the ominous legislation provided an escape: no one was empowered to traverse private property to verify the origins of slaves. The "oversight" was a boon for Cuban and Puerto Rican slaveholders.[48] Furthermore, nothing in the code forbade slave traffic from non-African ports. The Dutch Caribbean was the main source of the influx. The consul implored the Foreign Office for immediate instructions.[49] The situation was critical at three levels: his informants told him that omissions in the penal code of 1845 promoted the trade; the Anglo-Spanish treaty of 1835 referred only to Africa as the proscribed source of slaves; and the Anglo-Dutch treaty of 1818 outlawed only the use of Dutch carriers in the international transport of slaves.[50]

Puerto Rican missions to Dutch St. Eustatius and St. Maarten failed at first. Though Dutch maritime law permitted both internal and external slave sales, local laws forbade external sales without documented consent from the slaves and permits from the governor endorsed by the Hague. But in Curaçao, slave traders used Spanish vessels.[51] Lindegren registered disbelief at the rapidity of the expeditions. When he first notified the Foreign Office of the traffic in February, he thought it was barely in the planning stage. Of the count, he wrote, "I certainly did not expect the Governor to consent to it. He must have been strongly pressured, especially considering the want of females here. I hear that they want as many women as possible."[52] In May, he reported the success of the mission to Curaçao. The Spanish schooner *Bailear* landed some fifty slaves—mainly women—in Guayama in the south. After government agents collected duties, tolls, and head taxes, the slaves were distributed to local estates.[53]

When Palmerston returned to the Foreign Office, apparently Lindegren believed it necessary, in view of his blind spots, to demonstrate his expertise in Spanish law. After reiterating his conviction that the governor-count buckled under planter pressure, he noted that Spain must have relaxed its codes on slave commerce, given that on May 11, 1526, the Hapsburg monarchy forbade the importation of all slaves to its colonies who were not freshly extracted from Africa. And in 1804, still in the spirit of eighteenth-century reforms, on the one hand, and the exigencies of Napoleonic chaos, on the other, the Bourbons outlawed the import of Creole slaves. He also noted that in 1842, in the wake of havoc linked to Turnbull, and 1844, in the throes of the Conspiración de la Escalera, colonial law forbade the landing of all black foreigners in Cuba, except African slaves. Governor Leopoldo O'Donnell charged captains and supercargoes with bonds to assure that foreign blacks would not leave their ships no matter how long the ships docked.[54]

In his eagerness to impress Palmerston, which he did, Lindegren failed to note that the sixteenth-century initiative proclaimed not only blacks and mulattoes born in Spain personae non gratae in the colonies, it forbade the arrival of Hispanicized Africans as well. Moreover, once colonists adjusted to the New Laws of 1542—designed, among other things, to initiate the extinction of Amerindian slavery—restrictions on black slave traffic based on black alterity served no purpose. Respecting the turn-of-the-century Bourbon measure, Lindegren did not realize that it countered rising Spanish Antillean slaving interests and was therefore ignored. Last, unlike the penal code of 1845, laws forbidding the disembarkation of free foreign blacks in Cuba in 1842 and 1844 did not apply to Puerto Rico at all. Furthermore, Cuban authorities only applied them to Afro-Britons. Black mariners from the United States and the non-Britannic Caribbean and free Africans who worked on slave ships, such as the Kru of Liberia, were excluded from the restrictions.[55]

During the influx of 1847, Arístegüi occasionally suspended permits for slave imports. But this was not because Palmerston instructed Lindegren to remind the governor that inter-Caribbean slave traffic violated Anglo-Spanish treaties. Though Arístegüi had yet to halt the traffic, he heard rumors about the infiltration of rebels among the newcomers. But he continued to gamble. In early June, the *Bailear* brought slaves from Curaçao to Ponce, the only known instance in which *ponceños* benefited from the venture. It left others at Mayagüez, then proceeded to St. Thomas for more. Lindegren reported three additional voyages. Two ended in Cabo Rojo with an estimated thirty-five slaves and one in Mayagüez with twenty-nine. In July, the Dutch schooner *Esther* arrived in Mayagüez with slaves in violation of Anglo-Dutch accords. Shortly after, when an unnamed Puerto Rican planter went to Franco-Dutch St. Maarten and Franco-Swedish St. Barthèlemy, unspecified numbers of slaves arrived.[56]

Tapas and Tulips on the Thames

Diplomatic reactions varied as three nations exchanged a plethora of correspondence on five fronts, with as many intermediaries shuttling from one plenipotentiary to another. Arístegüi told Lindegren that the imports did not violate the treaty and that he would always uphold Spain's commitment to end the traffic with Christian and Castilian honor. Responding to the revelation of the Dutch-Spanish axis, Baron von Schimmelpenninck expressed surprise, considering that the Dutch islands could ill afford to export their slaves. As the Netherlands's largest slave-based economy, Suriname could afford to export them. But it ceased to import slaves, and its planters refused to sell those who remained. The baron added that he would do all in his power to stop the exodus.

Javier de Isturiz, Spanish ambassador to Great Britain, was apologetic and accommodating to Palmerston's protests, but John Bulwer, his British counterpart in Madrid, received a terse response from Palmerston's counterpart, Juan Francisco Penalva. Penalva argued that Spain knew nothing of such traffic and demanded proof. Dutch foreign minister Sarraz was more irate. When Palmerston instructed Henry Howard, British ambassador to the Netherlands, and his successor, Edward Disbrowe, to query the Dutch government, Sarraz summarized pertinent articles from the Anglo-Dutch treaties of 1814 and 1818. And after congratulating his compatriots for adhering to the accords and setting the example for Spain to do likewise—which in his words it did—Sarraz dismissed the British inquiry when he quipped, "Ne saurait fournir à la Grande Bretagne un just objet de plainte."[57]

Notwithstanding Sarraz's prickly defense, Anglo-Dutch exchanges proved the most telling. Palmerston was pleased with plans for the abolition of Dutch slavery in 1848 and with positive responses to British offers to buy Dutch leases on the Gold Coast. Not wanting to offend the Hague, he softened his tone, instructing Disbrowe to inform Sarraz that "Her Majesty's Government readily admit that the traffic in question is not contrary to any of the stipulations of the Treaty ... of 1818 nor ... the Treaty of 1814, which clearly apply only to slaves brought from Africa." He then discussed the "infringement of the great principle of humanity. . . . [I]t ought not to be lawful for a man to buy and sell his fellow man, for the purpose of carrying him away from the country of his birth, to be held in slavery in a foreign country. But that principle is violated, whether the unfortunate captive, who is the subject of the purchase and sale, was born in Africa or the West Indies."[58]

Though Palmerston's solicitude in the second letter was no less accusatory than the scolding tones of the first, it achieved its aim. Sarraz mellowed and revealed a facet of Dutch policy hitherto unknown to the British. Curaçao could export slaves even though other Dutch colonies outlawed it. In 1832, the Hague stipulated

> that only the exportation of specialized slaves would be allowed without special authorization, and only under those conditions. . . . [W]hile receiving from the British delegation a request from Curaçao demanding some clarification ... it was mentioned to the Governor of the said island that the conditional authorization of 1832 had been replaced by a more restrictive one, meaning that authorization to export slaves ... will be granted only in the most urgent of extraordinary cases.[59]

Though Disbrowe relayed Sarraz's assurance to Palmerston that slave export laws applied only in cases of drought and famine, he thought the decree was a "cruel measure ... so contrary to the spirit of those engagements by which the two Governments had promised each other ... to prevent the sale of man by man."[60] Palmerston expressed his gratitude for restricting Curaçao exports to cases of planter hardship. But he added that because slavery is slavery, be it in Africa or the Antilles, the traffic would give rise to slave breeding for exportation, "a practice replete with cruelty, and in the highest degree demoralizing to any country in which it is practiced."[61] Sensationalism did not disguise his true sentiments. If the Netherlands carried out its plan to abolish slavery in 1848— which, excepting St. Maarten, it did not—and if it took greater steps to abandon its settlements on the Gold Coast—which it did in 1850, 1868, and 1872—Great Britain stood much to gain. Abolition in the Dutch colonies would lessen market competition with mainland Suriname—the real center of Dutch slavery and sugar production. Dutch retreat from the Gold Coast would give the

British greater access to raw materials and at the same time the opportunity to monitor French interests in Togo and Dahomey.[62]

On September 23, Lindegren wrote that the influx stopped. Later he added that Arístegüi revoked all remaining permits. In December, Palmerston ordered the consul to thank the governor for withdrawing his permission. Sarraz kept his word to lobby for modifications in the law of 1832. Curaçao was now obliged to follow the example of other Dutch islands: no slave exports without consent from the slaves, except in cases of planter hardship. But in Lindegren's last report on the topic, he stated that Dutch planters petitioned the king to reinstate the original law and that more slaves had just arrived from Curaçao. Although most remained in Puerto Rico, eighty were rerouted to Cuba.[63]

Arístegüi's mastery of diplomatic deception was consummate. Though he complained often about Lindegren to his superiors, he withheld the full thrust of his dissatisfaction until he returned to Spain, where he recommended the consul's removal because "[h]is accusations are always based on rumors that later prove false." He added that the post was superfluous, *inncesario,* and as such, it should be dissolved. Failing that, a more sensible, reasonable person, *una persona más sensata,* should replace the incumbent. He concluded by returning to the uselessness of the consulate. "Given the strain of relations with Great Britain, it would not be convenient to affect new problems and [in any event] any other consul would behave in the same manner because they [the British] always appoint abolitionists convinced of their righteousness."[64] The governor's hyperbole warrants emphasis, for John Lindegren, head of Great Britain's first permanent diplomatic mission to Puerto Rico, was neither a John Brown, a David Turnbull, nor a Julio Vizcarrondo. Indeed, his record shows that he did not join the ranks of "righteous, die-hard abolitionists," *antiesclavistas convencidos,* as the governor called them, until the 1850s.[65]

9

Theories in Practice

The Inter-Caribbean Influx of 1847

Africans dominated the inter-Caribbean slave influx of 1847. Though non-Hispanic Creoles, especially women, ranked among them, most came from the Upper Guinea Coast, primarily Río Pongo. Regarding other possible African sources at this time—reliance on circumstantial evidence notwithstanding—additional captives came from Lower Guinea, especially Dutch Accra. The chapter's first section addresses immigration, slavery, and slave traffic as they relate to changing but ever-ambivalent notions of island security. Because most of the slaves were African reexports, it is obvious that demands for slave labor in Puerto Rico continued to outweigh fears of slave resistance. The second and third sections focus on large- and small-scale slave landings. The fourth section assesses the failure of British vigilance, for consular oversight contributed to the success of the influx.

Island Security

The penal code of 1845 left transatlantic corridors open by upholding the right to own private property. Foreign agents could not search for African captives on private estates in Spanish dominions. Shortly before the code was ratified, the governors of Cuba and Puerto Rico rejected Spain's proposal for free African contract labor. The Cuban government reasoned that the time was not propitious.[1] The Puerto Rican government developed a fuller explanation: more workers were not needed because conscripted peasants and vagrants reinforced slave labor.[2] Arístegui did not misrepresent the truth. There were high hopes for the local labor program, though it proved a failure. Still, were his response identical to that of his Cuban counterpart, he would have been on target. It was foolhardy to consider free African contract labor while slavery still existed. Socially and ideologically, the two systems were incompatible.

Under African and Creole leadership, Puerto Rican slaves showed their willingness to challenge slavery head-on. Year after year in the 1840s, Puerto Rico was jolted by the confrontational behaviors of slaves.[3] Nonetheless, Puerto Rico experienced nothing on the scale of the Cuba's Conspiración de la Escalera in 1844, an ethnic cleansing so sanguinary that anticolonial elements among Cuba's free black community did not resurface as a political group with its own agenda until the Guerra Chiquita of 1879—a failed plot that stemmed from dissatisfaction with terms that ended the Ten Years War. Slave dissidence in Cuba became less conspiratory and more spontaneous by the late 1840s. Lacking girth and organizational cohesiveness after 1848, slave resistance in Puerto Rico also grew in spontaneity, isolation, and individualism. While some free Puerto Ricans of color—divided unevenly between the well-to-do and the poor—expressed dignified sympathy and at times violent outrage over the plight of slaves, joint action across the socioeconomic chasm was unknown. Though color phobias were less pronounced in Puerto Rico than in Cuba, free blacks—be they island- or foreign-born Creoles or creolized Africans—were often viewed with suspicion. In addition, officials in Puerto Rico associated any form of slave unrest with Haitian intrigues against the Spanish reoccupation of Santo Domingo in the early 1860s.[4]

Albeit free African immigrants were to be bound by contract, the idea of their non-Westernized presence, unfettered by slave status, did not appeal to island administrators. A fecund imagination was not requisite to conjure up images of another St. Domingue. While there is no evidence to support the idea of political solidarity between Puerto Rican slaves and free blacks, records do show that Spain's formidable military presence was based as much on Afrophobia as on its fear of independence movements.[5] Puerto Rican slave dissent took its toll in lives and property.[6] But there were other reasons for Arístegüi's rejection of free African immigration. It was his aim to avoid responsibility for monitoring free Africans—a burden to which metropolitan authorities would have committed him without compromise. Finally, friction between the captaincy general and the intendancy remained keen. It is possible that he rejected the plan to chafe its aged catalyst, Intendant José Domingo Díaz.[7]

Did Arístegüi's rejection indicate his political and diplomatic growth, or was it consistent with his proslavery posture? Lindegren would have us believe that the governor was not in league with the planter class, that he fought slave traffic because he was committed to upholding Spanish honor by maintaining its international treaties, and that he was forced to yield to local and metropolitan pressures. This view does not bear up under scrutiny. There was no change in the governor's policy. There was no ideological deviation. In office less than a year when the consulate opened, Arístegüi proved his affinity with slaveholding elements from the beginning. He had already issued trade permits when Lindegren first reported the revival of traffic from the Pongo River in December 1844. He did not mislead his superiors when he stated that Puerto Rico did not need more slaves. High colonial officers were selected with care. As a result, most were quite shrewd. He meant, and was understood to mean, that in view of the penal code of 1845, he would permit an unspecified grace period for the acquisition of as many slaves as possible by way of foreign— but non-Britannic—Caribbean ports.[8] Then the traffic would halt. And when Arístegüi said the island did not need free African contract workers, he meant that he would not accept responsibility for thousands of foreign black workers unrestricted by the controls of institutional bondage.

By 1846, as permits for African slave trade expeditions increased, along with permits for inter-Antillean slave imports, a number of proslave trade factors were evident. First, the subjugation of landless peasants would not achieve its desired results. *Agregados*, as they were called, could not be coerced into meeting planter-class demands. Second, Aberdeen's anti-Palmerstonian politics, the variants of jihad politics vis-à-vis diminished non-Muslim resistance, the increasingly unified expansion of French commercial and political interests in West Africa, and competing European territorial designs in general—between France and Great Britain above all—combined to signal renewed interests in Senegambia and the Upper Guinea Coast as sources of slaves. Third, though the Spanish antislave trade law of 1845 caused a temporary slowdown in Cuba, for Puerto Rico it spelled out long-range contradictions. Though the African slave trade continued, the code marked the beginning of business and banking reservations over the profitability of slavery. As a consequence, several thousand slaves were sold from Puerto Rico to Cuba between 1848 and 1873, causing an eruption of boisterous protest from local officials, planters, the British, and the slaves.[9] Meanwhile, in an effort to forestall the close of the West African corridor, Arístegüi made it clear, though not clear enough for Consul Lindegren, that the landing of slaves directly from Africa was one thing, while the landing of slaves—be they African or Creole—from nearby ports was another.

Puerto Rico, more than Cuba, found itself in a quandary. Colonial leaders had no problem with violating codes and treaties to obtain new captives. Yet the African-born often led slave rebellions—some small-scale, isolated incidents; others, large-scale, with aims well-defined.[10] The reenslavement of British freedmen, popular in the 1830s, was too dangerous to continue. Planters in the French and Dutch islands were either ambivalent about exporting substantive numbers of their slaves or hostile to it. Slave numbers in Danish St. Thomas were too small to consider for export. And though St. Croix had more slaves, export was not broached there either. Of the French, Dutch, and Danish islands, however, those with free port status still served as intermediaries for the transfer of African captives. But the dilemma over African versus Creole slave character remained until the influx ceased in the fall of 1847. Until then, the governor was willing to take chances. Rather than alter a carefully hammered-out policy that favored Africans over Creoles, to avoid more irritating attention from the British, he examined each petition for its individual merit.

Dutch Treats

Between January and August 1847, Arístegüi received forty-four petitions from forty-eight individuals to import some 1,100 slaves from the French, Dutch, and Danish Caribbean islands. All were granted licenses. Thirteen petitioners requested small numbers ranging from 1 to 9, for a total of 51. Larger requests ranged from 10 to 60 per petitioner. Of these, ten applications were temporarily inactivated due to Lindegren's protests. All small-scale requests were for Creoles and *ladinos*, most of whom were destined for nonagrarian duties. Four of the 13 applicants owned a total of 20 slaves inherited from estates on other islands; six owned the slaves previously; and seven lived in the capital, far from the sugar-producing centers of the south and west. But in slave commerce, small figures are as suspect as large ones. There was nothing to stop the applicants listed in table 9.1 from selling their slaves for a considerable profit.

Without citing motives, Marcelino Classe, José María Sánchez, and Antonio Salvador de Vizcarrondo requested five slaves from St. Barthèlemy and St. Thomas.[11] More suspect were applicants citing "any island" as a source, intimating profiteering motives no matter how diminutive. Yet desperate planters, such as Nicasio Viña, had no intention of selling their slaves at this point. Some cited occupations that specified nonplanter identity. Schooner captain

Table 9.1. Petitioners for small-scale importations, 1847

Date	Petitioner	Municipality	No. of Slaves	Source
1/09	Juan Montaña	San Juan	1	St. Thomas
1/25	Ramón Cestero	Mayagüez	4	Any island
1/25	José Ramón Fernández	San Juan	2	St. Eustatius
2/27	Antonio Monserrate	Guayama	3[a,b]	St. Thomas
3/05	Claude Abraham	Guayama	4[a,b]	St. Thomas
3/06	Federico Hagenbergh	Guayama	6[a,b]	Venezuela[c]
3/12	Juan Liano	San Juan	2	St. Thomas
3/13	Marcelino Classe	Guayama	2[a]	St. Barthèlemy
3/25	José Antonio Sánchez	Guayama	7[b]	Curaçao[d]
3/30	Domingo Pelati	San Juan	8	Any island
8/04	José María Sánchez	San Juan	1[a]	St. Thomas
8/16	Nicasio Viña	San Juan	9	Any island
9/13	Salvador Vizcarrondo	San Juan	2[a]	St. Thomas

Sources: AGPR, GE:E, caja 66, and GE:C, cajas 66 and 222.

a. Slaves were owned by the petitioner previously.

b. Slaves formed part of an inherited estate.

c. Brought via Curaçao.

d. Brought via St. Thomas.

Juan Montaña asked for a single slave. Juan Liano, who owned ships for shuttle service between San Juan and the Danish Virgins, requested a carpenter and a caulker from St. Thomas.[12]

Most gave detailed explanations. Claude Abraham left St. Thomas to settle in Guayama after the death of his wife. His daughter, Antoinette, left in the care of relatives, inherited her mother's estate. It included four slaves: two adults, Daphne and Celestine; and two minors, Joseph and Thomas. Abraham stated that Antoinette was to be reunited with him, and since the four slaves were all raised as domestics in his former Thomian household, it would be cruel to leave them behind.[13] Federico Hagenbergh, a postmaster born in Arroyo of Prussian-Venezuelan parents, inherited six slaves from his mother, Maria Philippa, who died in Maracaibo. Because Federico was a minor at the time, his brother-in-law, Johann Vandersinger, was named trustee of the estate. Vandersinger took the slaves to Curaçao where he resided. Federico stated that, because he had reached the age of legal adulthood and because of the needs of his growing nuclear family, he was anxious to claim his slaves. They were: Platina, forty-five, and her two children, Pieter, six, and Andrés Corsino, four; Kato, twenty-four, and her son, Castile Alcée, two; and Herminia, nineteen.[14] Shoemaker Antonio Monserrate, also of Arroyo, petitioned on behalf of his wife, Louise Françoise, to import three slaves she inherited from her father in St. Thomas. Though the problem was resolved, their arrival was delayed because papers were sent to the governor without clearance from the military commandant, who was also chief customs officer.[15]

Guayama dominated both sets of applications as the most frequent port of entry and the most oft-cited municipality of legal residence. Requesting a total of 676 slaves, large-scale petitioners came exclusively from western and southern municipalities, including Guayama, with far fewer occupational variants among them. Most were planters and owned one or more sugar haciendas. A few produced both sugar and coffee. There were no claims for slaves as inheritance or for use as domestics. Many applicants filed in response to changing fortunes, good and bad. Of the seven indicating the Danish Virgins, five named St. Thomas specifically; of the fifteen citing Dutch provenance, thirteen spelled out Curaçao specifically. Though eleven had not yet made their purchases, they asked to bring 266 slaves from any neighboring island.[16] One petitioner tempted the governor with technological progress. Juan López de Alicea solicited twenty slaves for his sugar estate, newly overhauled with a state-of-the-art hydraulics system.[17] The remainder made no reference to modernization. Achilles Stuart petitioned for twenty slaves from St. Thomas in the name of his father-in-law, Pierre Danois. Debtors owed Danois large sums of money during his years as a merchant in French Guadeloupe and the Danish Virgins, but they could only repay him with slaves. Tito Patxot Gurnach was a Catalonian who emigrated with his sisters in 1831 from Gerona to Puerto Rico.[18] Like Danois, associates and clients in the non-Hispanic islands owed him money. But until the sugar crisis—that is, the suppression of the Atlantic slave trade—he saw no need to call in the debts. When debtors could not pay, he agreed to settle for a total of twenty-five slaves, all over eighteen years of age.

Patxot's narrative is especially significant in relation to the price index of slaves. It shows that even in times of internal economic crisis, slaves in Spanish colonies brought higher prices than did those in non-Hispanic colonies. Patxot was a businessman who knew that a coffle of prime slaves would sell in Puerto Rico for two or three times the original price elsewhere in the region. In the 1830s, he was an agent for Pedro Blanco's Cuban-assisted slave trade to Puerto Rico. His application did not state his present occupation, but his intention to sell the twenty-five slaves is borne out by the fact that he did not call himself a planter. A declaration of current or intended agricultural pursuits sped up most large-scale requests in 1847. Patxot made no such reference.[19]

José Saldaña blamed his misfortunes on slave illness and death. Thus, he was authorized to buy thirty slaves from Curaçao and the Windwards.[20] Antonio Cabasa, who lost livestock and sugar harvests for want of labor, requested forty slaves from St. Thomas and Curaçao. Filing his first petition in October 1846 with no results, he reapplied in February 1847. Permission came in March.[21] In attempting to prevent collectors from confiscating the property of his orphaned grandchild, Simón Moret underscored the uselessness of free workers and the lack of means to pay them in his petition to bring in fourteen slaves from St. Thomas and St. Croix.[22] Between 1835 and 1845, Antonio Canales of Guayama was identified as the captain of several slavers operating between the Upper Guinea Coast and Puerto Rico.[23] But his schooner, the Isabel, was destroyed in a mishap in Humacao in 1846, which prompted him to switch from seafaring to farming. To prepare for the change, he imported six slaves. After purchasing a farm, he asked for more.[24]

Ten of the petitions filed between January and August 1847 were placed on hold pending instructions from Spain. Their selection seems to have been arbitrary. The applications reveal no common threads. In addition, some requested unlimited numbers of slaves several weeks before Lindegren heard about them. It would seem, then, that individual applications were suspended at random to discourage consular denouncements. Arístegüi revoked permits he issued between September and October.

The large-scale influx reveals the irony and uncertainty of policy toward acquisition and behavior based on natal origins and resocialization. After a failed attempt in 1845, Luisa Belvis was twice granted permits to import thirty slaves in late 1846. By midsummer of the following year, only fourteen arrived; of those, six were labeled esclavos urbanos. Arístegüi required her to post a bond for their behavior.[25] This suggests that urban occupations were equated with Creole identity. The problem could have been related to clerical error, to an excess of Creoles among the African-born, or to efforts to further disguise the Africans as Creoles. Her case indicates that urbanites, Creoles, and ladinos (thus, all slaves except bozales assigned to field work)—long seen as corrupt but more expensive and less prone to violent resistance—lost their place of confused eminence. It also challenges the notion that they were ever preferred over new Africans.[26] In other words, the delay hints that Spanish authorities were indecisive over which type of slave they preferred. This problem centers on circumstances in the late colonial period that made slave origins a nonissue as an internal factor of social control.

Complications in the Belvis petition show that Spanish policy-makers equated urbanity with slave creolization in terms strictly negative rather than mixed.[27] For the 1847 influx, the equation was a useful ploy to discourage the import of Creoles—not because slave owners and lawmakers believed that Africans were suddenly less militant or given to a shorter transition from *bozal* to *ladino* but because Puerto Rico could not afford to upset cooperative governments by spiriting off their Creoles. As we have seen, while no longer able to purchase Africans, many non-Hispanic colonies still served as depots. The siphoning off of Creoles from foreign neighbors would have undermined Spain's objectives by alienating the very polities that continued to play supporting roles in the larger scheme of transatlantic operations—hence Arístegüi's increased communications with Madrid. The logic that motivated this bemused state of affairs merits emphasis. To prevent antislavery entanglements and at the same time to prevent the taking of umbrage on the part of foreign accomplices, it behooved Arístegüi to avoid the importation of bona fide Creole slaves from the French, Dutch, and Danish islands.

Despite drastic declines in prices, for example, the Dutch monarchy strictly forbade the selling of local slaves for export. Curaçao was the exception because its wealth, in the main, came from its status as a duty-free emporium. By the time Dutch planters gathered enough support to challenge the king's orders —no slave sales to foreign colonies without documented consent from the slaves—the Puerto Rican influx of 1847 had ceased, it seems. The Danish islands experienced a similar decline in slave prices. Moreover, St. Thomas did not have enough slaves to satisfy Puerto Rican needs. While St. Croix and the French islands had more than enough, they exhibited no trend in external sales, not even on the eve of abolition in 1848. To the contrary, rather than concede to Spanish supremacy in sugar production, Cruzian and French Antillean planters solicited free African labor, as did their counterparts in the British Antilles.[28] In certain quarters of the Danish, Dutch, and French governments, some lamented the fact that tax-paying colonists could no longer afford African captives because Spanish demands inflated slave prices. But until these governments abolished slavery, they attempted to counter losses in plantation revenues by allowing their colonies to continue as entrepôts for the home stretch in the African slave trade.[29]

Danish St. Thomas, Dutch Curaçao, and Dutch St. Eustatius were the islands

Lindegren and the petitioners named most frequently as entrepôts. The first two had few Creoles to sell because neither was a slave-based economy. Applicants never cited Danish St. Croix definitively, with its slave population of 16,706, a stout figure compared to its sister islands, St. Thomas and St. John, and the Dutch islands. So close to southern Puerto Rico, St. Croix would have made an ideal donor. Though Ponce's sugar industry was in decline, other towns continued to seek slaves. Attempting to pick up where Ponce left off, planters in neighboring Guayama would have been delighted to receive slaves from St. Croix, as table 9.2 suggests. Instead, on the eve of abolition in the Danish Virgins, Cruzian planters savored the idea of free African immigrants working alongside newly emancipated slaves.[30] Slave export hemmed in small sugar producers in Curaçao given that Spaniards kept slave prices high.[31] The Dutch planter dilemma was thorny: export slaves because of unimpressive sugar profits or retain them in hopes of future assistance from African contract labor. But the problem resolved itself when the influx appeared to stop between the summer and fall of 1847. More important, the Hague upheld its position that Dutch sugar production would stay concentrated in Suriname, where several thousand free African soldiers and farmers were settled.[32]

Proof of connections between West Africa and the non-Hispanic Caribbean in 1847 combines the empirical and the circumstantial. First, though Lindegren never voiced suspicions of a joint ploy, before he learned of the governor's permits, he reported that French, Dutch, and Danish Caribbean territories were identified as intermediate ports for African slave commerce in 1847. He stated specifically that the use of these ports sidestepped the penal code of 1845.[33]

Second, some applicants came close to admitting that the entire operation was a smoke screen to hide recent African provenance. For example, Juan Bentejeal stated, "I have 20 slaves in Curaçao and St. Barthèlemy.... [B]y virtue of the fact that the importation of said slaves is prohibited without sufficient authorization from your preeminent office ... I beg that you deign to permit them to enter."[34] Certain specificities and omissions are implicit here. Any reference to Creoles or *ladinos* would have expedited approval. "Sufficient authorization" suggests that he needed Arístegüi's full endorsement. High-level support was not needed to bring in Creole or creolized slaves from neighboring islands, except in cases of controversy. Furthermore, while some petitioners hinted that they knew the slaves, or had at least seen them, when they stated "todos son aplicables, laborosos y de buenas costumbres," not one applicant was in a position to swear that the slaves were *not* recent arrivals from Africa.

Table 9.2. Petitioners for large-scale importations, 1847

Municipality/petitioner	Slaves	Source	Motive
Guayama			
Isabel Batable	21	St. Thomas	Sugar production
Juan Bentejeal [sic]	20	Curaçao	Sugar production
Antonio Canales	50	Curaçao	Sugar production
Juan Luis Ramis	12	Any island	Factory work
Francisco Ramírez	12	Any island	Sugar production
Constantine Souteyran	10	St. Thomas	Sugar production
Jean Toubert	26	Any island	Sugar production
San Germán			
Luisa Belvis	30	Curaçao	Second request[b]
Manchani and Silva	30	Curaçao	Sugar production
Narciso Pujols	30	Curaçao	Sugar production
Giuseppi Romagnera	50	Dutch islands[a]	Sugar production
José Saldaña	30	Curaçao	Slave illness
Beltrán Saint Laureant	15	Curaçao	Sugar production[c]
Mayagüez			
Antonio Cabasa	40	Curaçao	Sugar production[b]
Nicolás Más	50	Curaçao	Sugar production
M. Ponce de León	40	Curaçao	Second request[b]
Naguabo			
James Byron	30	Curaçao	Sugar production[c]
Tito Patxot Gurnach	25	Curaçao	Debt collection
Mariano Polo	50	Dutch islands	Sugar production
Humacao			
Juan López Alicea	20	Any island	Sugar production
José María Ríos	50	St. Thomas	Sugar production
Achilles Stuart	20	St. Thomas	Debt collection
Vega Baja			
Casimiro Capetillo	15	Curaçao[d]	Sugar production

Sources: Same as table 9.1.
a. Also named the Danish islands.
b. No response to the first request.
c. Also cited coffee production.
d. Also named St. Thomas.

Were they certain of their Creole or creolized identity, they would have stated as much. To avow that "todos son criollos y ladinos" would have made their requests more attractive legally.

Third, only a few slaves were imported from St. Thomas; they were either local Creoles or creolized Africans, or they were new Africans landed in French or Dutch colonies first. For more than a decade, St. Thomas was one of the least desirable ports to land captives directly from Africa.

Fourth, French dominion was another matter. Ever sensitive to Anglo-French diplomacy, the Foreign Office was often powerless when French affairs corresponded to the slave trade. Indeed, there is evidence of slave traffic between Guadeloupe and Puerto Rico by way of the islets of Marie Galante and Vieques.[35] From Havana, in the 1840s and 1850s Pierre Fourçade orchestrated the arrival of several thousand captives from Upper Guinea. Most went directly to Cuba, but some, less than a hundred, were taken to Puerto Rico directly from Río Pongo.[36] Apparently, Fourçade maintained business relations with neither his native France nor its imperial appendages in Senegal, the Caribbean, and the Indian Ocean. His affinities were Spanish. This was verified when the British tried but failed to connect him to French immigration schemes.[37] They reasoned that *éngagés* recruited from Dakar to Benguela would be diverted from Martinique to the Spanish islands. However, at the height of the Nantes-based program in 1858, Fourçade was implicated in a separate plot to kidnap free Afro–Puerto Ricans for enslavement in Cuba.[38]

In 1847, French connections to Puerto Rican slave traffic seemed more direct, and with limited succor from Cuba. Lindegren wrote that British vessels were so rare in Senegambia that Spaniards purchased French slaves in Gorée.[39] But if any captives landed in Puerto Rico directly from West Africa in 1847, secrecy was consummate. Lindegren had not a clue. In 1844, 1845, 1846, and 1848, he had a great deal to say about direct landings from the Pongo. But in 1847, with one exception in February, he was silent. Nonetheless, if the slaves imported by Arístegüi's authority included Africans landed first in Martinique and Guadeloupe, their numbers were low. Only five petitions pointed to French Caribbean origins. Though slaves numbered nearly 50 percent of the nonwhite population of Martinique in the 1840s, the decade of French abolition, planters were not willing to part with them.[40]

From Jamaica, David Turnbull commented on the Dutch slave trade to Puerto Rico. He correctly identified several stimuli: Spanish fears of sex imbalances, the willingness of Spanish planters to pay top prices, and the willingness of Western consumers to import tropical staples produced by slaves. But in one of few miscalculations made in the course of his explosive career, he stated that Dutch planters sold their slaves to Puerto Rico out of the same fear that prompted the British in the 1830s: inadequate compensation.[41] His comparison is inappropriate because the times and their variables were different. Abolition in the Dutch Caribbean was too far off for compensation to have been a central issue. Though by 1841 Dutch planters could not afford to import slaves, slavery did not end until 1863.[42] The Dutch Crown had the delay of abolition in mind when it forbade external sales in 1818. But that law was altered by another, which permitted slave exports under conditions that might lead to planter impoverishment.[43]

Of all seven Dutch Caribbean colonies, mainland Suriname was most firmly rooted in slave labor. The others, Curaçao in particular, resembled Danish St. Thomas. Producing little surplus compared to genuine slave-based economies, many were small, prosperous free ports and international clearinghouses for manufactured items and tropical goods.[44] Slaves formed the minority in all the Dutch islands. In Curaçao, other groups consisted of Europeans and Dutch Creoles—Dutch Jews in particular—a multinational commercial sector, and a corpus of equally enterprising free blacks and Afro-Ashkenazim, that is, Creole Dutch Jewish mulattoes.[45] Hence, it would seem that these islands were ideal sources for the rerouting of slaves. Yet in 1832, St. Eustatius rejected the Hague's permission to export certain slaves. Furthermore, Puerto Rican efforts to buy large numbers from planters there failed.[46] The royal Dutch measure of 1818 was taken seriously wherever it was adopted, but in the 1840s, despite the compromise of 1832, Dutch planters petitioned the king to nullify the non-export act of 1818, which he refused to do.[47] It would appear, then, that the minuscule slaveholding class was willing to part with some of its slaves for top Spanish pesos. But in late 1847, when Lindegren reported their pleas, he failed to note that they excluded representation from St. Maarten, where slavery was abolished the following year.[48] Certain that slaves would flee to the French side, where slavery ended in 1848, the Dutch abolished it on the their side as well. Thus, St. Maarten was the only Dutch Antillean possession with an urgent motive to shed its bonded class. It would seem plausible, therefore, that slaves landed in Puerto Rico from there were indeed Creoles were it not for the fact that St. Maarten did not have a slave population large enough to match the numbers that arrived under Arístegüi.

The majority of the slaves bound for Puerto Rico were alleged to have originated in Curaçao, where the slave numbers were only slightly higher than those in other Dutch islands. But most planters in Curaçao were also reluctant to let them go. Some found ways to skirt the king's order against external sales. But with total emancipation sixteen years away, most preferred to keep them. In the 1840s, slaves in Curaçao did not exceed 7,000. Its slave market, however, was lively, with 853 transactions for more than 1,000 slaves between 1842 and 1851. Though petitions and transactions listed in tables 9.1–9.3 point to the importance of Dutch sources in the influx of 1847, statistics for Curaçao between 1842 and 1851 reveal the energy of internal sales.

In table 9.4, against the total slave population for each year, figures for births and deaths between 1845 and 1850 leave little room for demographic gains and

Table 9.3. Price, age, and sex distribution of slaves sold from Curaçao to Puerto Rico in 1847

Buyer/Seller	Price in guilders	Age of slave	Sex
Estéban Balaguer			
J. H. Moron [sic]	300	16	Male
Paulina de Wendt	310	22	Male
M. C. Henríques	300	17	Male
David Henríques	300	21	Male
H. van der Menlengh	300	20	Male
P. H. de Mesa	300	14	Male
Johanna Henríques	200	13	Male
Josefina de Lima	250	12	Male
F. Vidal	1,050[a]	23	Male
F. Vidal	—	24	Female
F. Vidal	—	19	Female
Antonio Canales			
B. da Costa Gomes	225	9	Female
D. A. Jesuran (?)	400	27	Female
D. A. Jesuran (?)	450	36	Male
P. F. Haseth	525	29	Male
David Mattey	350	14	Female
J. Torres	600	24	Male
P. F. Haseth	2,000[a]	27	Male
P. F. Haseth	—	27	Male
P. F. Haseth	—	21	Female
P. F. Haseth	—	18	Female
Nicolás Más			
A. Guilheux	450[a]	21	Female
A. Guilheux	—	3	Female
Louisa Jones	280	41	Female
W. Prince, Jr.	325	20	Female
Gertruida de Jongh	225	15	Female
C. L. van Alytrecht	325	22	Male

Buyer/Seller	Price in guilders	Age of slave	Sex
J. A. Haseth	300	33	Female
A. de Veer	300	13	Male
A. de Veer	500	23	Male
B. Daniat	425	16	Male
A. Bennjon	460	23	Female
W. G. Neuman	500	15	Male
E. Lopes	625	17	Male
W. Prince, Jr.	400	17	Female
F. W. Palm	450[a]	26	Female
F. W. Palm	—	7	Female
David Duval	950[a]	44	Female
David Duval	—	22	Female

Total: 20 males, 19 females

Source: Centraal Historisch Archief, Willemstad, Curaçao, Netherlands Antilles. Koloniale Secretary: Archief van het Notariaat, 1842–1851.

a. Group price, 20 males, 19 females, total 39.

Table 9.4. Slave births and deaths in Curaçao, 1845–1850

Year	Births	Births per 100 slaves	Deaths	Deaths per 100 slaves	Total slave population
1845	141	2.53	97	1.74	5,569
1846	228	4.06	141	2.51	5,619
1847	213	3.92	117	2.15	5,436
1848	253	4.62	93	1.70	5,479
1849	251	4.49	112	2.00	5,585
1850	283	5.02	139	2.47	5,638

Source: Same as table 9.3.

losses from slaves in transit. Furthermore, between 1846 and 1848, *De Cura-çaosche Courant*, the island's official government weekly, trivialized internal slave sales by citing smaller figures and fewer transactions. More important, though table 9.3 shows that the Dutch colonial secretary listed Puerto Rican buyers by name, the Curaçao newspaper failed to indicate any external sales.[49] These factors combine to perpetuate the question of slave origins in 1847. Despite its wispy dependence on slave labor, Curaçao received the services of Gold Coast Africans in the 1830s and 1840s. Though most went to Dutch Southeast Asia, they were trained in Suriname, and many were contracted to remain in Dutch Caribbean territories as a military force to keep slaves in check.[50] It is at this point in the discussion that the viability of continued trans-atlantic linkages is more evident.

As long as the Dutch maintained leases in Accra, which they did until later in the century, voyages—ostensibly for legitimate commerce—between the Antilles and the Gold Coast continued unfettered. In previous chapters I observed that the Dutch government protested British interference in its African affairs; Dutch officials prevented the British from inspecting French slavers docked in Accra for supplies; Dutch authority over the indigenous peoples of Accra was nominal; and Spanish slave traders operated in all European settlements along the Gold Coast. Though slave exports from the Gold Coast throughout the nineteenth century ranked among the lowest in Lower Guinea, it should be reiterated that African slaving ventures from one region of the Atlantic littoral to another—that is, from Upper Guinea to Lower Guinea to the Congo and Angola and back, before the start of inbound voyages to American destinations—were not unusual.[51] Bulking was a cooperative, cross-national operation to facilitate inbound voyages. Given that the Dutch Crown forbade civil service workers in Accra from buying and selling slaves—an utterly useless proscription—there was nothing to prevent these functionaries from receiving slaves in Senegambia, Bissau, Río Pongo, Sherbro, or Gallinas in Upper Guinea and combining them with their own captives—or with free contract laborers and military recruits—and sending them to the Caribbean under the guise of Dutch cabotage. Often the pretext of intrastate commerce tied the hands—but not the tongues—of British ministers, secretaries, and naval officers.

The free port status of many Dutch islands gave foreign slavers a different safety valve. If they escaped British patrols and the venture were disclosed after the Africans landed, their presence was legal. St. Thomas was the exception due to the underrepresentation of Danish officialdom. Lengthy and fruitless investigations surrounding the case of the *Con la Boca* cited in Chapter 6 would never have been allowed in any port of Dutch or French dominion—duty free or not. The combination of free port status and the sovereignty of cabotage trade rendered Curaçao an ideal location for the reexport of Africans to Spanish territories, especially—and almost exclusively—Puerto Rico.

Misjudgments

The gradual shift in acquisitions from the sparsely populated savannas of Upper Guinea to the densely populated forests of Lower Guinea was a major geo-demographic feature of the Atlantic slave trade from the sixteenth century onward. But slave trade experts are divided over the significance of the Upper Guinea Coast in the era of abolition. Curtin asserts that its west-bound traffic grew moribund, while Eltis, Moreno Fraginals, and Bergad et al. show that Upper Guinea lost little of its infamy as a source of slaves for Cuba. Though Cuba took more captives from other African latitudes, Puerto Rican itineraries were limited largely to Upper Guinea. As we have seen, the Creole families of Upper Guinea and an assortment of European and American nationals served Brazil in diminishing degrees by the 1840s and Cuba through the 1860s, albeit the latter relied heavily on Lower Guinea and the subequatorial zones. In the 1850s, British military interventions led to a consulate in Lagos, on the one hand, and augmented civil strife, on the other.[52] As a result, Yoruba captives from southwest Nigeria continued to land in Cuba for another twenty years.[53] According to Moreno Fraginals, captives from Lower Guinea—Ghana, Togo, Dahomey, and Nigeria—soared from about 41 percent between 1800 and 1820 to almost 49 percent between 1850 to 1870. For the same periods, captives from Senegambia and Upper Guinea—Guinea-Bissau, Guinea-Conakry, Sierra Leone, and Liberia—dropped from almost 27 percent to more than 11 percent.[54] This was not the case with Puerto Rico.

Table 9.5 shows that between 1834 and 1859, more than 50 percent of the vessels listed sought captives from the Upper Guinea Coast alone. For most of the 1840s, the British identified Río Pongo as an important source. Intermittently from 1844 to 1848, Lindegren warned the Foreign Office and the Admiralty that slave traders from riverine Upper Guinea were attempting to land captives in Puerto Rico.[55] But his trust in Arístegüi did not waver. "As long as the present governor remains, no slave will be allowed to be landed upon this island." He was oblivious to Arístegüi's responsibility to the planter class and, in turn, its obligations to the Spanish treasury through taxation. Nor did he envision links between the inter-Caribbean arrivals of 1847 and transatlantic activity from West Africa. Instead of following tips from British and Puerto Rican informants, he continued to express his conviction that the influx was entirely Creole.

A mixture of boons and obstacles to the suppression of the slave trade increased in the 1840s. In the words of one naval officer, "Reports are conflicting and contradictory...and too burdensome to unravel."[56] Slave ships sailed 2,195 miles of Atlantic African shoreline. With only twenty-four cruisers deployed in the service of the abolitionist cause, one vessel per 91 miles was insufficient.[57] They were also slow and often in bad condition—hardly a match for sleek

Table 9.5. Slave ships bound for Puerto Rico alone, 1834–1859

Vessel	African regions represented	Destination[a]
Arrogante Mayagüesana	Congo/Angola	PR
Josefa	Upper Guinea	PR
Zema	Upper Guinea	PR
Explorador	Lower Guinea, Congo/Angola	C/PR
Luisa	Upper Guinea, Congo/Angola	PR
Vigilante	Upper Guinea, Lower Guinea	C/PR
Preciosa	Upper Guinea	C/PR
Negrinha	Upper Guinea	PR
Fénix	Lower Guinea	PR
San Nicolás	Upper Guinea	PR
Descubierta	Upper Guinea	PR
Temerário	Upper Guinea	PR
Cinco Amigos	Upper Guinea	PR
Cobra de Africa	Upper Guinea, Lower Guinea	C/PR
Primoroza	Lower Guinea	C/PR
Vencedora	Congo/Angola	PR
Felicidade	Upper Guinea	C/PR
Princéza Africana	Upper Guinea	PR
Con la Boca	Upper Guinea	PR
Gertrúdes	Upper Guinea	PR
Merced	Upper Guinea, Lower Guinea	PR
Carranzano	Upper Guinea	PR
Casualidade	Upper Guinea	PR
Brilhante	Upper Guinea	C/PR
Segunda Rosario	Upper Guinea	C/PR
Jesús María	Upper Guinea	PR
Triunfo	Upper Guinea	PR
Majesty	Congo/Angola	PR

Source: Modified from table 6.2.

a. PR = Puerto Rico alone; C/PR = Cuba and Puerto Rico.

schooners from Baltimore and Barcelona so favored by slave smugglers serving Cuba and Brazil. Still, heavier brigs and brigantines, which dominated Puerto Rican voyages, could outrun the rusty tubs on which the British relied.[58] Pedro Blanco improved strategies and techniques. By the 1830s, his men could load a slaver in two hours. Honing his lessons to scientific precision, Blanco's disciples learned where and how to wait for chasers to exhaust their provisions and stamina.[59] Pursuit could only occur eight out of twenty-four hours, somewhere between dawn and 2 P.M. Darkness thwarted all efforts at capture; the culprits were fully aware that cruisers would not commence chase after midafternoon. Thus, the remaining sixteen hours belonged to them.[60] It is to the credit of the British Admiralty that any slave ship was overtaken at all—though at least one Briton thought otherwise.

After thirty-five years of foreign service to his country, Jonathan Rendall assailed the Foreign Office for its ignorance of Africa and its peoples. An expert on West African affairs, he observed that crews from condemned slavers were not as hapless as the Admiralty reported. More often than not, they assisted newly arrived slavers. Rendall also noted that from Senegal to Liberia, slave traders from the United States accommodated all in need of their services. He stated further that Great Britain underestimated the power of African leaders. According to Rendall, the British did not take them seriously, for the British neither consulted them in earnest nor followed up antislave trade treaties with formal state visits of peace and goodwill. He insisted that the suppression of slave traffic and the promotion of legitimate commerce were impossible without friendship. Until the early 1850s, few listened to Rendall's complaints. As fast as the British burned Spanish slave factories in the tiny kingdoms and paramount chieftaincies of Sherbro, Gallinas, and Cape Mount, new ones not only appeared in Guinea-Bissau and Guinea-Conakry, the old ones returned.[61]

The popularity of slave commerce from Río Pongo in the 1840s comes as no surprise. Its labyrinthine contours made it impossible to monitor efficiently. Gallinas and Sherbro, however, were more accessible and therefore more vulnerable, as table 9.5 indicates. Furthermore, by 1845 many Luso-Brazilian slave traders abandoned national interests in favor of aiding Cuba and Puerto Rico. In December 1847, for example, it was reported that no Africans from the area were shipped to Brazil that year. But more than 1,000 left directly from the Pongo River or indirectly by way of rivers and islets in Guinea-Bissau. Despite British reports, it is evident that Dom Caetano José Nozzolini placed little faith in the cultivation of peanuts.[62]

The Puerto Rican "Registro Central de Esclavos de 1872" (Slave Register of 1872) is a useful tool for extrapolations backward to 1847.[63] Of the 31,000 slaves it lists, less than 3,000 were foreign-born. Africans, however, accounted for 89 percent of this minority. At 7 percent, slaves of Dutch origin ranked a distant second. Slaves of British, Cuban, Danish, Portuguese Asian, and Venezuelan origin accounted for the remaining 4 percent. Table 9.6 demonstrates that Africans made an impressive showing in the largest sugar-producing areas.

Though the register corroborates the Arístegüi influx, it belies true provenance. Table 9.2 shows that the influx of 1847 was limited to the island's three major slaveholding municipalities. With figures gleaned from the register, table 9.6 shows that the same towns held the largest concentration of foreign-born slaves. Vestiges of the 1847 initiative are, therefore, certain, with 13 percent of the foreign slaves identified as French, Dutch, or Danish in origin. Proof that they arrived in Arístegüi's time is fairly easy to come by. The average age of all slaves in the register is approximately 25. The Arístegüi arrivals in table 9.3 average 20.7 years, a prime age for both heavy-duty field work and natural reproduction. The number of non-Hispanic Antillean slaves acquired prior to his influx—but still living and enslaved in 1872—must have been marginal. Older slaves either died by then or were freed because of the sexagenarian article of the Moret Law of 1870, which freed slaves over the age of 60.[64]

Table 9.6. Foreign-born slaves in three major sugar-producing municipalities, 1872

	Guayama	Mayagüez	Ponce
African	502 (31.5%)[a]	385 (41.4%)[a]	262 (26.6%)[a]
Inter-Caribbean			
Danish	7 (71.4%)	16 (87.5%)	2 (50.0%)
St. Thomas	5	14	2
St. Croix	0	1	0
Unknown	2	1	0
Dutch	23 (82.6%)	100 (86.0%)	10 (80.0%)
Curaçao	19	94	10
St. Maarten	3	0	0
Unknown	1	6	0
French	8 (100%)	9 (57.5%)	3 (66.6%)
Guadeloupe	3	2	0
Martinique	0	2	1
St. Barthélemy	2	3	1
Unknown	3	2	1
British	1 (100%)	2 (100%)	0 (0)%
Anguilla	1	0	0
Unknown	0	2	0
Total	541	512	277

Sources: Registro Central de Esclavos de Puerto Rico, 1872; National Archives, Washington, D.C. (microfilm).

Note: Omitted: Cuba 1; Macao 1; Venezuela 12.

a. (%) = percentage of female slaves.

By way of French, Dutch, and Danish ports, more than 1,000 slaves entered Guayama, Ponce, and Mayagüez over an eight-month period in 1847. Yet in 1872, in those same towns, 13 percent for non-Hispanic Caribbean slaves is a poor showing, despite the passing of two and a half decades. Less than a dozen were rerouted to other Puerto Rican municipalities or to Cuba. But even considering the possibility of individual manumission, cabotage, or death, if they were actually non-Hispanic Creoles and not Africans, their representation in the 1872 tallies should have been higher. The extenuating circumstances of 1847 required the import of slaves with French, Dutch, or Danish passports. The reporting of actual birthplaces did not matter at this level. But for government records, such as the Slave Register of 1872, truth was in the best interest of the slaveholder. To avoid fines from the apprehension of slaves suspected of sedition, for slave descriptions in state-controlled periodicals for reasons ranging from sale to marronage, and to collect insurance benefits when slaves died, documents demanded accuracy. While the importance of ethnic, national, cultural, and linguistic differences declined in the nineteenth century politically—but not socioculturally—the separation of *bozal* from *criollo* remained crucial. The crux of the matter is that an unknown number of slaves listed as African-born in 1872 formed part of the Arístegüi influx, but at the time of their arrival their passports identified them as non-Hispanic Creoles. Moreover, the arrivals of 1847 are but one aspect of a wider influx of African captives through junctions in the Eastern Caribbean.

Africans made up 86 percent of the foreign-born in Guayama, Mayagüez, and Ponce. Slaves classified as "others" totaled less than 1 percent.[65] When eliminating the two extremes, "Africans" and "others," the non-Hispanic focus looms large. Dutch slaves in Guayama outnumbered French and Danish slaves at 53 percent of the total, and of that figure, 82 percent came from Curaçao. In Mayagüez, 83 percent the non-Hispanic Caribbean slaves came from Dutch sources; 94 percent of those came from Curaçao. Ponce received few foreign slaves in 1847, but data from 1872 show that 69 percent were of Dutch origin, and all of them came from Curaçao.

Though Cuba and Puerto Rico responded differently to the penal code of 1845, both relied on old friends. In the 1850s, the United States provided Cuba with even greater assistance in direct Africa-to-Cuba transport than it did in the 1830s. Puerto Rico, however, could not maintain direct access to this corridor. Thus, beginning in 1845 but flourishing and peaking in 1847, it returned to the use of French, Danish, and Dutch Caribbean channels, which worked so well in the 1820s. This point leads back to the question of true versus immediate provenance in 1847. Dutch St. Maarten, along with the French and Danish islands, abolished slavery in 1848. Remaining Dutch Caribbean territories did not follow until 1863. Why, then, did Puerto Rican applicants for large-scale imports target Curaçao as their principal source? Their rationale was simple. The geographic extremes of Río Pongo and Accra were still reliable provenance zones, while Dutch Curaçao—with its legitimate imperial, albeit flaccid, connection to Dutch Accra—was a duty-free port.

In June 1847, Lindegren finally admitted that the governor issued more permits than he previously believed.[66] Soon after he reported that the Dutch schooner *Esther* brought thirty-four slaves from Curaçao to Mayagüez and that local planters went to Franco-Swedish St. Barthèlemy and Franco-Dutch St. Maarten for smaller cargoes.[67] He did not specify under whose auspices—Dutch, French, or Swedish—the slaves were exported from the two binational colonies. Though an applicant complained in October that the governor revoked his license, the consul advised his superiors that the traffic stopped in September.[68] Archival records in Puerto Rico and Spain show no activated permits dated after August.

As Arístegüi's tenure drew to a close, Lindegren implored his government to request Spain to grant the "abolitionist governor" another term of office. Arístegüi's successor, Juan Prim y Prats, the count de Reus, voiced little restraint in his support of the slave trade prior to accepting the royal commission in Madrid. Lindegren feared that once in Puerto Rico, Prim would manifest his passion for the maritime malaise. Arístegüi returned to Spain in December 1847. Prim held office less than a year. His term carried greater implications for the internal state slavery itself than the external affairs of trafficking. While interest in Río Pongo sources continued during his rule, he is more known for the suppression of slave revolts in Puerto Rico and St. Croix and for authoring the "Edict against the African Race," a proclamation that promised to prosecute Afro–Puerto Ricans, slave and free, for bearing arms and for any deed or utterance associated with lack of respect toward whites.[69]

All told, Arístegüi was no less supportive of the slave trade than was Prim. The former was civil, courteous, and falsely accommodating in foreign affairs, while the latter was loud, pretentious, and arrogant. Arístegüi was careful to avoid any link between Africa and the importation of slaves. Lindegren made but one reference to Río Pongo or any other source of African captives during the influx of 1847. Conversely, Prim was openly receptive to direct acquisitions, though the consul was never able to verify an actual landing. Prim did not eschew inter-Caribbean routes. Though petitions did not come forth during his term, he was prepared to entertain them. He simplified tariffs and duties by consolidating them into a single tax. In doing so, he reinscribed the *pieza de India*, a unit of measurement that resulted in the selling of slaves in groups rather than as individuals—a term rarely heard after 1820. But despite the brevity of Prim's tenure, the Pongo corridor gave Lindegren considerable diplomatic grief.[70]

With the exception of the *Majesty* in 1859, the slave trade to Puerto Rico seems to have ceased in 1847. Revisionists have shown that the collapse of slave commerce did not result from declining planter demands.[71] Several factors dictated that Puerto Rico would not benefit from the shifting political configurations in West Africa in the 1850s and 1860s, which permitted the continued flow of captives into Cuba until the 1870s. Merchants and speculators, not slaveholders, created the myth of waning Puerto Rican dependency on slave labor, making Cuba the last market for slave traffic from Africa and even Puerto Rico itself.[72] With the closing of African sources for Brazil between 1850 and 1854, Cuba was free of competition. Juan de la Pezuela was an additional factor. While his career in Puerto Rico, and later Cuba, has been explored elsewhere, suffice it to say that in the smaller colony, by fully endorsing intrastate traffic, he thwarted the purchasing power of planters who could still afford slaves.[73] Given that he was Puerto Rico's first abolitionist governor, linking Dutch slave traffic to his name may seem odd. However, while he boasted no captain would dare land a slave ship in Puerto Rico as long as he governed it, two years into his administration he had overstated his confidence. On the morning of October 21, 1850, Dutch authorities sighted a Spanish vessel in Curaçao filled with African captives.[74]

Good Neighbors

Dutch Caribbean ports were intermediary sites for the reexport traffic of African captives to Puerto Rico, beginning as a trickle in 1845 and ending with a flood in 1847. Only a few years separated the end of Dutch military recruitment from Ghana and the return of Dutch Caribbean assistance to Puerto Rico, almost exclusively to Guayama and Mayagüez. Dutch statistics reveal little about the traffic, least of all from Curaçao. As a major emporium, with multinational attributes similar to those of Danish St. Thomas, Curaçao was not a slave-based economy. Though it had sugar plantations—more than St. Thomas, in fact—its wealth was not centered on internal slave production.

Given that slavery in most Dutch Caribbean colonies was not abolished until 1863, few Dutch slaveholders exhibited a willingness to sell their slaves to Spanish Caribbean markets when the outflux occurred. With the exception of Suriname, which was never named as a source, Dutch Caribbean territories did not have slave populations large enough to meet Puerto Rican demands. Among the foreign-born, with the exception of those identified as African, slaves ostensibly of Dutch Caribbean origin dominate the Puerto Rican Slave Register of 1872. The Dutch Crown discouraged the sale of Dutch slaves to markets outside its dominions. But African captives in transit were not Dutch—anymore than their counterparts were Danish in St. Thomas. They were, therefore, omitted from internal statistics. French-directed free African contract schemes nearly succeeded in providing a cover-up for the enslavement of free Puerto Ricans in Cuba under the direction of Pierre Fourçade in the 1850s. In the heyday of African Dutch military recruitment, nothing prevented similar machinations in voyages between Ghana and the Caribbean, especially in the name of intrastate traffic between Dutch Accra and Suriname or Curaçao.

Important counterarguments accompany these assertions. For example, Lindegren stated that most slaves in the influx were women. A host of studies prove that males outnumbered females in the transatlantic slave trade from the sixteenth to the nineteenth centuries. African traders shaped the imbalance because local consumers placed higher value on female slaves. If the "Dutch" slaves were really newly landed Africans, did internal suppliers and the coastal brokers suddenly place a higher premium on male captives? Certainly not. Notarized Dutch records—never shown in Dutch newspapers—illustrate Puerto Rican transactions in Curaçao in 1847. Males slightly outnumbered females. If the sample represents sex distribution for the influx overall, women did not dominate. Lindegren was misinformed. Furthermore, between 1844 and 1848, when he reported numerous efforts to land captives in Puerto Rico, he never mentioned areas in Lower Guinea. Río Pongo was the only source named. Between 1846 and 1847, his Pongo reports overlapped with those for the inter-Caribbean influx. If most of the slaves were truly Africans rather than Dutch Creoles, as is asserted here, then Puerto

Rican business in West Africa remained tied to the Lightbourns, the Fabers, and the Fula in Río Pongo, not the Asante in Kumasi.

These issues would compromise the Gold Coast argument were it not for discrepancies in British and Dutch statements about slave traffic for export in and around Dutch Accra from the 1830s to the 1840s and our quantitative understanding of the area as a provenance zone during the same period. This means that studies showing comparatively small figures for the Gold Coast contradict texts used in this study that identify it as a beehive of slaving activity. Thus, it is not only certain that between 1845 and 1847 the Dutch Caribbean islands served as interim ports for the Puerto Rican influx of recent captives from the Pongo River in Upper Guinea; it is also likely that some of them came from Dutch Accra on the Gold Coast in Lower Guinea.

Epilogue

Cette Fin Qui N'en Est Pas Une

*It is truly lamentable that Great Britain and the United States should
be obliged to spend such a vast amount of blood and treasure for the
suppression of the African Slave Trade, and this, when the only portion
of the civilized world where it is tolerated and encouraged are the
Spanish islands of Cuba and Puerto Rico.*

Abraham Lincoln, May 28, 1860

This book has attempted to grapple with a variety of new problems while
shedding light on older ones left unresolved. In doing so, it has also considered the symbols, meanings, mobilities, and ironies endemic to slave commerce in the Age of Abolition and their implications for the sociocultural history of Puerto Rico and other Atlantic societies. Topics considered range from
European immigration to Puerto Rico to the politics of social and economic
change in West African societies from the interior to the coast; from tensions in
diplomatic relations between Great Britain and Spain to distributions of African captives and Creole slaves from the non-Hispanic Caribbean; from the
size and fittings of slave ships to the politics of interpersonal relations among
maritime outlaws who served the interests of slaveholding elites. This epilogue
offers a few final observations and comments.

Multiple Masters

Puerto Rico was a small Spanish colony with a nucleus of planter and nonplanter elites who continued to buy slaves and consume their labor in an age
that heralded the end of slavery. Thus, Puerto Rican slavery subscribed to many
of the same contradictions that informed politics and society elsewhere in the
Atlantic world. Nonetheless, its own brand of difference, conflict, and change

tempered the extent to which it followed the changing contours of slave commerce during the crisis of abolition. Spain endorsed the illegal traffic in the face of irregular opposition and support. While expatriates—especially Frenchmen—catered to Cuban and Puerto Rican markets without fanfare, official positions assumed by the governments of Denmark, France, and the Netherlands were contingent on political and economic relations with Great Britain. While British opposition to the trade was great, the enormity of the project often resulted in a damaging lack of internal cohesiveness. Frequently, the practitioners of British abolitionist politics and diplomacy were not on the same page.

Fluctuations in the Puerto Rican slave trade were not centered on Euro-American politics alone. Social, political, and economic forces endemic to West African affairs contributed to the dictates of the traffic. Among African Creoles, Muslims, and polytheists—across national, ethnic, and sometimes regional boundaries—power politics, social upheavals, cultural revolutions, and changing systems of trade were felt on the Puerto Rican slave market. Beyond points of embarkation within regional divides, the specificities of African provenance are difficult to determine. It is certain, nonetheless, that the majority of captives who landed on Puerto Rican shores came from the interiors of Upper Guinea in present-day Guinea-Conakry, Sierra Leone, and Liberia. While most were polytheists from small states, acephalous societies, and client polities not far the coast—such as the Pongo Susu and the Gangá of Sierra Leone and Liberia —some, such as the Fula and the Manding, were Muslims from larger and often newly centralized states between Futa Jallon and the Sahel at the Niger Bend. Lower Guinea representation is also worthy of note. However, it was limited almost entirely to the Niger Delta in southeastern Nigeria because independent Puerto Rican slave traders were not active in the Nigerian southwest. In essence, for Puerto Rico, in contrast to Cuba and Brazil, the Ibo outflux from the Bight of Biafra outdistanced the Yoruba outflux from the Bight of Benin.

Two questions warrant emphasis here. First, if captives from Senegal and the Gold Coast were sparsely represented in the slave trade to the Spanish Caribbean, where lay the strength and value of French, Dutch, and Danish succor in Africa vis-à-vis Cuba and Puerto Rico? Second, if Spain was determined to keep the slave trade in Spanish hands, why did foreign assistance continue? Responses to both concerns form the basis of operational differences between the two Spanish islands. Indeed, important strategic bifurcations begin with these questions. Such bifurcations contributed to Puerto Rico's unique position as a participant in the traffic. Marginal Senegalese representation among slaves in the Spanish islands did not point to the displacement of French slave traders. French nationals continued to serve Spanish Caribbean interests elsewhere on the coast of Africa. Several French merchants settled in Cuba and joined Spaniards in slaving expeditions that almost always involved voyages of direct return from Africa to Cuba. However, the African slave trade to Cuba was not dependent on relations with the non-Hispanic Caribbean. Conversely, Puerto Rican operations relied on them often. Therefore, due to a greater dependency on mixed channels—direct landings and reexport operations—French slave traders served Puerto Rico differently, lending the strength of their flag in the 1820s, without the consent of their government, and the strength of their business connections in the French Caribbean from the mid-1830s to the early 1840s.

A history of commercial relations with the French, Dutch, and Danish islands resulted in a longevity of reexport practices that supplemented ventures organized as voyages of direct return. British reports about slave ships detained or captured often lacked evidence to verify final destinations in the 1820s. However, when non-Hispanic Caribbean ports were mentioned, it is likely that Puerto Rico was slated as the final stop. This likelihood was compounded in the 1830s, when British authorities reported the proliferation of Spanish slave traders in the immediate hinterlands of the Gold Coast, where Danes, Dutchmen, and no small number of Britons supervised all manner of commercial subterfuge. Therefore, Spain's determination to rely on its own resources for the acquisition of African captives met with fractured success, with Cuba and Puerto Rico marking the line of division. From one Atlantic terminus to the other, the African slave trade to the larger island was, in the main, a Spanish affair, while the same activities in the smaller island continued to reflect mixed means.

Theory and Discourse

Relations predicated on antislave trade treaties between Great Britain and Spain constituted a series of unending maneuvers between diplomatic rupture and repair. Given that Great Britain imposed its abolitionist determinations on Spain, the treaty of 1817 began a series of plays based on diplomatic snags, tears, and fissures. What followed was a discursive battle of wills played out in Europe, Africa, the Caribbean, and the high seas. Great Britain established the discourse; that is, it authored conventions of communication that dictated who had the right to say what and do what to whom and when. There was nothing inherently Afrophobic about Spain's determination to maintain slavery. Nor—after two centuries of lucrative, slave-based imperialism—was Great Britain motivated by a sudden burst of Afrophilia in its determination to abolish slavery and the traffic that nourished it. Groups and individuals formed a parade of players that demonstrated the density of relational power, knowledge, difference, and resistance within the walls of both camps. Discursive discord at the international level failed to disguise internal dissent. Yet both powers made every effort to present public images of national uniformity. No matter how thin the surfaces of national agreement, Great Britain and Spain took turns in straining communications by breaking the rules.

In portions of this book I concur with conclusions drawn by other scholars about the slave trade in the nineteenth century. My efforts, for example, corroborate the works of those who assert that the slave trade to Puerto Rico began its irreversible decline in the 1830s. Other areas signal assorted points of departure. My concerns begin with understated opposition to the "friendly master" thesis. Throughout the book, it is taken for granted that Roman Catholicism and medieval Spanish law buffered neither slavery nor its traffic. Broader concerns counter postures that emphasize the positive force of British diplomatic and maritime intervention.

International abolitionism was not a monolithic crusade. In addition to facing ongoing resistance from a variety of external opponents, the movement was fractured at the internal level by overextended energies based on the impossibility of political uniformity among the crusaders themselves. Segmented victories overrode ideas about linear success on all sides of the campaign. In addition, given my sustained focus on the dynamics of African and inter-Caribbean trajectories and their impact on the island as a whole, the book does not correspond to microeconomic approaches—an important internal genre within the study of Spanish colonial Puerto Rican history that, among other things, assigns earlier dates to the decline of the external slave trade. By problematizing the obvious and substantiating nuances that characterize the not-so-obvious, this study has explored different concerns, chronologies, and trends. In doing so, it makes an effort to redirect the flow of premises established in canonical and revisionist readings of slave commerce in the nineteenth century. Thus, I underscore less the notion of closure than the need to identify the inscriptions, descriptions, and details about ideas and actions for or against movements toward closure.

Discourse and Metaphor

With the publication of *Capitalism and Slavery* in 1944, Eric Williams established himself as an epistemological provocateur. In 1971, his record for intellectual catharsis and controversy continued with the synthesis *From Columbus to Castro: The History of the Caribbean, 1492–1969*. Given that he focused as much on Caribbean people as he did on European wars, treaties, and colonial structures, his work marked a major break with canonical Caribbean historiography. But for my concerns, his synthesis represents something more, for in it he likened the Puerto Rican abolitionist movement to a sledgehammer used to kill a fly.

The layered complexity of Williams's metaphoric assertion, the very construction of its double voice, serves as a haunting echo, for we are not certain whether his rhetorical device identifies and conveys the course of the cause as difficult and arduous or facile and therefore superfluous. We need only envision an attempt to kill a fly with any type of hammer to begin to understand the strain of such an undertaking. The double-speak of this figurative execution folds back on an array of epistemic dualities, for everything about slavery interfered with its purpose—from the socioeconomic position of slave masters, whose status depended on slave labor, to the slaves themselves, whose very humanity and desirability subverted the myths their masters created to justify their enslavement. Daily practices of contradiction, of interference, of ideological slippage fed what resulted in the cross-purposes of slavery. Hence, dexterity was a key element for reinforcing the foundations of bondage during the Age of Abolition. With the force of figurative imagery, Williams recreated this element as historical hindsight in relation to the Puerto Rican experience.

As an economic institution, slavery remained consistent. As a social institution, however, its success and longevity hinged on maneuverability. Its politics thus operated on a sliding scale between the fixity of its economic demands and the malleability of its social practices. Opposition was not limited to tangible borders. Therefore, abolitionists throughout western Europe and the Americas fought as much against what they could not see as what stood clearly before them. Few white abolitionists could escape their deep-seated prejudices against the very people they wanted to liberate. (John Brown, Thaddeus Stevens, Joaquim Nabuco, David Turnbull, and Julio Vizcarrondo ranked among a minority of remarkable exceptions.) If slavery was a mixture of tangible and intangible elements of oppression and acquiescence, it follows that missions to undermine and destroy it were made of similar, if not identical, ingredients. As rising European imperialism in Africa suggests, even before the official partition of the continent in 1885, opposing hegemonies always used fire to fight fire. In other words, the cause against slavery was based on no simple construction of antagonisms between European and American Afrophiles promoting the liberation and humanity of black people and European and American Afrophobes in opposition to these efforts.

What, then, informs the Williams metaphor, the hammer to abolish the external slave trade or the hammer to abolish slavery itself? More important, as the British abolitionists reasoned, hoped, divined, and planned from the late 1700s onward, did one movement lead automatically to the next? These questions ultimately redirect us to umbrella questions related to arguments of cause, effect, and probability. Did the landing of the slave ship *Majesty* in 1859, for example, provide Madrid-based Puerto Rican abolitionists with additional impetus to push for the legal recognition of La Sociedad Abolicionista Española? Put another way, did the *Majesty* episode, with its many scandals, force the Spanish government to act on the bids of Puerto Rican abolitionists, bids that further divided Cuban and Puerto Rican politics for the remainder of the century? Or was it inevitable that Puerto Rican abolitionist activism would take center stage, with or without the *Majesty* affair? While these issues do not correspond directly to the greater concerns of this study, which include the identification and examination of the social, political, and logistic structures of Puerto Rican slave commerce in the Age of Abolition, they point to the location of breaks and openings that lead to thematic separations between international slave sales and the local consumption of slave labor, that is, distinctions between commerce as a promise and ownership as a performance.

Slavery was a commercial promise. Within it lay the hope of fulfilling that promise. Keeping the bargain depended on capture or collection, then transport, then delivery. Capture and transport initiated the transition from freedom to bondage. As such, the two stages contained some, but not all, of the elements that composed that which followed delivery: the performativity of slave ownership—an ontological confrontation of *moving* subject positions between the slave as the Self and the slave as the Other. Slave sales were based on hopes and promises at the level of marketing. Albeit slave ownership also came with hopes and promises, such expectations could not be tested to the fullest until reaching the site of labor consumption, be that site a dock in Havana, a cotton field in Natchez, a sugar mill in St. Lucia, a diamond mine in Minas Gerais, a textile factory in Tampico, a guano depository in Callao, or a convent kitchen in Buenos Aires. In the eyes of slaveholders, Africans were singular candidates for enslavement. Therefore, since the mid-sixteenth century—but not before—they were always already slaves. Based firmly on the watery foundations of racial essentialism, abolitionists faced opposition from a long-standing sociocommercial discourse that was embedded politically and culturally within the fabric of all Western slave-based economies regardless of size.

From the standpoint of maritime antislave trade vigilance after 1835, the sharpest teeth bit more selectively. British abolitionist forces concentrated more on African than on American shores. Within Cuban waters when necessary, Spanish officialdom could rely on a bevy of bureaucratic technicalities to discourage the continuance of British pursuit, in some cases, or to block capture and therefore prevent adjudication, in others. Topographic variation was a greater encumbrance. The Royal Navy lacked the support to monitor all cays, bays, inlets, isolated beaches, and other features that diversified Cuban shorelines. Puerto Rico's littoral lacked the hideaway features that facilitated Cuba's many secret landings. It was impossible to disembark slaves in any Puerto Rican district without its inhabitants' knowledge. But there was a trade-off: Puerto Rico had neither a Turnbull, a *Romney*, nor a Court of the Mixed Commissions. Most important, for both islands, after slave ships docked and unloaded their human cargoes, attempts to enforce abolitionist measures were futile. Spanish sovereignty prevented foreign abolitionist agents from searching for newly arrived captives on dry land. Dry land symbolized the legal ownership of private property, with all its rights and privileges. With each landing, a promise was kept, and the hammer missed again. African slaves were illegal commodities only when abolitionist forces intercepted their captivity and freed them. But for Puerto Rico between 1835 and 1845, successful interventions were limited almost exclusively to African waters.

Though fourteen years separated the landing of the *Majesty* from the abolition of Puerto Rican slavery, three and a half centuries forged a link between slave commerce and the consumption of slave labor. However small the influx of African slaves to the island from approximately 1510 to 1859, the outflux of more than a thousand Puerto Rican slaves to Cuba between 1848 and 1873, along with the fluctuations of internal sales, combined to form a singular, monotonal enunciation: the movement of chattels. As long as the traffic continued, whether legal or not, slaveholding marked an undifferentiated ontological space between commerce and consumption. From a legal standpoint, once reaching his or her destination, nothing distinguished an African captive from a Creole slave. Hence, in the Age of Abolition, when the African slave trade was outlawed, the very success of a slaving expedition rendered as legal commodities the illegal fruits of the enterprise.

Spain, Great Britain, and Puerto Rico

On June 16, 1598, George Clifford, third earl of Cumberland, attacked Puerto Rico and held it for two months. Shortly before the attack, in the course of a stirring pep talk he delivered to his men, he toasted the island lustily as "the maydenhead [sic] of Puerto Rico," that is, the penetrable shield that guarded the wealth of the Spanish Indies.[1] The English—soon followed by the Dutch but the French before them both—had coveted the island aggressively since the mid-1500s. Great Britain attempted to conquer it for the last time in 1797. Slaves and free Spanish subjects—Spaniards and Creoles—banded together and expelled them in a resounding defeat. The Britons took Spanish Trinidad instead. But times changed, and rather quickly. If given half a chance, under the right conditions, Great Britain (not to mention France and Belgium) would have taken Puerto Rico without hesitation anytime in the nineteenth century. But between 1815 and 1845, a different world order reduced British political desires to commercial exchange with the island, preferably within the context of a labor system freed from the shackles of slavery.

In January 1852, Mayagüez customs chief Blás Ginart submitted to Interim Governor Enrique España Taberner an eighteen-point plan to reverse Puerto Rico's troubled economy. He wrongly anticipated the appointment of a governor who would endorse the revival of African slave commerce. The seventh recommendation addressed his concerns more specifically:

> Allow the importation of slaves, and at the same time, demand that slaveholders obey the wise and philanthropic laws that spell out the mutual obligations of masters and slaves. This way, without pretentious fanfare, we will manifest the veracity of our humanitarian sentiments. We will maintain dominion over our island and see to its progress in the face of those invidious, hypocritical foreigners, whose predilections ignore the fact that people in glass houses should not throw stones.[2]

Ginart's poorly veiled jibes at the British are less impressive than the times he described, times that rendered compatible two incompatible discourses. Slave commerce in the Age of Abolition endorsed the politics of progressive backwardness. Ginart eschewed the argument of African inferiority as unjust and counterproductive. But at the same time he promoted the understanding of mutual obligations between masters and slaves. He advocated for Puerto Rico the continued production of internal outsiders through slave commerce, dismissing Great Britain's abolitionist campaign as a disingenuous display of Afrophilia everywhere except in its own colonies. Ginart was well aware of the social and economic failures of postemancipation politics in the British Caribbean. Thus, internal factors connected to cultural politics and external factors associated with Anglo-Spanish diplomacy delineated his cross-purposes simultaneously. There was no need for the Spanish government to take his advice seriously. The antislave trade component of the British diplomatic mission in Puerto Rico had already dissolved into a dubious fait accompli. Ginart spoke well for his own time and for times to come.

Abolitionism is associated with several eighteenth-century buzzwords: enlightenment, benevolent despotism, anticlericism, science, reason, revolution, and, ultimately, progress. Its eighteenth-century origins, nonetheless, fractured its nineteenth-century culmination by drawing qualitatively vague human boundaries between mercantilism and capitalism. Though the Age of Abolition functioned as a conductor for new ideas and practices, it did not purge the content of the form. In more ways than one, it simply rearranged it. In August 1862, Consul Augustus Cowper forwarded to London the translation of a letter signed by twenty-three Africans in Puerto Rico. Despite the semantic and syntactic interventions that punctuate the text as a lexical assembly—for history is not only historical, it is discursive and therefore linguistic—the basic concerns of the authorial collectivity are clear:

> The undersigned, and particularly Richard Latimer and Catalina de la Fosse, natives of the land of Cangá [sic], present ourselves to Your Excellency with much respect to entreat you to consider our present petition. Sufficient that we are children of another land, that a wretched fate brought us here, that after long years of labor, God has looked upon us with eyes of pity and enabled us to achieve our liberty; we have, however, few resources, and desire to return to our Country and, consequently approach Your Excellency ... to aid us in obtaining a free or cheap passage for us, remembering our poverty. We also wish Your Excellency to send us away as soon as possible, and we shall ever remember this service and pray that God may preserve you many years.[3]

Many Africans in Cuba and Brazil returned to the African continent. Some even reached their homelands or lands nearby. But the vast majority remained, as did the Puerto Rican–based authors of the petition above. Though the British Foreign Office, the Royal Navy, and at times the Spanish colonial government facilitated return voyages for *emancipados* and self-liberated Africans in Cuba, Foreign Minister Russell declined to act on this request, despite Cowper's urgent recommendations.[4] Although the perspectives and aspirations of African-born slaves, freedmen, and freedwomen are rarely seen in texts that document the history of slavery in Puerto Rico, Latimer, Fosse, and their companions verify the assumption that they had a great deal to say. Regrettably, we have heard but few of their own stories in their own words.

The history of slave commerce in the Age of Abolition is more than a study of false constructions of human biology founded on the inherent deceptions of race-based ideologies protected by the forces of politics and society. And it is more than a study of paradox, global politics, practices of cultural retention, the inevitability of cultural diffusion, and the diversification of humanity's inhumanity to itself. As a study of the mobility of fixity, it is one more signpost for the dynamic and ever-changing cooperative between hegemonic notions of progress and what constitutes the status quo between "the West and the rest,"[5] be the rest in the West or elsewhere.

Appendixes

1.1. Slavery and the Economic Transformation of Puerto Rico, 1816–1830

I was forcibly struck with the great improvements made on this island since my first voyage in the winter of 1816, especially on the south side, about Ponce, Guayanilla, Tiabo [sic], and all around this region. The south side of Puerto Rico was at that time but thinly inhabited, and only a small portion of the lands cultivated. There were but a few sugar estates and those on a very small scale. And now, after a lapse of fourteen years, I found immense cane-fields, large sugar plantations, everything thriving, and the country comparatively rich and prosperous; in fact, I could scarcely believe my own eyes, the change was so great. I was told that in the past ten or twelve years, Spain had adopted a very liberal policy, toward this colony, to induce immigration, by selling rich cane lands at very low prices. It also fostered and encouraged the slave trade, and, in a word, had granted every facility in its power to induce enterprising strangers to come here, to enrich themselves, and consequently, to augment the government revenue. These facilities, granted by Spain, had the desired effect; enterprising men had settled here from nearly all parts of the world; French, Germans, English, and Americans, had bought lands, and were cultivating them extensively. The island has now become rich and prosperous beyond anything I could have imagined.

Source: Coggeshall, *Thirty-six Voyages to Various Parts of the World between 1779 and 1841*, 507–8.

1.2. A Landing of Captives Directly from Africa, Mayagüez, 1831

They have been imported, into little bays of this part of Puerto Rico, within the last two months, three small cargoes of African slaves ... about 500 in number, men, women, and children. I saw the remnants of these cargoes for sale in three small enclosures. The best looking and the most healthy of these miserable beings had been sold to the planters and removed to their estates; the remainder were extremely thin and sickly, and were selling at very reduced prices ... if they showed any resistance ... they were driven like cattle. At the time I visited this island, there were so many obstacles to the African slave-trade that the owners of large vessels dared not risk sending them, and were therefore in the habit of employing small, fast-sailing pilot-boat schooners to elude the vigilance of men of war of different nations who were striving to prevent this inhuman traffic. These pilot-boats carried from 150 to 200 of these poor creatures.

Source: Coggeshall, *Thirty-six Voyages to Various Parts of the World between 1779 and 1841*, 507–8.

1.3. A Landing of Reexported African Captives from the Non-Hispanic Caribbean, Ponce, 1831

While here at Ponce, on the 18th of February, 1831, a large brig, under Spanish colors, arrived at a small port about a league to the eastward of this place, with 350 negro slaves from the coast of Africa. They were all landed under the direction of the government officers, and I was told that their owners paid a duty of 25 dollars per head. I went with my friend G. to see them landed; they were all taken to neighboring plantations and there exposed for sale. They were marched up from the vessel in parties of fifty; the men and women were all quite naked except for an apron which they wore about their loins; the children, both boys and girls, were in a perfect state of nudity, and as far as I could judge, they all, both men and women, appeared utterly unconscious of any impropriety in their want of clothing. They were healthy, sleek, and in good condition.... They all seemed to eat with a good appetite and enjoy their food. The planters from all of this part of the island, soon came to this depot to purchase according to wants or ability to pay; and here they were sold singly, in pairs, or in large numbers, as agreed upon by the parties.

Source: Coggeshall, *Thirty-six Voyages to Various Parts of the World between 1779 and 1841,* 507–8.

1.4. A Passenger Ship Encounters a Slave Ship between St. Croix and Puerto Rico, 1840

Toward the evening of this day we hove in sight of a brig, which, after viewing attentively, our people considered it to be of a very suspicious character. Some apprehensions were entertained that she might be a pirate; and I observed more or less the anxiety upon the countenances of the captain and some of our West India[n] passengers. This state of things continued for an hour or two, when on a nearer view, she was determined to be what the captain called a black bird, a slaver, bound undoubtedly for Puerto Rico from Africa. We came within a half mile of the ship, when we distinctly saw her windsails and between sixty and eighty men on the deck, who were supposed to be the fighting men of the crew. . . . We were not yet relieved of our apprehensions for we feared that if the slaver wanted water or provisions, she would, without ceremony, and without compensation, take from us. We therefore passed her in great silence, and were glad that she discovered by disposition not to intermeddle with us.

Source: Smith, *The Winter of 1840 in St. Croix, with an Excursion to Tortola and St. Thomas,* 7–8.

2.1. Tax Amnesty Plan for the Illegal Introduction of Slaves to Puerto Rico: Preamble, 1841

The interests of the colonial treasury should be upheld. But economic vigilance must be tempered with political rationale in order to discourage a national crisis. To that end, it is desirable that antislave trade accords include measures that do not jeopardize our national standards. It is well known that the African slave trade is prohibited; *that the shadow of this proscription has introduced exaggerated pretensions that have cost us no small effort to elude* [emphasis added]; and that abolitionist organizations are not satisfied with ending the traffic alone, but extend their mission to the universal emancipation of slaves, without considering the inevitable results of their obscenities. In the throes of this sad state of affairs, we consider the actions of the governor and the intendant most unwise. The authorization to circulate printed material which called attention to the presence of English-speaking slaves in Puerto Rico, and the subsequent measures adopted to prevent the future importation of said slaves, represents nothing less than a public confession of treaty violations, providing the enemies of slavery with ammunition to support their hypocritical opinions.

Source: Archivo Histórico Nacional, Madrid. Ultramar: Puerto Rico: Hacienda, legajo 1.071/4, 1841–44, expediente número 2.

2.2. The Spanish Government Authorizes the Use of Free African Contract Labor in Cuba and Puerto Rico, 1842

Here our recommendations would end, were it not for grave concerns expressed by the intendant over the destruction of Puerto Rican agriculture should the slave trade cease. According to him, there are other ways that Spanish possessions can supply themselves with labor. He understands that on February 15, 1841, a Mr. Barclay, under official British authorization, sailed from the Thames with three ships to procure Sierra Leonian blacks, bound by 4–year contracts to cultivate Jamaican plantations. These expeditions have been repeated, despite protestations to the Colonial Office by abolitionist societies. In view of this, we see no inconvenience in authorizing the captains general of Cuba and Puerto Rico to permit their inhabitants to proceed to the African coast, as is done in Jamaica, to procure and contract blacks from said coast, for compulsory labor on their haciendas for whatever period of time deemed convenient. These blacks are to be guided by the same regulations that apply in the British Caribbean, and once their contracts expire, they are to return to their homelands, unless they volunteer to remain.

Source: Archivo Histórico Nacional, Madrid. Ultramar: Puerto Rico: Hacienda, legajo 1.071/4, 1841–44, expediente número 2.

Note: Despite authorization, Spanish officials did not pursue the plan. Later, Spanish and Cuban Creole sugar producers submitted elaborate proposals for the recruitment of African and Asian contract workers in Cuba and Puerto Rico. The "coolie trade" to Cuba began in 1847. The Spanish government never engaged free African contract workers in its American colonies .

3.1. A Spanish Slave Ship Is Sighted in Dutch Curaçao, 1850

Official Report of the Meeting Held in the Government House, Monday, 21 October 1850, 11:30 A.M. *Present:* The Governor of Curaçao, the Naval Commander, the Garrison Commander, the Royal Solicitor, and the Colonial Secretary

The Governor announced that the assistant pilot of the port reported the following to him at 10:30 in the morning: At 7 o'clock this morning, the assistant pilot went out to direct a schooner, which was sailing under the Spanish flag and heading for the harbor into the port from the southeast. He was not permitted to board the schooner, however, and the vessel sailed past the harbor. During his short encounter with the ship, the assistant pilot got the impression, of which he was quite confident, that the schooner was a slaver. Since the telegraph on the west [side of the island] later reported that a schooner had anchored at Fishwives Bay, and no other ship had been seen, it was concluded that this schooner was the same vessel as the one earlier suspected by the assistant pilot. The Governor announced that he would meet with the persons named above to discuss the possible measures to be taken in the given situation.

After reviewing the existing treaties concerning the slave trade, the attendants named above agreed that current conventions only apply to Dutch and English vessels, equipment, and/or inhabitants. As far as they know, an applicable treaty between the Netherlands and Spain does not exist, and the treaties with England are not valid for Spanish vessels and/or Spanish subjects.

The Naval Commander, in concurrence with the others present at the meeting, decided that he should not be authorized to stop and seize a Spanish vessel. Thereupon, the Governor asked if the anchoring of the vessel, if indeed it was a slaver, related to the Royal Decree of 17 September 1818, specifically by the third article, which addresses the *importation* and *transport* of slaves. After much discussion about the true meaning of the above-mentioned article, it became apparent that those present were uncertain about the correct interpretation of the article. Regarding the importation and transport of slaves, legislators presumably meant "unloading." Though elsewhere the anchoring of a vessel would seem to be an attempt to unload slaves on land, such could not be the case in Curaçao, where such an act would immediately be detected, and where no one would partake in the illegal *buying* of slaves [emphasis added]. Furthermore, the outcome of a prosecution based simply on anchoring would be uncertain since the jurisprudence for such a case does not exist. In the case of a possible acquittal, Spanish authorities could file suit [against the Dutch Government], given that the covert tolerance of the slave trade to the Spanish Antilles is an important source of income for its officials.

Meeting attendants decided to send His Majesty's Brigantine *Ternate* to Fishwives Bay with the following instructions to the Naval Commander: (1) Ascertain whether the suspected vessel is anchored at the bay or docked at shore. (2) If either is the case, the Commander shall examine the schooner's papers, since the law permits commanders of warships to investigate a vessel's sea papers. (3) Should the papers be authentic [Spanish], and should the schooner under the Spanish flag indeed be a slave ship, the Captain of the vessel shall be instructed to leave the bay immediately and remove his ship from the colonial territory. (4) Or, if the vessel under Spanish colors does not possess authentic [Spanish] papers, but instead possesses Dutch or English sea papers, and is indeed a slaver, the schooner should be seized and brought back to the port. (5) If, however, upon the arrival of the *Ternate* at Fishwives Bay, the schooner should be in motion, that is, neither docked nor anchored, the investigation shall not take place. The commanding officer must ascertain, nonetheless, that the vessel in question has withdrawn from Dutch territory. (6) Furthermore, members of the Royal Military Police shall be sent to Fishwives Bay by land, in order to prevent communication between land and the schooner under the Spanish flag. This also allows the Commander of the

Ternate to report his findings more efficiently by way of the Royal Military Police.

Done in Curaçao.
[Signed]
-A.J. Rouwebuan [?] Elsevier, Jr.
-S.W.F. Frucht
-M. [illegible]
-Schotborgh M.

Hearing No. 144. Copy sent to the Colonial Minister as Official Document No. 169, dated 30 October 1850

Source: Centraal Historisch Archief, Willemstad, Curaçao, Netherlands Antilles, Uil: Koloniaal, Arbeid, inv. #22. (Translated from the Dutch by Eliane van Vliet.)

Abbreviations

AGPR	Archivo General de Puerto Rico
AHN	Archivo Histórico Nacional
AHU	Arquivo Histórico Ultramarino
AIH	*Anales de Investigación Histórica*
AMAE	Archivo del Ministerio de Asuntos Exteriores
ANC	Archivo Nacional de Cuba
BHPR	*Boletín Histórico de Puerto Rico*
BN	Biblioteca Nacional de España
BNJM	Biblioteca Nacional José Martí
C	Comercio
c	caja
CM	Comisión Militar
CO	Colonial Office
E	Esclavos
EST	Estado
exp	expediente
F	Fomento (Ultramar)
FO	Foreign Office
G	Gobierno (Ultramar)
GE	Gobernadores Españoles: Asuntos Políticos
GJ	Gracia y Justicia (Ultramar)
GSC	Gobierno Superior Civil
H	Hacienda (Ultramar)
HAHR	*Hispanic American Historical Review*
leg	legajo

M	Municipios
NHC	Non-Hispanic Caribbean
OG	Oficios de Guerra (Ultramar)
PA	Proceso Abolicionista
PP	Parliamentary Papers
PRO	Public Record Office
PSV	Partus Sequitur Ventrem
PUA	Possessões Ultramarinas: Angola
RCEPR	Registro Central de Esclavos de Puerto Rico
RCJF	Real Consulado y Junta de Fomento
RCO	Reales Cédulas y Ordenes
RSGPR	Records of the Spanish Governors of Puerto Rico
SDG	Santo Domingo, Gobierno
UC	Ultramar y Colonias
USNA	United States National Archives

Notes

Introduction

1. The mid-nineteenth-century estimate includes permanent residents and transients, Spanish subjects and foreigners. By the 1860s, two-thirds of the slave population worked in agriculture, producing sugar, coffee, and cotton. See Morales Carrión et al., eds., *El proceso abolicionista en Puerto Rico*, 1: 49 (PA). In Coll y Toste, *Boletín Histórico de Puerto Rico*, 4: 332 (BHPR), Puerto Rican census figures show the steadfast minority of slaves in the nineteenth century (see table A below).

But in the same tome, a reconfiguration of the nonwhite population reveals a different dynamic, one that speaks to the fear that the free black population empathized and sympathized with slaves. However, investigative efforts must begin with the recognition that social, political, and economic determinants divided free people of color (see table B below).

On free black and mulatto activism against intrastate slave traffic, see Dorsey, "Seamy Sides of Abolition." The Cuban population was not only larger, proportions between slaves and free people of color were reversed. From 1774 to 1872, slaves surpassed free blacks and mulattoes. For years comparable to those above, figures indicate that Cuba's black population was staggering. See Ortiz, *Hampa afro-cubana*, 321–22 and table C below.

A. Racial demographics in Puerto Rico: Distribution I

Year	Black and white	Slaves	Total population
1834	315,262	41,818	357,080
1846	391,874	51,216	443,090
1860	541,445	41,736	583,181

B. Racial demographics in Puerto Rico: Distribution II

Year	Whites	Free blacks and slaves
1834	190,619	168,217
1846	216,083	227,056
1860	300,439	282,751

C. Racial demographics in Cuba

Year	Slaves	Free blacks and mulattoes
1830	310,978	112,365
1846	323,759	149,226
1860	367,758	209,407

In 1872, Cuba's slave population of 379,523, combined with 235,938 free people of color, surpassed the total population of Puerto Rico.

2. The estimate of 6,000 slaves refers to the first six months of 1825. See González Vales, "Towards a Plantation Society," 99. Thomas Buxton's figure of 7,000 captives landed in 1836 derives from a preconsular system of *espinonage*. His informants included British residents and travelers, along with covert Puerto Rican abolitionists. See Buxton, *The African Slave Trade and Its Remedy*, 36. Morales Carrión's figure of 2,000 per annum stems from a lawsuit filed against Governor Miguel López de Baños in 1839. See chapter 4, note 9. Though the slave population was always small compared to other Caribbean and Latin American colonies, in the early years of settlement, blacks in Puerto Rico outnumbered other inhabitants incorporated into the colonial system. The first Puerto Rican census was taken in 1530. Because it omitted white women, children, and Indians not bound by work contracts, tabulations are faulty. There are two sources: Salvador Brau's *Colonización de Puerto Rico* (1908) shows 387 whites and 1,523 blacks (1,168 slave men and 355 slave women); Alejandro Tapía y Rivera's *Biblioteca histórica de Puerto Rico* (1854) reduced the white population by 50 and raised the black population to 2,292. Either way, thirty-seven years after Columbus first sighted Puerto Rico, black slaves from Spain and West Africa outnumbered the free population of Spanish settlers. But from 1765 onward, whites and free blacks outnumbered slaves.

3. For discussions of the African slave trade to the Spanish American colonies from 1521 to 1843, see Curtin, *The Atlantic Slave Trade*.

4. Alvarez Nazario, Díaz Soler, and Morales Carrión are not members of the Generation of 1973. Significant theoretical distinctions separate them from other scholars in this group. I chose to include Alvarez Nazario and Díaz Soler because publishers during the 1970s reissued their earlier works. Furthermore, I do not believe that the datedness of their pioneering work suffices to exclude them from the new generation of scholarship. I included Morales Carrión because his work in the 1970s forms, how-

ever tenuously, a transgenerational bridge between scholars who wrote about the history and culture of Puerto Rican slavery in the 1950s and 1960s and scholars from the Generation of 1973. I thank the anonymous referees for asking me to explain my choices.

5. Curet, "De la esclavitud a la abolición," 1–35, and Carbonell and Consuelo Vázquez Arce, "Las compraventas de esclavos en San Juan y Naguabo," 1–83.

6. Stein, *Vassouras: A Brazilian Coffee County, 1850–1900;* Freyre, *The Masters and the Slaves;* Tannenbaum, *Slave and Citizen;* and Williams, *Capitalism and Slavery.*

7. Tannenbaum posited that slavery in the Americas was divided into three systems. The Iberian system merged Spanish and Portuguese slavery under the banner of mildness. The British system, which he extended to the Danes and Dutch, was harsh. The French system fell midway between the extremes. The most significant flaw in this theory is its failure to recognize that black bondage in the Americas was based on a single system: chattel slavery, the outright physical ownership of one person by another, which privileged slaveholders with the right to buy and sell certain people at will, without legal interference. Variants such as languages, religious traditions, the national origins of slaveholders, circumstances of acquisition, distinctions in social relations between masters and slaves, and job differentiation among slaves never constituted separate systems of slavery in the Americas, as they did in premodern societies. In different parts of Africa, Asia, and the Near East, at different points in their histories, persons kidnapped from enemy states, children taken in war or conquest, children of slave couples, and children fathered by slaveholders with slave women, along with slaves classified as field workers, convicts, pawns, concubines, eunuchs, and soldiers, represented ten distinct systems of slavery, each governed by its own set of rules—which included, for some, the prohibition of sale. In many societies, only field workers were chattel slaves. Slaves such as pawns, concubines, and soldiers could not be sold at the whims of their masters. Premodern systems of bondage—including slavery in Europe and pre-Columbian America—were marked less by morphological similarity than by morphological diversity. There was certainly occupational variety among slaves in the Americas, as instanced in housekeeping; child care; concubinage; prostitution; gold, silver, mercury, and diamond mining; cattle ranching; carpentry; field work; porterage; and pearl diving. However, black slaves in this hemisphere were governed by the singular, systemic authority of chattel ownership. Geographic, climatic, temporal, occupational, political, and individual determinants diversified practices of black bondage, but its uniformity as a system of unmitigated property ownership remained the same. All differences considered, British, Danish, Dutch, French, Portuguese, Spanish, and Swedish practices in the Americas never constituted separate systems of bondage. This does not suggest that the systemic pluralities of premodern slavery rendered them kinder or milder. It simply foregrounds the force of historical difference, epistemological rupture, and the continuity of change.

8. Genovese, "Treatment of Slaves in Different Countries." Genovese was a Marxist

scholar when he published this article. Albeit he was, and perhaps remains, a fan of Hegelian phenomenology, he is no longer a Marxist. Moreover, he does not follow the text-oriented precepts of structuralism and poststructuralism. Least of all would he endorse their application to historical studies. Therefore, any association in his essay between slavery and morphology is inadvertent. I am responsible for reading this example of his work as an exercise in sociocultural morphology.

9. Lombardi, "Comparative Slave Systems in the Americas," 156–74, and Magnus Mörner, "Recent Research on Negro Slavery and Abolition in Latin America," 265–89.

10. Martínez-Alier's *Marriage, Class and Colour in Nineteenth-Century Cuba* and Cohen and Greene's *Neither Slave nor Free* are transsystemic histories. Picó's *Libertad y servidumbre en el Puerto Rico del siglo XIX* and Bergad's *Coffee and the Growth of Agrarian Capitalism* examine the uses, abuses, and failures of free labor systems in force concurrently with slavery. Thus, their histories are likewise transsystemic, as is Scott's *Slave Emancipation in Cuba.* Crossing into the first two decades of the twentieth century, Warren Dean's *Rio Claro: A Brazilian Plantation System* is both transsystemic and transgenerational. With themes that crisscross slave labor, free labor, and conscripted free labor—despite chronological and geopolitical variations—all authors cited here made use of transinstitutional approaches to explore the changing structures of nineteenth-century labor systems.

11. Davis, *Slavery and Human Progress,* and Patterson, *Slavery and Social Death.*

12. Conrad, *Children of God's Fire;* Russell-Wood, *The Black Man in Slavery and in Freedom in Colonial Brazil;* Karasch, *Slave Life and Culture in Rio de Janeiro;* Eltis, *Economic Growth and the Ending of the Transatlantic Slave Trade;* and Paquette, *Sugar Is Made with Blood.*

13. To name but a few: Miers and Kopytoff, *Slavery in Africa;* Lovejoy, *Transformations in Slavery;* Robertson and Klein, *Women and Slavery in Africa;* and Claude Meillassoux, *The Anthropology of Slavery.* See also the expanded version of Moses Finley's *Ancient Slavery and Modern Ideology.*

14. See, for example, Fleischner, *Mastering Slavery;* Andrews, *To Tell a Free Story;* and Painter, "Of *Lily,* Linda Brent, and Freud." Vera Kutzinski's outstanding work on the impact of biopolitics and biocultural hybridity on national identity, *Sugar's Secrets: Race and the Erotics of Cuban Nationalism,* emphasizes the literary dominion of slavery and race relations.

15. Among works by these authors, see Louis Althusser, *Lenin and Philosophy and Other Essays* (New York: Monthly Review, 1971); Hayden White, *The Content of the Form: Narrative Discourse and Historical Representations* (Baltimore: Johns Hopkins University Press, 1987); Julia Kristeva, *Powers of Horror: An Essay on Abjection* (New York: Columbia, 1982); Roland Barthes, *The Pleasure of the Text* (New York; Hill and Wang, 1976); Pierre Bourdieu, *Outline of a Theory of Practice* (Cambridge: Cambridge University Press, 1977); Homi Bhabha, *The Location of Culture* (New York: Routledge,

1994); Michel Foucault, *History of Sexuality* (New York: Vintage, 1990); and Jacques Derrida, *Of Grammatology* (Baltimore: Johns Hopkins University Press, 1976).

16. Amid many definitions and deployments of the terms "modernist" and "structuralist," most of which depend on variants in academic disciplines, I refer to the former historically to delineate the period between the postmedieval and the precontemporary, that is, from about 1500 to 1899 (or 1492 to 1910), and the latter to indicate a twentieth-century metatheory—a theory about theories—that envisions any object of inquiry as a structure. The heat of the postmodern controversy centers less on its complex and often inaccessible jargon and syntax than in its challenge to Eurocentrism. In *White Mythologies* (London: Routledge, 1990, 108–9), while drawing distinctions between the "postmodern" and the "poststructural," Robert Young postures postmodern history: "[W]hereas postmodernism seems to include the problematic of the place of Western culture in relation to non-Western cultures, poststructuralism as a category seems not to imply such a perspective. This, however, is hardly the case, for it rather involves if anything a more active critique of the Eurocentric premises of Western knowledge. The difference would be that it does not offer a *critique* by positioning itself outside 'the West,' but rather uses its own alterity [difference] and duplicity in order to effect its deconstruction. . . . Contrary, then, to some of its more overreaching definitions, postmodernism itself could be said to mark not just the cultural effects of a new stage of 'late' capitalism, but the sense of the loss of European history and culture as History and Culture."

17. For debates among Marxist scholars of slavery and race relations across the disciplines, see Patterson, *Slavery and Social Death*, 2–3; Davis, *Slavery and Human Progress*, 254; Meillassoux, *The Anthropology of Slavery*, 16–20, 292–93, and 324–25; Engerman and Genovese, *Race and Slavery in the Western Hemisphere*, 533–34; Robinson, *Black Marxism*, 105–6 and 135 n. 47; Fox-Genovese, *Within the Plantation Household*, 53–59; and Bhabha, *Location of Culture*, 16, 26, and 215–16. For an important critique of postmodern positions in Caribbean scholarship that focuses on women and slavery, see Hilary Beckles, "Sex and Gender in the Historiography of Caribbean Slavery" in Shepherd et al., *Engendering History*.

18. Moreno Fraginals et al., *Between Slavery and Free Labor*.

19. Martínez-Fernández, *Torn between Empires*; Ayala, *American Sugar Kingdom*; and Schmidt-Nowara, *Empire and Slavery*.

20. Dávila-Cox, *Este inmenso comercio*; Findlay, *Imposing Decency*; Kinsbruner, *Not of Pure Blood*; Matos Rodríguez, *Women and Urban Change in San Juan, Puerto Rico*; Martínez-Vergne, *Shaping the Discourse on Space*; and Picó, *Al filo del poder*. Kinsbruner's scope is neither municipal nor comparative by design. By examining specific districts to test the structured extremities of Ponce, for example—where slave-based sugar production dominated the social and political economy—and San Juan—where the slave population was smaller and nonagrarian—his conclusions carry implications

for islandwide representations of free people of color. Predating Kinsbruner's study, Picó's mosaic of Puerto Rican subalternity yields similar effects. However, while Kinsbruner highlights San Juan and Ponce, Picó's chapters that center on municipal loci— Camuy, Cidra, Utuado, and Río Piedras—lay outside areas where slave labor predominated, in contrast with two chapters that, in Althusserian terms, represent the island as an aggregate.

21. Pedro San Miguel, *El mundo que creó el azúcar: Las haciendas en Vega Baja, 1800– 1873* (Río Piedras, Puerto Rico: Ediciones Huracán, 1989); Luis Antonio Figueroa, "Facing Freedom: The Transition from Slavery to Free Labor in Guayama, Puerto Rico, 1860–98" (Ph.D. diss., University of Wisconsin–Madison, 1991); and Mariano Negrón Portillo and Raúl Mayo Santana, *La esclavitud urbana en San Juan: Estudio del registro de esclavos de 1872* (Río Piedras, Puerto Rico: Ediciones Huracán, 1992).

22. Quantitative controversy began with Robert Fogel and Stanley Engerman, *Time on the Cross: The Economics of American Negro Slavery*, 2 vols. (Boston: Little, Brown, 1974), and accelerated with Curtin's *The Atlantic Slave Trade*. On dissent from qualitative text experts, see Eltis and Richardson, *Routes to Slavery*. With the exception of Francisco Scarano's work, there are few extensively quantitative studies of Puerto Rican slavery. Though three Puerto Ricanists made quantitative contributions to the Moreno Fraginals et al. collection on emancipation adaptations, only one, Nistal Moret, used statistics to advance preemancipation arguments.

23. Eltis and Richardson, *Routes to Slavery*, 3.

24. Thornton's ability to interpret quantitatively without relying on numerical figures or their orthographic representations undermines the "scientific" exclusivity of statistical objects with textual subjects. Thus, between numbers and narratives he dismisses dialectical notions of binary opposition in favor of moving subject positions. In this manner, albeit inadvertently, his work lends itself to postmodernism, poststructuralism, and postcolonial theory. See his *Africa and Africans in the Making of the Atlantic World, 1400–1680*. For his discussions of works by qualitative and qualitative authorities, see 72–74 and 88–102. For a shorter example of Thornton's use of history as intertextual performativity, see his "African Soldiers in the Haitian Revolution" in the *Journal of Caribbean History* (1991): 25.

25. Scarano, *Sugar and Slavery in Puerto Rico*, 121. Here, Scarano probably refers to an assortment of administrative divisions and subdivisions and to the bureaucratic offices that represented them, which were largely identical between the two islands. However, the organization and the content of the islands' principal Spanish colonial collections—the Archivo Nacional de Cuba and the Archivo General de Puerto Rico —differ considerably. For example, Cuban prison files are dispersed throughout a myriad of separate records, while Puerto Rican files are centralized. Also, in the context of this study, the Registro Central de Esclavos de Puerto Rico de 1872, an assem-

bly of vital statistics for nearly 32,000 slaves on the eve of abolition, has no parallel in Cuba.

26. Ibid., 134–37.

27. Ibid., tables 6.3 and 6.4, 136–37.

28. "Creole" has many definitions. In Latin American history, it refers to Iberians born in the Americas, that is, whites born in the Spanish colonies and Portuguese Brazil rather than Europe. It also refers to slaves born in the Americas as opposed to African-born slaves. In African history, "Creole" refers to Europeanized Africans living in coastal communities that developed as a result of transatlantic commerce. Cape Verde, Gorée, Freetown, Ouidah, Lagos, São Tomé, and Príncipe were Creole African societies. With the exception of those who kept relations with local groups—especially through matrimony for the sake of trade—Creole Africans were disconnected from indigenous African traditions, languages, and lineages. As a coastal people, they had no bearing on political affairs in the interior, except when linked to trade. Historically, indigenous Africans, be they Islamic or polytheistic, and Creole Africans, who were ostensibly Christian, regarded each other with disdain. Creole Africans could be either black or mulatto, as with their counterparts in the Americas. The term was sociocultural, not biological.

29. See chapter 3 in Morales Carrión, *Auge y decadencia de la trata negrera en Puerto Rico, 1820–1860* (*Trata*). There are various renderings for the first surname of this governor: Miguel de la Torre (which is the most common), Miguel de Latorre, and Miguel de La Torre. I use the latter spelling, based on a collection named after him at the Archivo Histórico Nacional in Madrid. This is also the way he signed his name.

30. For a statistical analysis of Puerto Rican slave traffic prior to the treaty of 1817, see Adam Szasdi, "Apuntes sobre la esclavitud en San Juan de Puerto Rico, 1800–1811," *Anuario de Estudios Americanos,* Seville (1967), 24: 1433–77.

31. *Bozales* and *negros de nación* applied to the same people—African newcomers placed at the bottom of society. But unlike *bozales,* "wild/slow/muzzled/silent/silenced ones," the term *negros de nación* lessened, superficially, the ideological distance between the derision of bondage and the dignity of freedom. However, use of the latter term was not only superficial and ultimately inconsequential; frequently it was incorrect. While many African captives came from polities Spaniards identified as nations—such as the Wolof, the Bambara, the Manding, the Yoruba, the Hausa, and the urban Fula—others came from acephalous societies—such as the pastoral Fula, the Tiv, most Ibo, many but not all Congolese, and a small number of Berber nomads captured along the Sahel, the southern fringe of the Sahara, especially around the Niger Bend. For important discussions about Muslim captives in the Atlantic slave trade to Latin America and the Caribbean, including references to Sahelian Berbers and Tuaregs, see Alvarez Nazario, *El elemento afro-negroide en el español de Puerto Rico;* Barry, *Senegambia and*

the Atlantic Slave Trade; Curtin, *Africa Remembered;* Diouf, *Servants of Allah;* and Mendonça, *A Influencia Africana no Portugués do Brasil.* For a biography connecting the Antebellum South to the imamate of Futa Jallon in Guinea-Conakry, see Terry Alford, *Prince among Slaves* (New York: Oxford University Press, 1977).

32. Decreed on October 21, 1817, the Cuban Cédula de Fomento Blanco favored working-class settlers from Spain, especially farmers. But few came at this time. More newcomers were wealthy, conservative Spanish subjects fleeing independence wars in South America and an assortment of French and Spanish refugees from Haiti and Santo Domingo, many of whom settled in Mexico, Louisiana and, Florida first. Though the presence of French and Spanish elites reinforced slavery and Spanish colonialism in Cuba and Puerto Rico, the government solicited distinct groups of settlers for the two islands. Cuba, with its advanced sugar technology and planter-class conservatism, already had its share of landed gentry, agri-industrialists, and other bourgeois aristocrats. Its ever-expanding economy needed more workers, not more capitalists. Conversely, Puerto Rico needed both. Cuban planters sought white workers to supplement the anticipated decline in African slaves. For the moment, they failed to recognize slave trader resourcefulness. For Spain's working-class poor, the Cuban decree offered little that distinguished them from slaves. Thus, more white elites fleeing revolution in Haiti, Santo Domingo, and the Spanish American mainlands took advantage of the offer, paltry as it was by comparison. Two salient features separated the decrees. First, while the Cédula de Gracias permitted the immigration of free people of color, the Cédula de Fomento Blanco did not. Second, between 1810 and 1826, 31,000 free newcomers settled in Puerto Rico compared to 20,000 in Cuba during the same years. Though local administrators and bureaucrats trimmed the blandishments of the Puerto Rican *cédula*, it still offered greater incentives than the Cuban decree. On white immigration to Cuba, see Corbitt, "Immigration to Cuba," and Corwin, *Spain and the Abolition of Slavery in Cuba,* 32–33. For differences in the development of Cuban and Puerto Rican sugar production, see Scarano, *Sugar and Slavery in Puerto Rico,* 9–12 and 20–22. For figures comparing white immigration to the two islands, see Ulibarri, "Nineteenth-Century Puerto Rican Immigration and Slave Data."

33. Many Cuban planters took advantage of social, political, and juridical problems that marked the preparation and execution of abolition and apprenticeship in the British Caribbean between 1834 and 1838 by (1) inviting disgruntled slaveholders, mainly from Jamaica and the Bahamas, to relocate to Cuba with their slaves, of both sexes, between 1822 and 1833; (2) purchasing slaves of both sexes from British Caribbean masters, again, largely from Jamaica and the Bahamas between 1830 and 1833; and (3) endorsing the outright kidnapping of free-born blacks, as well as newly emancipated slaves—all young Jamaican men and boys—between 1834 and 1842. Puerto Rican interest groups carried out similar machinations at the same time, but on a smaller scale,

involving victims from the Eastern Caribbean rather than Jamaica and the Bahamas. See Dorsey, "Women without History."

34. Though few source materials document practices of African rituals and festivals in Spanish colonial Puerto Rico, in *Trata,* 112–13, Morales Carrión shares an important vignette from the 1840s. Perhaps the oldest reference to African spiritual practices dates back to 1594, when Nicolás de Ramos advised Philip II, "Syendo [*sic*] obispo de Puerto Rico, descubrí una gran compañía de *negros brujos,* que trataban con el demonio." Though they were all slaves, of both sexes, he did not indicate if they were African- or Puerto Rican–born; BHPR 3: 48. Scholars acknowledge the preeminence of Cuban and Brazilian folkloric traditions that came from Yoruba polities in Dahomey and Nigeria, on the one hand, and the Niger Delta polities, on the other. Yoruba practices are the more visible. More than cultural survivals, they offer living testimony to the destruction of Old Oyo early in the 1810s and the continuity of related conflicts up to the 1860s. For Yoruba and Ibo traditions, see João Sebastião das Chagas Varella, *Cozinha de Santo: Culinária de Umbanda e Candombé* (Rio de Janeiro: Editora Espiritualista Lta., 1972), and Clara Domínguez et al., *El cabildo carabalí Isauma* (Santiago de Cuba: Editoria Oriente, 1982). Classic studies include Lydia Cabrera, *El monte* (Havana: Ediciones CR, 1954); Rómulo Lachatañeré, *O mío Yemayá* (Manzanillo, Cuba: Editorial del Arte, 1938); Fernando Ortiz Fernández, *Hampa afro-cubana: Los negros brujos* (Madrid: Ruíz and Co., 1906); and his somewhat less essentializing *Hampa afro-cubana: Los negros esclavos.* For the incorporation of Yoruba terms into Cuban Spanish and for Ibo chants, see Lachatañeré, 199–210 and 37–56. Scholarship in English includes William Bascom, *Sixteen Cowries: Yoruba Divination from Africa to the New World* (Bloomington: Indiana University Press, 1980), and Joseph Murphy, *Santería: African Spirits in America* (Boston: Beacon, 1993). Outstanding accounts of Santería and Candombé are found in fiction, film, and theater. See Jorge Amado's magnum opus, *War of the Saints* [Sumiço da Santa] (New York: Bantam, 1993), and the Cannes-winning play-turned-film "The Given Word" [O Pagador de Promessas] by Alfredo de Freitas Dias Gomes and Anselmo Duarte in 1962. See also *María Antonia,* a Cuban play, in Eugenio Hernández, *Teatro* (Havana: Letras Cubanas, 1989), 94–106; for excerpts in English, see "María Antonia" in Pedro Pérez Sarduy and Jean Stubbs, eds., *Afrocuba: An Anthology of Cuban Writing on Race, Politics, and Culture* (Melbourne, Australia: Ocean Press, 1993), 169–79; a video-taped performance in Spanish is available through Amazon.com. For an underdeveloped effort to juxtapose Marxist intellectualism with Candombé as a social semiotic, see the Brazilian vignette, "Hesed," in Umberto Eco, *Foucault's Pendulum* (New York: Harcourt Brace Jovanovich, 1989), 161–216. For discussions of African traditions in Puerto Rican popular culture, see Edward Zaragoza, *St. James in the Streets* (Lanham, Md.: Scarecrow, 1995).

35. Eyewitness accounts of either Christian or traditional African religious beliefs

and practices among black people in Puerto Rico prior to the abolition of slavery are rare. During hearings against a recalcitrant planter in Isabela in 1841, a priest testified that the accused allowed an illiterate slave to baptize other slaves. He quoted the slave, ridiculing his pronunciation, "[Y]o te batizo en gloria Patri et Filia e Espita Santa." PA 1: 154–55. Concerning religious syncretism among Puerto Rican slaves, Leopold Krug —pro-Spanish and proslavist vice consul of Mayagüez in the diplomatic service of Sweden, Norway, Prussia, and Great Britain—informed the Foreign Office in 1866, "As regards their . . . religion, the least said about it, the better, as it is next to nothing. [A]ll they know . . . is that there are lots of Saints and the Blessed Virgin. The amulets which most of them wear belong partly to Catholicism and partly to Paganism. Some old females may be able to say part of a [Christian] prayer, but without understanding its meaning." PA 1: 50–51. For his devotion to the Spanish Crown and his lack of support for the abolitionist movement, Krug was awarded Spain's highest honor, La Cruz de Isabel la Católica. See Archivo Histórico Nacional, Ultramar: Gobierno de Puerto Rico, legs. 5098/31, 5100/19, and 5106/62. Anthropologically, we may speculate that (1) Krug's reference to the slave's awareness of the proliferation of Catholic saints suggests the possibility of syncretism with African divinities; (2) his reference to amulets—instead of scapulars, crucifixes, and other wearable symbols linked to Catholicism—conjures Western images of gris-gris and other adornments associated with African polytheistic beliefs; and (3) the singling out of elderly female slaves suggests neo-African religious leadership from the ranks of senior women—a common form of leadership among black people, slave and free, in the United States, the non-Hispanic Caribbean, and Brazil. We must approach these possibilities with extreme caution, for we are faced not only with the lack of empirical evidence in the area of African religious retentions during the time of slavery in Puerto Rico. Geographic patterns of African slave acquisition gleaned from available sources also militate against drawing parallels with larger slaveholding polities. In other words, Krug's observations do not suffice to prove the existence of Puerto Rican parallels to Jamaican obeah (conjuring), Bayou gris-gris (charms to provoke or protect), Brazilian *mães do santo* (Yoruba female cult leaders), or Cuban *prendas* (Gangá-Congolese implements for the preparation or casting of spells) and *orizas* (Yoruba gods). In all probability parallels were there, albeit in subtle forms and on a much smaller scale. In *Esclavos rebeldes,* 66, 96, and 120, for example, Baralt tells us that some slave conspirators used the Bomba, now revered as a Puerto Rican national dance form, as a signal to carry out various brands of resistance. There could have been religious implications in the performance of the dance. Believed to be Bantu in origin, denoting drum, drummer, or a certain kind of percussive movement, the word was pronounced with phonetic variation in Cameroon, Congo-Brazzaville, the Republic of Congo, Angola, and Mozambique, according to Alvarez Nazario, *El elemento afro-negroide en el español de Puerto Rico,* 57–59, 291, and 303–9. However, until concrete sources come to light or until we begin to read more closely documents already at our disposal, we must rely on anthropological theory, linguistic evidence, and postslavery narratives to grasp the cultural particulars of specific African provenance in nineteenth-century Puerto Rico. Alternatives include fin-de-siècle memoirs, interviews with the elderly, and—with a modest background in West African and subequatorial language patterns—the poetry of Luis Palés Matos. See his *Tuntún de pasa y grifería* (San Juan: Biblioteca de Autores Puertorriqueños, 1937).

36. Documents for the *Majesty* affair—in Spanish, French, British, Cuban, and Puerto Rican archives—are capable of generating volumes of historical studies. However, with the exception of comparative references and statistical discussions, its engaging story is not pursued in this book for several reasons. In terms of the timing of its arrival, the number of captives it brought, and the uniformity of their ages and their provenance (all came from areas around the Lower Congo), it was an exception rather than a rule. Furthermore, because of the bounty of documents available, it will take a team of interdisciplinary scholars several years to render the case the analytical justice it deserves. For practical reasons, a minority of interested scholars elected to approach some of its many angles in segments, in journal articles or chapters of larger works that focus on broader themes. See, for example, Rosa Martínez, "Los negros del brick-barca Majesty," and Teresita Martínez-Vergne, "The Regulation of Time and Space: 'Liberated' Africans at Midcentury," in *Shaping the Discourse*, 72–90.

Chapter 1. "Such an Obscure Colony"

1. Morales Carrión, *Puerto Rico and the Non-Hispanic Caribbean* (NHC).

2. For excerpts of O'Reilly's report in English, see Wagenheim and Jiménez de Wagenheim, *Puerto Rico*. For the original Spanish version, see BHPR 8: 108–30.

3. Quoted in the preface of this study, Raynal's reference to Havana as "the boulevard of the New World" comes from Hugh Thomas, *Cuba: The Pursuit of Freedom* (New York: Harper and Row, 1981), 12. For Raynal's assessment of Puerto Rico, see NHC, 97.

4. See NHC, especially chapters 2–4.

5. Agustín Iñigo Abbad y Lasierra, *Historia geográfica, civil, y natural de la isla de San Juan de Puerto Rico* (Río Piedras, Puerto Rico: Editorial Universitaria, 1970), 182–83. On his expulsion, see Isabel Gutiérrez del Arroyo's introduction to the edition cited here; BHPR 7: 147–50; and Díaz Soler, *Historia de la esclavitud negra en Puerto Rico*, 93. Abbad's discussions of race relations are rich in detail, though occasionally, in accordance with the times, he fails to distinguish *negro*, meaning "slave," from *negro*, meaning "black man," which creates semantic and contextual uncertainty.

6. For examples of Abbad's observations of contraband commerce, see *Historia geográfica, civil, y natural de la isla de San Juan de Puerto Rico*, 135–36, 147–48, and 168–71.

7. Signed in 1817, the Anglo-Spanish treaty for the abolition of the African slave trade went into full effect in 1820. Between the two dates, the treaty outlawed slave

trading above the equator. With the exception of the *Majesty* in 1859, there is no concrete evidence that African captives were landed in Puerto Rico after the summer of
1847, albeit documents verify numerous attempts.

8. For examinations of sugar production and class transformation in Puerto Rico
from the late 1700s to the late 1800s, including references to immigration resulting
largely from the Cédula de Gracias, see San Miguel, "Tierra, trabajadores, y propietarios"; Gregorio Villegas, "Fluctuaciones de la poplación de Guaynabo, 1780–1830,"
Anales de Investigación Histórica (AIH) 8: 91–126; Lydia Martínez de Lá jara, "Repar-
timiento de Tierras de Salinas en el siglo XIX," AIH 2: 48–81; María Libertad Serrano
Méndez, "La clase dominante en San Sebastián, 1836–1853," AIH 2: 82–143; and Ben-
jamín Nistal Moret, "El Pueblo de Nuestra Señora de la Candelaria y del Apóstol San
Matías de Manatí, 1800–1880: Its Ruling Classes and the Institution of Black Slavery"
(Ph.D. diss., State University of New York, Stony Brook, 1977). Scarano assesses the
Cédula de Gracias in Ponce in *Sugar and Slavery in Puerto Rico,* 18–20. For a shorter
discussion see Kinsbruner, *Not of Pure Blood,* 41–42. For the full text of the decree in
Spanish, see BHPR 1: 297–307. For the Cuban Cédula de Fomento Blanco of 1817, see
Corbitt, "Immigration to Cuba." Though the Cuban *cédula* forbade the immigration of
free blacks, until the mid-1830s the proscription was ignored. Free Afro-Venezuelans
and Afro-Mexicans, along with free blacks from the United States and the non-Hispanic
Caribbean, figured among Cuba's black bourgeoisie, especially in Havana and Santiago.
When Leopoldo O'Donnell decreed the expulsion of all free foreigners of color in 1844,
many who petitioned to remain were allowed to do so, provided they were not emancipated slaves. See ANC: CM, leg. 50, no. 3.

9. Cifre de Loubriel, *Catálogo de extranjeros residentes en Puerto Rico en el siglo XIX,*
87; Ulibarri, "Nineteenth-Century Puerto Rican Immigration and Slave Data"; and
Hernández, "Inmigrantes italianos de Puerto Rico durante el siglo XIX."

10. Many non-Hispanic Caribbean workers began to settle in Puerto Rico when
slavery was abolished in 1873. See Cifre de Loubriel, *Catálogo,* 115, 119–30, and 140–
51. All Chinese contract workers came from the south and southeast between Fukien
and Canton; most were convicted of homicide in Cuba between the 1850s and the
1880s. Archivo Histórico Nacional (AHN), Ultramar: Puerto Rico, Gobierno (PRG),
leg. 5.082/1–2. On other Asians in Puerto Rico, see PA 1: 57–63.

11. Public Record Office, Foreign Office, Series 84, 674 and 1046, Papers Related to
the Slave Trade (FO 84) and Cifre de Loubriel, *Catálogo,* 40. For Boulogne and the
Bellevue brothers, see AHN, PRG, leg. 5.104/47. For more of Beaupied's schemes, see
Dorsey, "Seamy Sides of Abolition."

12. In Cifre de Loubriel's *Catálogo,* statistics demonstrate *cedulario* settlement, along
with the numbers of slave *cedularios* introduced under the Fernandine decree. However,
they do not demonstrate relocations after arrival or the numbers of slaves bought and
sold after arrival. Such trends are evident in the collection "Extranjeros en Puerto Rico,

1815–1845," Record Group T1170, Microfilm Publication Rolls, United States National Archives, Washington, D.C. (USNA, Extranjeros).

13. USNA, ibid. Raw data on Irish *cedularios* are misleading. The few who had reported large sums of money on "entry" had settled in Puerto Rico before 1815. Though most Irish slaveholders were concentrated between Loíza and Cangrejos, Irishmen between Fajardo and Humacao were farmhands without property. For example, only one Irishman in Fajardo owned slaves in 1838. See Archivo General de Puerto Rico (AGPR), Gobernadores Españoles, Asuntos Políticos: Esclavos (GE:E), "Censo de la Poplación Esclava."

14. Cifre de Loubriel, *Catálogo*, 87.

15. Hernández, "Inmigrantes italianos de Puerto Rico durante el siglo XIX," 31. In 1819, Laura was an alderman on the town council of Ponce. Later, the same body ratified his permit to sell medicines. See Ilia del Toro Robledo, ed., *Actas del Cabildo de Ponce, Puerto Rico, 1812–1823* (Ponce, Puerto Rico: Gobierno Municipal Autónomo, 1993). Despite María's "demonstrated affection," her master must have suspected that she would leave him had he freed her before his death.

16. Scarano, *Sugar and Slavery in Puerto Rico*, 18–20.

17. Cifre de Loubriel, *Catálogo*. For the figures discussed here, I cross-referenced Cifre de Loubriel's main entries with those of her addenda for that same compilation and with the entries for her more detailed *Inmigración a Puerto Rico durante el siglo XIX*, tercera parte (*Inmigración*). This technique revealed a few statistical irregularities. Thus, the figures for Table 1.1 of the present study vary from those listed in Cifre de Loubriel's *Catálogo* and *Inmigración*. The Archivo General de Puerto Rico, for example, contains *cedulario* records for immigrants who do not appear in her copious lists and biographical sketches. Cifre de Loubriel's many works on immigration to nineteenth-century Puerto Rico are extensive but not exhaustive. She relied more on data in Spain than in Puerto Rico.

18. See Nelson Hernández, "La administración de Miguel de la Torre y Pando" (master's thesis, Universidad de Puerto Rico, 1983).

19. Scarano, *Sugar and Slavery in Puerto Rico*, 19.

20. AGPR, GE:Comercio, caja 222.

21. The plot was masterminded by Ducourdray Holstein, an Alsatian émigré, and his brother-in-law, Pierre Binet, a Thomian resident of unknown birth. Baralt, *Esclavos rebeldes*, 47–49, and Diaz Soler, *Historia de la esclavitud negra en Puerto Rico*, 212–13.

22. AGPR, GE:C, caja 222. Spanish law required passports for travel from one municipality to another, even within the same colony.

23. Ibid.

24. Ibid. He gave no reason for keeping Gerónimo. Perhaps he was his son or his valet.

25. Ibid. Pedro was listed as *lucumí*, the Cuban term for the Yoruba of southwest

Nigeria. In *El elemento afro-negroide en el español de Puerto Rico,* his analysis of African influences on Puerto Rican Spanish, Alvarez Nazario notes that it was also used in Mexico and South America. Though he mentions its use in Puerto Rico, without citing his source, it must have been rare. Unless referring to Cuban slaves, it appears nowhere in documents used for the present study. "Ollu" (perhaps a Luso-Spanish corruption of Oyo, the largest of the Yoruba kingdoms) appears occasionally in documents for the early nineteenth century.

26. AGPR, GE:E, caja 66. Joseph Danois owned fifty-seven slaves. About 20 percent were from the French Caribbean; nearly half were African-born. GE: Municipios, "Censo de Esclavos de Fajardo, 1838."

27. AGPR, GE:E, caja 66.

28. Ibid.

29. Ibid. and Cifre de Loubriel, *Inmigración.*

30. Cifre de Loubriel, ibid.

31. AGPR, GE:C, caja 222. The narrative is silent on paternity, but there is ample room to suspect that Juliana was Jean Dizac's daughter. His family probably pressured him because he did not own her and because he separated her from her mother.

32. Ibid.

33. Ibid.

34. Ibid.

Chapter 2. Early Anglo-Spanish Diplomacy

1. Nistal Moret, *Esclavos prófugos y cimarrones,* 173–74.

2. After more than a decade in Puerto Rico, Justo knew that laws allowed him to sue his master for kidnapping and brutality. In theory, slaves in Spanish dominions had certain civil rights, but they were predicated on group objectification for the benefit of the slaveholding class, not the individual subjectivity of slaves. Thus, in practice they had no rights at all. During the nineteenth century in the Spanish Caribbean, hundreds of slaves filed lawsuits against their masters for transgressions that ranged from inadequate rest periods, excessive beatings, and rape to broken promises, theft, and wrongful enslavement. In nearly every instance, slave litigants lost. For Puerto Rico, see Dorsey, "Seamy Sides of Abolition"; PA 2: 231–73, "Reclamo de libertad de los esclavos"; and Nistal Moret, "Catorce querellas de esclavos de Manatí." For Cuba, see Dorsey, "Women without History," and, more recently, María Elena Díaz, *The Virgin, the King, and the Royal Slaves of El Cobre: Negotiating Freedom in Colonial Cuba, 1670–1780* (Stanford, Calif.: Stanford University Press, 2000).

3. Corwin, *Spain and the Abolition of Slavery in Cuba,* 26.

4. Ibid., 24–25. For detailed discussions of antislave trade maneuvers and counter-maneuvers involving all nations represented at the Congress of Vienna, see Thomas, *The Slave Trade,* 583–90.

5. Corwin, *Spain and the Abolition of Slavery in Cuba*, 28.

6. Ibid., 29.

7. Dorsey, "Women without History."

8. BHPR 9: 376–77.

9. Ibid., 377.

10. Ibid.

11. Ibid., 4: 90–93.

12. Ibid., 91–92.

13. AHN: EST, leg. 8040/9.

14. Ibid., leg. 8033/16.

15. Corwin, *Spain and the Abolition of Slavery in Cuba*, 29.

16. "Interrogatorio de Mr. R. R. Madden, 17 de septiembre de 1829," in José Antonio Saco, *Historia de la esclavitud de la raza africana en el Nuevo Mundo* (Havana: Cultural, SA, 1938), 4 vols, 4: 330–40. Madden was the first diplomat Great Britain assigned to look after the welfare of Africans liberated by the Court of the Mixed Commissions in Havana. David Turnbull was the second. Preferring to cultivate the confidences of influential white Cuban Creoles with abolitionist leanings, Madden was not very effective in his official duties—though his testimony during the *Amistad* trials in the United States helped prove that the litigants were newly landed African captives, not Creole slaves. Delmonte headed and hosted Cuba's literary abolitionist circle. When Madden interviewed him, he asked pointed questions about all aspects of life in Cuba, including slavery, the African slave trade, the Roman Catholic Church, and the tenor of the island's relationship with Spain. As indicated in his reply to the question of taxes, the planter-abolitionist never minced words. Twentieth-century experts in nineteenth-century Cuban history and literary criticism frequently discuss Delmonte's political relations with Madden, the centrality of his role in the creation of literary abolitionism, and allegations of his complicity in the Escalera conspiracy.

17. BHPR 4: 91; emphasis added.

18. Ibid., 92–93.

19. AHN: EST, 8030/88–90.

20. Corwin, *Spain and the Abolition of Slavery in Cuba*, 39. My assertion of what motivated the delay is tentative. Future research may reveal that the Royal Navy did pursue vessels bound for Cuba prior to 1823.

21. Ibid., 13–14.

22. BHPR 13: 361.

23. While the authors of published slave trader memoirs had much to say about Cuba and Brazil, they rarely mentioned Puerto Rico or Puerto Rican destinations. See Drake, *Revelations of a Slave Smuggler*, 92, and Canot, *Adventures of an African Slaver*, 242. For the illegal period, the works of Drake and Canot are the most famous of the genre; they are also the most unreliable. While both authors had little to say about

Puerto Rico, when they did, they were vague. In 1829, for example, Canot spoke of his crew's attempted mutiny on board a nameless schooner sailing to Cuba with captives from the Pongo River in Upper Guinea. He described the beginning of that near-fatal day. "It was a sweet afternoon when we were floating along the shores of Porto Rico, tracking our course upon the chart." An inbound slave vessel with Cuba as its destination would have no reason to be in Puerto Rican waters unless a portion of the captives were slated to land there. Furthermore, British and Spanish archival sources prove that Canot lied with precision about when he quit the slave trade. Of his participation in the voyage of the *Volador* in 1840, he stated, "*This was the last cargo of slaves I ever shipped!*" To the contrary, the voluminous ledgers of Pedro Blanco, lord of the Spanish slave trade, reveal that Canot continued to service Cuba and Puerto Rico well into the 1840s. See ANC, Miscelánea, leg. 535 AD. Drake also took liberties with details. See note 26 below. Both memoirs were published while transatlantic slave commerce still existed. While publishers couched both books deceptively within the context of "death-bed confessions," Canot, Drake, and their editors were aware of the need to obfuscate certain facts to prevent the authors from incriminating themselves and to discourage acts of revenge on the part of current slave traders.

24. PA 1: 7. The document cites "Boni" as the point of embarkation. The Bonny River forms part of the Niger Delta. Though Ibibio may have ranked among the captives, most were probably Ibo. Both come from southeast Nigeria.

25. Baralt, *Esclavos rebeldes,* 31–32.

26. Drake, *Revelations of a Slave Smuggler,* 91–92. Drake states that the *Panchita* was slated for Brazil. However, the identity and legal residence of the captain, together with the details he offers to describe the subterfuge involved in the ship's registration papers, suffice to establish that it was bound for Puerto Rico.

27. PA 1: 7–8.

28. Ibid.

29. For assessments of first three events, see Scarano, *Sugar and Slavery in Puerto Rico,* 129–39. Regarding the fourth, though the British decision briefly slowed slave traffic to Cuba and Brazil, it had a lasting impact on Puerto Rico. See Great Britain, *Extracts,* 9–13. The *Casualidade* was the last slaver bound for Puerto Rico alone under the Portuguese flag. The British captured it in July 1839. See Table 6.2.

30. Díaz Soler, *Historia de la esclavitud negra en Puerto Rico,* 237; Coll y Toste, ed., and Cuchí Coll, comp., *Historia de la esclavitud en Puerto Rico,* 165–67 (Coll y Toste); Morales Carrión, *Trata,* 82–85; and Scarano, *Sugar and Slavery in Puerto Rico,* 130.

31. Great Britain, *Parliamentary Papers: Slave Trade,* vol. 10, Class B, dispatches 1–4 (PP); and AHN: Estado, leg. 8.031/22 (EST).

32. Ibid.

33. PP, vol. 13, Class B, subenclosure K in Palmerston to Villiers, December 12, 1835, and vol. 16, Class B, López to Hope, March 9, 1838.

34. PP, vol. 16, Class B, Colebrook to Glenleg, April 25, 1838. No one raised the real issue here: compensation was not considered for the owners of black Britons enslaved in Puerto Rico after August 1, 1834. For this reason alone, less than a hundred slaves were sent to San Juan for repatriation.

35. PP, vol. 14, Grey to Backhouse, November 20, 1835.

36. PP, vol. 16, Class B, López to Hope, March 9, 1838.

37. Ibid., López to Colebrook, March 2, 1838.

38. Ibid., Hope to Colebrook, March 16, 1838.

39. Ibid., López to Hope, March 9, 1838.

40. Ibid., Beg to López, subenclosure K, and Coll y Toste, 165–67. On Monsanto, see Cifre de Loubriel, *Catálogo,* 22.

41. British reports state that seven slaves were freed and repatriated. Initial Spanish dispatches name but two, Andrés and Phoebe. Subsequent Spanish letters refer to a third, Olivier, or Oliver, whose name, like Phoebe's, is absent from the list López circulated. See EST, legs. 8.036/3 and 8.045/9.

42. PP, vol. 16, Colebrook to Glenleg, April 25, 1838.

43. Ibid., López to Hope, March 9, 1838.

44. Ibid., Palmerston to Villiers, July 11, 1838, subenclosures G–M.

Chapter 3. Friendly Fire, Enemy Fire

1. For a radically different assessment of the founding of the British consulate, see Morales Carrión, *Trata,* 123–25.

2. Classic examinations of the Spanish intendancies include John Lynch, *Spanish Colonial Administration: The Intendant System in Río de la Plata* (London: Athlone, 1958), and J. R. Fisher, *Government and Society in Colonial Peru: The Intendant System* (London: Athlone, 1970). For early intendancies in Puerto Rico, see Córdova, *Memorias,* vols. 3 and 4.

3. For the duties of governors, intendants, and appellate judges in the Spanish Caribbean, see Luis de la Rosa Martínez, *Lexicón Histórico-Documental de Puerto Rico, 1812–1899* (San Juan: Centro de Estudios Avanzados de Puerto Rico y el Caribe, 1986); Rodríguez San Pedro, *Legislación ultramarina;* José Serapio Mojarrieta, *Ensayo sobre juicios de residencia* (Madrid: Alhambra y Compañía, 1848); and Zamora y Coronado, *Biblioteca de la legislación ultramarina.* For legal adjustments between the abolition of Puerto Rican slavery and the end of the Spanish American empire, as well as entries related to all legislative aspects of slavery from the Middle Ages to the abolition of slavery in Cuba, see Joaquín Escriche, *Diccionario razonado de legislación y jurisdicción* (Paris and Mexico: Bouret, 1888); Mariano Granados and Gregorio Peces-Barba, *Legislación Española* (Madrid: Editorial Lex, 1934); and León Medina and Manuel Marañón, *Leyes Penales de España* (Madrid: Reus, 1936).

4. This became evident between February and April 1837, when parliamentary peers

declared that Cuba and Puerto Rico would not be governed by the Constitution of 1812 but by "special laws." See Corwin, *Spain and the Abolition of Slavery in Cuba,* 64–66. For the behaviors of the governor of Cuba, Miguel Tacón, and La Torre of Puerto Rico during the tumult, see BHPR 2: 29–32 and Morales Carrión, *Trata,* 68–69. The exclusion of Cuban, Puerto Rican, and Filipino participation in constitutional reforms resulted not only in the ejection of the Asian and Caribbean Creole delegates from the Palacio de las Cortes. In Puerto Rico, it led to a failed coup in the summer of the same year. The conspiracy was planned and betrayed when Moreda was governor, but the trial of its authors took place under López. Thus, authorities interpreted the plot as another example of his incompetence. It is referred to as the "Conspiracy of 1838." Two decades passed before Spain attempted to undo the damage incurred by the exclusion of colonial delegates. See BHPR 10: 368.

5. On these reforms and others, see Rodríguez San Pedro, *Legislación ultramarina,* vol. 2. Some have asserted that Francisco González de Linares was the island's first civilian governor in 1822. In that year, he was appointed *jefe superior político,* a constitutional title that did not mean the same thing as governor. Immediately he named La Torre captain general. But González's position collapsed, along with the constitutional government. Later he solicited the governorship but was denied. AHN: PRG, leg. 5065/7–10. Between La Torre and López, Francisco Moreda y Prieto served as governor and captain general from January to December 1837. Though his appointment was official, the combination of its pioneering brevity and uneventful tenure likened it to an interim. Subtle exceptions were revelations that exposed La Torre—to no avail—not the incumbent Moreda. See PA 1: 9–11 and Morales Carrión, *Trata,* 77 and 95. See also note 4 above. African slaves continued to arrive during Moreda's term. However, with the exception of the voyage of the *Vencedora,* discussed in Chapter 6, vis-à-vis slavery and its traffic, his office was relatively quiet. Brief terms of service did not necessarily result in uneventful terms, of course. Though Juan Prim y Prats served less than a year in 1848, he left unforgettable marks on the history of slavery and race relations by supporting the slave trade openly, by crushing a slave revolt in St. Croix, and by issuing his infamous "Edict against the African Race."

6. AHN: Gracia y Justicia (PRGJ), leg. 2020/10.

7. AHN: Hacienda (PRH), leg. 1072–79 and 1074–152.

8. Morales Carrión, *Trata,* 87.

9. Ibid., 98–100.

10. Ibid., 106–8. Both cases pose the compelling question: How often did governors disagree with the Audiencia over slave litigants? At this point, my own field work suggests that such instances were rare. However, inasmuch as most slaves charged with serious crimes, including homicide, were tried in upper and lower civil courts, with governors simply rubber-stamping verdicts from the Audiencia, the second case poses an additional question related to the social economy of slave identity. Military trials for

slaves and free civilians were reserved for treason. In the Spanish Caribbean from the 1820s to the 1870s, sedition was a treasonous offense. Hence, the second question, in terms of those who controlled the discourse, here, the political protocols of social communication: Was it possible for slaves to betray the government that endorsed their bondage? The second case suggests that this possibility was in a state of discursive decline until the late 1840s, when Prim ruled. Both conflicts are important because they identify a general mood that helped shape the foundations of Puerto Rican abolitionist thought—or at least in comparison to top-level Spanish and Creole bureaucrats in Cuba, they demonstrate a greater sense of repugnance toward the institution of slavery. Perhaps Morales Carrión had this in mind when he summarized the two cases in *Trata* and placed a sample of the original text from one of them in PA, vol. 1. In this vein, I suggest that the late Morales Carrión came to be less a disciple of Tannenbaum and Díaz Soler than a leader in the cause against the construction of history on metaphysical foundations. In other words, he opposed the detractors of Tannenbaum and Díaz Soler less than he opposed the conflating tendencies of theories and methods that reconstructed the history of black slavery in the Americas as monolithic and therefore essentialist. The totality of his scholarship must be seen in the context of matters left unexplored after the furor of counter-Tannenbaumian criticism ran its course, for there exists a historiographic gap between counter-Tannenbaumian research and the non-comparativist scholarship that slowly silenced it. For an acknowledgment of this epistemological problem, see Paquette, *Sugar Is Made with Blood,* 112.

11. AHN: PRH, leg. 1119–153, "Memoria sobre la administración económica de la Isla de Puerto Rico, redactada por el Intendente Núñez a su sucesor, el Señor López de Acebedo [*sic*]" (Núñez to López), and legs. 1065–77, nos. 2 and 3. Strengthening of the captaincy general was associated with efforts to recapture the mainland colonies Spain lost in the wars of independence—especially in Venezuela. In further efforts to prevent the spread of independence movements to Cuba and Puerto Rico—especially from Venezuela—between 1822 and 1826, Ferdinand empowered the Caribbean captaincies general with sweeping, emergency authority reminiscent of the viceroyalties of old. For Cuba, see Hortensia Pichardo, ed., *Documentos para la historia de Cuba* (Havana: Editorial de Ciencias Sociales, 1977), 289, Documento 36, "Reales Ordenes Concediendo Facultades Omnímodas al Capitán General de Cuba." For Puerto Rico, see Córdoba, *Memorias geográficas, históricas, económicas,* 4: 432–34.

12. AHN: PRH, leg. 1.071/4 and 39.

13. Ibid., leg. 1.071/39.

14. Ibid., leg. 1.071/5. The Francophone slaves could have come from French Martinique and Guadeloupe—or even St. Domingue, especially if they were older. But most were probably natives of British Dominica and St. Lucia, where French patois was and is still spoken. Puerto Rican masters had nothing to gain by giving up able-bodied slaves who did not come from the British islands.

15. Ibid., leg. 1.071/4, no. 2.

16. Ibid. On the belated reimbursement, see leg. 1.071/5.

17. Ibid., leg. 1.071/11

18. Ibid., leg. 1.071/4, no. 2.

19. Colonial amendments to metropolitan orders were common. In *Sugar and Slavery in Puerto Rico,* 18–19, Scarano discusses local changes in the Real Cédula de Gracias of 1815. In *Marriage, Class and Colour in Nineteenth-Century Cuba,* Martínez-Alier observes that Spanish laws against cross-group matrimony were amended differently in Cuba, Argentina, and Mexico.

20. For a slaveholder's financial responsibilities at the level of legality rather than morality, philanthropy, or common sense, see article 4, chapter 7, of the "Reglamento Sobre la Educación, Trato, y Ocupaciones que Deben Dar a sus Esclavos los Dueños o Mayordomos de ésta Isla" in Coll y Toste, 129. It is fairly certain that, in the name of cost effectiveness, the famous slave rebel Martín Xiorro died by his master's hand. Nistal Moret, *El cimarrón.* I thank Luis de la Rosa Martínez, retired director of the Archivo General de Puerto Rico, for pointing out this practice to me.

21. AHN: PRH, leg. 1.071/4, no. 4.

22. PP, vol. 15, subenclosure D in Colebrook to Leith, December 26, 1837.

23. AHN: PRH, leg. 1.071/4, no. 4.

24. Ibid.

25. Ibid.

26. Ibid., leg. 1.071/4, no. 2.

27. Ibid.

28. Ibid. On runaway slaves from the non-Hispanic Antilles see Díaz Soler, *Historia de la esclavitud negra en Puerto Rico,* 233–35.

29. British efforts to convince Spain to outlaw inter-Caribbean traffic are discussed at length in subsequent chapters. In Spain, *ladinos* were "New Christians," Hispanicized peoples of non-European descent, specifically, Africans from both sides of the Sahara, as well as Jews. Later, in the colonies, the term was used to identify creolized or partially creolized African-born slaves, to distinguish them from *bozales,* newly landed African captives.

30. AHN: PRH, leg. 1.071/4, no. 2. For the full text of this preamble, see Appendix 2.1.

31. Ibid.

32. British references to Puerto Rican abolitionist informants increased after 1845. Though they were never named, it is probable that white Creole intellectuals and activists such as Alejandro Tapía y Rivera and Julio Vizcarrondo y Coronado ranked among them. Both loathed slavery and challenged the heavy-handedness of Spanish imperial rule. Governor Juan de la Pezuela exiled Tapía y Rivera because he, like other Puerto Rican antislavists, advocated immediate abolition. Vizcarrondo fought more effectively

in New York, Philadelphia, and eventually Madrid, where—with two compatriots—he created Spain's first public abolitionist organization, La Sociedad Abolicionista Española. In their insistence on the immediate rather than gradual termination of slavery, Puerto Rican abolitionists differed from their counterparts in Cuba. On Vizcarrondo and his compatriots, Corwin reflected, "[T]he Puerto Ricans in Madrid would become the spearhead of the [Spanish] emancipation movement. . . . A purely economic explanation would scarcely suffice. . . . Puerto Rican liberalism was not quite the same as that of Cuba, even if the same sources of ideas were drawn upon" (154–55). For further abolitionist comparisons between Cuba and Puerto Rico, see his *Spain and the Abolition of Slavery in Cuba*, 154–61. For recent discussions, see Schmidt-Nowara, *Empire and Slavery*, 117–19 and 136–37.

33. The Brazilian branch of the Mixed Court also used the term *emancipados*. British officers called them "recaptives."

34. AHN: PRH, leg. 1.071/4, no. 2. This ruling may explain, but not justify, O'Donnell's overbearing behavior toward black Cubans in 1844, along with Prim's menacing but less sanguinary "Edict against the African Race," promulgated in 1848.

35. Ibid.

36. Ibid.

37. Ibid.

38. EST, 8037/18.

39. Baralt, *Esclavos rebeldes*, 93–100. For a selection of primary sources on the Ponce conspiracy of 1841, see PA 1: 136–39.

40. "Africanization" referred to two fundamentally antithetical concerns in nineteenth-century Cuba. A minority of white Creole intellectuals used it to identify the sociopolitical dread associated with the Atlantic slave trade. It voiced the fear that rising numbers of blacks—slaves, *emancipados*, and free people of color—would ban together and destroy Cuba's "white civilization," be that civilization Spanish and therefore colonial or republican and therefore independent. This group promoted the gradual abolition of slavery and the immediate cessation of the slave trade. On the other hand, white Creole sugar producers, and the Spanish financiers who supported them, viewed "Africanization" as any law, political activity, or passing utterance that threatened the status quo, including British abolitionism, ubiquitous rumors of secret plans for aggregate emancipation, and grievances against Spanish colonial rule—especially during the early 1850s, when Pezuela was governor. Though both groups cited Cuba's potential to become "another Haiti," due to Spain's formidable military presence, the latter voiced less concern for the numerical superiority of nonwhites. Thus, until the late 1860s, the African slave trade functioned as a counterpoise against independence from Spain. See Corwin, *Spain and the Abolition of Slavery in Cuba*, 115–22, and C. Stanley Urban, "The Africanization of Cuba Scare, 1853–1855," HAHR 37 (February 1957): 29–45. In the minds of white Creole elites, independence would have been prefaced by the withdrawal

of troops, which would have threatened white Creole hegemony in relation to the larger population of nonwhites. In reality, the island's nonwhites—three groups of black people dominated numerically by heterogeneous African-born slaves in addition to nearly 25,000 heterogeneous Chinese contract workers at that time—were too divided by social, cultural, and economic variants to achieve the political unity ruling whites feared. Perhaps Spaniards placed greater faith than white Creoles in the political force of nonwhite divisiveness.

41. Turnbull, *Travels to the West.*

42. The United States feared the Foreign Office would coax the Spanish regency into immediate abolition and British annexation. In the interests of its Spanish allies, Washington dispatched a man-of-war to Cuba. See Paquette, *Sugar Is Made with Blood,* 194–200, and Corwin, *Spain and the Abolition of Slavery in Cuba,* 77–78. The creation of the superintendency of liberated Africans was illegal. Spain refused to recognize it and protested its authority for the whole of its short existence. The British hulk *Romney* further fanned the flames of Spanish outrage. It was docked in Havana, ostensibly to shelter and care for *emancipados.* Its crew consisted of Africans manumitted by the Mixed Court at Havana and Freetown. While these men were invaluable as interpreters for *emancipados* during and after Mixed Court proceedings in Havana, Spanish soldiers and local police forces treated them severely. See PP, vol. 17, Palmerston to Clarendon, January 29, 1839; Clarendon to Palmerston, February 2, 1839, especially the second enclosure; and PP, vol. 22, Turnbull to Aberdeen, January 31, 1842.

43. Paquette, *Sugar Is Made with Blood,* 152–60. A foreign eyewitness likened O'Donnell's persecution of Afro-Cubans to the "Reign of Terror" in Paris during the French Revolution.

44. PP, vol. 16, Colebrook to Mason, April 28, 1838; Colebrook to López, April 27, 1838; and Cifre de Loubriel, *Inmigración,* 249.

45. EST 8031/7 and 22. Historians disagree on the role of British vessels in this case. Compare, for example, Ward, *The Royal Navy and the Slavers,* 124–25, and Ortiz Fernández, *Hampa afro-cubana,* 163–64.

46. EST 8028/23.

47. Puerto Rico's use of agents in Curaçao to report subversive activities emanating from Venezuela and Santo Domingo peaked between 1844 and 1852. See AHN: PRG "Correspondencia de los capitanes generales de Cuba y Puerto Rico y de la Primera Secretaría de Estado," leg. 3524, nos. 5 and 63.

48. EST 8035/1 and 12. When Tacón's term ended, he had amassed 500,000 pesos in bribes from slave traders. Fernando Portuondo, *Historia de Cuba* (Havana: Pueblo y Educación, 1965), 347.

49. EST 8036/3.

50. EST 8015/38.

51. Asiegbu, *Slavery and the Politics of Liberation,* 34–47.

52. PP, vol. 14, Villiers to Palmerston, October 14, 1835, and vol. 16, Palmerston to Villiers, July 11, 1838, and Colebrook to Glenleg, April 25, 1838. See also Turnbull, *Travels to the West*, 568–71, and Díaz Soler, *Historia de la esclavitud negra en Puerto Rico*, 119–20 n. 44. The delay was due to changes in British strategy toward slave traffic to Brazil and the prosecution of slave ships bearing the Portuguese flag beginning in 1839.

53. Spanish, British, and Cuban archives have many files on Turnbull. Records on his political relations with liberated Africans, Afro-Cubans, and Afro-Britons in Cuba are abundant. For samples of documents that connect him to slave unrest, see ANC, Comisión Militar (CM) 1844, leg. 5, and FO 84/608, Aberdeen to Turnbull, February 10, 1842. For his efforts to free black Britons enslaved illegally in Cuba, see Dorsey, "Women without History."

54. For overlappings in the chronology of Cuban and Puerto Rican slave revolts, see Baralt, *Esclavos rebeldes*, chapters 7–9. See also Arturo Morales Carrión, "La revolución haitiana y el movimiento antiesclavista en Puerto Rico," *Boletín de la Academia Puertorriqueña de Historia* 8: 139–56; and Nistal Moret, *El cimarrón*, as well as his *Esclavos prófugos y cimarrones*. Though many have discussed Turnbull's years in Cuba, biographical histories devoted to his life and his efforts have yet to appear. For his Cuban activities, see Mário Hernández y Sánchez-Barba, "David Turnbull y el problema de la esclavitud en Cuba," *Anuario de Estudios Americanos* 14 (1957): 241–99. Historians continue to debate his connection to slave rebellions that led to the Conspiración de la Escalera, an exercise in ethnic cleansing. Paquette's *Sugar Is Made with Blood* offers the most thorough examination to date. For other treatments, see Corwin, *Spain and the Abolition of Slavery in Cuba;* Philip Foner, *A History of Cuba and Its Relations with the United States*, vol. 1 (New York: International Publications, 1962); Hall, *Social Control in Slave Plantation Societies;* Edward Mullen, ed., *The Life and Poems of a Cuban Slave* (Hamden, Conn.: Archon, 1981); and Murray, *Odious Commerce*. See also Deschamps, *El negro en la economía habanera del siglo XIX*, and Francisco González del Valle y Ramírez, *La conspiración de la escalera* (Havana: Siglo XX, 1925).

55. Leslie Bethell, "The Mixed Commissions for the Suppression of the Transatlantic Slave Trade," *Journal of African History* 12: 79–93, and Martínez-Fernández, *Fighting Slavery in the Caribbean*.

56. For more examples of indecisiveness over the court's transfer, see PP, vol. 14, Villiers to Palmerston, October 14, 1835, and AGPR, GE:E, caja 66.

57. EST, 8025/17.

58. Corwin, *Spain and the Abolition of Slavery in Cuba*, 79–81; Knight, *Slave Society in Cuba during the Nineteenth Century*, 63; and Bandiel, *Some Account of the Trade in Slaves from Africa*, 224–336.

59. PP, vol. 30, Sotomayor to Aberdeen, May 30, 1845, with eight enclosures; Aberdeen to Sotomayor, December 19, 1845; and ANC, Real Consulado y Junta de Fomento, leg. 148.7306.

60. PP, Kennedy and Dalrymple to Aberdeen, March 20, 1844.

61. EST, leg. 8025/17.

62. AGPR, GE:E, caja 66.

63. Paquette, *Sugar Is Made with Blood*, 209.

64. AHN: PRG, 5064.

Chapter 4. Teamwork

1. AHN: PRG, leg. 5.070/29, no. 23.

2. Dorsey, "Women without History."

3. Scarano, *Sugar and Slavery in Puerto Rico*, 122, 124, and 144–54. See also Hall, *Slave Society in the Danish West Indies*, and Sonesson, *Puerto Rico's Commerce*.

4. Morales Carrión, *Trata*, 39–44.

5. Ward, *The Royal Navy and the Slavers*, 139.

6. The principal organizers of these networks were Pedro Blanco, Pedro Martínez, and Julián Zulueta. For slave merchants in Puerto Rico, see ANC, Miscelánea, leg. 535 AD. My use of this hefty set of hardbound documents is limited strictly to Cuban assistance in Puerto Rican slave trading. For a novelization of Blanco's career, see Novás Calvo, *Pedro Blanco, el negrero*. For updated assessments of all three, see Eltis, *Economic Growth and the Ending of the Transatlantic Slave Trade*.

7. See Buxton, *The African Slave Trade and Its Remedy*, 155–57, for eyewitness accounts in 1831.

8. See Corwin, *Spain and the Abolition of Slavery in Cuba*. Politics surrounding the marriage of Isabel II was predicated on British interference vis-à-vis relations with France and Italy.

9. Great Britain exerted a greaet deal of diplomatic pressure on all major Western powers. France and the United States were especially offended by British political tactics. In the long run, all nations making suppressionist agreements with Great Britain found ways to violate them. For British antislave trade treaties with Denmark, France, and the Netherlands, see PP, vols. 8 and 19–21. The international implications of the destruction of Spanish slave factories on the Upper Guinea Coast are discussed in Asiegbu, *Slavery and the Politics of Liberation*, 120–24; Ward, *The Royal Navy and the Slavers*, 178–81; and Novás Calvo, *Pedro Blanco, el negrero*, 207–12. References to Spanish slave-trading establishments along the West African littoral should not be confused with "legitimate" territorial claims recognized by European treaties. Spain claimed no territories in sub-Sahara Africa until 1777, when it purchased the islands of Fernando Poo and Annobon from Portugal.

10. For one of numerous examples for the crossing of legitimate and illegitimate (read slave) commerce, see PP, vol. 21, Lewis and Hook to Palmerston, April 21, 1841.

11. Wiley Bell, ed., *Slaves No More: Letters from Liberia, 1833–1869* (Lexington:

University Press of Kentucky, 1980); Horatio Bridge, *Journal of an African Cruiser* (London: Dawsons of Pall Mall, 1968); and Melville, *A Residence at Sierra Leone.*

12. On diplomatic tensions surrounding these treaties, see Emmer, "Abolition of the Abolished," and Daget, "France, England, and the Suppression of the Illegal Trade." See also Daget, "British Repression of the Illegal French Slave Trade."

13. On Dutch resistance to multinational antislave trade treaties, see Emmer, "Abolition of the Abolished," 180–81. See also PP, vol. 13, Palmerston to Falek, October 7, 1831; PP, vol. 15, Palmerston to Disbrowe, August 11, 1837; PP, vol. 23, Aberdeen to Disbrowe, December 31, 1842; and PP, vol. 25, Schenley to Aberdeen, September 5, 1843.

14. PP, vol. 50, "Report on the Condition of the Gold Coast," 544–63.

15. Daget, "British Repression of the Illegal French Slave Trade," 419–22.

16. While the Anglo-French treaty of 1831, amended in 1833, forbade slaving between 15 degrees north latitude and 10 degrees south latitude (Cape Verde to Angola), specifications omitted East Africa except Madagascar. PP, vol. 11, 1844. See also Ward, *The Royal Navy and the Slavers,* 121.

17. For the *Diosa,* see PA 1: 328–30. Nistal Moret devotes a chapter to scarification patterns on African-born slaves in Puerto Rico. See *Esclavos prófugos y cimarrones,* 123–35. The collection of documents includes precise graphics based on descriptions.

18. On abolition and the British occupation of the Dutch West Indian territories, see Emmer, "Abolition of the Abolished," 179. On Anglo-Dutch treaties, see PP, vol. 8, 19–21. See also Ward, *The Royal Navy and the Slavers,* 78.

19. PP, vol. 11, Williams to Canning, April 4, 1826.

20. Ibid.

21. PP, vol. 11, Reffel to Canning, January 27, 1827, with enclosed report of the *Fortunée.* For a different assessment of the same case, see Emmer, "Abolition of the Abolished," 182.

22. PP, vol. 11, Reffel to Canning, ibid.

23. Ibid.

24. In 1823, the Netherlands accepted the equipment clause in an addendum to the Anglo-Dutch treaty of 1818.

25. Daget, "France, England, and the Suppression of the Illegal Trade."

26. PP, Naval Officers to the Commissioners of the Admiralty, May 6, 1825. British intelligence varied greatly from one year to the next. After calculating an average of thirty ships per annum in 1823, the following year reports reduced it to ten. Estimates for Puerto Rico at this time were educated guesses at best.

27. For the first two centuries of Portuguese colonization in the Gulf of Guinea, see Garfield, *A History of São Tomé.* On the frequency of foreign vessels that visited São Tomé in the early 1800s, see Arquivo Histórico Ultramarino, Lisbon, Portugal (AHU), and Colecção Sá da Bandeira, Papéis sobre a abolição da Escravidão Africana, and

Possessões Ultramarinas, Angola (PUA), Navios Estrangeiros. Both collections show that most ships docking in São Tomé registered British, Dutch, French, and United States nationality. On Corisco and Cuban slave traffic in the 1830s, see Ibrahim Sundiata, *From Slaving to Neoslavery: The Bight of Biafra and Fernando Po in the Era of Abolition* (Madison: University of Wisconsin Press, 1996), 45–47.

28. Though the Royal Navy targeted Spanish, Dutch, and Luso-Brazilian slavers, the Foreign Office had yet to supply the Admiralty with specific instructions for French transgressors. Ward, *The Royal Navy and the Slavers,* 103–7, and Daget, "France, England, and the Suppression of the Illegal Trade."

29. PP, vol. 13, Fleeming to Burrow, September 7, 1829, in Aberdeen to Addington, April 23, 1830.

30. PP, vol. 11, The *Fortunée* Report.

31. Ibid.

32. Ibid.

33. Ibid.

34. Emmer, "Abolition of the Abolished," 180–81.

35. See Great Britain, *Extracts.*

36. PP, Kennedy and Schenley to Palmerston, April 21, 1838.

37. Scarano, *Sugar and Slavery in Puerto Rico,* 127–29.

38. Emmer, "Abolition of the Abolished," 184.

39. Coggeshall, *Thirty-six Voyages,* 523.

40. Anthony Trollope, *The Caribbean and the Spanish Main* (New York: Harper Bros., 1858). See also Hall, *Slave Society in the Danish West Indies.*

41. On Danish Accra, see PP, vol. 34, Palmerston to Wynn, December 31, 1847. On trade between St. Thomas and San Juan, see Sonesson, *Puerto Rico's Commerce.*

42. Scarano, *Sugar and Slavery in Puerto Rico,* 122–30.

43. On natural and manmade factors that resulted in the destruction of many Puerto Rican records for the Spanish colonial period, see Gómez Canedo, *Los archivos históricos de Puerto Rico.*

44. Coggeshall, *Thirty-six Voyages,* 507–8. See also Appendix 1.1.

45. Appendix 1.2.

46. Appendix 1.3.

47. Smith, *The Winter of 1840 in St. Croix, with an Excursion to Tortola and St. Thomas.* See also Appendix 1.4.

48. Ward, *The Royal Navy and the Slavers,* chapter 2.

49. Morales Carrión, *Trata,* 87.

Chapter 5. Moving Meridians and Parallels

1. S. Green-Pedersen, "Economic Considerations behind the Danish Abolition of the Slave Trade," in Gemery and Hogendorn, *The Uncommon Market.*

2. S. Green-Pedersen, "Slave Demography in the Danish West Indies," in Eltis and

Walvin, *The Abolition of the Atlantic Slave Trade,* 231–57, and Hall, *Slave Society in the Danish West Indies,* 126.

3. PP, vol. 15, Palmerston to Wynn, December 15, 1836; Wynn to Palmerston, January 12, 1837, with enclosure Wynn to Krabbe, December 27, 1836; and PP, vol. 17, Wynn to Palmerston, February 17, 1839, with enclosure Krabbe to Wynn, n.d.

4. PP, vol. 15, Wynn to Palmerston, January 12, 1837, with enclosure in dispatch 155, Krabbe to Wynn, n.d.

5. On Dutch slave flight to British territories, see PP, vol. 28, Aberdeen to Disbrowe, December 31, 1844, and PP, vol. 27, Schenley to Aberdeen, March 28, 1844. For Dano-British accords on runaway slaves, see PP, vol. 15, Wynn to Palmerston, May 31, 1837.

6. PP, vol. 15, Scholten to Light, May 1, 1837, in Wynn to Palmerston, May 21, 1837.

7. Ibid.

8. Slaves burned property, but no whites were killed. Fearing the revolt would spread to Puerto Rico, Governor Prim ordered tortures and executions. AHN: PRG, leg. 5.069/ 3–7.

9. Works on this general topic include James Duffy, *Portuguese Africa* (Cambridge: Harvard University Press, 1961), and Donald Burness, ed., *Critical Perspectives on Lusophone African Literature* (Boulder, Colo.: Three Continents, 1981). The British purchased Freetown from indigenous lords in 1797 and established it as a place of exile for Caribbean maroons and a settlement for conscripted royalist slaves from the newly independent North American colonies. In the nineteenth century, it was used as a Europeanization center for Africans freed from intercepted, westbound slave ships. British authority was confined to the settlement's borders. Beyond them, slave trading in the rest of Sierra Leone continued. See, for example, Mavis Campbell, *Back to Africa: From Nova Scotia to Sierra Leone* (Trenton, N.J.: Africa World Press, 1993).

10. PP, vol. 12, "Report by Captain Lucas, Commander of the Abolitionist Patrol at Accra," October 7, 1829, subenclosure A in Baget to Aberdeen, August 21, 1830.

11. PP, vol. 21, Palmerston to Wynn, January 18, 1841, with four enclosures.

12. Ibid.

13. Ibid., Tucker to O'Farrill, October 29, 1840, in Palmerston to Wynn, January 18, 1841. *Mongo* applied to slave traders working the West African coast, African Creoles—black and mulatto—as well as European whites.

14. PP, vol. 20, Dall to Tucker, September 24, 1840, in Palmerston to Wynn.

15. Ibid.

16. Ibid.

17. PP, vol. 21, Krabbe to Wynn, July 9, 1841, in Wynn to Palmerston, July 15, 1841.

18. Ibid., Wynn to Palmerston, July 15, 1841; Palmerston to Wynn, August 9, 1841; and Wynn to Palmerston, August 19, 1841.

19. PP, vol. 36, Palmerston to Wynn, December 31, 1847.

20. Ibid., Palmerston to Wynn, January 13, 1848.

21. PP, vol. 11, Williams to Canning, March 20, 1826, with four enclosures, and April 4, 1826, with twelve enclosures; PP, vol. 12, The Lucas Report, October 7, 1829, and the Gold Coast Report, 1812–1824, in PP, West Africa, vol. 18.

22. Boahen, "Asante and Fante in the Nineteenth Century." See also Ivor Wilks, *Asante in the Nineteenth Century* (Cambridge: Cambridge University Press, 1989). Though Wilks discusses Anglo-Dutch relations on the Gold Coast, as well as conflicts between Asante and Anglo-Fante forces, his study does not address the external slave trade in the 1830s.

23. Flint, *The Cambridge History of Africa,* vol. 5, 1790–1870, chapter 6.

24. Boahen, "Asante and Fante in the Nineteenth Century." On Gold Coast exports over time, see Curtin, *The Atlantic Slave Trade,* and Eltis, *Economic Growth and the Ending of the Transatlantic Slave Trade.* For Mina slaves in Cuba—compared to the Ibo, Yoruba, Gangá, and Congolese—see statistics in Moreno Fraginals, "Africa in Cuba," and, more recently, Bergad et al., *The Cuban Slave Market,* 72–75 and 199–206. See also note 68 below. Statistics in Bergad et al. substantiate arguments throughout the present study that circum–Sierra Leonian importations to the Spanish Caribbean were higher than earlier findings suggest.

25. PP, vol. 12, The Lucas Report.

26. Ibid.

27. PP, vol. 12, The Report of Lt. Col. Last, Commandant of the Dutch Possessions on the Coast of Guinea in Bagot to Aberdeen, August 21, 1830.

28. Ibid.

29. Ibid.

30. Ibid.

31. Ibid.

32. Ibid.

33. Ibid.

34. Ibid.

35. Ibid.

36. Ibid.

37. Akinjogbin, *Dahomey and Its Neighbors,* and Polanyi, *Dahomey and the Slave Trade.*

38. PP, vol. 12, The Lucas Report.

39. PP, vol. 18, The Gold Coast Report.

40. The Mixed Court in Paramaribo freed the *Snow* captives in 1823. True liberation was delayed for more than two decades. PP, vol. 25, Schenley to the Governor of British Guiana, August 29, 1843.

41. For an example of this consular ploy, see the discussion of Mary Gordon in Dorsey, "Women without History."

42. PP, vol. 15, Palmerston to Disbrowe, June 30, 1837. Palmerston relied on an

earlier report from the London Committee for Gold Coast Merchants: Malck to Palmerston, August 27, 1831.

43. PP, vol. 22, Dedel to Aberdeen, November 22, 1841, and Aberdeen to Dedel, December 31, 1841.

44. PP, vol. 18, The Gold Coast Report.

45. PP, vol. 15, Palmerston to Disbrowe, August 11, 1837, and the Gold Coast Committee to Stephens, June 27, 1836, in Palmerston to Disbrowe, July 28, 1836.

46. PP, vol. 15, Verstolk Soelen to Disbrowe, September 6, 1837.

47. Ibid. Verstolk's reply came from the apologetic in Verveer to the Minister of the Colonial Department, August 29, 1837.

48. Verveer cites William Topp, Vice President of the British Possessions of Guinea [British Accra]. PP, vol. 15, Verveer to the Colonial Minister, August 29, 1837, and PP, vol. 20, Verstolk to Disbrowe, November 9, 1840.

49. Ibid.

50. PP, Samo to Palmerston, June 29, 1840.

51. Ibid.

52. PP, vol. 15, Verstolk de Soelen to Disbrowe, November 9, 1840. Baron Verstolk must have enjoyed citing this quote; it originated from Verveer's report of his visit to Belize. For ethnic distributions of slaves in Suriname, see Höetink, "Suriname and Curaçao," 60–61.

53. PP, vol. 18, The Gold Coast Report.

54. PP, vol. 20, "Extract de la Matricule des Recrués d'Afrique Destinés au Service Militaire dans les Indes Occidentales, Contenant la Liste des Hommes Dèja Revenus de l'Isle de Java avec Pension," in Verstolk de Soelen to Disbrowe, November 9, 1840.

55. Ibid., Samo to Palmerston, June 29, 1840. I stress the possibility of a small number of Africans over larger numbers. Dutch legal quandries over the export of slaves to Puerto Rico were limited to the islands. Unlike St. Maarten or Curaçao, for example, mainland Suriname was not a part of the argument simply because its planters refused to sell their slaves. If some Asante military trainees were rerouted from Suriname to Puerto Rico as slaves, their numbers were small by necessity; the movement of larger numbers for reexport would have alerted Surinamese planters, who would have made every effort to keep them. Furthermore, a larger movement would have been impossible to hide from British diplomatic and naval surveillance. See Chapter 9 in this study for Dutch slaves in Puerto Rico.

56. Emmer, "Abolition of the Abolished," 188–90.

57. The Anglo-French dispute over the legality of free African emigration dominates Foreign Office correspondence from January 1857 to May 1860. The first émigrés—from the Congo—arrived in Martinique. PP, vol. 44, Lawless to Clarendon, January 20, 1857.

58. See the cases of the *Charles* and *L'Amable Claudine* in PP, vol. 11, Williams to Canning, March 20, 1826.

59. PP, vol. 22, Valentine to the Governor of Senegal, August 20, 1841, in St. Aulaire to Aberdeen, November 24, 1841. Vis-à-vis the transatlantic slave trade, the relationship between Islamic expansionism and Creole West African commercial hegemony is discussed in Chapter 7 of this study.

60. Ibid.

61. Daget, "British Repression of the Illegal French Slave Trade," 419–25, and Daget, "France, England, and the Suppression of the Illegal Trade," 193–97 and 201–5.

62. Ibid.

63. Ibid.

64. For every adult African landed in Martinique, the company received 129 francs from the French government and 221 francs from planters; for every minor, 110 and 210, respectively. PP, vol. 44, Lawless to Clarendon, January 20, 1857.

65. *New York Times,* February 27, 1858, in ibid., Napier to Clarendon, February 28, 1858.

66. "Memorandum Respecting the Slave Trade under the French Flag," in ibid., Clarendon to Cowley, December 5, 1857.

67. Great Britain's Caribbean crisis in emancipation adaptation refers to the failed socioeconomic transition from slave labor to free labor. Planter-class failures included the reluctance of ex-slaves to continue to labor in the sugar sector, which led to reprisals against them, on the one hand, and free contract labor recruitment from West Africa, India, and South China, on the other. For broad overviews, see Asiegbu, *Slavery and the Politics of Liberation,* and Craton, *Empire, Enslavement, and Freedom.* On free African recruitment, see Monica Schuler, *Alas, Alas, Kongo: A Social History of Indentured African Immigration into Jamaica, 1841–1865* (Baltimore: Johns Hopkins University Press, 1980). On free Asian recruitment, see Walton Look Lai, *Indentured Labor, Caribbean Sugar: Chinese and Indian Migrants in the British West Indies* (Baltimore: Johns Hopkins University Press, 1993).

68. In *El ingenio: Complejo económico social del azúcar* (Havana: Editorial de Ciencias Sociales, 1978), 9, Manuel Moreno Fraginals calculates Mina representation at 3.9 percent of the African-born slave population in Cuba in the 1850s. In Bergad et al.'s *The Cuban Slave Market,* the Mina do not figure at all for the years 1790–1880, unless they are included unnamed in the category of "others," at 10 percent. For the same years, the Bergad collective shows that Upper Guinea exports (largely Gangá and Manding, aka Mandingo and Mandinka) accounted for 25 percent of all Africans arriving to Cuba. Captives exported from Lower Guinea (principally from Old Oyo in the southwest and the Delta polities in the southeast, that is, the Yoruba through Lagos in the Bight of Benin and the Ibo and Ibibio between Calabar and the Bonny River in the Bight of

Biafra) accounted for 36 percent. Those embarked from Angola and the Congo accounted for 28 percent. See Bergad et al., *The Cuban Slave Market*, 72. Their samplings confirm that among Lower Guinea embarkations, the Bight of Biafra, at 27 percent, surpassed the Bight of Benin, at 9 percent. This means that more Ibo than Yoruba arrived in Cuba. Thus, their findings more closely resemble those of Moreno Fraginals than Curtin's. This is to be expected given that they, like Moreno Fraginals, used Cuban archival sources, while Curtin relied on published materials. However, if their samplings prove to represent the whole of illegal slave commerce to Cuba, new studies, foremost from anthropologists, will have to demonstrate why Yoruba rather than Ibo traditions have openly dominated Afro-Cuban cult practices for nearly two centuries. A part of the answer lies in radical differences between the two cultures as ethics systems, not to mention differences in their political structures. Yoruba polities were centralized states, while most Ibo polities were acephalous.

69. Alvarez Nazario, *El elemento afro-negroide en el español de Puerto Rico*, 20–23 and 49–50.

70. See note 68 above.

71. Alvarez Nazario, *El elemento afro-negroide en el español de Puerto Rico*, 205–8, and Baralt, *Esclavos rebeldes*. The absence of an African surname does not eliminate the possibility of African birth. Consider the inventory for the Hacienda Carmen in Vega Alta when it was sold in 1873. PA 1: 379–80. It includes fifty-two slaves. While only two have surnames indicating African birth—Vicente Matamba and Calixto Nangobá—the remaining fifty could represent any combination of Africans and Creoles.

72. Coll y Toste's BHPR, Morales Carrión's PA, and Nistal Moret's *Esclavos prófugos y cimarrones* are the most useful collections of documents.

73. Alvarez Nazario, *El elemento afro-negroide en el español de Puerto Rico*, 206. For Mina participation in the slave conspiracy of 1826, see Baralt, *Esclavos rebeldes*, 66–67.

74. Alvarez Nazario, *El elemento afro-negroide en el español de Puerto Rico*. Albeit Alvarez Nazario was a linguist par excellence, with a penchant for anthropology, he was not a semiologist. His work was published before experts began to engage Saussurean semiology and later negate the linguistic separability of synchrony and diachrony.

75. See note 42 above for examples.

Chapter 6. African Rivers

1. Morales Carrión, *Trata*, 241–42.

2. David Turnbull gleaned this misinformation from George Dawson Flinter and included it in his *Travels to the West*. Flinter—an Irishman and a counterabolitionist with Spanish royalist sympathies—visited Puerto Rico between 1829 and 1831. The books he published as a result of his stay misrepresented Puerto Rican slavery as benign and nondependent on external acquisitions, though Africans represented approxi-

mately 50 percent of the island's slave population when he was there. For a discussion of the impact of Flinter's distortions on Turnbull and others, see Scarano, *Sugar and Slavery in Puerto Rico*, 26–29, and Morales Carrión, *Trata*, 100–103.

3. For nineteenth-century memoirists, see Canot, *Adventures of an African Slaver*, and Drake, *Revelations of a Slave Smuggler*.

4. Bruce Mouser assesses female slave traders in "Women Slavers of Guinea-Conakry," 329–39.

5. See Canot, *Adventures of an African Slaver*, and Great Britain, *Extracts*.

6. Eltis, *Economic Growth and the Ending of the Transatlantic Slave Trade*, 98–99.

7. For statistics that illustrate United States trading interests in subequatorial Africa, see AHU: PUA, Navios Estrangeiros, "Mappas de Entradas e Saidas."

8. PP, vol. 15, Lewis and Campbell to Palmerston, September 5, 1836. Naval reports for the Foreign Office and the memoirs of the slave traders Drake and Canot all assert that Francisco de Souza was a mulatto born and raised in the Brazilian interior. On the other hand, writer Bruce Chatwick insists that he was a white. See Chatwick's *Viceroy of Ouidah*, a novelization of Souza and one of his many Dahomean-born offspring. Unlike Maryse Condé's *Segu* and *Children of Segu*, which depict Creole African societies in Upper and Lower Guinea in the Age of Abolition, Chatwick's novel is limited to a single creoledom in Lower Guinea, and it segues into the twentieth century.

9. PP, vol. 15, Pedro Blanco, "Letter of Instructions," April 14, 1835, in Lewis and Campbell to Palmerston, September 5, 1836.

10. Ibid., first enclosure.

11. Ibid.

12. Ibid., Lewis and Campbell to Palmerston, December 24, 1836.

13. Ibid., June 18, 1837.

14. Ibid.

15. PP, vol. 18, Macaulay to Doherty, November 15, 1839.

16. Ibid., "Letters on Board the Schooner *Brilhante*."

17. Ibid.

18. Ibid.

19. Ibid.

20. Ibid.

21. Ibid.

22. Ibid.

23. Ibid.

24. Ibid.

25. Ibid.

26. Ibid.

27. Ibid.

28. PP, vol. 18, Macaulay and Lewis to Palmerston, March 20, 1839.

29. Ibid.

30. See Table 9.2.

31. PP, vol. 20, Macaulay and Lewis to Palmerston, July 11, 1839. Underground abolitionist activity at this early date is plausible but not yet verified, though indirect evidence is impressive. Tip-offs such as the one mentioned here were common. In addition, after 1844, British consuls in San Juan used local informants, whose detailed accounts were almost always reliable. Furthermore, missing Puerto Rican slaves occasionally turned up as freedmen in the United States, especially in Boston and Philadelphia. See AHN: EST, 8039/8. I strongly suspect that Julio Vizcarrondo directed covert abolitionist activities in Puerto Rico and the United States before and after he founded Spain's first openly abolitionist organization in 1859.

32. PP, vol. 20, Macaulay and Doherty to Palmerston, July 31, 1839.

33. On the initiatives of individual Frenchmen in the intrastate slave trade from Puerto Rico and Cuba, see Dorsey, "Seamy Sides of Abolition."

34. PP, vol. 18, Macaulay and Lewis to Palmerston, July 12, 1838. On Juan and Felipe Lavaca, see Cifre de Loubriel, *Inmigración,* 212; on the commercial affairs of Pedro de Arana, see AHN: PRH, leg. 1. 138/2.

35. PP, vol. 17, "Minutes of Evidence, Police Courts of St. Thomas" in Wynn to Palmerston, July 7, 1838 ("Minutes").

36. PP, vol. 20, Macaulay and Lewis to Palmerston, May 30, 1839.

37. Ibid. On Anglada, see Cifre de Loubriel, *Inmigración,* 22.

38. PP, vol. 20, Tucker to Lafarque and Anglada, June 30, 1839, in Macaulay and Lewis to Palmerston, July 20, 1839. I translated Tucker's letter from pidgin English.

39. Ibid.

40. On Beaupied and Fourçade, see Dorsey, "Seamy Sides of Abolition."

41. PP, vol. 20, Palmerston to Guizot, August 5, 1840.

42. Ibid., Palmerston to Granville, July 31, 1840, and Palmerston to Guizot, August 5, 1840.

43. Daget, "France, England, and the Suppression of the Illegal Trade," 203–4.

44. Rodney, *A History of the Upper Guinea Coast,* chapters 3 and 7; Charles R. Boxer, *Race Relations in the Portuguese Colonial Empire, 1415–1825* (Oxford: Clarendon, 1963); and A.F.C. Ryder, "The Re-establishment of Portuguese Factories on the Costa da Mina to the Eighteenth Century," *Journal of the Historical Society of Nigeria* 1 (December 1958): 157–83. Nineteenth-century eyewitness accounts include, Drake, *Revelations of a Slave Smuggler,* and Melville, *A Residence at Sierra Leone,* letters 5, 17, 26, 27, 29, and 33.

45. PP, Sierra Leone Mixed Courts Reports, Naval Officer Reports, and Reports from the Vice-Admiralty Courts, 1840–1860.

46. Ibid. Spanish-language skills were not limited to Africans on the coast. In the case of the *Jesús María,* some of the captive children rescued near Ponce spoke Spanish well

enough to serve as interpreters for their Gangá compatriots at the Mixed Court in Havana. This indicates that Spanish slave traders knew Sierra Leone beyond its littoral. See PP, vol. 22, Palmerston to Aston, May 25, 1841, eighth enclosure.

47. ANC, Reales Cédulas y Ordenes (RCO), leg. 101.85.

48. PP, Kennedy and Dalrymple to Palmerston, February 20, 1841; ANC, RCO, legs. 161.80 and 121.73; and Miscelánea, 536 AD.

49. Eltis, *Economic Growth and the Ending of the Transatlantic Slave Trade*, 98–99.

50. For graphs and tables on Sierra Leonian slaves in Cuba, especially the Gangá, see Bergad et al., *The Cuban Slave Market*, 72–75.

51. Eltis, *Economic Growth and the Ending of the Transatlantic Slave Trade*, 166.

52. Ibid.

Chapter 7. South Atlantic East

1. See Hall, *Slave Society in the Danish West Indies*, and Birgit Sonesson, "El Papel de Santomás en el Caribe hasta 1815," *Anales de Investigación Histórica* 4, nos. 1–2 (1977): 42–80.

2. Morales Carrión, *Trata*, 52–60.

3. Scarano, *Sugar and Slavery in Puerto Rico*, 136.

4. See tables in Chapter 9 for comparative slave demography in Ponce, Guayama, and Mayagüez.

5. George E. Brooks, "A Nhara of the Guinea Bissau Region: Mãe Aurélia Correia," in Robertson and Klein, *Women and Slavery in Africa*.

6. For a brief biography of Esther, see Canot, *Adventures of an African Slaver*, 56–62.

7. Mouser, "Women Slavers of Guinea-Conakry." In his analysis, Mouser does not distinguish Bailey Lightbourn's activities from those of her daughter, Isabel, for whom there is greater documentation. If his naval sources are correct—that Bailey was born in 1800—it is difficult to understand how her daughter had adult sons in 1841, as stated in parliamentary sources in notes 9 and 17.

8. Ibid., 320–26.

9. PP, vols. 21 and 22, Kennedy and Dalrymple to Palmerston, February 26, 1841; Lewis and Melville to Palmerston, August 2, 1841; and Valentine to the Governor of Senegal, August 20, 1841, in St. Aulaire to Aberdeen, November 24, 1841.

10. Canot gives the only detailed account of Ormond's death. His authorship alone suffices to raise doubt about the circumstances. Dates also vary. Canot, *Adventures of an African Slaver*, 169, placed his death in 1828. Using British Admiralty sources for his "Women Slavers of Guinea-Conakry," Mouser says 1833. The Mixed Court commissioners at Freetown state 1840 in PP, vol. 21, Jeremie and Lewis to Palmerston, December 31, 1841.

11. PP, vol. 21, Jeremie and Lewis to Palmerston, December 31, 1841. The British were elated over the revolts. They hoped the Bangalang freedmen would form the

basis of another Freetown to halt rising French commercial influence in the Pongo region.

12. Ibid., Jeremie and Lewis to Palmerston, December 31, 1841, and Mouser, "Women Slavers of Guinea-Conakry," 330–31. See also Barry, *Senegambia and the Atlantic Slave Trade*, 133–44.

13. PP, vol. 21, Lewis and Hook to Palmerston, April 21, 1841; Lewis and Melville to Palmerston, August 2, 1841; and PP, vol. 36, Hotham to the Secretary of the Admiralty, December 5, 1848.

14. For the British destruction of Tucker's slave factories, which led to the signing of treaties, see Ward, *The Royal Navy and the Slavers*, 175.

15. PP, vol. 37, MacDonald to Palmerston, December 2, 1850.

16. See references to the *éngagé* program in Chapter 2.

17. Three members of the Lightbourn clan signed an antislave trade treaty with the British on March 20, 1861. Stiles Lightbourn, reputed author of the accord, stated that he was the son of Mrs. Lightbourn and that the cosigners, Benjamin Lightbourn and William Emerson, were her grandsons, as seen in the proceedings of the *Segunda Rosario* twenty years before. Distinction between Bailey and Isabel remains elusive insomuch as Benjamin and William were said to be grandsons of the latter. Parliamentary reports, including input from naval officers, failed to identify the matriarch by her given name, Bailey, though they stated that she was born in 1800. It does not seem possible that a woman born in that year could have great-grandsons old enough to author and sign an international treaty in 1861. Perhaps Stiles was Isabel's son, not her brother, that Benjamin was his son, William his nephew—the son of his unnamed sister who married the Briton Emerson—and, that over time, bad record keeping or local mythology blended Isabel and Bailey into a single identity.

18. Díaz Soler, *Historia de la esclavitud negra en Puerto Rico*, 203–4 and, in particular, 226. For a pioneering synthesis of the impact of Islam on slave formations in the Americas, see Diouf, *Servants of Allah*. Her reference to a Fula presence in post–St. Domingue Puerto Rico raises critical questions about slave traffic to the island between the 1790s and the 1810s.

19. According to several sources, which include newspaper notices and prison records, *negros de nación* in nineteenth-century Puerto Rico were classified by the following taxonomy: Islamic = Mandinga, Yambo; Upper Guinea = Bangua, Gangá, Mandinga, and Yambo; Lower Guinea = Bembé, Longoba, Mina, and Ollu; Bantu = Bembé, Congo, Longoba. For the generally outdated nomenclature cited here—except Ollu—see Curtin, *The Atlantic Slave Trade*. For samples of their application, see Baralt, *Esclavos rebeldes*. For Ollu, see PA, vol. 1.

20. Spanish sociocultural and commercial reconstructions of African identity, from heterogeneous and national to homogeneous and ethnic, were evident prior to the internationalization of the antislave trade campaign in 1815. If known, the naming of

specific African provenance was still given in public notices for marronage. But the blanket label *bozal*—newly landed African—grew increasingly acceptable. Consider the following advertisements from the *Gaceta de Puerto Rico*. Of the four, only one refers to African identity beyond the generic *bozal:*

• En la oficina de ésta imprenta darán razón de quien bende [*sic*] una negra bozal como de edad de 19 a 20 años, de sana salud y de buena conducta. 14 de julio de 1813, no. 23, vol. 8.

• Quien quisiere comprar un negro de 14 a 15 años, nación congo, buena salud, puede ocurrir a la imprenta donde dará razón D. Valeriano San Millán. 18 de junio de 1814, no. 13, vol. 9.

• Quien quisiere comprar un negro bozal, pero aclimatado con 6 años de estancia en ésta isla e impuesto en sus labores y trabajos, acuda al Teniente de Milicias Don Fernando Delgado quien dará razón. 16 de julio de 1814, no. 21, vol. 9.

• Quien quisiere comprar tres negras bozales de buena salud y un negro de ocho meses, acudirá a Don Marcelino Cabrera de la Calle de la Fortaleza, esquina a la Marina. 13 de agosto de 1814, no. 29, vol. 9.

21. Unlike Bissau, Pongo suppliers fed the slave trade to Cuba throughout the 1850s. PP, see the following reports: for 1841, vol. 21; 1842, vol. 25; 1844, vol. 29; 1845, vol. 32; 1846, vol. 33; 1847, vol. 34; and 1848, vol. 36. My assertions in this discussion are frequently at odds with conclusions drawn by experts who also rely on British sources. Mouser, "Women Slavers of Guinea-Conakry," 229–33, for example, credits the Fabers as the most powerful slave-trading dynasty on the upper Pongo after the death of Mongo John, citing the Lightbourns as important allies but perhaps less powerful than the Fabers. Though Eltis, *Economic Growth and the Ending of the Transatlantic Slave Trade,* 165–68, emphasizes the Lightbourns, as I do, his discussions do not stress the Spanish presence in the Pongo with the same consistency as those in the present chapter. Furthermore, neither author explores the ongoing connection between the Pongo families and the Fula imamate after Mongo John died. Albeit both strongly suggest that the entire area was a cluster of client polities controlled by Futa Jallon, Eltis states that by 1822, the Núñez, rather than the Pongo, was the most important corridor to Atlantic slave commerce for the Fula, while Mouser (and Canot) assert that Mongo John successfully courted Fula favor. Given, as Eltis also observes, that the Núñez River was more vulnerable to British abolitionist monitoring, it is likely that sometime during the early 1820s, Mongo John had little difficulty in redirecting slave traders to his domain in the Pongo. These differences in interpretation stem from my emphasis on Puerto Rico rather than on Cuba, my efforts to tie Islamic politics and Fula commerce in the interior to Creole African brokerage on the coast, and the fact that primary sources frequently contradict themselves.

22. For an examination of this traffic, see Dorsey, "Seamy Sides of Abolition."

23. Sá da Bandeira, *O Trabalho Rural e a Administração Colonial.* Many of Sá de

Bandeira's abolitionist writings—largely opportunistic proposals veiled as liberal Christian philanthropy—remain unedited and unpublished in Lisbon's Arquivo Histórico Ultramarino in "Colecção Sá de Bandeira, Papéis sobre a Abolição de Escravidão Africana."

24. Mouser, "Women Slavers of Guinea-Conakry," 331–32, and Barry, *Senegambia and the Atlantic Slave Trade,* 94–101.

25. Rodney, *A History of the Upper Guinea Coast,* 232–39 and 257, and Barry, *Senegambia and the Atlantic Slave Trade,* 133–38.

26. Curtin et al., *African History,* 210.

27. Klein, "The Impact of the Atlantic Slave Trade on Societies in the Western Sudan," and Barry, *Senegambia and the Atlantic Slave Trade,* 116. Barry, 165–66, further notes that by converting the Pongo into a protectorate of Futa Jallon, the Fula brought about a brand of political stability that allowed Creole families more time to mix slave commerce with surplus agricultural production. See also Curtin et al., *African History,* 232–33; Rodney, *A History of the Upper Guinea Coast,* 236–37; and Canot, *Adventures of an African Slaver,* 63–70 and 133–41.

28. Canot, *Adventures of an African Slaver,* 53–59; Mouser, "Women Slavers of Guinea-Conakry," 330–31; and Rodney, *A History of the Upper Guinea Coast,* 257–68.

29. Jules Saint-Père, "Creation du Royaume du Fouta Djallon," *Bulletin du Comité d'Etudes Historiques et Scientifiques de l'Afrique Occidentale Française* 2 (1929): 484–555, and Guebhard, *L'Histoire du Fouta Djallon et des Almamys.*

30. Canot, *Adventures of an African Slaver,* chapters 10–28.

31. Mouser, "Women Slavers of Guinea-Conakry," 331–32.

32. Ibid. Between the late 1860s and the early 1870s, the Lightbourns bowed out of the Atlantic slave trade. Corresponding with the ending of African slave traffic to Cuba, it seems they were the last Creole African family in Upper Guinea to do so, switching fully to agrarian production for export based on the labor of local slaves. See note 8 above and Eltis, *Economic Growth and the Ending of the Transatlantic Slave Trade,* 167–68 and 314–15. Again, my assertion of Lightbourn hegemony runs counter to others who stress the Fabers. I base my position on British records that habitually connect the former alone to Spanish markets from the 1840s to the 1860s. See, for example, PP, Naval Officers Reports, vols. 21, 25, and 29. It is possible that British abolitionists focused on the Lightbourns because Isabel was married to British merchant Benjamin Campbell.

33. PP, vol. 21, 1841. Naval Officers Report for 1840.

34. PP, vol. 36. On the British occupation of Bulama, see Hargreaves, *Prelude to the Partition of West Africa,* 47–49.

35. PP, vol. 25, Naval Officers Reports.

36. Mouser, "Women Slavers of Guinea-Conakry," 332–33.

37. PP, vol. 29, Naval Officers Reports.

38. PP, vol. 40, "The Journal of Commander G. A. Seymour," and vol. 43, "Consular Reports for the Bight of Benin."

39. PP, vol. 21.

40. PP, vol. 34. Subsequent discussions will show that the Lightbourns of Río Pongo did not sign antislave trade accords with Great Britain until later.

41. Ibid. However, Sherbro participation declined between 1841 and 1850. See Table A.10 in Eltis, *Economic Growth and the Ending of the Transatlantic Slave Trade,* 253.

42. On the expulsion of Spanish slave traders from Gallinas in 1848, see PP, vol. 37. Eltis, *Economic Growth and the Ending of the Transatlantic Slave Trade,* 167, notes that soil quality in Gallinas was poor from the coast to as far as twenty miles inland. Therefore, the economic transition from illegal slaving to legitimate agrarian surplus production was difficult. On Vai efforts to recover from the financial loss of the Spanish slave trade from Gallinas, see Svend Holsoe, "Slavery and Economic Response among the Vai," in Miers and Kopytoff, *Slavery in Africa.* For British succor to the Spanish colonies, see Colin Palmer, *Human Cargoes: The British Slave Trade to Spanish America, 1700–1739* (Urbana: University of Illinois Press, 1981), and Curtin, *The Atlantic Slave Trade,* 141 and 145–46. On the presence of Mande-speakers in Puerto Rico and other parts of Spanish America, see Alvarez Nazario, *El elemento afro-negroide en el español de Puerto Rico.*

43. PP, vol. 36.

44. Ibid.

45. Ibid. Legitimate Spanish vessels were rare in Angola until Portugal abolished slavery in its African colonies in 1875. This date suspiciously approximates the close of slave traffic to Cuba. See AHU: PUA, Navios Estrangeiros for the years 1840 to 1880.

46. Hiskett, "Nineteenth-Century Jihads," 5: 151–54.

47. Curtin et al., *African History,* 230 and 232–33, and Rodney, *A History of the Upper Guinea Coast,* 233–39.

48. Hiskett, "Nineteenth-Century Jihads," 162.

49. Ibid., 155–60; Curtin et al., *African History,* 383–86; and T. A. Osae et al., *A Short History of West Africa* (New York: Hill and Wang, 1973), 202–3.

50. For major works, see Flint, *The Cambridge History of Africa,* 5: 546–49.

51. Hiskett, "Nineteenth-Century Jihads," 157–61.

52. On French aid to Tal's enemies, see Hargreaves, *Prelude to the Partition of West Africa,* 99–103 and 122–26, and Guebhard, *L'Histoire du Fouta Djallon et des Almamys.* For loopholes in the penal code of 1845, see Knight, *Slave Society in Cuba during the Nineteenth Century,* 138–39. For annual Cuban slave trade figures, see Eltis, *Economic Growth and the Ending of the Transatlantic Slave Trade,* 245.

53. Hargreaves, *Prelude to the Partition of West Africa,* 122–26. The mysterious Gangá or Canga, whose numbers dominated the slave trade to Cuba and Puerto Rico in the nineteenth century, are an important example of the girth of Muslim territorial expan-

sion. According to limited ethnological studies, they were expendable subjects of Islamic Manding suzerains in Sierra Leone and Liberia, as well as Vai chieftains of the Gallinas River. More reliable are Mixed Court cases aired in Freetown and Havana, which strongly suggest that their homelands were not far from the coast. Jihad maneuvers among the Tukulor were visible on the coast of Senegal. The same holds true for the Manding and Fula vis-à-vis the coastal waters of Guinea-Bissau and Guinea-Conakry. If the Gangá were Manding subjects based near the littoral, as Mixed Court cases suggest, then Muslim expansionism also had a hand in slaving activities at Gallinas, the main outlet for Gangá captives destined for the Spanish Caribbean.

54. Barry, *Senegambia and the Atlantic Slave Trade,* 153.

55. See Klein, "The Impact of the Atlantic Slave Trade on Societies in the Western Sudan," on peanut production vis-à-vis declining slave exports. For African traffic to the Spanish Caribbean in the 1840s, see Curtin, *The Atlantic Slave Trade,* 234, and Eltis, *Economic Growth and the Ending of the Transatlantic Slave Trade,* 249.

Chapter 8. South Atlantic West

1. The heading of this section—"Two Wings, One Bird"—paraphrases the words of Lolita Rodríguez de Tió, a nineteenth-century Puerto Rican *independentista* who lived in Cuba. The Cuban patriot José Martí co-opted her politically accurate but culturally exaggerated conflation of Cuban–Puerto Rican identity. It is still frequently and wrongly attributed to his authorship. In Baralt's study of militant slave resistance in Puerto Rico from 1795 to 1873, it seems that most movements involved a variety of African and Creole slaves as well as ex-slaves and free-born blacks. When we focus alone on the names Baralt cites—with two exceptions, the "Congolese" conspiracy of 1826 in Ponce and the "Longoba" conspiracy of 1843 in Toa Baja—his study suggests that African-born slaves did not band together according to natal ethnicities and language groups. (For the years 1835 and 1847, see his *Esclavos rebeldes,* 85–144. See also note 7 below.) However, this may not have been the case. The absence of African national or ethnic surnames in Spanish records does not guarantee Creole birth. Unless documents state birthplaces specifically, a slave called "Angel," "Altagracia," or "Juan Nepomuceno," for example, could have been Creole or African. On the other hand, a document citing "Dámaso Criollo" or "Julio Gangá Carabalí" would signal Creole birth, while "Mauricio Mina," "Eusebio Congo," or "Leocadia Mandinga" would indicate African birth. However, it seems that slaves with double African surnames—an indication that they were Creoles born of African parents from distinct geopolitical areas—were rarely recorded as such. I have found less than a dozen in Cuban records and none in Puerto Rican records. Vis-à-vis cultural and political conflict between assimilation and resistance, it would prove helpful to learn who was responsible for assigning double African surnames: the slaves themselves, one or both of their parents, their owners, or general standards for Spanish colonial record-keeping.

2. The greatest of the revolts—believed unrelated to unrest that began in 1841—took place in Matanzas on November 5, 1843, on Triunvirato and Acana Plantations. ANC, CM leg. 30, 3–4. The Gangá and the Ibo were the principal participants named. They were followed by the Yoruba and a few Bantu-speaking Congolese who may have been Angolans. See note 6 below.

3. On the black Cuban middle class, see Deschamps, *El negro en la economía habanera del siglo XIX*. Yucateco conscripts in Cuba numbered less than a thousand. Scott, *Slave Emancipation in Cuba*, 101–2. Entrepreneurial Spaniards and white Creoles promoted Asian immigration to both islands from the 1840s to the 1860s. It is not known when Asians first arrived in Puerto Rico. However, in her *Catálogo*, 25, Cifre de Loubriel cites the death of a Chinese inmate in the Presidio Provincial in 1802. Fifty-five of the fifty-seven Chinese listed—all men—died of various diseases between 1872 and 1891. Most were convicts from Cuba. When Spain reoccupied Santo Domingo, the Samaná Peninsula was a penal colony for Cuban convicts serving long-term sentences. Local rebel forces, with backing from Haitians and rebel Spanish soldiers, forced Spain to abandon Santo Domingo once again between 1863 and 1864. As a consequence, many Chinese convicts from Cuba were transferred to Puerto Rico. Despite testimonies suggesting otherwise, all Asian contract workers in Spanish dominions came from the depressed provinces of South China, especially Amoy, Fukien, and Canton. See AHN: PRGJ, legs. 2.080/6, 11, 13, 14, and 26–28. See also Joseph Dorsey, "We Bowed Our Heads in Submission: Identity, Resistance, and Social Justice among Chinese Contract Workers in Nineteenth-Century Cuba," in *Latin American Perspectives* (forthcoming).

4. Kinsbruner, *Not of Pure Blood*, and Martínez-Alier, *Marriage, Class and Colour in Nineteenth-Century Cuba*.

5. PA 1: 50.

6. Groups cited in note 2 above participated in slave revolts in November 1843. Greater African diversity is seen in revolts between 1842 and 1844: the Gangá (from the border of Sierra Leone and Liberia), the Mina (all slaves embarked from present-day Ghana), the Carabalí (from southeast Nigeria, the Ibibio, and occasionally the Efik, but mainly the Ibo), and the Mandinga or Mandinka (the designation for all Muslim slaves from the Western Sudan, including the Manding, Fula [Peul], Tukulor, Soninke [Sarakole], Dyula, and sometimes Berbers and Tuaregs). But the majority of the conspirators were identified as Lucumí, the Yoruba of eastern Dahomey and southwest Nigeria. Thus, excepting Cote d'Ivoire, which was rarely a source of transatlantic slave traffic, all of West Africa proper was represented. Regarding southern Africa, some Mozambicans were implicated, but few Congolese groups were named. This sampling was taken from ANC, CM, 1842, legs. 27 and 28; 1843, legs. 29 and 30; and 1844, legs. 44 and 52.

7. Most nineteenth-century African-born militants in Puerto Rico whose nationalities or ethnicities were mentioned were labeled Gangá and Mandinga from the Upper

Guinea Coast or Bantu-speakers from the Congo and Angola. Baralt, *Esclavos rebeldes*, 121–26, cites conspiratory input from the *longoba* or *longobá*. I have not been able to identify the origins of this group. They do not appear in Alvarez Nazario's linguistic study, *El elemento afro-negroide en el español de Puerto Rico*, though he refers to *los nangobá*, 55–56, 216–18, and 258, Bantu-speakers from areas between southwest Cameroon and Río Muni in Equatorial Guinea.

8. Identical stereotypes existed in Brazil. See Degler, *Neither Black nor White*. For opposing views based on firsthand observations, see Barnet, ed., *Estéban Montejo*. For comparative prices of Congolese slaves in Cuba, see Bergad et al., *The Cuban Slave Market*, 72–75. For Congolese participation in Puerto Rico slave revolts, see Baralt, *Esclavos rebeldes*, and Nistal Moret, ed., *Esclavos prófugos y cimarrones*. For a vignette on nonmilitant Congolese leadership in San Juan, see Morales Carrión, *Trata*, 112.

9. This influx is detailed in the next chapter.

10. On comparative fertility, see Herbert Klein, "African Women in the Atlantic Slave Trade," in Robertson and Klein, *Women and Slavery in Africa*. See also Scarano, *Sugar and Slavery in Puerto Rico*, 134–43. Though some scholars now dispute the numerical dominance of males over females among Africa captives—a given for the entire history of the Atlantic slave trade—it is sure that males dominated for the whole of the illegal period in the nineteenth century.

11. For a different view of the founding of the British consulate in San Juan, see Morales Carrión, *Trata*, 123–25.

12. PP, vol. 14, Palmerston to Villiers, November 25, 1835.

13. For O'Donnell's complicity in clandestine slaving, see Corwin, *Spain and the Abolition of Slavery in Cuba*, 80–81; Knight, *Slave Society in Cuba during the Nineteenth Century*, 53; and Paquette, *Sugar Is Made with Blood*.

14. See Chapter 3 of this study.

15. PP, vol. 28, Kennedy to Dalrymple to Palmerston, March 20, 1844, and AGPR, GE:E, caja 66, Estévez al Secretario del Señor Ministro de Guerra, October 15, 1844.

16. AHN: PRH, leg. 1.152/2, "Estado Comparativo de la Esportación [*sic*] de las Principales Producciones de la Isla de Puerto Rico por sus Puertos Habilitados . . . 1846 y 1847."

17. The exception was María del Carmen Colón, née Mary Pleasant Gordon, of British St. Kitts. Her case is discussed in Dorsey, "Women without History."

18. Respecting his praise for the governor, it made no difference whether his superior was Palmerston or Aberdeen.

19. PP, vol. 30, Lindegren to Aberdeen, June 11, 1845.

20. Ibid.

21. Ibid.

22. Díaz Soler, *Historia de la esclavitud negra en Puerto Rico*, 136–48.

23. On ways in which the Spanish military regulated itself, see Joaquín Llaverías, *La*

Comisión Militar Ejecutiva y Permanente de la Isla de Cuba (Havana: Academia de la Historia de Cuba, 1929). For juridical procedures against slave and military subversives during the term of López de Baños between 1838 and 1841, see Morales Carrión, *Trata*, 85–86 and 106–8.

24. FO 84/578, Lindegren to Aberdeen, January 25, 1845.

25. Persons not affiliated with the British government reported slaving activity on the Pongo to the Mixed Court at Freetown that year. PP, vol. 32, Melville and Hook to Aberdeen, December 31, 1844.

26. Despite direct proof, it seems that the *Triunfo* formed part of the same efforts cited in the following note.

27. PP, vol. 32, Melville and Hook to Aberdeen, March 5, 1845, and December 31, 1845. The commissioners reported the presence of the Aldeçoa brothers on the felucca *Huracán* and the schooner *Venganza*. Pierre Fourçade organized both ventures, with input from Julián Zulueta. Though both vessels were slated for Cuba, a portion of the slaves were destined for Puerto Rico.

28. FO 84/578, Lindegren to Aberdeen, January 25, 1845.

29. Ibid., May 9, 1845.

30. Ibid.

31. PP, vol. 33, Lindegren to Aberdeen, March 10, 1846.

32. Ibid., November 8, 1845.

33. Ibid.

34. Ibid.

35. On cruiser shortages and other naval problems, see PP, vol. 36, Naval Officers Report, December 5, 1848.

36. PP, vol. 33, Crawford to Aberdeen, February 24, 1846.

37. Ibid., Aberdeen to Lindegren, April 28, 1846; for the Goff report, Turnbull and Hamilton to Aberdeen, March 2, 1846.

38. Ibid., Lindegren to Aberdeen, June 6, 1846.

39. Ibid.

40. Ibid., June 26, 1846.

41. See Chapters 1 and 3 of this study.

42. PP, vol. 33, Lindegren to Aberdeen, July 11, 1846.

43. Turnbull revealed that Mixed Court commissioners James Kennedy and Campbell Dalrymple owned slaves and *emancipados*. PP, vol. 22, Turnbull to Kennedy, January 12, 1841, and Turnbull to Palmerston, March 12, 1841.

44. PP, vol. 30, Lindegren to Bidwell, June 26, 1845.

45. The main plaintiff was Maclovio, aka Toribio, a Congolese teenager assigned to field labor at Hacienda Buenavista in Carolina, where William was an overseer. On his treatment of slaves and *emancipados*, see AGPR, GE:Municipios, cajas 430 and 573, and AGPR, Audiencia Territorial: Civil, caja 9. Though the consul died four years before the

landing of the *Majesty,* it is possible that the odd tones that marred his reports during his first six years as consul were linked to efforts to hide or protect his entrepreneurial affairs or those of family members such as William. Charles Lindegren assumed the affairs of his father's estate in 1855 and functioned as acting consul.

46. FO 84/674, Lindegren to Palmerston, February 10, 1847.

47. Ibid.

48. Knight, *Slave Society in Cuba during the Nineteenth Century,* 142–43.

49. PP, vol. 35, Lindegren to Palmerston, March 26, 1847.

50. PP, "Instructions . . . to Act under the Treaty between Great Britain and the Netherlands for the Abolition of the Slave Trade, 4th of May, 1818."

51. PP, vol. 35, Lindegren to Palmerston, March 26, 1847.

52. FO 84/674, Lindegren to Palmerston, February 10, 1847.

53. PP, vol. 35, Lindegren to Palmerston, May 25, 1847.

54. Spain strengthened these laws in response to the British Superintendency of Liberated Africans and the presence of the British hulk *Romney* in the harbor of Havana.

55. On his continued misunderstanding of Spanish imperial laws, which he was so fond of citing, see PP, vol. 34, Lindegren to Austen, June 10, 1847, in Austen to the Admiralty, July 10, 1847.

56. PP, vol. 35, Lindegren to Palmerston, June 10, 1847, and July 13, 1847, and Palmerston to Howard, July 16, 1847.

57. Ibid., Sarraz to Disbrowe, August 20, 1847, in Disbrowe to Palmerston, August 23, 1847; Disbrowe to Sarraz, September 27, 1847; Disbrowe to Palmerston, October 12, 1847; Palmerston to Disbrowe, October 27, 1847; and Schimmelpenninck to Palmerston, August 7, 1847.

58. Ibid., Palmerston to Disbrowe, September 24, 1847.

59. Ibid., Sarraz to Disbrowe, August 20, 1847, in Disbrowe to Palmerston, August 23, 1847.

60. Ibid.

61. Ibid., Palmerston to Disbrowe, August 24, 1847.

62. In Lower Guinea, France acquired Togo, Dahomey, Gabon, and, later, Cameroon.

63. FO 84/721, Lindegren to Palmerston, March 22, 1848. On Dutch Caribbean slaves sent to Cuba in 1847, see ANC leg. 945, no. 33320.

64. AHN: EST, leg. 8.042/2

65. The limits of Lindegren's abolitionist intelligence cannot be attributed wholly to Aberdeen's counter-Palmerstonian diplomacy. When Palmerston returned as foreign secretary, the wording of Lindegren's reports still rang off-key. Palmerston, for example, directed him to forward the names of Britons in Puerto Rico who owned slaves. As we have seen, these were typical instructions directed at British consuls worldwide since the mid-1830s. After abolition in the British Caribbean, under stiff penalty, be they at home

or abroad, all British subjects were forbidden to own slaves. Lindegren complied, but not without asking Palmerston to substantiate his orders according to British law. PP, Lindegren to Palmerston, January 22, 1849. This was the same suspicious question he posed to Aberdeen in June 1845. Usually tough on his overseas staff, the imperious Palmerston replied to Lindegren's impertinence with surprising restraint, a form of consideration he never extended to Richard Madden during his tenure in Havana. On the other hand, until Turnbull brought Anglo-Spanish relations to the brink of disaster, Palmerston gave him carte blanche. But Turnbull and Lindegren did not subscribe to the same abolitionist style. Lindegren became bolder, however, in the 1850s, as instanced in the case of María del Carmen Colón cited in note 17 above.

Chapter 9. Theories in Practice

1. Knight, *Slave Society in Cuba during the Nineteenth Century,* 142.

2. On the conscription of free, ostensibly white workers in Puerto Rico, see González Vales, "Towards a Plantation Society," 102–6.

3. Baralt, *Esclavos rebeldes,* 13–20 and 101–34.

4. For Spain's short reoccupation of Santo Domingo and the Haitian politics that permeated much of it, see AHN: Ultramar, Santo Domingo, Gobierno, "Correspondencia de los Capitanes Generales de Santo Domingo, 1861–1865," leg. 425–565 (SDG). For an example of free black Puerto Rican activism against the slave trade, see the case of Gregoria and her children in Dorsey, "Seamy Sides of Abolition." In Puerto Rico between 1848 and 1873, homicides against brutish overseers grew increasingly popular. See Baralt, *Esclavos rebeldes.* For original documents, see PA, vol. 1.

5. Again, this is not to suggest that cooperative social and political relations did not exist between individual slaves and free people of color, especially the poor. See, for example, "The Troubles at Porto Rico," 71–73, in Wagenheim and Jiménez de Wagenheim, eds., *Puerto Rico.* The size of the Spanish army in Puerto Rico was sufficiently impressive prior to the Puerto Rican, Cruzian, and Martinican slave revolts of 1848. Archivo de Museo Naval, Matrículas Generales, MSS 10250, "Nueva División de la Isla de San Juan Bautista de Puerto Rico, en Provincias Marítimas, y Subdivisión de éstas en Distritos, para el Mejor Régimen y Gobierno de las Matrículas de ella, Cuidado y Vigilancia de sus Costas, Calas, Ensenadas y Surideros," 1830. Troops and fortifications increased to discourage engagements in independence politics and to control the island's "negradas y mulaterías," its black and mulatto masses, slave and free. Madrid, Archivo del Servicio Histórico Militar, Serie: Asuntos Generales, América Central, expediente 6.880, "Consideraciones generales sobre Puerto Rico: Sistema de servicio adoptado actualmente, reformas que necesitan y ventajas que resultarán," 1849. For this project and others, staff members in this vast military repository have always exhibited unlimited attentiveness.

6. For a sampling of military mortality in slave revolts, see AHN: PRH, leg. 1.071/6–10.

7. On governor-intendant friction between 1812 and 1840, see Chapter 3. For the years 1848 to 1856, see Dorsey, "Seamy Sides of Abolition."

8. Arístegüi's concern for the well-being of the planter class is evidenced in "El Conde de Mirasol al Señor Secretario de Estado y del Despacho de Marina, Comercio y Gobernación de Ultramar, November 30, 1844." Typed from the original document. Archivo Personal de Luis de la Rosa Martínez, Director Jubilado del Archivo General de Puerto Rico. (The original letter is damaged and therefore retired from public use at AGPR.)

9. For immediate Cuban responses to the penal code of 1845, see Knight, *Slave Society in Cuba during the Nineteenth Century,* 140–42.

10. Baralt, *Esclavos rebeldes,* demonstrates that slave rebellions changed from large- and medium-scale liberationist efforts to small-scale, individual, and often spontaneous acts of resistance such as arson and assassination. Chapter 7 of his study addresses overt African resistance specifically.

11. AGPR, GE:C, caja 222.

12. AGPR, GE:E, caja 66.

13. AGPR, GE:C, caja 222.

14. AGPR, GE:E, caja 66.

15. Ibid.

16. Ibid.

17. AGPR, GE:E, caja 66; AGPR, GE:C, caja 222; and AGPR, GE:M, caja 406.

18. AGPR, GE:E, caja 66.

19. Ibid. For references to Puerto Rican–based Spaniards in Blanco's slave trade ledgers, see ANC, Miscelánea, leg. 535 AD, and discussions and tables in Chapter 6 of this study.

20. AGPR, GE:E, caja 66.

21. AGPR, GE:M, caja 406.

22. AGPR, GE:E, caja 66.

23. The British never caught Canales. See table 6.2.

24. AGPR, GE:E, caja 66, and GE:C, caja 222.

25. AGPR, GE:E, caja 66.

26. On Spanish laws governing distinctions between Creoles and Africans, especially during the Hapsburg dynasty, see Díaz Soler, *Historia de la esclavitud negra en Puerto Rico,* 20–21 and 210–14. On Lindegren's misunderstanding of these laws, see PP, vol. 35, Lindegren to Palmerston, May 25, 1847.

27. As a Puerto Rican model, the homogenization of black slave identity—that is, the conflation of African and Creole identity, as well as diminishing emphasis on African heterogeneity—reinforces the biopolitical postures assumed in Ann Stoler's important

Foucauldian study, *Race and the Education of Desire* (Durham, N.C.: Duke University Press, 1995).

28. Le Gouvernement du Roi a appris que le Gouvernement Impérial de France a importé dernièrement dans ses Colonies aux Antilles et dans l'Amérique du Sud, plusieurs cargaisons de laboureurs libres de la République Libéria. Ou, le Gouvernement du Roi est tenté de suivre cet exemple. J'ai donné reçu l'ordre, M. le Comte, de prier votre Excellence de vouloir bien me faire part de l'arrangement qui a été fait par le Gouvernement Français avec le Gouvernement de Sa Majesté Britannique pour assurer aux batiments porteurs de ces laboureurs un libre passage à travers les croiseurs Anglais, et de me dire si un certificat des autorités en Danemark, et aux Antilles Danoises, ou bien du Consul que le Roi nommerait à Libéria, ne suffira pas pour protéger contre les croiseurs Anglais les batiments chargés des nègres volontaires enrolés pour se rendre aux Antilles Danoises. PP, vol. 44, Reventlow to Clarendon, September 17, 1857 in Clarendon to Newnham, October 14, 1857. The governments of France and the Netherlands went so far as to posture that African emigration to the West was the only way to end the Atlantic slave trade: PP, vol. 44, Cowley to Malmesbury, March 23, 1858.

29. On high Spanish prices for slaves, see "Memorandum respecting the Slave Trade which is Carried on under the French Flag," in PP, vol. 44, Clarendon to Cowley, December 5, 1857. For further evidence of the complicity of Dutch, Danish, and French nationals in the Spanish slave trade, see Wise to Grey, September 13, 1858, also in vol. 44.

30. H. C. Johansen, "The Reality behind the Demographic Arguments to Abolish the Danish Slave Trade," in Eltis and Walvin, *The Abolition of the Atlantic Slave Trade,* 224.

31. On the planter dilemma in Curaçao, see FO 84/721, Lindegren to Palmerston, March 22, 1848; PP, vol. 36, Palmerston to Disbrowe, May 8, 1848, and Disbrowe to Palmerston, June 13, 1848. For Dutch slave demographics, see Höetink in Cohen and Greene, *Neither Slave nor Free,* 335–36. Even in the face of declining slave labor dependency, slaves in Curaçao increased substantially between 1833 and 1863, while the reverse held true for Suriname between 1830 and 1863.

32. In "Abolition of the Abolished," 187, Emmer observed that by 1841, Suriname could no longer afford to import slaves. In PP, Disbrowe to Palmerston, August 11, 1846, an extract from the *Journal de l'Haye* confirms Emmer's assessment. "Documents Statistiques et Commerciaux: Etat Civil et des Esclaves" demonstrates that the combination of high slave mortality and moderate manumissions was more than double the number of slave births in Suriname in 1845. In Curaçao that same year, slave deaths and manumissions surpassed slave births by only twenty-one, or 1.13 percent. For a colony that generated wealth from its free port status and not from agrarian production, the Hague's response was straightforward: slavery could not survive in Curaçao, but it was not sufficiently jeopardized to warrant immediate abolition, and, in the context of sugar production, unlike Suriname, it was not important enough to entertain African immigration.

33. J.F.A. Ajayi, "West Africa in the Antislave Trade Era," in Flint, *The Cambridge History of Africa*, 5: 202–21.

34. AGPR, GE:E, caja 66

35. FO 84/674, Mirasol to Lindegren, May 9, 1847, and Lindegren to Palmerston, May 11, 1847.

36. See the case of the *Atalanta*, alias *Robert Wilson*, PP, vol. 33, Dalrymple and Kennedy to Crawford, November 27, 1845.

37. Fourçade is discussed in Chapter 1 of this study.

38. FO 84/1046, Ratti-Menton to the Admiral of the French Navy, October 20, 1858, and Ratti-Menton to Bordère, October 20, 1858, in Hunt to Malmesbury, December 8, 1858.

39. FO 84/674, Lindegren to Palmerston, February 10, 1847.

40. For the demographics of slavery in the French Caribbean, see the appendix in Cohen and Greene, *Neither Slave nor Free*, 337.

41. PP, vol. 37, Turnbull to Palmerston, January 1, 1848.

42. See reference to Emmer in note 32 above.

43. PP, vol. 35, Sarraz to Howard, August 20, 1847, in Disbrowe to Palmerston, August 23, 1847.

44. See notes 31 and 32 above.

45. Höetink, "Suriname and Curaçao."

46. PP, vol. 35, Lindegren to Palmerston, June 10, 1847; Palmerston to Schimmelpenninck, August 6, 1847; Disbrowe to Palmerston, October 12, 1847; and Palmerston to Disbrowe, October 27, 1847.

47. FO 84/721, Lindegren to Palmerston, March 22, 1848.

48. Ibid.

49. *De Curaçaosche Courant*, 1812–1848, microfilm, the Caribbean Collection, University of Florida Libraries. I thank Robert Paquette for leading me to this Dutch periodical and my students Leontyne Hillenaar and Eliane van Vliet for combing the years 1845 to 1848 to locate the information I needed. Regarding other primary sources in Dutch, when I visited Curaçao in 1995 I could not have secured the statistics for Tables 9.3 and 9.4 without the assistance of Emy Maduro, who located them and expedited photocopying procedures, and Richenel Ansano, who translated the text from Dutch to English and mailed the documents to me.

50. On Spaniards in Dutch Accra, see Chapter 5.

51. Ibid. For statistics on westbound slave traffic from Ghana, see Curtin, *The Atlantic Slave Trade*; Eltis, *Economic Growth and the Ending of the Transatlantic Slave Trade*; Moreno Fraginals, "Africa in Cuba"; and Bergad et al., *The Cuban Slave Market*.

52. British interventions in the coastal affairs of Nigeria between Lagos and Old Calabar brought about the gradual halt of slave exports across the Atlantic, but they discouraged neither internal slavery nor its traffic. Slavery in British colonial Nigeria

remained well into the twentieth century. For a regional example, see Victor Uehendu, "Slaves and Slavery in Iboland, Nigeria," in Miers and Kopytoff, *Slavery in Africa*.

53. Moreno Fraginals, "Africa in Cuba." See also Bergad et al., *The Cuban Slave Market*, compared to Curtin, *The Atlantic Slave Trade*, and Eltis, *Economic Growth and the Ending of the Transatlantic Slave Trade*.

54. Moreno Fraginals, "Africa in Cuba."

55. For general slaving activity in Río Pongo, see PP, vols. 36 and 37, Slave Trade Reports for 1848. For traffic from Río Pongo to Puerto Rico, see PP., vol. 30, Lindegren to Aberdeen, April 9, May 9, and November 8, 1845; PP, vol. 33, April 28, June 6, June 26, and July 11, 1846; and Lindegren to Palmerston, FO 84/674, February 10, 1847; FO 84/721, January 7, 1848; and PP, vol. 37, January 18, 1848.

56. PP, vol. 37, Naval Officers Report, December 5, 1848.

57. Ibid.

58. Ward, *The Royal Navy and the Slavers*, 24–29, and Table 2.1 in this study.

59. See note 56 above.

60. Ibid. See also Eltis, *Economic Growth and the Ending of the Transatlantic Slave Trade*, chapters 6 and 7, for economic, diplomatic, and technological obstacles to the British campaign.

61. PP, vol. 36, The Rendall Report, January 1847.

62. PP, vol. 37, Slave Trade Report of 1848.

63. "Registro Central de Esclavos de Puerto Rico" (RCEPR), United States National Archives, Washington, D.C., microfilm.

64. For documents on the Moret Law, see PA, vol. 2. Applying the Moret Law could be difficult. Some masters misrepresented the ages of Creole slaves. African birth made deception even easier because the ages of new captives were based on estimates.

65. RCEPR. Entries for Ponce in the microfilm version are incomplete.

66. PP, vol. 35, Lindegren to Palmerston, June 10, 1847.

67. Ibid., July 13, 1847.

68. Ibid., October 27, 1847.

69. For the edict and its addenda, see Coll y Toste, ed., 175–81. For assessments, see Díaz Soler, *Historia de la esclavitud negra en Puerto Rico*, 218–22, and Baralt, *Esclavos rebeldes*, 127–34. The bark of this proclamation was worse than its bite. It was not fully enforced, nor was it intended to be. Had it been followed to the letter, its targets—a considerable demographic chunk—would have responded with mass hostility, and the Spanish government would have held Prim responsible. Puerto Rican Creoles—white, black, slave, and free (along with a few African-born slaves)—established a vibrant tradition of verbal insubordination, that is "sassing" or "talking back" to Spaniards, mainly, soldiers. Expletives included references to the person addressed, the person's mother, God, and the Virgin Mary. Fines and prison sentences failed to stem these

fluid utterances of contempt and defiance. Prim's menacing edict put no dent in this tradition. His successor had the good sense to nullify it as soon as he arrived.

70. On Prim and the slave trade, see FO 84/721, January 7, 1848, Lindegren to Palmerston. On his tax reforms vis-à-vis slave commerce, see AHN: PRH, leg. 1.071/11.

71. Scarano, *Sugar and Slavery in Puerto Rico,* chapters 1, 2, and 6.

72. Dorsey, "Seamy Sides of Abolition."

73. Ibid.

74. Curaçao freed itself of complicity. See Appendix 3.1. To Pezuela's credit, it is probable that the slaver did not unload captives on Puerto Rican soil, albeit he claimed to be ill at the time. It is certain that he was notified of its arrival, however, given Puerto Rico's excellent spy system with Curaçao. Since the 1820s, authorities in San Juan relied on agents in Willemstad to report abolitionist and anticolonial activities in British Guiana, Colombia, Panama, and especially Haiti, Santo Domingo, and Venezuela between 1844 and 1865. This system of espionage climaxed when Pezuela was governor. See AHN: SDG, leg. 3525/52–55.

Epilogue

1. Quoted from Aida Caro Costas, "The Organization of an Institutional and Social Life," in Morales Carrión et al., *Puerto Rico: A Political and Cultural History.*

2. AHN: PRH, leg. 1.119/53, "Apuntes sobre la Riqueza y Administración de la Isla de Puerto Rico," January 28, 1852.

3. PA 1: 166–67, Cowper to Russell, August 23, 1862. The remaining cosigners were Juan Díaz, Juan Nava, Francisco Benales, Juan Mestrón, Julián Guas, Manuel Couvertier, Matilde Gense, Francisco Couvertier, Antonio García, María Antonia de la Cruz, Tomasa Chiquez, Ramón Villas (with an unnamed daughter), Eleuterio Rijo, José Colvaño, Antonio Buset, Miguel Gonzáles, Ignacio Gonzáles, Agustín Supero, Juan Aula, and Juan Auris.

4. For *emancipados* and other freed Africans who left Cuba, see Canot, *Adventures of an African Slaver,* 397–98; Rodolfo Sarracino, *Los que volvieron a África* (Havana: Ciencias Sociales, 1988); Joseph Dorsey, "Cuba y el auge de la colonización española en el Golfo de Guinea: El influjo de presos políticos y presos criminales a Fernando Poo, 1850–1898," lecture delivered at the Casa de las Américas, Instituto de Historia Cubana, Havana, Cuba, June 1989. Even after consulting an ex-slave who told him otherwise and gave him a date, Fernando Ortiz denied emphatically that ships from Cuba took freed Africans back to Africa. He wrote, "Jamás han salido de Cuba barcos con expediciones de repatriados africanos." His ex-slave informant alluded to the *Farol,* which made three trips from Havana to Fernando Poo in 1866 with several hundred *emancipados* he identified as Yoruba (*lucumí*) and Fon (*arará*). While these groups were well represented in the mission, the passenger manifest for each voyage shows that *congos* predominated.

Cuba's most famous "repatriation" initiative was the case of *San Antonio,* alias *Caimán,* which, under the suspicious auspices of Pedro Blanco, set sail for Sierra Leone from Havana in early 1845, as Afro-Cubans continued to feel tension from the Conspiración de la Escalera. Its passengers consisted of seventy *emancipados* and other liberated Africans, with twenty-nine Cuban-born dependants. Most settled among other liberated Africans in Freetown. See Sarracino, 113–24. According to British officials who seized the vessel and tried it as a slaver at Freetown, many of the passengers were Gangá. The term "repatriation" must be used with caution. British steamers were known to have carried freed African individuals from Cuba to Freetown. After 1850, British mail junkets between Sierra Leone and Nigeria were frequent enough to allow the *lucumí* and *carabalí* safe passage to Lagos and the Delta, with the hope of finding their families in the interior. But given the lack of British political authority and hegemony south of the equator, many freed Africans who landed in Freetown lacked the means to return to their true homelands, those from the Congo, Angola, and Mozambique in particular. For examples of liberated Africans who remained in Freetown, see Curtin's *Africa Remembered.* For liberated Africans who left Brazil for Togo, Dahomey, and Nigeria, see Pierre Verger, "Nigeria, Brazil, and Cuba," *Nigeria Magazine* 66 (October 1960): 113–23.

5. My wording here is derived from the title of a political analysis authored by Chinweizu, *The West and the Rest of Us: White Predators, Black Slavers, and African Elites* (New York: Random House, 1975).

Bibliography

Primary Sources: Archival Documents

Archivo Histórico Nacional, Madrid

Estado: legajos 8015/38, 8020/45, 8025/17, 8030/88–90, 8031/7 and 22, 8033/16, 8035/ 1 and 12, 8036/3, 8039/8, 8040/9, 8045/9.

Ultramar:

Gobierno: legajos 5.065/12 and 19; 5.069/3–7; 5.070/29; 5.072/28, 32, and 38; 5.076/15 and 24; 5.079/16; 5.082/1–2, 9–10, and 29; 5.088/25 and 26; and 5.104/47.

Gracia y Justicia: legajos 2.060/29 and 42; 2.080/6, 11, 13–14, and 26–28; and 2.960/42.

Hacienda: legajos 1.065/77; 1.071/4–11, 14, and 39; 1.082/10; 1.100/28; 1.119/53; 1.38/ 2; and 1.152/2.

Guerra: legajos 6.347/1 and 6.348/9.

Archivo del Ministerio de Asuntos Exteriores, Madrid

Ultramar y Colonias: legajos 2967 and 2968.5.

Archivo del Museo Naval, Madrid

Matrículas Generales, MSS: 10250.

Archivo de Servicio Histórico Militar, Madrid

Asuntos Generales, América Central: legajo 6.880.

Archivo de las Cortes Españolas, Madrid

Sesiones de las Cortes: Sesiones sobre la Abolición de la Esclavitud.

Archivo General de Puerto Rico, San Juan

Audiencia Territorial: Civil, caja 9.

Departamento de Justicia, Confinados: Esclavos, caja 1.

Gobernadores Españoles: Asuntos Políticos: Esclavos, cajas 63 and 66–69; Comercio: caja 222; Municipios: cajas 57, 406, 430, 444, 480, and 495–96.

Archivo Nacional, Havana

Comisión Militar: legajos 5, 11, 27–30, 44, 51–52, 78, and 83.

Gobierno General: legajo 565.27942.

Gobierno Superior Civil: legajos 941.176 and 941.33176.

Miscelánea: legajo 535 A, Libros de Contabilidad.

Real Consulado y Junta de Fomento: legajo 148.7306.

Reales Cédulas y Ordenes: legajos 101.73, 75, and 85; 121.73 and 75; 161.58 and 180; and 164.396.

Arquivo Histórico Ultramarino, Lisbon

Colecção Sá da Bandeira: Papéis sobre a Abolição da Escravidão Africana.

Possessões Ultramarinas, Angola: Navios Estrangeiros, Mappas de Entradas e Saidas.

Centraal Historisch Archief, Willemstad, Curaçao

Koloniale Secretary: Archief van het Notariaat. Contains listings of slaves registered and sold in the Netherlands Antilles, 1842–51.

National Archives, Washington, D.C.

Records of the Spanish Governors of Puerto Rico: Filaciones de Negros Emancipados, Puerto Rico, 1859, microfilm; Extranjeros en Puerto Rico, 1815–1845, Record Group T 1170, Microfilm Publication Rolls.

Public Record Office, London (Kew Division)

Foreign Office: Papers Relative to the Slave Trade, Series 84: 578, 674, 721, 838, 874, 902, 907, 935, 964, 965, 988, 1046, and 1080.

Consular Reports: 72/770.

Primary Sources: Published Documents

Coll y Toste, Cayetano, ed. and comp. *Boletín Histórico de Puerto Rico*. 14 vols. San Juan: Tipografía Cantero Fernández, 1914–26.

Coll y Toste, Cayetano, ed., and Isabel Cuchí Coll, comp. *Historia de la esclavitud en Puerto Rico*. San Juan: Cuchí Coll, 1977.

Córdoba, Pedro Tomás. *Memorias geográficas, históricas, económicas, y estadísticas de la isla de Puerto Rico*. 6 vols. San Juan: Ediciones Borínquen, 1968.

Curtin, Philip, ed. *Africa Remembered: Narratives by West Africans in the Era of the Slave Trade*. Madison: University of Wisconsin Press, 1967.

Great Britain. *Extracts from the Evidence Taken before Committees of the Two Houses of Parliament Relative to the Slave Trade*. New York: Negro Universities Press, 1969.

———. *Parliamentary Papers: Slave Trade*. 90 vols. Dublin: Irish University Press, 1969.

Morales Carrión, Arturo, et al., eds. *El proceso abolicionista en Puerto Rico: Documentos para su estudio*. 2 vols. San Juan and Río Piedras: Instituto de Cultura Puertorriqueña and Centro de Investigaciones Históricas, 1974–78.

Nistal Moret, Benjamín, ed. *Esclavos prófugos y cimarrones: Puerto Rico, 1770–1870*. Río Piedras: Editorial de la Universidad de Puerto Rico, 1984.

Rodríguez San Pedro, Joaquín. *Legislación ultramarina*. 14 vols. Madrid: Ministerio de Ultramar, 1865–69.

Zamora y Coronado, José María, comp. *Biblioteca de legislación ultramarina.* 7 vols. Madrid: Alegría y Charlain. 1844–49.

Secondary Sources

Ajayi, J.F.A., and Michael Crowder, eds. *A History of West Africa.* 2 vols. London: Oxford University Press, 1974.

Akinjogbin, I. A. *Dahomey and Its Neighbors.* Cambridge: Cambridge University Press, 1972.

Alvarez Nazario, Manuel. *El elemento afro-negroide en el español de Puerto Rico.* San Juan: Instituto de Cultura Puertorriqueña, 1974.

Andrews, William. *To Tell a Free Story.* Urbana: University of Illinois Press, 1988.

Asiegbu, Johnson U. J. *Slavery and the Politics of Liberation, 1781–1864: Liberated African Emigration and British Anti-Slavery Policy.* New York: APC, 1969.

Ayala, César. *American Sugar Kingdom: The Plantation Economy of the Spanish Caribbean, 1898–1934.* Chapel Hill: University of North Carolina Press, 1999.

Badillo, Jalil Sued, and Angel López Cantos. *Puerto Rico Negro.* Río Piedras, Puerto Rico: Editorial Cultural, 1986.

Bandiel, James. *Some Account of the Trade in Slaves in Africa.* London: Frank Cass, 1968.

Baralt, Guillermo. *Esclavos rebeldes: Conspiraciones y sublevaciones de esclavos en Puerto Rico, 1795–1873.* Río Piedras, Puerto Rico: Ediciones Huracán, 1982.

Barnet, Miguel, ed. *Estéban Montejo: Biografía de un cimarrón.* Havana: Academia de Ciencias Sociales, 1966.

Barrow, Christine, ed. *Caribbean Portraits: Essays on Gender Ideologies and Identities.* Kingston, Jamaica: Ian Randle, 1998.

Barry, Boubacar. *Senegambia and the Atlantic Slave Trade.* Cambridge: Cambridge University Press, 1998.

Benítez Rojo, Antonio. *The Repeating Island: The Caribbean and the Postmodern Perspective.* Durham, N.C.: Duke University Press, 1996.

Bergad, Laird. *Coffee and the Growth of Agrarian Capitalism in Nineteenth-Century Puerto Rico.* Princeton, N.J.: Princeton University Press, 1983.

Bergad, Laird, et al. *The Cuban Slave Market, 1790–1880.* Cambridge: Cambridge University Press, 1995.

Bethell, Leslie. *The Abolition of the Brazilian Slave Trade.* Cambridge: Cambridge University Press, 1970.

Boahen, A. A. "Asante and Fante in the Nineteenth Century." In *A History of West Africa,* ed. J.F.A. Ajayi and Michael Crowder. London: Oxford University Press, 1974.

Buxton, Thomas. *The African Slave Trade and Its Remedy.* London: Dawsons, 1968.

Camuñas Madera, Ricardo. *Epidemias, plagas, y marginación: La lucha contra la adversidad en Puerto Rico en los siglos XVIII y XIX.* Santo Domingo, Dominican Republic: Universidad de América, 1992.

Canot, Theodore. *Adventures of an African Slaver.* New York: Dover, 1969.

Carbonell, Rubén, and María Consuelo Vázquez Arce. "Las compraventas de esclavos en San Juan y Naguabo." *Anales de Investigación Histórica* 3:1–83.

Cibés Viadé, Alberto. *El Gobernador Pezuela y el abolicionismo puertorriqueño, 1848–1873.* Río Piedras, Puerto Rico: Ediciones Edil, 1978.

Cifre de Loubriel, Estela. *Catálogo de extranjeros residentes en Puerto Rico en el siglo XIX.* Río Piedras: Universidad de Puerto Rico, 1962.

———. *La inmigración a Puerto Rico durante el siglo XIX.* San Juan: Instituto de Cultura Puertorriqueña, 1964.

Coggeshall, George. *Thirty-six Voyages to Various Parts of the World between 1779 and 1841.* New York, 1844.

Cohen, David, and Jack Greene, eds. *Neither Slave nor Free: Freedmen of African Descent in the Slave Societies of the New World.* Baltimore: Johns Hopkins University Press, 1972.

Conrad, Robert, ed. *Children of God's Fire: A Documentary History of Black Slavery in Brazil.* Princeton, N.J.: Princeton University Press, 1983.

Corbitt, Duvon. "Immigration to Cuba." *Hispanic American Historical Review* 22 (1942): 280–307.

Corwin, Arthur. *Spain and the Abolition of Slavery in Cuba, 1817–1886.* Austin: University of Texas Press, 1967.

Craton, Michael. *Empire, Enslavement, and Freedom.* Princeton, N.J.: Markus Wiener, 1997.

Crowther, Samuel. *Vocabulary of the Yoruba.* London: Longmans, 1843.

Cruz Monclova, Lidio. *Historia de Puerto Rico: Siglo XIX.* Río Piedras: Universidad de Puerto Rico, 1957.

Curet, José. "De la esclavitud a la abolición." *Cuadernos* 7:1–35.

Curtin, Philip. *The Atlantic Slave Trade: A Census.* Madison: University of Wisconsin Press, 1969.

———, et al. *African History.* New York: Longman, Inc., 1978.

Daget, Serge. "British Repression of the Illegal French Slave Trade." In *The Uncommon Market: Essays in the Economic History of the Atlantic Slave Trade,* ed. Henry Gemery and Jan Hogendorn. New York: Academic Press, 1979.

———. "France, England, and the Suppression of the Illegal Trade, 1817–1850." In *The Abolition of the Atlantic Slave Trade: Origins and Effects in Europe, Africa and the Americas,* ed. David Eltis and James Walvin. Madison: University of Wisconsin Press, 1981.

Dávila Cox, Emma. *Este inmenso comercio: Las relaciones mercantiles entre Puerto Rico y Gran Bretaña, 1844–1998.* San Juan: Universidad de Puerto Rico, 1995.

Davis, David Brion. *Slavery and Human Progress.* New York: Oxford University Press, 1984.

Dean, Warren. *Rio Claro: A Brazilian Plantation System.* Stanford, Calif.: Stanford University Press, 1976.

Degler Carl. *Neither Black nor White: Slavery and Race Relations in the United States and Brazil.* New York: Macmillan, 1971.

Deschamps Chapeaux, Pedro. *El negro en la economía habanera del siglo XIX.* Havana: Unión de Escritores y Artistas de Cuba, 1971.

Díaz Soler, Luis Maldonado. *Historia de la esclavitud negra en Puerto Rico*. Río Piedras, Puerto Rico: Editorial Universitaria, 1974.

Diouf, Sylviane. *Servants of Allah: African Muslims Enslaved in the Americas*. New York: New York University Press, 1998.

Dorsey, Joseph C. "The Presence of Absence: Rape and the Avoidance of Rape among Slave Women in the United States and the Spanish Caribbean." Paper presented at the 24th annual conference of the Caribbean Studies Association, Panama City, Panama, May 1999.

———. "Seamy Sides of Abolition: Puerto Rico and the Cabotage Slave Trade to Cuba, 1848–73." *Slavery and Abolition* 19, no. 1.

———. "Women without History: Slavery, Jurisprudence, and the International Politics of *Partus Sequitur Ventrem* in the Spanish Caribbean." *Journal of Caribbean History* 28, no. 2.

Dorsey, Joseph C., and Robert Paquette. "Cuban Slave Resistance." *Slavery and Abolition* 15, no. 3.

Drake, Philip. *Revelations of a Slave Smuggler, 1807–1857*. Northbrook, Ill.: Metro Books, 1972.

Eltis, David. *Economic Growth and the Ending of the Transatlantic Slave Trade*. New York: Oxford University Press, 1987.

Eltis, David, and David Richardson, eds. *Routes to Slavery: Direction, Ethnicity, and Mortality in the Atlantic Slave Trade*. London: Frank Cass, 1997.

Eltis, David, and James Walvin, eds. *The Abolition of the Atlantic Slave Trade: Origins and Effects in Europe, Africa and the Americas*. Madison: University of Wisconsin Press, 1981.

Emmer, Pieter. "Abolition of the Abolished: The Illegal Dutch Slave Trade and the Mixed Courts." In *The Abolition of the Atlantic Slave Trade: Origins and Effects in Europe, Africa and the Americas*, ed. David Eltis and James Walvin. Madison: University of Wisconsin Press, 1981.

Engerman, Stanley, and Eugene Genovese, eds. *Race and Slavery in the Western Hemisphere: Quantitative Studies*. Princeton, N.J.: Princeton University Press, 1975.

Findlay, Eileen. *Imposing Decency: The Politics of Sexuality and Race in Puerto Rico, 1870–1920*. Durham, N.C.: Duke University Press, 2000.

Finley, Moses. *Ancient Slavery and Modern Ideology*. Princeton, N.J.: Markus Wiener, 1998.

Fleischner, Jennifer. *Mastering Slavery: Memory, Family, and Identity in Women's Slave Narratives*. New York: SUNY Press, 1996.

Flint, J. E., ed. *The Cambridge History of Africa*. 8 vols. Cambridge: Cambridge University Press, 1976.

Fox-Genovese, Elizabeth. *Within the Plantation Household*. Chapel Hill: University of North Carolina Press, 1988.

Fox-Genovese, Elizabeth, and Eugene Genovese. *Fruits of Merchant Capital*. New York: Oxford University Press, 1983.

Freyre, Gilberto. *The Masters and the Slaves*. New York: Knopf, 1946.

Garfield, Robert. *A History of São Tomé, 1470–1655*. San Francisco: Mellon Research University Press, 1992.

Gemery, Henry, and Jan Hogendorn, eds. *The Uncommon Market: Essays in the Economic History of the Atlantic Slave Trade*. New York: Academic Press, 1979.

Genovese, Eugene. *Roll, Jordan, Roll: The World the Slaveholders Made*. New York: Random House, 1974.

———. "Treatment of Slaves in Different Countries: Problems in the Applications of the Comparative Method." In *Slavery in the New World: A Comparative Reader*, ed. Laura Foner and Eugene Genovese. Englewood Cliffs, N.J.: Prentice-Hall, 1969.

Gilroy, Paul. *Small Acts: Thoughts on the Politics of Black Cultures*. London: Serpent's Tail, 1993.

Gómez Canedo, Lino. *Los archivos históricos de Puerto Rico*. San Juan: Instituto de Cultura Puertorriqueña, 1960.

González Vales, Luis. "Towards a Plantation Society." In *Puerto Rico: A Political and Cultural History*, ed. Arturo Morales Carrión et al. New York: Norton, 1983.

Guebhard, Paul. *L'Histoire du Fouta Djallon et des Almamys*. Paris: Comité de l'Afrique et Le Comité du Maroc, 1909.

Hall, Gwendolyn Midlo. *Social Control in Slave Plantation Societies*. Baltimore: Johns Hopkins University Press, 1971.

Hall, Neville. *Slave Society in the Danish West Indies*, ed. Barry Higman. Baltimore: Johns Hopkins University Press, 1992.

Hargreaves, John. *Prelude to the Partition of West Africa*. New York: St. Martin's, 1963.

Hernández, Pedro. "Inmigrantes italianos de Puerto Rico durante el siglo XIX." *Anales de Investigación Histórica* 3: 1–63.

Hiskett, M. "Nineteenth-Century Jihads." In *Cambridge History of Africa*, ed. J. E. Flint. Cambridge: Cambridge University Press, 1976.

Höetink, H. "Suriname and Curaçao." In *Neither Slave nor Free: Freedmen of African Descent in the Slave Societies of the New World*, ed. David Cohen and Jack Greene. Baltimore: Johns Hopkins University Press, 1972.

Inikori, Joseph, and Stanley Engerman, eds. *The Atlantic Slave Trade*. Durham, N.C.: Duke University Press, 1992.

Jones, Howard. *Mutiny on the Amistad: The Saga of a Slave Revolt and Its Impact on American Abolition, Law, and Diplomacy*. New York: Oxford University Press, 1987.

Karasch, Mary. *Slave Life and Culture in Rio de Janeiro, 1808–1850*. Princeton, N.J.: Princeton University Press, 1986.

Kinsbruner, Jay. *Not of Pure Blood: Free People of Color and Racial Prejudice in Nineteenth-Century Puerto Rico*. Durham, N.C.: Duke University Press, 1996.

Klein, Herbert. *The Middle Passage: Comparative Studies in the Atlantic Slave Trade*. Princeton, N.J.: Princeton University Press, 1978.

Klein, Martin. "The Impact of the Atlantic Slave Trade on Societies in the Western Sudan." In *The Atlantic Slave Trade*, ed. Joseph Inikori and Stanley Engerman. Durham, N.C.: Duke University Press, 1992.

Knight, Franklin. *Slave Society in Cuba during the Nineteenth Century*. Madison: University of Wisconsin Press, 1970.

Kutzinski, Vera. *Sugar's Secrets: Race and the Erotics of Cuban Nationalism*. Charlottesville: University Press of Virginia, 1993.

Lalinde Abadía, Jesús. *La administración española en el siglo XIX puertorriqueño*. Seville: E.E.H.A.S., 1980.

Lombardi, John. "Comparative Slave Systems in the Americas: A Critical Review." In *New Approaches to Latin American History*, ed. Richard Graham and Peter Smith. Austin: University of Texas Press, 1974.

Lovejoy, Frank. *Transformations in Slavery*. Cambridge: Cambridge University Press, 1983.

Manning, Patrick. *Slavery and African Life*. Cambridge: Cambridge University Press, 1990.

Martínez-Alier, Verena. *Marriage, Class and Colour in Nineteenth-Century Cuba*. Cambridge: Cambridge University Press, 1974.

Martínez-Fernández, Luis. *Fighting Slavery in the Caribbean: The Life and Times of a British Family in Nineteenth-Century Havana*. New York: Sharpe, 1998.

———. *Torn between Empires: Economy, Society, and Patterns of Political Thought in the Hispanic Caribbean, 1840–1878*. Athens: University of Georgia Press, 1994.

Martínez-Vergne, Teresita. *Capitalism in Colonial Puerto Rico: Central San Vicente in the Late Nineteenth Century*. Gainesville: University Press of Florida, 1992.

———. *Shaping the Discourse on Space: Charity and Its Wards in Nineteenth-Century Puerto Rico*. Austin: University of Texas Press, 1999.

Matos Rodríguez, Félix. *Women and Urban Change in San Juan, Puerto Rico, 1820–1868*. Gainesville: University Press of Florida, 1999.

Meillassoux, Claude. *The Anthropology of Slavery*. Chicago: Chicago University Press, 1991.

Melville, Elizabeth. *A Residence at Sierra Leon*. London: Frank Cass, 1968.

Mendonça, Renato. *A Influencia Africana no Portugués do Brasil*. Rio de Janeiro: Civilização Brasileira, 1973.

Miers, Suzanne, and Igor Kopytoff, eds. *Slavery in Africa: Historical and Anthropological Perspectives*. Madison: University of Wisconsin Press, 1977.

Morales Carrión, Arturo. *Auge y decadencia de la trata negrera en Puerto Rico, 1820–1860*. San Juan: Centro de Estudios Avanzados de Puerto Rico y el Caribe and Instituto de Cultura Puertorriqueña, 1978.

———. *Puerto Rico and the Non-Hispanic Caribbean*. Río Piedras: University of Puerto Rico, 1952.

———, et al., eds. *Puerto Rico: A Political and Cultural History*. New York: Norton, 1983.

Moreno Fraginals, Manuel. "Africa in Cuba." In *Comparative Perspectives on Slavery in New World Plantation Societies*, ed. Vera Rubin and Arthur Tuden. New York: New York Academy of Science, 1977.

———. *The Sugarmill: The Socioeconomic Complex of Sugar in Cuba, 1760–1860*. New York: Monthly Review, 1976.

————, et al., eds. *Between Slavery and Free Labor: The Spanish Caribbean in the Nineteenth Century*. Baltimore: Johns Hopkins University Press, 1985.

Mörner, Magnus. "Recent Research on Negro Slavery and Abolition in Latin America." *Latin American Research Review* 13 (1978): 265–89.

Mouser, Bruce. "Women Slavers of Guinea-Conakry." In *Women and Slavery in Africa*, ed. Claire Robertson and Martin Klein. Madison: University of Wisconsin Press, 1983.

Murray, David. *Odious Commerce: Britain, Spain and the Abolition of the Cuban Slave Trade*. Cambridge: Cambridge University Press, 1980.

Nistal Moret, Benjamín. "Catorce querellas de esclavos de Manatí, 1869–1873," *Sin Nombre* 6, no. 2 (1973): 78–100.

————, ed. *El cimarrón*. San Juan: Instituto de Cultura Puertorriqueña, 1979.

Novás Calvo, Lino. *Pedro Blanco, el negrero*. Madrid: Colección Austral, 1955.

Ortiz Fernández, Fernando. *Hampa afro-cubana: Los negros esclavos*. Havana: Revista Bimestre Cubana, 1916.

Painter, Nell. "Of *Lily*, Linda Brent, and Freud: A Non-Exceptionalist Approach to Race, Class, and Gender in the Slave South." In *Half Sisters of History*, ed. Catherine Clinton. Durham, N.C.: Duke University Press, 1994.

Paquette, Robert. *Sugar Is Made with Blood: The Conspiracy of the Escalera*. Middletown, Conn.: Wesleyan University Press, 1988.

Patterson, Orlando. *Slavery and Social Death: A Comparative Study*. Cambridge: Harvard University Press, 1982.

Pescatello, Ann, ed. *The African in Latin America*. New York: Knopf, 1975.

Picó, Fernando. *Al filo del poder: Subalternos y dominantes en Puerto Rico, 1739–1910*. Río Piedras, Puerto Rico: EDUPR, 1993.

————. *Libertad y servidumbre en el Puerto Rico del siglo XIX: Los jornaleros utuadeños en vísperas del auge del café*. Río Piedras, Puerto Rico: Huracán, 1979.

Piñeiro de Rivera, Flor. *Arthur Alfonso Schomburg: A Puerto Rican's Quest for His Black Heritage*. San Juan: Centro de Estudios Avanzados de Puerto Rico y el Caribe, 1989.

Polanyi, Karl. *Dahomey and the Slave Trade*. Seattle: University of Washington Press, 1966.

Robertson, Claire, and Martin Klein, eds. *Women and Slavery in Africa*. Madison: University of Wisconsin Press, 1983.

Robinson, Cedric. *Black Marxism*. London: Zed, 1988.

Rodney, Walter. *A History of the Upper Guinea Coast, 1545–1800*. London: Oxford University Press, 1979.

Rosa Martínez, Luis de la. "Los negros del brick-barca Majesty." *Revista del Centro de Estudios Avanzados de Puerto Rico y el Caribe* 3 (1986): 45–57.

Rubin, Vera, and Arthur Tuden, eds. *Comparative Perspectives on Slavery in New World Plantation Societies*. New York: New York Academy of Science, 1977.

Russell-Wood, A.J.R. *The Black Man in Slavery and in Freedom in Colonial Brazil*. New York: St. Martin's, 1982.

Sá da Bandeira, Bernardo de. *O Trabalho Rural e a Administracão Colonial*. Lisbon: Impresa Nacional, 1873.

San Miguel, Pedro. "Tierra, trabajadores, y propietarios: Las haciendas de Vega Baja, 1828–1865." *Anales de Investigación Histórica* 6: 1–51.

Scarano, Francisco. *Sugar and Slavery in Puerto Rico: The Plantation Economy of Ponce, 1800–1850*. Madison: University of Wisconsin Press, 1984.

Schmidt-Nowara, Christopher. *Empire and Slavery: Spain, Cuba, and Puerto Rico, 1833–1874*. Pittsburgh: Pittsburgh University Press, 1999.

Scott, Rebecca. *Slave Emancipation in Cuba*. Princeton, N.J.: Princeton University Press, 1985.

Shepherd, Verene, et al., eds. *Engendering History: Caribbean Women in Historical Perspective*. Kingston, Jamaica: Ian Randle, 1995.

Smith, James. *The Winter of 1840 in St. Croix, with an Excursion to Tortola and St. Thomas*. New York, 1840.

Smith, Robert. *Warfare and Diplomacy in Pre-Colonial West Africa*. Norwich, England: Methuen, 1976.

———. *Yoruba Warfare in the Nineteenth Century*. Cambridge: Cambridge University Press, 1964.

Sonesson, Birgit. *Puerto Rico's Commerce, 1765–1865*. Los Angeles: University of California Press, 2000.

Stein, Stanley. *Vassouras: A Brazilian Coffee County, 1850–1900*. Cambridge: Harvard University Press, 1957.

Tannenbaum, Frank. *Slave and Citizen*. New York: Knopf, 1946.

Thomas, Hugh. *The Slave Trade*. New York: Simon and Schuster, 1997.

Thornton, John. *Africa and Africans in the Making of the Atlantic World, 1400–1680*. Cambridge: Cambridge University Press, 1992.

Turnbull, David. *Travels to the West: Cuba, with Notices of Puerto Rico and the Slave Trade*. London: Longmans, 1840.

Ulibarri, Jorge. "Nineteenth-Century Puerto Rican Immigration and Slave Data." National Archives and Record Services, Paper no. 64. Washington, D.C.: General Services Administration, 1973.

Wagenheim, Kal, and Olga Jiménez de Wagenheim, eds. *Puerto Rico: A Documentary History*. New York: Praeger, 1973.

Ward, W.E.F. *The Royal Navy and the Slavers*. New York: Schocken, 1970.

Williams, Eric. *Capitalism and Slavery*. Chapel Hill: University of North Carolina Press, 1944.

———. *From Columbus to Castro: The History of the Caribbean, 1492–1969*. New York: Harper and Row, 1971.

Zenón Cruz, Isabelo. *Narciso descubre su trasero: El negro en la cultura puertorriqueña*. San Juan: Instituto de Cultura Puertorriqueña, 1974, and Humacao: Editorial Furidi, 1974.

Index

Joseph Dorsey teaches Caribbean history, African history, and African American studies at Purdue University. His articles on race relations, gender systems, language, institutional structures, foreign diplomacy, and transnational identity in the Spanish seaborne empire have appeared or are forthcoming in the *Journal of Caribbean History, Latin American Perspectives, Slavery and Abolition, the West African Review,* and two edited collections. In 1999, he was awarded the John Garber Drushel Visiting Associate Professorship at the College of Wooster, and in 1996 he received the Lydia Cabrera Award for Research on Cuban Historical Studies from the Conference on Latin American History. He has also received grants from the American Philosophical Society and the National Endowment for the Humanities. Two of his projects in interdisciplinary history are near completion: "Puerto Rico and Its Others: Essays on Slave Commerce, Cognition, and Culture, 1508–1873," and "Dissident Tao: Subjects, Objects, and Rebels among Chinese Contract Workers in Nineteenth-Century Cuba."